CRANE

CRANE

SEX, CELEBRITY, and MY FATHER'S UNSOLVED MURDER

ROBERT CRANE
AND CHRISTOPHER FRYER

UNIVERSITY PRESS OF KENTUCKY

The University Press of Kentucky

Scholarly publisher for the Commonwealth,
serving Bellarmine University, Berea College, Centre College of Kentucky,
Eastern Kentucky University, The Filson Historical Society, Georgetown
College, Kentucky Historical Society, Kentucky State University, Morehead
State University, Murray State University, Northern Kentucky University,
Transylvania University, University of Kentucky, University of Louisville,
and Western Kentucky University.
All rights reserved.

Editorial and Sales Offices: The University Press of Kentucky
663 South Limestone Street, Lexington, Kentucky 40508-4008
www.kentuckypress.com

Library of Congress Cataloging-in-Publication Data

Crane, Robert David.
  Crane : sex, celebrity, and my father's unsolved murder / Robert Crane
and Christopher Fryer.
     pages cm
  Includes index.
  ISBN 978-0-8131-6074-0 (hardcover : alkaline paper) —
  ISBN 978-0-8131-6076-4 (PDF) — ISBN 978-0-8131-6075-7 (ePub)
  1. Crane, Bob, 1929-1978. 2. Television actors and actresses—United
States—Biography. 3. Murder—Investigation—Arizona—Scottsdale.
4. Cold cases (Criminal investigation)—-Arizona—Scottsdale. 5. Crane,
Robert David. 6. Crane, Bob, 1929-1978—Family. 7. Fathers and sons—
United States—Biography. 8. Fame—Social aspects—California—Los
Angeles. 9. Sex—Social aspects—California—Los Angeles. 10. Hollywood
(Los Angeles, Calif.)—Social life and customs. I. Fryer, Christopher.
II. Title.
  PN1992.4.C73C736 2015
  791.4302'8092—dc23   2014043934

This book is printed on acid-free paper meeting
the requirements of the American National Standard
for Permanence in Paper for Printed Library Materials.

Manufactured in the United States of America.

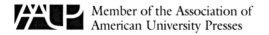 Member of the Association of
American University Presses

To Anne, Chuck, Debbie, and Karen

I am a camera with its shutter open, quite passive, recording, not thinking.

—Christopher Isherwood,
The Berlin Stories: Goodbye to Berlin

Contents

Author's Note

This book is a work of memory, and as such there may be other people who have different recollections of these events. I have written what I remember to be true and accurate. Some names have been changed for reasons that will be obvious. Some quotes from Greg Kinnear, Paul Schrader, and Willem Dafoe regarding *Auto Focus* were taken from a variety of sources, and not necessarily from one specific evening's conversation. They do, however, convey the essence of what was said.

Robert Crane

I

Reveille, 1978

On Thursday, June 29, 1978, I was twenty-seven years and two days old. I had just interviewed the hottest star in Hollywood for Playboy's new Euro-hip *Oui* magazine. I was living in Westwood, California, the epicenter of movies, nightlife, and all things cool in Los Angeles. Life was almost perfect for a young man in my position—almost, because twelve hours earlier, someone had crept into the room where my dad, TV star Bob Crane, was sleeping and bashed in his head with a blunt object. I was about to find that out.

It was 3:00 in the afternoon. I was home alone at the apartment my dad and I shared. Westwood was an eclectic mix of neighborhoods. UCLA student apartments and frat houses mixed genially with the grander estates of L.A.'s elites. In fact, Dad owned a large, handsome house that was less than a mile from the two-bedroom apartment he was sharing with me.

At the time Dad was going through very heated divorce proceedings and needed a safe-house. I guess most divorce proceedings are heated, but his marriage had become Chernobyl on the Pacific. The meltdown had begun six months earlier in December 1977 when he stepped off a United Airlines jet at LAX from Cincinnati, where he'd been directing and performing in his dinner theater workhorse *Beginner's Luck* over the previous month. Since the cancellation of *Hogan's Heroes* in 1971, live theater had been paying most of my dad's bills. At the airport, he wasn't greeted by a driver or a loving family member; a man walked up to him and asked, "Are you Bob Crane?"

"Yes," he answered, pen ready, thinking the guy wanted an autograph.

"These are for you," the guy said, and slapped divorce papers against his chest.

Like most boys in distress, he retreated to his mother. A widow, Rose lived in a one-bedroom apartment just down the street from mine. Dad couldn't go back to his own house because Patti, his second wife who was now suing him for divorce, was in residence there with her teenage daughter from her first marriage and with Scotty, my six-year-old half brother. The house is a half-timbered Tudor affair, draped on the hillside like a spider's web, and Patti had taken up her position in its center, guarding her realm.

When my dad and Patti collided, I had been living alone in my own Westwood apartment. Dad asked me to move in with him at his new digs, and I did—going literally half a block up the street. The 1930s building had nice big windows and hardwood floors. We set up the living room as a little theater for projection TV, which was the newest craze, with those primary-color lights that broadcast the entire television spectrum. We each had a bedroom. The kitchen area was very small, which was fine because we didn't cook. It was all TV dinners and takeout for us. The dining room was the postproduction room. The guests at our dining table were my dad's equipment: Sony VHS and Beta video recorders, a monstrous three-quarter-inch cassette video deck, an Akai quarter-inch audiotape recorder, a Sony handheld video camera, hundreds of video and audio cassettes and vinyl records, a turntable, microphones, a Nikon F still camera, camera tripods, RCA and Sony television monitors, a metal bar for cutting video and audio tape. All the new and exciting techno-gear of 1977 and '78 was on that table.

So at 3:00 p.m. on June 29 I was alone at the apartment writing up the interview I had just done with Chevy Chase for *Oui.* Chevy had emerged as the first star of the mold-shattering, late-night television revue *Saturday Night Live,* and he was about to become a big-time movie star. *Oui,* owned by Hugh Hefner's Playboy Enterprises, badly wanted him in the magazine, and I was the lucky guy on the assignment. I was sitting there transcribing tape—which, for the uninitiated, meant turning on a Panasonic portable cassette recorder, listening to a sentence or two, turning it off, typing the words on my Smith-Corona electric typewriter, turning the tape on again, and repeating the process over and over for an endless number of hours. It was important to me to have the interviewee's words transcribed perfectly so there could be no mistaking the subject's "voice." Not exactly a glamorous life, sitting in a room by yourself rolling tape, but Chevy was making me laugh with his candid observations of his former cast mates.

My dad was in Scottsdale, Arizona, doing his play *Beginner's Luck* for the thousandth time. I had talked to him two days earlier, on my twenty-seventh birthday. I was feeling pretty good when the phone rang. It was John Henry Carpenter, a salesman for Sony and Akai and my dad's best buddy. Carpenter, fiftyish, stood a stocky five foot eight and had Native American blood in his veins, which gave his face and especially his hooked nose a chiseled look. He looked almost Incan. He kept his longish hair synthetically black, wore Beatle boots, shirts with long pointed collars, and tight flared pants. Carpenter was married, but minimally. He had relationships with teenaged girls. He had relationships with guys, too, I would find out later. He did it all—threesomes, orgies, you name it. He would meet up with my dad on the road, ostensibly on a business trip. His salesman position with Sony and Akai was more than his job description implied—it gave him entrée to the stars, supplying Hollywood's bold-faced names with the latest cutting-edge gadgetry.

This was a new business at the time, all predigital, very primitive compared to today's toys. Carpenter hooked my dad up with all his newest and most advanced gear. Others in Carpenter's Rolodex included Tommy Smothers, Sammy Davis Jr., Richard Dawson (who was also on *Hogan's Heroes*), and other film industry people who were interested in the next wave of whizbang gizmos. Everybody had a stereo, everybody had speakers set up, and home video was the next big thing. It was no longer eight-millimeter and Super 8 film. It was now videotape, with cameras that resembled space junk from Russia that fell to earth from Cosmo-7. It took no small effort to move them around. You could hand-hold them, but you were still tethered by cables to the tape deck, so there was virtually no mobility. The best way to use the video camera was to put it on a tripod so you could at least swivel it. We're so spoiled now by having cameras in our phones, iPods, iPads. It's Dick Tracy stuff now, but that's where we were in '78.

So there I am in front of the typewriter, headphones on, cassette recorder clicking on and off, on and off, transcribing my interview when the phone rings. Carpenter would often call me before hitting the road on a business trip when he could maneuver a detour in his itinerary to visit my dad. He'd say, "Your dad wants me to bring that new multiheaded cable he's got that hooks up to the back of the Akai tape deck," or "I've gotta stop by and pick up some extra Beta cartridges to take with me." It was always before his trip he phoned, never after. Calling me when he got back never happened until June 29.

"Hey, John, what's going on?" I asked.

"Nothing much. I just wanted you to know I was back in L.A."

"Yeah. Okay. How was the trip?"

"Good, Bobby, good. Listen, if there's anything you need, call me."

The whole conversation lasted less than a minute. After Carpenter hung up it was like a scene from a movie: I just stared at the phone, replaying what had just happened. There was something off, something out of sync.

My dad and Carpenter had a weird symbiotic friendship. Carpenter would help my dad solve videotape or camera problems by bringing him new parts from L.A. to those dinner theater capitals like Warren, Ohio, Fort Lauderdale, Florida, or Lake Charles, Louisiana. In return, my dad offered Carpenter the opportunity to hang out with a celebrity and experience the nightlife, such as it was, of Paramus, New Jersey, El Paso, Texas, or Traverse City, Michigan. They would go clubbing, meet women, and, odds were, get lucky.

After that uncomfortable phone call I went back to Chevy's wild riffs on life at the top of the Hollywood heap. Half an hour went by. For some reason, I don't know why, I just had the urge to call my dad, to check in with him, say "Hi," see how he was doing, hear his voice. I called his apartment in Scottsdale, which was loaned along with a big American sedan to the "star" of each production that played the Windmill Dinner Theatre there.

A woman answered. That was not uncommon.

"Hi. Is Bob Crane there?"

"No. He's not here right now."

"Who's this?"

"Victoria."

Victoria was Victoria Berry, who was costarring in *Beginner's Luck* at the time. She played the bimbo role, the squeaky-voiced blonde whose main character traits filled out the front of her dress. Her character was onstage for maybe ten minutes. My dad's character, a low-level IBM executive, attempts to have his first extramarital affair with her but fails, and all hell breaks loose with his marriage in the two-act comedy.

"Can you tell him his son Bobby called? Nothing important. Just ask him to call me when he gets back."

"Sure."

I hung up and blithely went back to transcribing my tape.

4

2

Oh, Pioneers, 1955–1956

In 1955 Bridgeport, Connecticut, was a working-class town. My mom and dad had a two-story apartment in a drab brick complex that looked like some kind of institutional housing project.

My dad was on the radio—WICC in Bridgeport. He had started as a staff announcer but evolved into the morning personality because of his catching sense of wildness and fun. Listeners preparing for another humdrum day wanted a laugh, a smile to help kick things off. My dad provided giddiness, humor, and perhaps even the motivation to get out of bed. I was too young at four years old to figure out that he was different from other dads, but I knew he enjoyed what he did and he earned enough money to support us. He would spend hours in a small, soundproofed room talking fast and loud into a big microphone, and people would hear his voice in their cars or at home. I found that fascinating and became obsessed by the notion that on the radio no one could see you, but they could hear your voice. My dad had already done announcing work at a couple of smaller stations—WLEA in Hornell, New York, a town so small and rural in the early '50s that cows were often seen being herded across the main street. Then he worked at WBIS in Bristol, Connecticut. Bridgeport was closer to Stamford, where my parents had grown up and where their families lived. Being away in those small towns, separated from his Annie and Bobby back in Bridgeport, had made my dad lonely and sad. There were also temptations for him living alone, but I wouldn't find out about those until much later.

My dad had a quarter-inch reel-to-reel tape machine at home. I had been given a little brown microphone of my own, and I would imitate him—talking fast and loud, laughing, trying to make people happy, and showing my audience that I was having a good time. It was the *Bobby Crane Show.* I would tell silly jokes, relate stories and news from the apartment complex, and sing songs from shows like *The Mickey Mouse Club.* I

Bobby at WICC microphone, Bridgeport, Connecticut, 1956 (author's collection).

recorded my shows and played them back, listening to them with earphones. No one could see me. I thought that was exciting.

My dad played one of my tapes for my mom and grandparents and they laughed at the inane things I said, the observations I made with my semi-English accent. "Bird" was "bahrd." It was not an affectation; it was just the way I talked. God knows where I picked it up. I was cute, unpredictable, and funny.

My dad thought it was time to put me on the real radio. Little Bobby being coached by dad to make the residents of Bridgeport laugh. I did commercials. At four I was ready for prime time. In February 1956, I sang the theme for Borden's Milk. I still have the 78-rpm disc containing the spot. The vinyl looks like it's a quarter inch thick and the grooves were produced with a nail. I was just being a kid—raw thoughts originating in the underdeveloped mass of wiring in my brain streamed out through my mouth onto the airwaves. No editing. No inhibition. No denial. No restrictions. And, most attractive of all, anonymity. Nobody could see me. But they could hear me. I thought it was the world's best job.

My dad supported my mom and me by being funny, playing music, and reading commercial copy. Pretty neat. My occasional appearances on his show as cute little Bobby were as close as I ever got to doing what my dad did.

I still love radio very much. The big-time radio personalities, the Rush Limbaughs of the world who are bringing in hundreds of millions of dollars, now broadcast out of home studios. Rush can spew his venom in his underwear. Behold the dangers of TV simulcasts.

Family life was almost perfect in small-town Connecticut, not far from the mother ships, my parents' parents. But my dad saw a road that led out of Bridgeport. Being a DJ at WICC was not going to be the endgame for him. He refused to settle in his career. He had seen his father, Al, settle for his weekly paycheck at the furniture store. Food on the table, church on Sunday, to live and die in small-time suburbia. My dad had bigger ideas.

He kept mailing his demo reel out to radio station managers in New York City, the number one media center of the country, if not the world. That's where Arthur Godfrey was. Where Jack Paar was. In that mecca were radio, television, stage, and movies. The station managers kept turning my dad down. There was no interest in a twenty-seven-year-old, fast-talking, quick-on-his-feet personality. The stations in New York had radio icons that had been on the air for decades.

However, CBS's flagship radio station on the West Coast, KNX, was searching for a strong candidate for the morning show in the nation's number two market. Ralph Story was leaving to host a revitalized edition of the famously crooked game show *The $64,000 Question*, which was being morphed into *The $64,000 Challenge*. CBS in New York was aware of my dad's demo tape and the buzz in Connecticut about this morning guy, Bob Crane. Though there weren't any slots available at WCBS in New York, the company wanted to get him into the CBS family and stop

Bob Crane, KNX
publicity shot,
Hollywood, 1956
(author's collection).

the loss of listeners in the tristate area to this little broadcaster out of
Bridgeport. So CBS sent the reel to Bob Sutton, the general manager of
KNX in Los Angeles. Sutton loved what he heard—fun, light, upbeat,
music—a good way to kick off the day. KNX/CBS hired my dad to be its
6:00 to 10:00 a.m. morning drive guy, six days a week, Monday through
Saturday, the host who accompanies you on your drive from the Valley to
downtown Los Angeles.

My parents became the pioneers of our family, traveling across the
country not in a Conestoga but in an Oldsmobile complete with radiator
bag on the front grille. They'd never been out of the Connecticut/New
York/New Jersey area except for their honeymoon on Cape Cod in 1949.

I remember seeing photographs of Mom in her short shorts, wavy blonde hair almost reddish, sporting sunglasses, posing next to the Olds off the main highway in Oklahoma.

I stayed with Nan (pronounced "Non"), my mom's mom, at her modest home in the Belltown section of Stamford. Nan was born Ellen Elvira Nikander in Helsingborg, Sweden, and met her future husband at the Feldman Estate in Tuxedo Park, New York. My grandfather, Alexander Terzian, was an Armenian Turk who lost his family in the genocide of 1915. Tuxedo Park was carved out of the Ramapo Mountains north of New York City in the 1880s to serve as a resort for blue-blooded members of New York society. Some of the early notables who lived behind the great stone gates of Tuxedo Park were J. P. Morgan, William Waldorf Astor, Adele Colgate, and Augustus Juilliard.

Nan was a domestic and my grandfather a chauffeur. Nan was a handsome woman with a short hairdo that required little maintenance. She had small blue eyes behind a pair of plain eyeglasses. She wore dentures. Her clothing was functional. She had a stolid personality reflecting a perpetual insecurity. She was an immigrant who was never quite able to accept herself as equal to "real" U.S. citizens. Nan sometimes behaved as though she was a fugitive whom someone in authority might ask for papers. Occasionally she would laugh over a good joke or something silly on television until she cried. That always led to a sneezing fit. She and my grandfather married, settled in Connecticut, and had two daughters, Ellen (nicknamed Bunny to avoid confusion with her mom and also because she loved the many rabbits that populated the family backyard) and my mom, Anne. My grandfather traded in his chauffeur's uniform for chalk and tape to work in a tailor shop. In 1950 he went into the hospital for a routine operation and never came out—a victim of negligence; he contracted an infection that stampeded out of control. Today a member of the legal profession would be on that faster than you can say, "Weitz & Luxenberg." But in those days, the wife with the thick Swedish accent just accepted her fate, buried her husband, and asked no questions. I never met my grandfather.

In the summer of 1956 my parents reached California and saw the Pacific Ocean for the first time. They stayed at the Malibu Surf Motel, on the inland side of Pacific Coast Highway in Malibu. It's still there today. My folks liked what they saw in Los Angeles. They liked the weather. No chains needed to keep the Olds on the road in the winter. Everyone seemed to have a swimming pool or know someone who did. They met with Bob Sutton, a pleasant man with a Gorbachev-like birthmark on his face, who would become a father figure for my dad. My dad was excited by the unending possibilities that L.A. offered to his career. What's more, my parents sensed in Los Angeles a new freedom, a shaking loose from the conservative customs and button-down rules of the East Coast. They decided to make the move. The downside was that they had no family on the West Coast and only one acquaintance from the East, my mom's longtime friend Rose Curcio. But they decided it was time to leave the smallness of Bridgeport, Beardsley Park, Morokses Hamburger Stand, and WICC, time to explore the relative newness and social lawlessness of the wild, wild West.

My dad signed the KNX deal for $50,000 a year, pretty big money in 1956. My parents rented a three-bedroom home with a small yard on Fulton Avenue in Sherman Oaks in the San Fernando Valley. They drove back to Connecticut, and, like returning astronauts who have walked on the moon, they tried to explain to the tethered family what this new terrain looked like, what life might be like without snow and humidity, that houses could be constructed not to look like minimum security prisons, that orange trees were not only real but ubiquitous, that the alien from *The Day the Earth Stood Still* hadn't destroyed city hall after all.

My parents got out of their apartment lease, and my mom and I temporarily lived at Nan's house, while my dad packed up the Olds and drove across the country a second time to start his new job. My mom said sad good-byes to family and friends, and I said good-bye to my five-year-old girlfriend. We took a train out of Grand Central Station in New York City bound for Union Station, just blocks from the not disintegrated Los Angeles City Hall. I was excited because I had never taken a trip beyond New Haven. The mother and son journey gave us the opportunity to see new things together even though our transcontinental track took us through some of the worst parts of the country, the hairy backsides of every major and minor city and town. Mom was leaving the daughter and sister roles to star in the mother and wife roles while she prepared for her newly created celebrity wife role.

A few days later our train pulled into Union Station. I was in Los Angeles for the first time. There was excitement abounding, but there was no Dad to meet us. My mom and I walked through the crowded depot along with the other settlers. We made our way out to the curbside. Still no Dad. Mom had two phone numbers for him—KNX and the house on Fulton Avenue. He couldn't be reached at either. My mom, alternately disappointed, angry, and sad, hired a cab, and she and "the little man" lit out for the Valley, where a much different life awaited us.

3

No Good-byes, 1978

Transcribing tape requires lots of breaks. A little past 3:30 p.m. on June 29 I had to leave the apartment to pick up my grandmother, my dad's mom, and take her out to Tarzana in the San Fernando Valley to visit my mom, Anne, and stepdad, Chuck Sloan. Chuck and my mom had been married for five years. Chuck was an only child and had no children of his own, though he had previously been married for twenty years. He grew up in Boyle Heights, East L.A., when it was a white neighborhood. High school graduate. Air force, stationed in Tampa with stays in both Kansas and Greenland. His father had died at sixty-nine; his mother was deaf and in a care facility. His cousins, the Worthingtons, were his main family. When he married my mom, he took on a new lot of relatives—three children, me and my two younger sisters Debbie and Karen; an ex-husband, my dad; my mom's ex-mother-in-law, Rose; and my other grandmother, Nan, his mother-in-law. His dance card was full, but Chuck was ever buoyant. A salesman with a contagious smile, he first sold television sets, then stocks, then single-family houses, which is what he was doing when he met my mom. Our family's house in Tarzana had become too big and carried the taint of my parents' divorce, so my mom had visited the Braemar development in the hills of Tarzana with an eye to downsizing the family abode.

Chuck ran the sales office, and though my mom didn't buy a new house from him, she did find a caring, patient man. A physically diminutive figure at five six, Chuck is nevertheless always a dominant presence at any gathering through his wise advice or his commanding silence. He seems ageless, with his hair thinning and turning gray just now in his eighties. He looks like he could be Bob Newhart's younger brother.

So I was taking my dad's mother out to visit her ex-daughter-in-law and present husband. Relations between Rose and my mom had cooled after my parents' divorce (Rose took her son's side, of course), but, now, years later, everyone had become friendly again. We pulled up in front of my mom and Chuck's house, a comfortable one-story, three-bedroom with a million-dollar view of the Valley that Chuck designed and built three years earlier.

"Bobby, get in here," Chuck yelled in an uncharacteristically harsh tone.

I hustled in, leaving my grandmother to be greeted by my mom, Nan, and my sister Karen. I usually had genuine laughs with Chuck, but clearly this was not going to be one of those times. Creases formed between his eyebrows as he said abruptly, "Call Lloyd Vaughn."

Vaughn was my dad and stepmother's business manager and was currently involved (with attorney Bill Goldstein) in negotiating their divorce settlement. I dialed his number.

"Bobby, there's a rumor your dad has been shot," Vaughn said unemotionally. "Bill and I are going to Phoenix. Do you want to come?"

Hearing the perfunctory announcement in Vaughn's businesslike voice made me feel staggered and hollow at once. The shock of Vaughn's words was otherworldly. I had no experience to draw from to deal with them. Mechanically and unthinkingly I said, "Yes, I'll go."

I hung up and told everyone in the room. Rose shrieked. Instantly, other voices cried out. "Oh, my God." "I can't believe this." Chuck and I looked at each other. He'd stay home while I went to Phoenix.

I drove to Burbank Airport and met Vaughn and Goldstein, who had booked the flight to Phoenix. They were concerned personally as well as professionally—they considered themselves friends of my dad. They sat next to each other on the flight talking, even laughing. Their hour flight went quickly. Mine, not so much. I felt isolated.

I played out a thousand scenarios in my head. How could my dad have been shot? By whom and why? He was an actor, for God's sake. What did it feel like to be shot? How many times? What part of his body was hit? Where did it happen? When? In the middle of the day? Sleepy Scottsdale was a bedroom community, for chrissakes.

The pilot informed us that it was 110 degrees in Phoenix. We were met at Sky Harbor Airport by Barry Vassall, a Scottsdale Police Department liaison. As we drove into town, Vassall turned to the three of us and announced, "Gentlemen, I've got to inform you that Mr. Crane is deceased."

Vaughn, Goldstein, and I looked at each other. Their expressions mirrored my own reactions, alternately vacant, angry, and incredulous. I reviewed my dad's life in milliseconds—his upbringing, family, friends, coworkers, one-night pickups, first wife, divorce, second wife, second divorce in progress, career. My self-centered life tipped from thinking about my next date and which movie I was going to see to my dad's abrupt and permanent exit. Handshakes, hugs, smiles, laughter—they were all just memories now. In the blackness, the door had shut behind my dad. There was no possibility of a good-bye. I would never speak with him again.

How the hell could this have happened?

4

One Happy Little Family, 1956–1964

I was five when we moved to California, so I started school in the City of Angels. The highlight of my six-month tenure in kindergarten at Dixie Canyon Elementary was seeing a kid come to school one day in his pajamas. "Wow. We're not in Connecticut anymore."

It was the three of us as the little family unit. My dad was doing his morning show as well as 250 luncheons a year all over his Southland listening area where he would speak and do his comedy routine using his tape recorder. Those appearances were all done gratis as an opportunity to promote both his radio show and himself. For instance, when the Culver City Chamber of Commerce had its annual luncheon at the Elks Lodge, my dad would be there as the emcee. He'd do ten minutes of stand-up or just appear as a special guest. "Let's give a warm Culver City welcome to KNX's new morning man, Bob Crane!"

His routine consisted mainly of stories he told on the air, like the time he asked everyone in the San Fernando Valley to mail in ten dead flies to help clear up the Valley fly problem—the postmaster in Hollywood was not amused. Sometimes he would follow his own material with a punch line lifted from one of the many comedy albums of the day featuring Jonathan Winters, Stan Freberg, Mike Nichols and Elaine May, Shelley Berman, or Bob Newhart. At the beginning, he used a great deal of Jonathan Winters because he thought Winters was hysterically funny, though bordering on clinically insane. My dad would set up a story or joke, press the "play" button on the tape machine at the luncheon or drop the needle on a vinyl record in the studio, and the recorded voice would deliver the punch line—"I love you" or "Chicken fat and booze." Or he would use a sound effect of a building collapsing

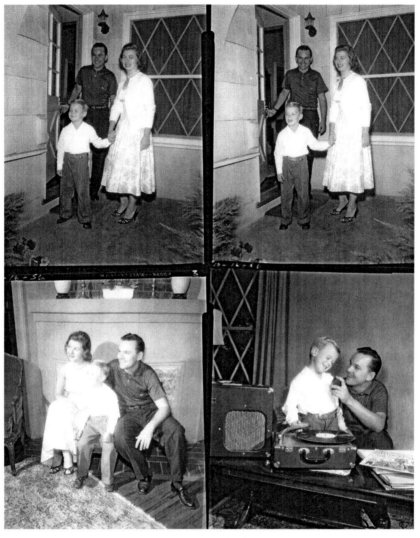

Bob, Anne, and Bobby Crane, KNX publicity layout, Sherman Oaks,
California, 1956 (photo by Walt Davis; author's collection).

or an automobile accident. My dad called these voices and sounds
"gimmicks."

When my dad had guests like Jerry Lewis or Nichols and May in the
studio, they would tape original lines and songs that he could use later in
person or on the radio. For live events, my dad would lift the vocal track
or sound effect off a vinyl record, transfer the bit to quarter-inch reel-to-

reel tape, physically cut the tape using a razorblade on a metal edit bar, and then use white stick 'em tape to butt the two heads of tape together. He knew exactly where each voice or effect was on the tape and what he would have to say to lead up to the payoff. Most audience members at those Chamber of Commerce and Elks Lodge events had a couple of drinks in them at lunch and were looking to have a good time, some laughs. This is how Southern California and Bob Crane met in person.

The downside of all those luncheons for my dad was that he gained a fair amount of weight that year because of all the rubber-chicken/rich-dessert affairs. After a year or so, he cut back on the personal appearances and shed the extra pounds. My dad also became a walking Thomas Guide/GPS for Southern California—Eastside, Westside, Valley, Southbay, Orange County. It starts to sound like a Randy Newman tune.

The dog and pony show, as he called it, helped to establish his name. Anybody who listened to Los Angeles radio in 1956 soon became aware of Bob Crane. He was the morning man on one of the leading radio stations in the second-largest media market in the United States. He was now part of the Tiffany Network—CBS. When his show ended at 9:55, after national and local news, Arthur Godfrey, another hero of my dad's, was on the air from New York. Pat Buttram, who would go on to *Green Acres* fame, had a show on later in the day. My dad's chief competition on morning radio was a longtime Los Angeles staple, KMPC's Dick Whittinghill, who presented a less manic drive-time show, a no-gimmicks, less hip, more traditional production in terms of the music he played and his sense of humor.

My dad defied the popular description of a disc jockey because he did more than just spin Top 10 records. He did comedy, interviewed celebrities, played mainstream music, and applied his gimmicks to the lifeblood of the show—commercials. Most company men enjoyed his playful jabs at their products, though some did not. The sales executives at Hertz got a kick out of their "We'll put you in the driver's seat" ad followed by the sound effect of a loud car crash, whereas the hierarchy at 20th Century Fox did not appreciate its sixty-second spot promoting "a new kind of thrill sensation," the critically reviled western/horror feature *The Fiend Who Walked the West* starring Robert Evans, ending with a hail of machine-gun fire.

My dad was in a studio by himself except when he had guests in the 9:00–10:00 hour. On his left he had one turntable for vinyl, a cabinet containing the gimmicks, his records, and a partial drum set (snare, hi-hat, cymbal), and on his right two more turntables. He wore a horse collar with a microphone on it so he could swivel in his chair, stand up and reach for a record, sit down, turn around, drum, and not be stuck with talking into a stationary microphone. Straight ahead of him in another room behind glass was his engineer, Jack Chapman, who was a bit older than my dad. He played the music and the commercials, which were on both vinyl and cartridge tapes. That was the setup. There was a lot of pointing—"Go!" "Cut!"—there were intercoms, station employees, ad men, and visitors peering into the studio through porthole windows. Chapman and my dad had great communication with only sporadic minor disagreements. My dad was twenty-eight years old in 1956, and he and Chapman were an odd couple, my dad loud, freewheelin', and improvisational, Jack buttoned-down and monosyllabic, but they worked really well together. Chapman was a great engineer because he anticipated my dad but never second-guessed him.

With my dad's radio salary providing comfort, my parents searched for a permanent base they could own—the American Dream, pride of ownership, their first house. They found an unpretentious three-bedroom on Donna Avenue in Tarzana, in the west San Fernando Valley. Edgar Rice Burroughs, the creator of *Tarzan,* used to have a large estate in the area on what is now Reseda Boulevard. Back in the '20s and '30s, the Valley consisted of immense orange groves and looked very much like scenes from *Chinatown.*

The Ventura Freeway (the 101) didn't exist; there were only surface streets. To get into Hollywood, one traveled Ventura Boulevard past the hamburger stands, car washes, and liquor stores. During school breaks, I would ride shotgun with my dad through the early-morning darkness into the big city to be in that radio environment that I loved from Connecticut—but the stakes were larger now.

My dad had only a tenuous relationship with punctuality, and most mornings found him racing the clock to the studio. His usual routine was to wake up at 5:00, take a shower, jump in his car, and at 5:45, though sometimes later, roar down the surface streets to Hollywood, his Cadillac hitting speeds of seventy-five miles per hour, to be on the air at 6:05. I never saw my dad drink coffee in the morning. He ran on pure adrenaline. He was writing that day's show in his head from the moment he opened his eyes.

Jack Chapman would fill the early minutes of the show by playing music. Some mornings listeners might not actually hear my dad's voice until 6:15. It got a little better when the Ventura Freeway was extended to the West Valley in 1957 and '58.

My dad did a promotion for his radio show on the Ventura Freeway in the Tarzana area before the freeway was officially opened. He staged an elephant race with jockeys "racing" four elephants eastbound on the new stretch of tarmac between Tarzana and Encino. The press ate it up. Once the freeway finally opened, my dad could get on at Vanalden Avenue, head east at eighty or ninety miles per hour (depending on how late he was) into Hollywood, exit at Gower, and turn right for Sunset Boulevard.

Columbia Square at Sunset Boulevard and Gower Street was an art deco structure that housed historic studios where Jack Benny, Bing Crosby, George Burns, and Edgar Bergen had broadcast their radio shows. KNX Radio and CBS's TV station, KNXT Channel 2, were the main tenants. Columbia Records had a recording studio in the basement of the building. I knew this was the big time, if only because the lobby of the building had a hot-chocolate machine that provided me with a much-loved treat every morning I went there.

I liked that it was dark outside when we entered the building and light when we left. I felt like I had lived a full day and it was still not even noon. The mornings I went to work with my dad felt like our little secret. It might have been our secret, but since my dad had the number one morning show on Los Angeles radio, it was a secret we shared with half a million other Angelenos.

My dad had the opportunity to meet many of the most popular, influential, and important celebrities of the day as they accepted the invitation to be his special guest during the last hour of his show. Marilyn Monroe, Bob Hope, Jack Lemmon, Charlton Heston, Steve Lawrence, and Eydie Gormé all trouped through his studio.

A thrill for my dad was having Jonathan Winters perform live in his studio. Over the years, Winters appeared on the show twenty-five times. The comedy album was king at the time, and veteran comics like Shelley Berman, Mort Sahl, and Alan King as well as up-and-comers like Bob Newhart, Bill Cosby, and George Carlin would book the show to promote a record, a TV show, a movie, or an appearance at the Cocoanut Grove at the Ambassador Hotel.

Word got around to publicists, managers, and agents that the *Crane*

Show was an easy, quick, and fun venue with an ever-growing audience for their clients. Generally, the last segment would feature two quite disparate guests like Dick Van Dyke and John Carradine, two very different actors though stars in their own right. My dad enjoyed mining information from each individual and setting up a dynamic between two opposite personalities.

My dad's television hero was Jack Paar. He loved the often weird combinations of guests from the arts and beyond, and how Paar extracted morsels of knowledge and oddball facts from people you might admire but know nothing about. The guests were at ease because Paar was a conversationalist, not an interviewer, emotional rather than intellectual. My dad identified with Paar, who was an open book on the air, sometimes crying, sometimes sharing with the audience what he did at home and on vacation with his wife and daughter. Paar behaved like a close friend. My dad emulated that behavior, and over the years on his radio show he would tell listeners stories of his home life with my mom. She would get upset, small-town Connecticut kicking in, and say, "Bob, it's nobody's business." But he, like Paar, became an open book on the air. He signed off his show everyday by saying, "Bye, hon." I always thought (and hoped) that he was talking to my mom, but as the years progressed, I realized he might have been talking to a few other "hons" in the audience as well.

As a kid in Los Angeles hanging around adult professionals, I became aware of my dad's appreciation of women, particularly actresses. This appreciation was expressed as a hug, a touch on the arm—nothing creepy. The fun-time mood of the radio show carried over to impromptu photo sessions with the guests and my dad. If the guest was Marilyn Monroe or an attractive newcomer like Stefanie Powers, all the better. One time my dad rolled up his pants for an interview he did with a bikini-clad Jayne Mansfield in her pool. After each interview was over, Jack Chapman would produce his Rolleiflex and strobe light and document the event. That's where I first noticed the touch, the kiss. This was important to me because the woman sharing that touch or kiss with my dad was not my mom. In Connecticut, I was aware of my dad kissing only my mom, his mom, and other female members of our extended family. The women he was kissing in Hollywood he had known only for an hour.

Film and television producers like Jerry Wald listened to my dad's show on their way in to the studio. They knew Bob Crane's morning radio show was a popular place to promote new movies and TV shows. Crane interviewed their stars in a light, easy manner, and besides, they thought he was funny, even wacky at times. Why not throw him a low-risk acting crumb here and there and have their projects talked about on the radio for weeks? So for example, on *The Twilight Zone,* my dad would be cast as the voice of a disc jockey; in *Return to Peyton Place,* he played an Ed McMahon–like talk show sidekick; in *The New Interns* (filmed across the street at Columbia), he played a drunken prankster; and on the *GE Theatre,* he appeared when future president Ronald Reagan was the host of the show.

My dad would walk around studio lots, hoping to run into an agent or producer or, if there was a god, Jack Lemmon or Gig Young. Sometimes I'd accompany him on his studio lot saunters, a cute little kid walking around with his dad. He didn't see this association as a liability at that time. Being a young, handsome actor with a youngster in tow demonstrated his virility, his being the head of a tribe. But as I got older my presence would reflect the aging process of a struggling actor.

Our happy-go-lucky show business family theme worked for a while. My family appeared in the ubiquitous fan magazines, the goal being to promote the product, Bob Crane. One time my dad, mom, and I performed a well-rehearsed short routine during intermission at the Ice Capades show at the Pan Pacific Auditorium. We also rode in a convertible during the Hollywood Christmas Parade along Hollywood Boulevard with my dad throwing 45-rpm records to the crowd. Mickey Hargitay, who was Mr. Universe as well as Jayne Mansfield's husband, once taped a week's worth of his exercise/workout television shows at our house, though I have no idea why.

One of the reasons my dad really admired Jonathan Winters's career was because Winters was a hyphenate—he did comedy albums, television, movies. My dad wanted a hyphen of his own. He loved radio, but he wanted to be an actor. He wanted to be a radio personality–actor.

His first live acting job was a supporting role in *Who Was That Lady I Saw You With?* at the Valley Playhouse in Woodland Hills across the street from where I would later attend William Howard Taft High School. It was a small theater with only a couple hundred seats. His character made his entrance walking through the tightly packed audience, literally knocking knees with the delighted theatergoers. He loved the instant gratification of live laughter, something he didn't hear doing radio except when he cracked up Jack Chapman or the live guests, who were amazed watching a human octopus in action.

The six-week run of *Who Was That Lady?* sold out thanks to my dad's constant promotion on the air. Most attendees were seeing my dad in the flesh for the first time at that barn in Woodland Hills. Up until that time he was just a zany voice coming from their dashboards. The material was light, my dad was charming, his part was brief. What was not to like? The experience was the equivalent of a delicious but low-calorie dessert.

In those days Dad was often away from home, what with 250 luncheons and dinners a year, a radio show six days a week, a couple of small television and movie roles, a play at night and matinees on the weekend. I was back to being "the little man" Bobby, who spent many hours alone with his mother, the mother who would always serve as the rock of our family. From the house we rented, my mom had walked me back and forth to kindergarten and to local stores along Ventura Boulevard. When we moved to Tarzana, she got a car, a beige Volkswagen bug. She loved that car, and in it we got out a lot more, mother and son, to parks, to movie theaters, to hamburger stands.

I was seven years old, less cute but still full of myself. I was getting cocky, too. I'd done one too many radio appearances. I depended on the same bits, which had become predictable—the bad jokes, the overly self-assured smile that could be cranked up at a moment's notice for a photo. I knew I was a fraud. I was feeling the early burnout that so many child actors experienced precisely because the one or two or three hooks they depended on were exploited until they were reeled in, bait gone and only an old boot hanging on the barb where an audience should have been. When the kid cast out for more, there was nothing there, just a pedestrian education, a lack of perspective, and a hollowness from the "me, me, me" preening that stage parents and set handlers helped create. While I was not a child star or even a child actor, I had, by virtue of my guest appearances and proximity to my dad's luminosity, started to take on some of the child star's foibles. Luckily, I also had the self-awareness to know that my cute days were past their sell-by date, even though it's tough to realize you're washed up and still can't even ride a two-wheeler.

When they made their first home purchase, my parents decided to shake off a bit of East Coast tradition, shed another skin, and move toward becoming full-fledged Angelenos. They decided to build a pool. An honest-to-goodness, precious water–holding, rebar-reinforced, cement-encased,

Bobby, Anne, and Bob Crane, Tarzana, 1958 (author's collection).

tile-accented ode to the New California. We were gonna have us a real cement pond, not one of those aboveground plastic tanks. A pool in Southern California is an expression. It's a way of life. It brings humanity to L.A.

With the construction of our kidney-shaped pool at the Donna Avenue house complete, all that was needed was a mere ten thousand gallons of precious Southwest water. This was an exciting moment in the life of a newly baptized Southern California family. We were talking serious pride of ownership as the water level approached the top step.

The ten-year-old son of our pool contractor was standing on the still-dry step, proud of his father's work. I was jealous that this kid, this stranger, this son-of-a-contractor was stealing my spotlight. How dare he stand on the top step of our new pool during the inauguration ceremony! I should have been standing there, not that alien. The contractor father stood on the deck at the deep end of the pool. He glanced over in our direction as I stealthily advanced toward his son from behind. When he looked away I gave the unknowing victim a full, two-handed push. Fully clothed, the boy disappeared into the green, unfiltered water. I looked at the splash zone, then at the father, and lit out for the territories. I headed for my bedroom and went to ground under the bed. My dad, who was in the front yard, heard the splash and the outrage and ran to the backyard. There was gasping and crying and yelling and angry pointing in the direction of my exit stage left.

"Bobby!" yelled my dad.

How could Anne Frank have remained hidden so long? I was disinterred in less than three minutes.

My parents asked me, "Why did you do that?" To this day, I still don't have a legitimate answer, just fragments of feeling about how that kid was stealing my thunder, replacing me somehow in my own kingdom. I think I can understand a little how Prince Charles must have felt about the public adoration of Princess Diana, albeit on a Tarzana-sized scale.

I was made to apologize to my victim, who was drenched and a little slimy. Ironically, his father's company was called Celebrity Pools.

My façade had cracked. My cuteness, cockiness, and self-absorption were coming to an end. I had to straighten up and be just an ordinary schoolkid, studying to someday receive a high school diploma, as my parents had, and maybe go off to college. At seven years old, the only thing I knew about college was that USC football games were on KNX radio.

After the splash heard 'round Tarzana, I made fewer and fewer appearances on my dad's radio show. The shine was off my apple. The cute phase was over. My dad recognized my transition from cuteness to pain in the ass and pulled the plug. Short career, but I was too young to know what *bitter* meant. More important, small-town radio was a few years ago. This was Hollywood, baby, and so it was from that point onward my dad's show would serve a higher purpose for me—an intimate venue where I could meet my heroes, stars of stage and screen like George Maharis of *Route 66* and Vic Morrow of *Combat!* I continued to visit the show during summer and school holidays. I didn't want to miss school because of the increasingly important social aspect of it—that is to say, girls. We were not an academic family, so my parents were pleased that I enjoyed going to school, even if I liked it just so I could see my friends.

I felt I was king of the roost for the first eight years of my life, but in 1959 my mom became pregnant with my sister Debbie. This tolled the end of my monarchy. Decades later I found out that I could have had a sibling closer in age to me, back when we lived in Bridgeport. One day when I was four, I sensed there was something physically wrong with my mom. She sent me to get the neighbor, a nice but extremely loud Italian woman who rushed over to our apartment and helped my mom, who had just suffered a miscarriage. My dad didn't find out until later that day.

With our family about to expand, my parents found a Richard Neutraesque three-bedroom with a pool, a big yard, and lots of driveway on Vanalden Avenue just a block over from our Donna Avenue house. Nan, who was still living in Stamford, sold her home for $18,000, packed up, and moved west to be with her younger daughter. My aunt Bunny remained with her husband and two kids in Noroton Heights, Connecticut.

My parents paid $50,000 for the modern home, complete with multiple levels, high ceilings, and severe exterior angles. When I heard the amount they paid, it seemed like a million bucks to me. Our small-town Connecticut family was morphing in many ways: my dad's salary was more than his father could ever have imagined earning; the small, two-story apartment in Bridgeport was a distant memory; the Oldsmobile and Volkswagen were gone, replaced by an ultra-finned Cadillac and a Lincoln Continental with suicide doors. I got a go-cart for Christmas and raced it for hours along the lengthy driveway, which was really the site of the Tarzana Grand Prix, complete with hairpin around the palm trees, much to the neighbors' consternation.

Although my parents always remained devoutly un-Hollywood, meaning no maids, no chauffeurs, no assistants, and, mostly, no pretenses, the family was blossoming. The obvious material advancement of a new home and new cars brought an uneasiness that was almost an embarrassment to me. I didn't want my dad's ballooning bank balance and the things that could be acquired with it to make me conspicuous among my friends. On the other hand, my dad's increasing financial success brought a level of comfort to my parents' lives that they had worked hard for and, at least in my considered opinion, really deserved.

In the '50s and '60s it seemed the average American family had three kids. In 1960 we joined that standard with the addition of Karen, my youngest sister, born eighteen months after Debbie. My dad related a blow-by-blow description of the birth on his radio show, much to my mom's chagrin.

More important, at least to me, 1960 spawned the Pool League, created by my dad and me. I was nine. The way it worked was I would stand in the shallow end of our pool when I was at bat, and my dad stood mid-

Bob and Bobby Crane at home pool, Tarzana, 1960 (author's collection).

pool as the pitcher. We used a rubber ball and a short wooden bat. My teams were the Dodgers, Pirates, Braves, and Cubs. My dad represented the Giants, Reds, Cardinals, and Phillies. Those eight teams constituted the entire National League in 1960. My dad, as the Reds, won the pennant that year and played the Yankees, who were always designated as the

American League champs. As the Yanks in that first Tarzana Pool League World Series, I was able to win four games to two. We kept a blue binder for box scores and standings, and my dad wrote a column reporting on and analyzing the ball clubs in his interesting combination of printing and handwriting. Innumerable summer weekends were spent playing the Pool League. At one point during the season, the bottoms of my toes bled because my skin was rubbed raw on the gunite bottom of the pool, but there was no going on the disabled list. My dad and I were the boys of summer. Those hundreds of hours of yelling, cheering, and laughing were among the best times of my life.

I was also in the Tarzana Little League, but I rarely played because I wasn't very good, though I still got to wear the Tigers uniform and pretend I was a baseball player. All the fathers took turns being the PA announcer for an audience of fifty bored parents, siblings, and friends. My dad took his turn at one of our games, comfortable behind the microphone doing funny ad-libs but completely lacking when it came to the recitation of the Pledge of Allegiance. I shriveled in the dugout, but I consoled myself with the fact that at least he was there. He tried, and all I wanted was to belong. I wanted to be a member of the team. I wanted to be like everyone else.

There were plenty of actor dads and actress moms sitting in the stands rooting on their sons, but I didn't want to be part of that. I didn't feel comfortable being a show business kid. When my dad botched the Pledge of Allegiance, it got a laugh, of course, and that instant response made him feel good. I think I was the only one in the audience who felt discomfort, though at the same moment pride mingled with my uneasiness. I wanted my family to be perfect, and I was worried my teammates would think my dad was an idiot, and therefore, so was I. But on the flip side, how did my dad feel watching his kid whiff on three forty-mile-per-hour fastballs? I'll never know. My dad never said, "Good game, Bobby, nice effort. You'll get 'em next time," or any of the other verbal back-pats that dads are supposed to dispense to sons who can't hit worth a damn.

In 1962 a TV series about a military school called *McKeever and the Colonel* was on NBC on Sunday nights. Unbeknownst to me at the time, they were looking for kids to be on the show, and my dad, who had met the producer or one of the writers, arranged an interview for me. But he neglected to tell me why we were going to Four Star Productions in Studio City. I was supposed to be energetic and bombastic, funny and

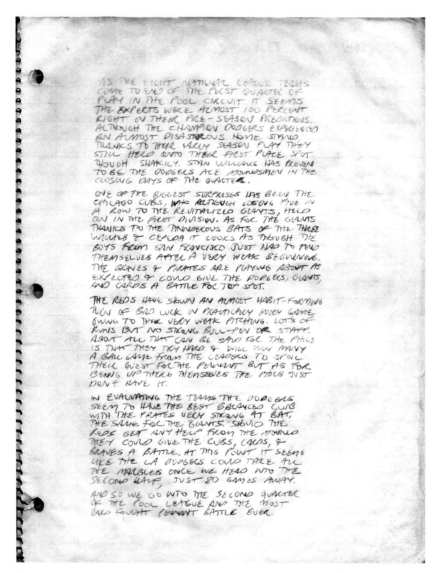

Two pages from the Pool League binder, 1960 (author's collection).

cute—and I just sat there like a lump because I thought my dad was meeting with these people for something to do with him.

When Dad told me why we had been there after we left the studio, I was really upset. I have the feeling now, on reflection, that my dad acted as he did because he was thinking, "Well, Bobby, I got you in the door. The rest is up to you." His parents knew nothing about show business

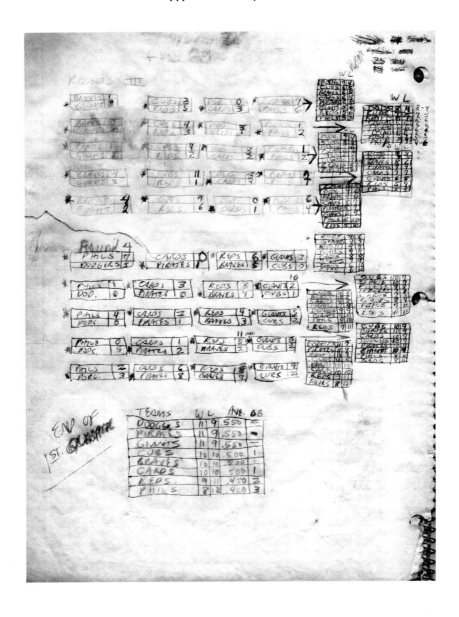

and had never helped him in his career—he made his own breaks and created his own opportunities. So getting me into that interview was more help than he had ever had, but still, he could've given me a clue about what was going on. I could have displayed my vast arsenal of charm, talent, and wit instead of sitting there like a ventriloquist's dummy. It also strikes me now as almost cruel, a passive-aggressive behavior that was setting me up for failure. Maybe I should've asked what we were doing there in the first place. Maybe I should just forget about it.

Before there was home video, there were eight-millimeter, Super 8, and sixteen-millimeter films. In one of our other homegrown activities at Camp Crane, my dad wrote, directed, photographed, and edited eight-millimeter movies with added post-production soundtracks. One summer we shot a film called *I Was a Teenager for the FBI*. I, aged eleven, played a very tough FBI agent. I wore a suit, and I had my own office. My secretary was played by my cousin Sandra. The villain was Dangerous Dan, played by my dad, and another cousin, Jack, played his hostage. I managed to save the hostage, but my secretary ran off with Dangerous Dan.

We shot at my dad's KNX office at night, and we used the streets of Hollywood for our exterior scenes. When we finished filming, which we did over a few weekends, we added all the sound, the dialogue, the music, and special effects like a credit roll even though the viewer could see the actual roller drum rotating. We were able to shoot the credits over existing footage because we could wind back the camera and create double images. It was pretty wild and imaginative stuff considering early '60s technology. The experience was great fun, and my dad had some memorably telling lines as Dangerous Dan, foreshadowing his yet-to-come lifestyle.*

At the end of the nine-minute film, there were coming attractions for a war film and a comedy starring the rest of our family members. Viewing the coming attractions now, the title that resonates most is *Get Me out of This House,* starring Anne Crane. There was a kind of subliminal message in that, a communication that the rest of us didn't see or understand at the time.

The hub of our productions was a ten-by-twelve room at the northeast corner of our Vanalden house that was known as the back room. It was the original man cave. Standing in the doorway and panning left to right, you would see one large speaker, a Ludwig drum set, two turntables, cassette and reel-to-reel audio tape machines, a vinyl mastering machine, three-quarter-inch and half-inch videotape machines, and then another large speaker in the far corner. There was a cobweb of wiring connecting the units in that room to speakers in the den and patio. The

---

*Dangerous Dan: "I'm so mad and sadistic, but most of all lovable. When Dangerous Dan comes, the girls always fall for him."

southern wall consisted of shelving that contained thousands of record albums. On the walls above all the gear were eight-by-ten glossies of my dad and some of his radio show guests: Rock Hudson, Ed Begley, and Johnny Mathis. There was also a large photograph and showcard from his first appearance on film in *Return to Peyton Place.*

The back room was used initially as an editing suite for my dad when he cut quarter-inch reel-to-reel audiotape containing celebrity interviews for his "Best of" radio show, which aired on Saturdays. I used to perch on a stool next to him and silently watch as he physically cut miles of tape, fascinated by how he could take a forty-minute conversation with Angie Dickinson, shorten it, and capture the essence of her in the limited amount of time he had to replay it. He took the week's interviews and boiled them down to eight- or ten-minute segments. So Tuesday's fifty-minute interview with Lawrence Welk and Bob Barker became an eight-minute piece for Saturday's show. The editing choices were all important. The inclusion of one funny or revealing answer and the exclusion of another depended on diverse factors such as length and flow. My dad could take a line from early in the interview and edit it next to an answer to a question thirty-five minutes later and make it sound like a continuously flowing conversation between the host and his guest.

The process made the editor godlike. It was about control. A successful wrinkle-free joining of separate sentences or thoughts was exciting. My dad removed breaths, dead air, and verbal stumbles to create a coherent and concise package. I would watch and ask, "Why are you cutting from there to there?" He would say, "The second line is funnier and faster than the first line" or "You need a beat there, a pause, because it makes the answer funnier." The results he achieved sounded seamless. Except for spotting the white edit tape rolling past the sound head, I wouldn't have been able to identify where the edits were. Later my dad would cut half-inch reel-to-reel videotape on his Sony player to create "Best of Carson" reels—the funniest and most touching moments from Johnny Carson's *Tonight* show. He created these for the pleasure of his dad and mom, who were always asleep by 11:30. My dad loved everything about the editing process: physically cutting the tape, splicing it, seeing the jokes come together. The times my dad was editing tape and film and making music were when I saw him at his happiest, most joyful, and most contented.

My dad received thousands of complimentary albums and singles from record companies promoting their latest band or artist. He would bring home a new batch every week. Each album jacket had a little hole punched in the corner designating it as a demonstration copy that could not be sold. I would watch for him to pull into the driveway at night and help him unload boxes of new records: vocal, big band, jazz, comedy, and rock. When I first heard The Beatles' "We Can Work It Out" single I played it a dozen times one morning before school. The back room was the best record store in the world.

My dad's popularity on the radio brought other perks. I was a Beatlemaniac and on Sunday evening, February 9, 1964, had watched their U.S. debut on *The Ed Sullivan Show* along with 73 million other people. My dad took black-and-white Polaroids of their performance off the television screen, which I cherished for decades. I saw all three of their *Sullivan* appearances, and their album *Meet the Beatles* was played nonstop at my schoolmate Pete Walker's make-out parties. I watched from the periphery as those progressive Encino girls gave long, soulful kisses to their steadies. I bought John Lennon's book *In His Own Write,* which I found hysterically funny, and my cousin Sandra and I went to see *A Hard Day's Night* at the Pix Theatre on Hollywood Boulevard three times in one day because the audience kept screaming through the movie and we couldn't make out all the dialogue.

In August 1964 the Beatles were going to play the Hollywood Bowl. I felt I had to see them live and in person. My dad mentioned on his radio show that his son longed to see the Beatles at the Bowl and if any listener had extra tickets for the soldout show he'd buy them. A woman called KNX and said she had four tickets that she couldn't use. The tickets were $5.50 each, and my dad, my mom, my aunt Bunny, and I were witnesses to the wild abandon of eighteen thousand young people and adults. It was a wonderful madness. To me, selfishly relishing the electrifying atmosphere of the Bowl full of Beatles, I realized there was definitely a plus side to my dad's celebrity. I temporarily forgot the discomfort I usually felt about my dad's fame.

Two summers later, my dad would make a call to the Wallach brothers, who were only slightly more than casual acquaintances. One brother was an executive with Capitol Records and the other ran the most successful record store chain in Los Angeles, Wallach's Music City. The result of that phone call had Dave Arnoff and me sitting in the first row behind the visitors' dugout at Dodger Stadium while our pals the Beatles took the stage set up at second base. This concert turned out to be their penultimate live show. Arnoff and I sat as close to them as one could get in a stadium rock show. Forty-five thousand of us hung on every note, not realizing that the closest we'd ever get to seeing the Beatles perform live together again would be the *Let It Be* film of their impromptu jam from the rooftop of Apple Records in London in January 1969. And that was it. Though there were still several brilliant albums to come, the innocent joy that was Beatlemania was unofficially over. I felt a real sense of loss thinking I'd never see those carefree moptops together again.

5

CSI: Crime Scene Ineptitude, 1978

Every four weeks, a new stage production opened at the warehouse-like Windmill Dinner Theatre at 10345 North Scottsdale Road in an unattractive commercial section of Scottsdale, which otherwise is an upscale Phoenix suburb. The productions were retooled Broadway dinosaurs or, in the case of Norman Barasch and Carroll Moore's *Beginner's Luck*, something that never got close to Broadway but somehow spoke to its leading man, my dad. He had made it his own vanity project, which he also directed, and he could recite the lines backward and forward. A cast of four, a couple of sets, ninety minutes, and time after the performance for the audience to enjoy a brief stand-up and autograph session with Colonel Hogan himself. These road warrior plays were fronted by former semistars like Forrest Tucker or Hugh O'Brian, who had had their bread-and-butter TV shows cancelled. The job could pay $3,000 to $5,000 a week, but the dinner theater circuit was about as far out as one could orbit show business and still technically be in it. Showbiz-wise, Scottsdale dinner theater was just beyond the rings of Saturn.

Apartment 132A at the Winfield Apartments complex a few miles down the road reflected just how far an actor or actress on the marquis had fallen. Instead of staying at the Arizona Biltmore, Hotel Valley Ho, or the Royal Palms, the star was supplied a nondescript sedan to get him or her from the warehouse to a cramped, dark, two-bedroom rental with a tiny kitchen in a lackluster group of buildings that could be part of any inner city. Parking spaces were not enclosed. There was no security. Many of the residents at the Winfield complex knew the comings and goings of their new neighbor, Bob Crane, aka Colonel Hogan. This was life off, off, way off Broadway.

34

THE WINDMILL

presents

BOB CRANE
in
BEGINNER'S LUCK
BY NORMAN BARASCH AND CARROLL MOORE

DINNER
THEATRE

Windmill Dinner Theater program, Scottsdale, Arizona, 1978 (author's collection).

I saw waves of heat rising from the blacktop as our car slowly moved down the driveway toward apartment 132A. There were no medical examiners, no crime scene investigators in jumpsuits, no yellow crime scene tape, no barriers for the crowds—and in fact, no crowds. There was no press, no field reporters jockeying for position, no flashbulbs blazing. It could have been the scene of a domestic disturbance on just another hot summer day in Scottsdale. As Officer Vassall led our party into the apartment, I was surprised there was nobody else there.

My dad's body had been removed in a zippered bag before my arrival. It had been wheeled across nine hundred square feet of cheap carpeting and wafting cigarette smoke through the open front door and onto the sizzling pavement where the medical examiner's vehicle idled, waiting for the return trip to the morgue.

The apartment had a cheap 1950s feel. There was JC Penney artwork on the walls, flower-print bedspreads, a plaid couch in the living room, a brass lamp on a pressed-wood end table. The cavelike space resembled a mad scientist's lab or a crash pad for a down-and-out rock group doing one-nighter club gigs. The place was trashed—a whiskey bottle and Booth's gin on the kitchen counter (I had only ever seen my dad drink two screwdrivers during an evening out at a club, and he never drank at home). There was a pack of cigarettes and an ashtray full of cigarette butts (my dad never smoked), mail, magazines, newspapers strewn about on the couch and coffee table in defiance of a tall, silver kitchen trash can, car and apartment keys, shirts, pants, shoes on tables, couch, and floor throughout as well as pool towels, suntan lotion, swim trunks, and a videotape containing an edited version of *Saturday Night Fever* sitting stacked in the hallway.

Dominating the small living room was the video equipment. It was mostly RCA and Sony products. There was a television monitor on a moveable stand, a three-quarter-inch video cassette recorder placed on top of the monitor, a metal shipping case standing vertically with "BC fragile" stenciled on one side that supported a VHS video recorder connected to a large, blue video camera with a carrying strap mounted on a metal tripod, a Beta video recording deck, stacks of Zenith videocassettes, AC power boards supporting a spider's web of wires, cables, attachments, converters, and adapters. I picked up three-quarter-inch videotape boxes. I touched the video camera that was mounted on a tripod. I opened my dad's travel case for the cumbersome videotape deck.

Vaughn, Goldstein, and I walked through the apartment, examining, touching, handling items in plain view of Vassall. We added our fingerprints, footprints, and hair samples to an already contaminated, lackadaisically investigated, casually considered location of a human being's last being. This was a murder scene.

Later I found out that when I had called my dad's apartment earlier that afternoon Victoria Berry was surrounded by Scottsdale Police Department officers and detectives as she played personal secretary. She was smoking as she answered the phone. Crime scene contamination was already well under way.

Berry had had an appointment at 2:00 at my dad's apartment to rehearse her scene in the play. When she arrived the front door was unlocked. The apartment was dark despite the bright Arizona sun outside. She whispered, "Bob?" There was no answer. She raised the volume. "Bob?" She looked in the bedroom and saw someone in the bed. The face and hair were so matted with blood Berry was unable to say whether it was her costar. She went screaming from the apartment and got a neighbor to call the police.

As I walked through the apartment I peeked in the spare bedroom. It didn't look as though it had been occupied anytime recently. In one of the bathrooms, a portable darkroom was set up, using the tank lid and toilet seat cover as workspace. There were strips of negatives containing thirty-six exposures hanging from the towel rack.

I walked down the narrow hallway and stopped just outside the doorway of my dad's bedroom. I didn't have any idea how to prepare myself for the actual murder scene. I turned ninety degrees to face the reality of it head-on. The lamp, nightstand, dresser, and generic paintings all had the transient feel of a motel that changed its occupants daily. What a lousy place to die, I thought. I had to keep reminding myself that this lifeless place didn't represent my dad.

A pair of eyeglasses, pocket change, and an open calendar book with "meeting with Victoria Berry at 2 p.m." marked down for the day sat on the nightstand. The investigators had stripped the bed of its sheets. The bare mattress reminded me of the Japanese flag—a large red circle surrounded by white. On the wall behind the head of the bed was a dervish-like blood splatter that showed, on closer examination, brain tissue. I felt I needed to see this. I had to bury my nose in this sad, sad, anticlimactic set piece. I had to register how the smell of that overflowing ashtray and those half-empty liquor bottles permeated the drapes, the tacky carpet, even the walls themselves. I felt it was my duty to be my dad's ambassador to the living, to report back to the troops on the home front accurate descriptions of the battlefield I was witnessing.

After walking those fields, I had to see my dad. I wanted to make sure that he was really dead. I couldn't rely on the announcement of his demise from a source I didn't know, didn't trust. My dad, my best friend, had been taken away, but I needed confirmation. I had to see it with my own eyes.

My only experience with shocking tragedies like this were those played out on the news at night, safely removed from reality. "Poor SOB," I'd sigh, and reach for a beer. Television created a safe distance between tragic events and the sanctuary of your own living room. I had for many years watched the 11:00 news during the Vietnam War, and Tom Brokaw, who was the local NBC anchor during those dismal days, often started his broadcast with the body count from Hue or Da Nang or some other hellhole. I would think about the guys out there, guys my age dying in a miserable misadventure and of the grief of their families back home, but the pain they must've felt was always unimaginable to me. Not anymore.

There had been unanticipated death in my family before, such as my grandfather's, but nothing so horrifically *wrong* as cold-blooded murder. I was staggeringly ill prepared for this. I had no background, no experience of any kind to help me deal with it.

To television fans it was the death of Colonel Hogan; to my family—a son, a brother, an uncle, a cousin, a former husband. To my sisters and me, our dad. It felt final and unfinished at the same time.

We left the crime scene. On my way out I took a six-pack of beer out of the refrigerator. That was another item that was out of place for my dad. He never drank beer. But it was going to be a hot night in Scottsdale. I figured it was also going to be a long one. The police officer in the apartment watched me take the beer and said, "Yeah, that's fine. Go ahead."

We drove to the morgue. I noticed that life was still being enjoyed by the local residents, running in their yards, spraying each other with hoses, children selling lemonade at the curb, couples riding bicycles. There were butterflies, hummingbirds. The sun was shining. It all seemed impossible. Death was a long way from their front yards.

At the morgue, Vaughn and Goldstein stayed behind as I was led into a cold, barren, uniquely unfriendly room. The sun never saw this place. My dad was lying on his back on a concrete slab. For the first time in his life, he was silent. No laughter. No nervous energy. No nothing. Just complete and absolute stillness, and it was that stillness that confirmed to me his death was real. My dad was lifeless. Life less.

I wasn't going to read about this in a newspaper, or watch some Barbie doll anchor work up the solemnity to stare into the camera and announce "Hollywood's loss." I wouldn't get the awkward phone call from a friend or relative who was unsure whether or not to tell me about it. There he was. Laid out on a slab.

I walked up to him. He was nude. I looked him over from head to toe. He was cleaned up. There was no blood on him. I stared at his face. I waited for him to open his eyes, look over at me, and start laughing, but it didn't happen. I leaned over and kissed him on the cheek. His skin felt like clay, the gray modeling clay I had played with in elementary school. It was cool to the touch. I panned his body, taking note of his thick head of hair, flat ears, chewed fingernails, hairless chest, uncircumcised penis, thin legs, long toes. He looked normal to me. How could he be dead? I felt numb. I didn't cry. I didn't experience an emotional upheaval. I was too occupied with mentally recording everything I saw—my dad, the slab, the room's décor. All lacked sensation. The scene was as removed from me as a dreary police procedural on television. I looked over my dad's body again, head to toe, toe to head. This was an animated person in life who was now dull and forever nullified. Somewhere outside the room someone was laughing.

I didn't know at the time that I was standing on the wrong side of the slab to see his wounds. He had been clobbered twice behind his left ear, and when I saw him I was on his right side. Later the police would show me photos taken at the murder scene that illustrated how copiously he had bled out. The tableau of that scene gave the impression that chocolate sauce had been sprayed all over the place. It wasn't like movie blood, red and vibrant. It was dark and thick.

The mass that looked like my dad, motionless as though he were having his makeup applied before filming, still didn't seem real. Was this the musician who played the drums with such passion and abandon? Was this the radio comedian who always had a quick-witted response to any situation? Was this the dad who created an entire baseball league we played in our swimming pool over several summers? Was this Dad? Motionless.

Cold. Humorless. Was my dad dead? It was impossible. We had a lot of stuff to do together yet.

After taking one more frame for my mind's eye, I turned away from that cadaver impersonating my dad. From that moment on, there would only be the long wait for answers.

6

Uncle Daddy, 1964–1965

My dad, dubbed the KNXtrovert Bob Crane by the radio station, enjoyed most of his guests, though actor Glenn Ford once asked no one in particular, "What am I doing here?" A relationship developed with some of them leading to multiple appearances every year: composers Henry Mancini and Bronislau Kaper; comedians Bill Dana (aka Jose Jimenez), Phyllis Diller, and Steve Allen; singers John Gary, Carol Lawrence, and Wayne Newton. He looked forward to having one guest in particular—Carl Reiner, the writer, producer, and actor who had just created *The Dick Van Dyke Show*.

My dad, like millions of other television viewers, admired the *Van Dyke Show*. The series was the classiest of its day, featuring wonderful dialogue for the talented actors and actresses and creating troublesome but clever situations from which the Petries (Van Dyke and Mary Tyler Moore) had to extricate themselves. Reiner always spent an enjoyable hour swapping quips with the whizbang host who asked him saucy questions about Van Dyke and Moore, tickled his commercials with gimmicks, drummed along with one or two records, and generally had fun so godawful early in the morning. Reiner always liked Bob Crane, whose nuttiness reminded him of Sid Caesar and Howie Morris.

Reiner took a flyer by casting my dad, based on an hour-long audition at KNX, in the guest role of a philandering husband in the upcoming "Somebody Has to Play Cleopatra" episode of the *Van Dyke Show*. Any actor chalking up a guest role on the Emmy-winning *Dick Van Dyke Show* noted a quick uptick in his or her career. The guest appearance was exactly what my dad wanted at that point. Working with Van Dyke, Moore, Reiner, producer Sheldon Leonard, and director John Rich—this was the Big Leagues.

My mom and I attended the filming at Desilu Cahuenga. There were three cameras, each loaded with ten-minute magazines, shooting in front of a live audience. Roles like my dad's part, of the good-time, life-of-the-party friend and/or neighbor, had always been abundantly in demand in television and film. Tony Randall and Gig Young had based careers on this seemingly simple role. Again, my dad fed off of the immediate laughter of the three hundred spectators in the bleachers. The response that Martin Ragaway's clever and snappy dialogue elicited suddenly made every hour on the air in Hornell, New York, every appearance at the Chamber of Commerce luncheons, every elephant race on the Ventura Freeway worth it.

My dad's performance caught the attention of Donna Reed's husband/producer, Tony Owen, who was producing *The Donna Reed Show* on ABC (everyone in the industry watched the *Van Dyke Show*). If *The Dick Van Dyke Show* was a dry martini with a couple of olives, *The Donna Reed Show* was lukewarm milk. It had been running for five years and was starting to curdle. It badly needed either an infusion of fresh, sassy honey or to be left to turn into yogurt. Owen and Reed were looking for a couple of new supporting characters for Reed and came up with Dr. Dave Kelsey (a cohort of Carl Betz's character) and his wife. Owen made an offer to my dad and Ann McCrea to play the roles in a seven out of thirteen episodes deal. That meant they would appear on the show every other week. If a season consisted of twenty-six episodes, my dad and McCrea would bring their neighborly charms to fourteen of them. Owen and Reed were sly show business veterans, but while they wanted new kids in town, they weren't prepared for the strong, pure energy that was about to be unleashed on the stale, tired series.

Donna Reed was a big-time Hollywood actress who had won a Supporting Oscar for her role in *From Here To Eternity* and had costarred with Jimmy Stewart in *It's a Wonderful Life*. My dad certainly appreciated her stature, but after filming a couple of episodes he became acutely aware that *The Donna Reed Show* was not *The Dick Van Dyke Show*. The writing was sweet but corny, and certainly not at all hip. It was a one-camera show. There was no live audience, and an irritating laugh track tried to spice up the otherwise unfunny dialogue and situations. It was a comfortable but unexciting program. The veteran crew just went through the motions and cashed their weekly checks. Most of them had probably been around since Harry Cohn ran the Columbia Studios lot. On the plus side, my dad could continue to do the morning KNX show, then walk fewer than a hundred yards diagonally across the street and enter Columbia

Pictures, where *The Reed Show* was filmed. He was off the air at 9:55 and in makeup by 10:00. He was making more money than he or his relatives back in Connecticut could ever have imagined. He had the number one morning radio show in Southern California and was a regular on a network series working with a motion picture star. The only problem was that my dad couldn't resign himself to performing pap after his *Dick Van Dyke* experience.

After that first season on *The Donna Reed Show*, my dad continued his emulation of Jack Paar by telling stories out of school about working on the Reed set. Producer Tony Owen didn't appreciate his smart-alecky candor. He felt the young upstart was biting the hand that partially fed him. Owen had given him an opportunity most youngish actors would have given their capped teeth for, but my dad wanted to be Dick Van Dyke or Jack Lemmon or Gig Young, and just couldn't settle for Carl Betz.

It was a snake pit audience at the Crane household. My mom was just happy that my dad was working and making good money. My grandmother Nan was still figuring out how my dad could appear on television while he was home watching it. My five-year-old sister Debbie and I (thirteen) sensed my dad's frustration with the bland scripts and acting style of *The Donna Reed Show*, and we seized every opportunity to pile on disdain for the entire enterprise like a couple of linebackers jumping on the stack of players after the whistle. Our baby sibling Karen was four and more accepting of the show's sugarcoating. Debbie and I made loud, obnoxious comments about how corny the show was, with little knowledge of or respect for how difficult an actor's life was. We were a despicable audience, rude to my dad. He was doing the best he could with what he had to work with. It was not his series, he didn't write it, and he was just a supporting character. His earnings put our family in a comfortable zone, and we were ungrateful wiseasses. Unable to resist his own instincts, my dad related some of his children's worst insults about the *Reed Show* on his radio program, and of course, Owen and Reed heard about it. Tony Owen, rightfully, didn't appreciate the bad-mouthing, but he allowed my dad to play out his two-year contract. Ann McCrea remained a wacky neighbor without a wacky doctor husband after those two seasons.

If *The Donna Reed Show* was a mediocre cloud, then at least it had a bronze lining. After my dad got the heave-ho, his agent at William Morris called him and said, "Bob, have I got an interesting script for you. Prisoner

Bobby, Bob, Anne, Karen, and Debbie Crane poolside, 1964 (author's collection).

of war camp during World War II. Nazi commandant, German shepherds, gun towers, the whole strudel." This was late 1964.

My dad said, "Thanks, but I want to do comedy. I want to be Dick Van Dyke. I want to be Jack Lemmon. I want to be Gig Young. I'm not a dramatic actor."

"Bob, what are you talking about?" the agent said. "This *is* a comedy. These are the funny Nazis."

"The Heroes," as *Hogan's Heroes* was originally titled, was created by Bernard Fein and Albert Ruddy, who would later produce the Oscar-winning Best Pictures *The Godfather* and *Million Dollar Baby*. In its first incarnation the show was set in a contemporary federal prison. Fein and Ruddy took it to ABC, where they did not get a lot of interest from the executives in their funny thieves, rapists, and murderers. The premise just didn't work, so they rewrote it, borrowing heavily from *Stalag 17*, a Billy Wilder film starring William Holden. There was a Sergeant Schultz in *Stalag 17*, and there was a Sergeant Schultz in "The Heroes." But what really made it work was filching a little bit from the James Bond franchise, since *Dr. No, From Russia with Love,* and *Goldfinger* had all recently been huge hits.

The idea was to have the POWs at Stalag 13 create all kinds of whiz-bang gadgets, all in the service of getting the better of their nincompoop captors—the Allied prisoners would be running their own base of clandestine and underground operations from a POW camp during WWII. The creators renamed the show *Hogan's Heroes* after Colonel Hogan, the American officer who led his crazy quilt of captives—the Frenchman LeBeau, the Cockney Newkirk, the Americans Carter and Kinchloe, and whichever guest stars happened to drop in at the Stalag that week—on various exploits. Originally, they also had a Russian POW who was played by an actor named Leonid Kinsky, but it turned out he was too old for the group, so they let him go after shooting the pilot.

The pilot was shot in black-and-white, the interiors at Paramount Studios and the exteriors at 40 Acres/Desilu in Culver City. It was the last pilot made and the first pilot sold for CBS's new fall 1965 season. William Paley and the executives at Blackrock, CBS headquarters on Fifty-second Street in Manhattan, were ecstatic. They loved it. They were jumping into the troop movement started two years earlier by *The Great Escape,* a huge hit set in a German prisoner of war camp and starring Steve McQueen, James Garner, Richard Attenborough, and an all-star international cast, and 1965's *Von Ryan's Express,* which starred Frank Sinatra and was set in an Italian POW camp.

In television and motion pictures, the stories, trends, and stars run in cycles, so it made sense that CBS would hop on the POW bandwagon, albeit employing relative unknowns and a weekly schedule. Blackrock hoped a large viewing audience would root for the Allied prisoners serving their countries by conducting missions behind enemy lines. They would blow up bridges, steal secrets, and generally confound the enemy, all with a laugh track. The stark black-and-white cinematography helped with the look of the pilot episode, but more and more TV series were going to color so, of course, *Hogan's* had to be in color as well. I never thought *Hogan's Heroes* and *Combat!* looked as good in color as they did in black-and-white, but they had to conform for commercial reasons. Viewers were buying color television sets, and damn it, they wanted color programming.

After numerous test audience screenings, CBS felt that *Hogan's Heroes* was going to become one of its most popular new weekly series.

The strong buzz emanating from CBS programming executives traveled crosstown to Madison Avenue and the all-important advertisers, who in those days sponsored entire episodes. General Foods bought up commercial time and planned to use *Hogan's Heroes* cast members to sell Jell-O.

Filming began in June 1965. My dad would go live on KNX at 6:05 in the morning, finish at 8:00, drive to Paramount or Culver City, depending on the three-day shooting schedule, and film all day and often into the early evening. Sometimes stunts involving tanks, trucks, and even airplanes would take the filming late into the night. My dad taped the 8:00 to 9:55 segments of his radio show at night after filming *Hogan's* or on the weekends for the upcoming week. My mom, sisters, and I saw so little of him during the filming of the first eight episodes he was known as "Uncle Daddy" at our house.

CBS publicity created an onslaught of television, radio, and print ads for the show. Satirist Stan Freberg created a radio campaign:

Freberg: "So, can we say if you loved World War II, you'll love *Hogan's Heroes?*"

Crane: "No, we better not say that."

Visiting the set became de rigueur for General Foods, Philip Morris, and Madison Avenue executives. There were also visits from American film master John Ford and English pop invader Dave Clark. There was a sense of fun in the air on the set as well as, more important, a scent of success.

For my dad, this was a long way from "Voice of Disc Jockey" on *The Twilight Zone* and a million light years from his small bedroom, consumed by a full drum set, at his parents' Stamford, Connecticut, house. These could have been heady times for him, but there were no spare minutes to consider the changes afoot as the fame factor invaded our lives over the next few weeks. *Hogan's Heroes* and KNX ate up his days.

Reluctantly, my dad met with Bob Sutton, who ran KNX and had hired him nine years earlier, to announce that he physically could not continue performing both jobs. Sutton took it well; like everyone else at KNX, he had heard nothing but great comments about the television series, not to mention the Freberg radio commercial spots for the show, which were running on the air all the time. Besides, CBS owned KNX so my dad wasn't abandoning that family.

My dad was on his way to being Jack Lemmon, but he wouldn't have minded being Buddy Rich or Louie Bellson either. He wasn't in the Rich

Buddy Rich, Bob Crane, and Louie Bellson, Redlands, California, 1978 (photo by Karen Crane; author's collection).

or Bellson category, but he was a pretty damn good drummer. He had started out playing in his high school band at Stamford High, which is where he met my mom. She played the glockenspiel. He went on to play timpani with the Connecticut Symphony Orchestra for a while but was bored by it. His goal when he was a teenager was to be in the big bands, playing with Tommy Dorsey, Benny Goodman, or Stan Kenton.

At fifteen I put together a rock band with two friends, Dave Arnoff and Ron Heck. We were a power trio. Ron played lead, Dave was on bass, and I played the drums. I used my dad's spare Gretsch drum set that he had at home for the band, but I was only a fair to average drummer. I could keep the beat and sing on key, but I couldn't do any of the pyrotechnics that my dad could. Ron Heck always impressed me because he played the same type guitar, a Rickenbacker, that Jim McGuinn of the Byrds played, except Ron was left-handed, and Arnoff was a great character because he had the longest hair and the oddest demeanor, a kind of Dylan meets Hendrix persona.

My garage band days coincided with the beginning of home video for my dad. He would bring out the new Sony camera and video deck, half-inch tape, reel-to-reel, and make videos of our band playing in the living room.

It was the mid-'60s, with all the craziness over the Beatles, the Byrds, the Stones. I loved what was happening. I loved the English invasion— the Kinks, the Animals, the Zombies. I thought I was going to be a rock musician for about five minutes, not knowing anything about what it took to get out of the living room and get a real, paying gig at the Troubadour or the Whisky A Go-Go or Gazzari's on the Strip.

Toward the tail end of my dad's KNX show in the summer of 1965, when he was doing double duty performing on the radio and shooting *Hogan's* at the same time, I was with him one evening at the basement entrance to the radio building at Columbia Square. Suddenly we were surrounded by five longhaired guys as my dad was trying to find his keys. I was slyly looking at each of them in turn as my dad finally got the door open. We let them into the building, and they headed to the Columbia Records studio as we took the elevator up to my dad's office.

"Dad, do you know who those guys were?" I asked.

"No, Bobby, I don't."

"That was the Byrds."

"Who?" As much as he knew about music, he didn't follow what was happening in rock 'n' roll.

The Byrds had just come out with the *Mr. Tambourine* album. David Crosby, Jim (later Roger) McGuinn, Gene Clark, Michael Clarke, and Chris Hillman. I had been standing there in the presence of greatness.

Two years hence, the Byrds' "So You Want to be a Rock and Roll Star" would address lazy wannabes like me. It's one thing to play in the living room with your buddies, and another thing to get out in the trenches. We did have a few gigs—a birthday party at somebody's house in the hills above Tarzana, the Corbin movie theater before a Saturday matinee, and a bar mitzvah at a restaurant in Encino called the Queen's Arms—but my rock stardom ended with a ten-minute jam of "Hava Nagila."

My dad's farewell KNX morning show aired August 16, 1965, a month before *Hogan's Heroes* debuted. It was a "Best of," where he played his favorite interviews and music, drummed to a few tunes, and rattled his sponsors one last time with his witty, bite-the-hand-that-feeds-you gimmicks. He was thirty-seven years old, late for emergence as an actor, but perfect for the role of Colonel Hogan.

Hogan's Heroes became an instant popular hit with its debut at 8:30 on Friday night, September 17, 1965. The series would finish number nine in the Nielsen ratings for that first season. Although many critics liked it, an equal number thought the show was in bad taste. It was, for them, still Nazis with a laugh track. Some critics felt World War II was still too fresh for comic treatment. The war had ended just a scant twenty years earlier. Compounding the issue, when *Hogan's Heroes* premiered, some members of the press misunderstood or misconstrued the premise of the show, confusing a prisoner of war camp with a concentration camp, and took great umbrage. The editors of *TV Guide* remain offended to this day, calling the show one of the worst series in television history.

But *Hogan's Heroes* takes place in a POW camp housing American, French, British, and other Allied soldiers. They are performing heroic deeds behind enemy lines. Some critics and viewers just didn't see it, or couldn't see it, or perhaps didn't want to see it. I concede that maybe the memories of World War II hadn't receded sufficiently. Interestingly, *M*A*S*H* appeared twenty years after the Korean War, and both the movie and television series won nominations and awards because, in between golfing, sipping martinis, and smoking marijuana, the medics kept expressing how awful war is. The critics loved it!

The war in Vietnam has spawned a lot of drama—*Platoon, Apocalypse Now, The Deer Hunter, Drive, He Said,* and *Coming Home*—but Hollywood has never found any humor in the jungles of Southeast Asia. Maybe one day we'll get the wacky and zany hijinks of "Ho's Heroes."

The truth is that the producer of *Hogan's Heroes*, Edward H. Feldman, and many of the directors, writers, and cast members were Jewish. Robert Clary, who played LeBeau, was in a concentration camp. He had a number tattooed on his forearm. The actors who played the Germans—Klink, Schultz, Burkhalter, and Hochstetter—were all Jewish. They caught the humor and cashed the paycheck. Werner Klemperer, a real liberal, won two Emmys playing the befuddled camp Kommandant, Colonel Klink, even while he spent much of his free time protesting against the Vietnam War.

The San Fernando Valley, where my family lived, and which many of L.A.'s Westside residents already viewed as foreign soil, supported the third-largest population of Jews in the world after Israel and New York City. During the High Holy Days in September or October, my high school was a ghost town. The reason I mention this is to point out that some of my Jewish classmates were heavily influenced by what was obviously being said at home. That sometimes put me on the receiving end of looks of disapproval, disappointment, or anxiety. "Hey, that's the kid whose father's in the show making fun of concentration camps. Get him!" I felt like there was a swastika tattooed on my forehead long before Charlie Manson thought of it as a fashion statement.

I had been in love since the third grade with a girl named Karen Nudell, the smartest, cutest girl in my class. In fact, when my parents were searching for a name for my youngest sister, they settled on Karen after I suggested it as a tribute to the girl who owned my nine-year-old heart. But would Karen Nudell ever want any part of a goy whose father was an actor on a show that mined laughs from the Luftwaffe? I think not.

Producer Edward H. Feldman's premise was that however unreal the series appeared to some critics and viewers, everyone involved in the production was to play it as though the situations were real. If the viewers could weather the laugh track behind a prison camp and care about the characters, the Allied soldiers, and their plight, then they were onboard. And whether you liked *Hogan's Heroes* or not, it was a landmark idea, with a good cast, funny scripts, and a respectful attitude toward its audience, which is why it's still playing fifty years later.

My dad had relied on himself—his intuition, his judgment, his sense of the room—throughout his radio career at KNX. When he started *Hogan's* it was no longer a case of microsecond processing of ideas and speaking as it had been on the radio. He needed to trust the person at the top of the pyramid, and that person was Feldman. Feldman had extensive experience in television production, responsible for hiring and firing actors, writers, directors, costumers, and editors. Based on his experience on the pilot episode that sold the series, my dad invested his trust in Feldman, who ultimately was the barometer of class and taste for the show. Ed Feldman hired New York stage actors; movie veterans; some old-timers in cinematography, wardrobe, and makeup; some TV warhorses in writing and directing; and a pair of young film editors for pacing. Feldman had my dad's complete trust, but *Hogan's* would be the only

Bob Crane, Ivan Dixon, and Bobby Crane on *Hogan's Heroes* set, Hollywood, 1969 (author's collection).

endeavor my dad undertook in which he trusted someone else more than himself. After *Hogan's* run, the creative trust reverted solely to my dad and his own instincts, and that's where his trouble began.

My dad was almost never home, portraying Hogan five days a week, fifteen-hour days locked up at Stalag 13 in Culver City. My dad enjoyed those thousands of hours on the set with the cast—Colonel Klink (Werner Klemperer), Sergeant Schultz (John Banner), Corporals LeBeau (Robert Clary) and Newkirk (Richard Dawson), Sergeants Carter (Larry Hovis) and Kinchloe (Ivan Dixon)—all sharing laughter and good times in character and out. The *Hogan's* production team was cranking out thirty-two episodes a season in the first few years. Nowadays, a show like *Dexter* or *Damages* produces ten episodes and calls it a season. The production had limited time and money. An episode was filmed in three days with a $90,000 budget. Hell, today that probably doesn't even cover Charlie Sheen's weekly budget for cocaine.

In addition to my dad's grueling weekday schedule, on the weekends, there were promotional trips to CBS affiliates around the country, "meet and greets" with fans, and visits to New York for appearances on CBS programs like *What's My Line?* and *The Arthur Godfrey Show.* So while all those fun-loving POWS and their German captors were winning the hearts and minds of America, my mom was left to hold the home front together, still just Annie from Connecticut (as she always will be). My mom bristled sometimes having her mother under the same roof, and there were clashes now and again. My dad didn't really appreciate having his taciturn, judgmental Swedish mother-in-law always within earshot, but he was home less and less. The upside for all of us was that Nan was there all the time taking care of my younger sisters. She was the built-in babysitter, tsk-tsker, and Dean of Discipline. I became the little man again, the only male in the house for extended periods of time.

7

Round Up the Usual Suspects, 1978

When we left the Scottsdale morgue, detectives Ron Dean and Dennis Borkenhagen, who were put in charge of the red-hot case, swapped possible murder scenarios with us. It wasn't quite a sit-down interview, just a trading of information. I ran through a list of people I thought were possible suspects. My first thought was there was a jealous boyfriend or husband out there, but then again, the women my dad fooled around with were not really the kind of women who had jealous boyfriends or husbands. Maybe my dad just fell into bed with the wrong woman this time. The Scottsdale apartment was what the police described as "a very passionate murder scene," not some cold-hearted Mafia hit. Someone had wielded a blunt instrument with enough force to kill my dad with two anger-filled strikes. Dean and Borkenhagen's prime suspect was the roving video equipment salesman John Henry Carpenter. They felt he had means, opportunity, and the physical strength to have inflicted the fatal blows. What they didn't have was a motive.

Then I thought about my stepmother, Patti. When *Hogan's Heroes* debuted in 1965, the German Kommandant, Colonel Klink, had a curvaceous secretary called Helga, played by an actress named Cynthia Lynn. She mysteriously left the show after the first raucous season, replaced by another buxom actress wearing blonde pigtails and tight sweaters. It wasn't until years later I found out that the reason Cynthia Lynn abruptly left the show was because she and my dad were having an affair, and her husband discovered the liaison and gave her an ultimatum: leave the show or divorce. She chose her marriage and cancelled her career. Unfortunately, her marriage got a pink slip a few years later, anyway.

So Helga became Hilda, and Cynthia Lynn dissolved into Sigrid Valdis. Valdis as Hilda would say, "Ja, mein Colonel" from the second season through the 168th and final episode. Valdis as Hilda would appear with Klink and Schultz on my dad's one and only record album cover. Valdis as Hilda would treat those on-set kisses with Colonel Hogan in Klink's outer office as a rehearsal, a prelude to an insurance policy on an acting career that was as doomed as the Third Reich. Valdis as Hilda would become my stepmother.

Sigrid Valdis was the nom de guerre of Patricia (Patti) Olson, sprung from the onion fields of Bakersfield to occupy the fertile beds of Hollywood. She landed the role of Hilda shortly after her first husband died from a brain aneurysm. They had been married just under ten years and had a young daughter, Melissa. Patti had worked with James Coburn in *Our Man Flint* and with Frank Sinatra and Dean Martin in *Marriage on the Rocks,* playing small roles requiring large cleavage. On the *Hogan's* set her talents attracted the immediate attention of Richard Dawson, but Patti was not going to hitch her ample wagon to the corporal when the colonel might be available for a hookup.

On a TV series, actors begin as coworkers, but if you're lucky enough to be a regular cast member on a hit show, the series actors can spend what amounts to years together rehearsing, filming, socializing— breaking for lunch and sometimes for dinner, too. The actors become real friends, second family members, and in the case of my dad and Patti, lovers.

Their time spent filming together segued into evening meetings at restaurants, which then morphed into quick, discreet sexual encounters in my dad's dressing room in the production building, and finally into full-blown carnal knowledge at Patti's apartment in Westwood on my dad's way home to a much more chaste Tarzana.

As my mom played both parental roles at home, Patti played the hyphenate roles of friend-lover-wife-mistress at work and on the road. My dad was also playing a multitude of roles: good Catholic son, high school sweetheart, husband, father, Casanova, and most important, Colonel Robert E. Hogan, lead character on a flourishing network television series beloved by millions.

Patti not only seemed to understand my dad's needs and proclivities; she nurtured them, fed them, and even participated in them. Their relationship began while my mom and dad were still married, and while I can't cite it specifically as the cause of my parents' divorce, Hogan and Hilda were a force that would not be denied.

As far as we knew at that moment in Scottsdale, Patti had neither means nor opportunity, but she alone did have a motive.

8

Zero to Ninety, 1965–1966

My dad was on autopilot as his recognition factor went from zero to ninety in a month, which naturally impacted the rest of the family. A dramatic change was in the air for the Crane household. Walking through a crowded Du-Par's to get a hamburger suddenly became disconcerting as we heard tittering, whispering, or even a rebel yell—"Hogan!" My dad was less concerned.

Soon, too, we had strange people showing up at the Vanalden house. An electric gate was installed. One attractive woman in her thirties somehow got through the gate and rang the front doorbell. The fact that there was someone at the front door signaled something odd. Everyone who knew us, who visited us at the house, came in through a side door that opened into the kitchen. My mom nervously answered as I stood guard nearby. The woman showed us a photo of a young child and said she wanted to see the father—my dad. My mom, in her low-key style, managed to get the woman off the property. If there was any fallout between her and dad over this, I never heard about it, and to my knowledge no one ever heard from the woman again. The members of my family— mom, sisters, grandmothers, grandfather, aunt, uncle, cousins—had no experience in dealing with these kinds of occurrences. There was no guidebook, no *Celebrity for Dummies*, we could reference.

My dad's anonymity was forever gone, but he felt he had earned the notice. Good or bad reviews aside, he had taken the next step, a big one, and there was no point in looking back. My dad was securely in the present. Being recognized was a Nielsen-like test of popularity. His face was the product he was selling, and if it didn't get recognized, hightailing back to radio would have been an ego destroyer for him. He wanted to attain a certain level of performance quality whereby he could, at least in his own mind, see the taillights of Jack Lemmon, Gig Young, and Tony Randall off in the distance. To him, the loss of privacy resulting from being on a hit TV show was a necessary evil, even as the intensity of his celebrity grew exponentially over the next few years.

Besides, his work was creative, he was making more money than his family had ever known, and he felt he was demolishing the small-town thought processes that had held him back. His only real disappointment was having to give up the radio show. Performing live on radio was his purest form of expression because the only script was in his head and there wasn't a supporting cast, only funny voices or sound effects on vinyl. It was all his creation, with the assistance of his "fine engineer, Jack Chapman." That was a pure creative process for my dad, and he was sad to give it up. But it was physically impossible to do a daily four-hour radio show and a one-camera filmed television series at the same time. So he took the plunge and put all his chips on making fun of the Third Reich.

Still, he would never completely shake the burg mentality engrained in his DNA. He would drive over to the Hollywood branch of Bank of America and stand in line to make a deposit on his lunch break, still wearing his Hogan uniform. It would never have occurred to him to send someone to do this chore. He picked up his own dry cleaning, went to the DMV, and always drove himself or had me drive him to the airport. There was never a VIP contingent for him.

CBS was riding a ratings-grabbing wave. It was a big-time network with big-time hit shows, and my dad was a part of that. *Hogan's Heroes* finished in the top ten in the ratings in its first season. There were Emmy nominations: for the show itself, for Werner Klemperer's Colonel Klink as Best Supporting Actor, and for my dad as Best Actor in a Comedy Series (the first of two nominations). Unfortunately, he was up against Don Adams in *Get Smart* and Dick Van Dyke, who was the eventual winner. Even though my dad didn't win, he was pleased to have been nominated, to have been recognized. It validated his move from his number one radio show.

At home Mom was keeping everything as low-key as possible, almost pretending all the hoopla wasn't even happening. Occasionally, however, she would succumb to the Hollywood sirens' call, getting out the fur coat and attending industry and charity event dinners with my dad. She went to the Emmy Awards. She did participate, but she certainly had no aspirations to be a Hollywood wife or even to be part of Hollywood. For God's sake, we lived in Tarzana, which *TV Guide* called "the unfashionable Tarzana, California," when it did an article on my dad. My folks enjoyed the perception that it was unfashionable. We were living in a town so named because the guy who created the "Lord of the Jungle," Edgar Rice Burroughs, happened to be raising sheep on a hill off Reseda Boulevard. People expected TV stars and film people to live large in Bel-Air or Beverly Hills, not out in the foothill recesses of the San Fernando Valley, which in the 1950s and '60s was more like Mayberry with oranges.

I was attending Gaspar de Portola Junior High School, and more and more kids were making the connection between Colonel Hogan and me, between Bob Crane and this kid named Bobby Crane who was in their English or industrial drafting class. I started to withdraw a bit because giggling kids at school I'd never met were awkwardly approaching me to ask, "Is your dad Colonel Hogan?" I didn't like being prejudged depending on whether people liked *The Donna Reed Show* or *Hogan's Heroes* or KNX or disliked wacky neighbors or laughable Germans or radio. My classmates' prejudgment was an automatic response, sometimes stoked at home by parents. After all, most fourteen-year-olds' opinions are just reflections of those of their parents.

Coincidentally, Portola was the same school Dick Van Dyke's two sons, Chris and Barry, attended. I didn't really know Chris, but I knew Barry a little bit. Barry always handled being Dick Van Dyke's son with ease, it seemed to me, and Dick Van Dyke was a major star. Not only did he have a hit TV series, he had just starred in *Mary Poppins*. He was truly a big star, and yet Barry handled it with style. All the kids at Portola knew who he was, but he was completely unflustered by it. I didn't know how he did that, and I envied him his cool. He was also part of the fast, hip crowd, at least as fast and as hip as thirteen- and fourteen-year-olds in the Valley could be. Barry's crowd had the best parties at the neatest houses in Encino. Maybe that was part of it. Barry was an Encino kid. I was a Tarzana kid. There was in my mind a big difference. I thought Encino was more of a show business community, more upscale and hipper than Tarzana. I mean, Dick Van Dyke drove a Jaguar XKE. My dad drove a Cadillac. Barry Van Dyke was like the chief ambassador for show biz kids, and I didn't quite get what my role at school was supposed to be. I didn't know what my role in life was supposed to be. It was like Barry was the ambassador to London and I was the chargé d'affaires in Ouagadougou.

I had once been, long ago, a cute radio kid, but now I was just an eighth-grade student trying to figure out algebra and worrying about how many sit-ups I could do in one minute without farting. I was positive that if Barry Van Dyke farted during a sit-up test in gym class, he'd handle that like a pro, too.

9

Seeing Orange, 1978

After seeing my dad at the morgue I knew I had to call home. This was as close as I would ever come to being a war correspondent calling the international desk, reporting on the day's casualty count. I could only imagine how many tears had already been spilled in anticipation of the worst. Certainly, there had been no phone call from my dad to my mom and Chuck clearing up the police blotter rumor. How did military messengers deliver the bad news? I'd much rather have done it in person. There is a coldness to a voice traveling through copper wire.

Luckily, Chuck answered the phone. I told him that my dad had not been shot; he'd been hit with something. I confirmed he was dead. I said I saw him. I said I saw him dead. I tried to keep my emotion in check like a good foreign correspondent. We weren't on the phone long. I spoke, too, to my mom. She was sobbing. I could hear my dad's mom in the background, her low moaning.

My family had been getting calls from friends and acquaintances who had heard something about the crime on the radio. That was long before CNN and the twenty-four-hour news cycle. The only reason the media even found out about the murder was because someone in the Scottsdale Police Department faxed the preliminary report to a reporter at the *Arizona Republic,* and it mushroomed from there. Still, it was nothing like what would happen now in the twenty-first century.

Vaughn, Goldstein, and I checked into a nearby motel for the night. We were going to talk to the police again the next morning. It was still June 29, the evening of a very long day. I went out to the motel pool and collapsed into a chaise longue. I drank a couple of the beers I had liberated earlier from the crime scene and stared at the sky. I had never felt lonelier.

Just one week earlier my dad had attended a high school graduation party for my sister Karen held at my mom and Chuck's house. Dad had canceled his play for that evening just so he could be there, and in the course of the afternoon he had a conversation with Chuck about his upcoming fiftieth birthday. He confided that he was seeing things differently, even mundane things. He told Chuck he was seeing the color orange for the first time, appreciating it—he believed he was on a different path. Today pundits would call it a sea change. He was going to try to reconstruct his life after getting out of his marriage to Patti. He'd already taken the first step by putting a $5,000 deposit on a house in Sherman Oaks, another Valley community. My dad had very few friends, yet despite that, it was my feeling that jettisoning John Carpenter was to be part of his planned rejuvenation. Dad had told me he felt Carpenter had devolved from being a fun-seeking friend to a hanger-on, a parasite. He was seeing a new horizon and was excited about it.

That image is burned in my brainpan: Chuck and my dad sitting in the backyard, looking out over the San Fernando Valley below. I thought at the time how strange that tableau was. It was uncomfortable for me to see my dad and my stepdad talking to each other (they had both made love to my mother, for one thing), but on the other hand how nice it was that they could have that quiet, intimate moment together without any animosity. I think they appreciated each other. They were two very different men, much like the kind of guests my dad liked to book on his radio show—one frenetic and funny, the other quiet and thoughtful—but there they were making the best of it for the family.

Although they were the same age, Chuck had the serene confidence and demeanor of a teacher, whereas my dad seemed always to be on a quest, like a young student. They had both been married twenty years to their first spouses. My dad was the father of four children and stepfather of one, and Chuck the stepfather of three. Chuck was the anticelebrity with no ego. He lived his life according to a strong moral code. He took his time thinking things through before reaching a decision, and his judgments were correct almost all of the time. My dad lacked patience and jumped in feet first, though I never saw him dive headfirst. He always anticipated the best and shrugged off the worst.

I tried to reconcile myself to the fact that my dad was dead, and I wondered about the changes coming into all the lives connected to him. My dad wouldn't see his children get married. He wouldn't see any of our achievements. He wouldn't see us get older, mature. We would miss seeing him get older. He was now going to be locked in forever at forty-nine,

Robert Crane and Chuck Sloan at home, Tarzana, mid-1980s (author's collection).

two weeks shy of fifty. He wouldn't see the changes he had talked about with Chuck actually happen. I wanted him to see the color orange. I wanted him to see new things because he could not have continued down the path he had been on much longer. What we've come to know as sex addiction wasn't talked about at that time. We didn't even talk about alcoholism in public. There was no Betty Ford Clinic, no *Celebrity Rehab* on television, no Doctors Phil or Drew. Those were all big-sky thoughts, lying there in the warm night staring at the stars through misty eyes.

Then I was also confronted by practical questions. Where would I live? I would have to move out of the apartment. I didn't earn enough money as a freelance writer to afford a two-bedroom in Westwood. What would happen to all my dad's equipment? He was in the middle of a divorce, but he was still married, technically, and I was guessing Patti still had certain rights. I worried about all this and about getting on a plane the next day, flying back to Burbank, getting in my car and driving back to the apartment I share with my dad. My dad who's dead.

10

Living la Vita Hogan, 1967

After shooting the first two seasons at Paramount Studios, the *Hogan's Heroes* company moved west a few blocks to the smaller Desilu Cahuenga lot. *The Andy Griffith Show, That Girl,* and *The Dick Van Dyke Show* all maintained soundstages and offices there. My dad had a small dressing room onstage, filled to bursting with a drum set, turntable, stereo equipment, and hundreds of albums. Between takes or while the crew was lighting the next scene, he would crank up the volume and drum to his heart's content. It was a stress release for him as well as the other actors and technicians who were within earshot. When the second assistant director would signal to him that they were ready to film the next setup, off went Harry James or Quincy Jones, and the stage would return to its whisper-quiet mode.

My dad was struggling with playing two distinct and conflicting roles. First, he was the sociable host of the amusement park for grown-ups known as the *Hogan's Heroes* set. It was a land where everyone had a great time. The cast and crew all got along really well, with the glaring exception of Richard Dawson and my dad. The chief reason for their simmering animosity was that Dawson had read for the starring role of Hogan but wound up in the supporting role of the Eastender Newkirk. He did a decent job, considering he was basically a comedian and not an actor, but Dawson always believed he should have been Hogan and my dad was the pretender on his throne. My dad's other role was that of the Catholic, churchgoing husband and father in charge of house and home, though he had relinquished much of that duty to my mom a long time before.

As the crow flies, the *Hogan's* set and not-so-posh Tarzana were fewer than twenty miles apart, but they represented two divorced worlds. My dad's frenetic days were spent in the wacky POW camp, complete with steak lunches, laughter galore with the actors from both Allied and German forces, and visits to the set from the likes of Lucille Ball, John Wayne, and an unending phalanx of models. These daytime labors were followed by evenings spent with a civilian wife, a critical mother-in-law, three rank-and-file kids, a German shepherd named Penny, and a small, gray poodle of indeterminate heritage named Candy, who had a habit of hacking up some kind of pellet whenever anyone but my mom tried to pet her. For my dad it wasn't just a different world, it was a different galaxy, and he tried mightily to keep the artificial pyrotechnics of the set from becoming emotional explosions on the home front.

In addition to his on-set digs, my dad also had a larger dressing room offstage in the building that housed producer Edward H. Feldman and his production staff. That petite white bungalow included a small living room and kitchen area, and could have doubled for the *Hogan's Heroes* editing room, just yards away, where the real work was done. Film editors Jerry London, who later directed ten episodes of the series and *Shogun*, among a hundred other credits, and Michael Kahn, who later became Steven Spielberg's editor beginning with *Close Encounters of the Third Kind* and who has, to date, won three Academy Awards, helped shape each episode. They were integral parts of a successful series. At the end of each season, London, Kahn, and my dad would go through all the out-take footage—where actors flubbed their lines or started to laugh in the middle of a scene or when a light stand fell or there were costume malfunctions—and put together the best bits for a gag reel, which they showed at the season's wrap party. The *Hogan's* blooper reel became a highly anticipated yearly staple, and my dad would make copies for everyone in the cast and crew.

While legitimate work was being done in London and Kahn's room, Colonel Hogan's dressing room had a very different mission statement. It reflected a growing fanaticism with gadgets and a private, personal obsession that would later threaten to undermine everything this workaholic man had built from nothing. My dad was losing his perspective, developing a dangerous tunnel vision. He was raising a curtain of hypocrisy that had clouded his true self, but his new behavior was becoming counterproductive to achieving his aspirations.

For one thing, my dad's dressing room was turning into porn central. There were strips of film, negatives, film cans, still and video cameras everywhere. The red light was always on in my dad's makeshift film-processing lab in the bathroom. He spent his "off-duty" time developing hundreds of photographs of the actresses and Playboy Playmates who were always stopping by the set—ostensibly to visit Brit bachelor-about-town Richard Dawson, but they soon became enamored with his commanding officer. It seemed word was out that the *Hogan's* set was the place to market your wares if you were young, shapely, and of the female persuasion.

Dawson's friend John Henry Carpenter, a Sony video equipment salesperson, aided and abetted my dad, helping to transform his dressing room into a makeshift movie theater where the latest sixteen-millimeter porno films were projected onto a wall and copied to videotape by means of a Sony video camera taping the film, much the way first-run films are pirated today. This crude version of the Deluxe, Fotokem, or CFI labs could be dismantled in minutes if need be.

When I was sixteen and visiting the *Hogan's* set that summer, I was exposed to an "actress" named Candy Barr's talents when my dad set up his sixteen-millimeter projector to premiere her latest sextravaganza. Candy Barr had been arrested in Texas for performing oral sex, so she refused to do that on film, but she did just about everything else before my unblinking teenaged eyes. This might have been my dad's clumsy, Hollywood way of having a "birds and bees" talk with his coming-of-age son, but what strikes me now looking back is that his equipment-laden room was another in a series of tech-heavy habitats that grew progressively darker. What started in the bright innocence of the back room of our house with all its music and editing paraphernalia eventually transferred to the dim Westwood apartment with its snare of wires, monitors, and videotape decks, then ultimately morphed into the grisly crime scene in Scottsdale with its lablike display of oversized video camera, metallic freight luggage, and strips of film negatives hanging spent and passionless in the makeshift darkroom/bathroom.

It was as though the same set designer and set dresser had been hired at all these locations but over the years had grown jaded and weary in his work. I only wish the Scottsdale apartment had been a set and the tawdry drama that played out within its walls a long-forgotten made-for-TV movie.

My dad's relationship with Carpenter created an intimacy and dependency that each assumed had no consequences. As my dad's popularity level rose, he became less and less certain of what his own life meant, both to himself and to his family. His Carpenter-assisted *cinéma du Hogan* could take place only in Hollywood, far from the friendly confines of the Vanalden house, where the only titillating artworks were the occasional seminude jazz or soul album cover and a substantial stack of *Playboy* magazines tucked away in the back room closet.

I began spending more and more hours alone in the back room. The siren sound of the thick wooden closet door's plastic rollers sliding over their metallic track bracketed my visits to the hidden flesh palace within. One day my mom decided to drop in while I was enjoying a layout featuring a healthy, freshly scrubbed maiden from Takemyclothesplease, USA. Mom rapidly deduced I wasn't drumming, playing records, or watching television since I was sitting cross-legged in front of the closet—and not because my interest in anatomy was going to lead to a career in medicine. I noticed her reddish-blonde hair first as she peeked around the corner of the wall of record album shelving. With no time to bid adieu to the lassie from Lascivious, Ohio, my face turned communist red. I was busted.

Embarrassed, Mom yelled, "Wait till your father gets home!"

Yeah, right, I thought. If she only knew.

As my skin color and body temperature returned to normal, I felt ashamed, and I mentally flogged myself for being such a disappointment to my mom. At that moment it was unfathomable to me that I would one day not only regularly write for *Playboy*, but actually *read* the magazine as well.

In that faraway nebula of Tarzana, my days were spent at William Howard Taft High School in Woodland Hills, where I persisted in my B academic world with no career objective on the horizon, although I was occasionally tickled by a creative writing, photography, or art class. I spent an exorbitant amount of effort trying to fly below the radar, trying to fit in, trying to hide the fact that my dad was a television star on a popular series on a major network. This was back in the day when a hit show pulled in 30 million viewers a week.

It was okay if kids disliked me because I was a jerk, but not because they thought my dad's TV show sucked, or he sucked as an actor, or that World War II sucked, or that Germans are a sweet, fun-loving group of people who just enjoy invading other countries. I always wondered if the son of someone like the heart surgeon Michael DeBakey would ever get knocked for the association. "Man, your dad's transplants suck!" But when you're performing in the arts or sports, you're wide open to the critics, the fans, the crazies, the people who are infatuated with you or resent you simply because they aren't in the spotlight. And they should be, dammit!

Junior high had been fun, but high school seemed a long road paved with life's mediocrity that lay ahead and the immediate fear of ridicule. Just to persist through the three years, grades 10, 11, and 12, was a survival test. Some kids had Scouts or Pony League or the school marching band to escape into away from problems at home or the hurt generated by mocking schoolmates. More and more, I enjoyed decamping behind the barbwire of Stalag 13 during my teenage years. It was a safe, insulated sanctuary apart from the judgment of my peers. It was also a great escape.

With *Hogan's Heroes* a big hit on CBS, the executives at Black Rock in Manhattan looked for creative avenues to exploit the series' popularity. Someone working for William Paley, head of the corporation, had seen my dad drum on *The Red Skelton Hour* and said that he wasn't half bad. Calls were made to agents in Los Angeles, and soon my dad was drumming with musical veterans like Ray Brown on bass, with Ernie Freeman arranging and Stu Phillips producing. Some of the players had worked with Sinatra. My dad filmed *Hogan's* during the day and recorded music at night.

The resulting album of television theme music, produced by Epic Records, a subsidiary of Columbia Records, which was owned by CBS, was called *Bob Crane (Colonel Hogan), His Drums, and Orchestra Play the Funny Side of TV*. Some of the theme songs, like those for *Get Smart* and *F Troop*, featured gimmicklike voices and sound effects not unlike those my dad had used on his radio show. John Banner did a spoken-word cameo as Sergeant Schultz on the *Hogan's Heroes* track. The album was recorded in the Columbia Records studio in the basement of the KNX Radio building at Sunset and Gower. My dad had returned to the scene of his earlier radio success but now as a television star. I went to the sessions, bringing along my school homework, as if I was going to work on it. Some of those sessions went late into the night. My dad was ecstatic, back in the world of the big band, laughing and playing alongside some of the best session players in Los Angeles.

Naturally, Epic Records wanted a *Hogan's Heroes* tie-in for the cover artwork so CBS could place ads for the album in *TV Guide* and other extensively circulated magazines. The result was a drum set being placed in the middle of the Stalag 13 set—Hogan behind the drums—surrounded by Colonel Klink, his secretary, Hilda, and Sergeant Schultz, all in costume, of course. The photographer, Gene Howard, suggested using an extra German soldier, weapon menacingly pointed in their direction, to give the tableau an "authentic" look. Since I was visiting the set in Culver City my dad pitched me as the guard. Or, rather, strongly suggested that I could deliver what Howard needed for the photograph. I was sixteen, so perhaps too young to play a German soldier convincingly, but I gave it my best shot, turning on a glowering look of intimidation. As I was getting into my storm trooper uniform, complete with helmet and machine gun, my thoughts returned to childhood days spent playing army with Ron Heck, emulating *Combat!* and Vic Morrow as Sergeant Chip Saunders, spending hours in our backyards fending off imaginary onslaughts of "Jerries." Now here I was, kitted out as the young Aryan who would have been machine-gunned or blown up by my *Combat!* hero. It seemed like an honor.

I didn't have to learn any lines. I didn't have to speak. I just had to stand there with my rubber machine gun pointed at the stars of *Hogan's Heroes.* Howard went through a couple of rolls of film capturing what the publicity department at Epic Records was after.

I thought it was great that my dad included me in his project, even if it was just throwing me a bone. His unyielding father had never thrown him so much as gristle. There was a price for laughter in that family—a laugh had to be earned. I think my dad may have developed his quick wit as a form of rebellion against his stern, stoic Connecticut family. In Culver City on that photo shoot, the laughs were plentiful and easy, and my rubber Mauser and I were a part of the fun.

Despite the ads in *TV Guide,* Bob "Colonel Hogan" Crane's album stiffed, notwithstanding his gimmicks, sounds effects, and drumming sessions with some of the best musicians in town. Listening to Hogan drum to the *My Three Sons* theme song couldn't draw a $5 bill out of even the most dedicated fan's wallet. Still, my dad thought the experience was worth it. His one and only album completed his recording contract. And I thought it was cool. I mean, the Yardbirds recorded for Epic Records. Years later, Epic would become home to some squeaky-clean, moonwalking kid from Gary, Indiana, name of Jackson.

Despite *Hogan's* being a hit and generating millions of dollars for CBS, Paramount, and Bing Crosby Productions, my dad didn't seek out

Bob Crane album cover: Bobby Crane, Werner Klemperer, Bob Crane, Sigrid Valdis, and John Banner, Culver City, California, 1967 (photo by Gene Howard; author's collection).

perks. He didn't get driven to the set of *Hogan's Heroes* in a limousine; he preferred to drive his own car, memorizing his lines for the day's scenes on his way to Hollywood or Culver City. When I got a driver's license, I would drop him off at the airport when he was going out of town, and he would make his own way through the check-in protocol without studio publicity department handlers or airline VIP escorts. That may have been the movie star world, but it wasn't Planet Crane. My parents were self-reliant, just like the pioneers they once were. That changed when my dad met Patti in *Hogan's* second season. Then it was as though he ceded all control of his destiny to her.

11

Happy Father's Day, 1978

I don't recall ever going to bed on the night following my dad's murder. I was sitting out by the pool of the Hellhole Motel on the fringe of Scottsdale, staring at the stars and thinking about the impact of my dad's death on Patti and her son and daughter and how the whole radioactive scene of her divorce from my dad had just been hosed down, demagnetized like so much used videotape. And all of it to Patti's advantage.

My dad had phoned me the day after Father's Day, June 18. "Bobby, you'll never believe who showed up here yesterday," he said. I could almost see him shaking his head.

I immediately started thinking of all the actresses or other women of interest to my dad. Gina Lollobrigida. Lee Remick. Stripper Angel Carter from the Classic Cat in Hollywood. There was a cast of thousands. "I have no idea," I said finally.

"Patti and Scotty," he said.

"You're kidding! How did that happen?"

"They spent the night. It was very uncomfortable for everybody. I went out for a while with Scotty. We went to the park in the neighborhood. I was pretty relieved when they left."

My dad was put off balance by Patti's sudden appearance. He sounded completely bewildered to me, which was remarkable because he was almost never at a loss like that. My dad and Patti were just weeks from the decree finalizing their divorce. They were in the middle of World War III. Why would Patti do that after all the vitriol? Six months earlier, in her divorce petition, she had called my dad an unfit father who, among other grievances, showed his young son pornographic videotapes. The press had jumped all over that—"Hogan's a Pervert!" Of course, my dad denied those accusations, and that's when attorneys became involved and things turned really ugly. Maybe Patti was trying to con my dad into thinking they still had a marriage, but that was a lost cause. My dad was gone on that issue. He was moving ahead, getting on with his life. Perhaps she did it as a show for the attorneys or even for the court, but Patti never lost sight of the fact that there was a lot of property at stake for her.

To this day I don't know how she knew where he was staying. Patti knew my dad was going to be in Scottsdale only for a couple more weeks, and she was uncertain what was going to happen when he got home. She did not like uncertainty. I think she was there on a combination reconnaissance mission and a kind of perverted, half-assed attempt to show her son what a wonderful mother she was by taking him to see his dad, even though it was the worst possible time to do that. I think it was all for show. Her visit was especially odd considering that the only intercourse Patti and my dad were having was the volley of threatening letters that ricocheted between their divorce attorneys.

Was she getting the layout of enemy territory? Was she the scout for the agent or agents of destruction that would follow in her wake? Did she just want a few minutes alone in my dad's apartment to look for something or things known only to her? After the murder it was discovered that one of the two sets of keys for the apartment was missing. Did Patti pick them up while she was there? The police never found the keys, nor did they ever seriously investigate Patti's possible participation, active or otherwise.

In the morning, Lloyd Vaughn, Bill Goldstein, and I had breakfast together before going to the Scottsdale Police Department. I felt a little wobbly emotionally. We talked to Detective Dennis Borkenhagen and Lieutenant Ron Dean, who were leading the investigation. While they were asking me about jealous boyfriends of cocktail waitresses I kept reiterating that they needed to take a closer look at Patti's motives and movements. They ignored me. They had their noses down on their own trail of clues.

Vaughn, Goldstein, and I boarded a plane and flew back to Burbank. I thanked Lloyd and Bill for all their help, got in my car, and drove to the Westwood apartment I had shared with my dad. I knew my time there was on life support. A security guard was standing outside the front door. I didn't know who he was, who he was affiliated with, or on whose behalf he was there. The guard was about my age, with bad skin, and we talked for a minute. He was just there doing his job and didn't know anything about anything. His job was to secure the apartment. He was, it turned out, hired by Patti to make sure nothing was taken from the apartment, and in performing his duties he refused to let me into my own home. I showed him my key, explained I had been living there for the past six months with my dad, and told him I needed to go into the apartment. He went in to phone his superiors, leaving me standing on the front step, door shut in my face, like an unwanted peddler. Somebody contacted Patti. After what seemed like hours of haggling I was allowed into the apartment—provided that the first night I was there the guard stayed inside the apartment too.

I went into my bedroom and locked the door. It was surreal to me that my dad had just been killed by person or persons unknown while he slept, and here I was in my apartment all night with a gun-toting stranger in the next room. I didn't sleep much that night, either.

12

Divorce, Tarzana Style, 1968–1969

The role of the lothario had hovered over my dad's career since his walk-on in *The New Interns* as Drunk Guy at Party with up-and-coming contract players like George Segal, Michael Callan, and Stefanie Powers. That epic was shot at Columbia Pictures at Sunset and Gower across the street from his morning gig at KNX and was an early opportunity for him to spend a few hours on a set. From there it was the break offered by Carl Reiner to appear as a philandering husband on *The Dick Van Dyke Show* followed by two seasons as Carl Betz's good-time dentist friend on *The Donna Reed Show*. Then there was Colonel Hogan, a role that was as close to playing his hero, Jack Lemmon, as my dad would ever experience. Besides squeezing out some Lemmon, my dad gave Hogan the appropriate look of the day—a combination of James Garner, Robert Culp, Robert Vaughn, Robert Conrad, and Gig Young.

After a few seasons of *Hogan's Heroes*, which by then was a well-oiled machine and a favorite at Black Rock in Manhattan, my dad jumped at the chance to costar in a motion picture with the red-hot European bombshell Elke Sommer. The script for *The Wicked Dreams of Paula Schultz* had never had any fingerprints of Garner, Culp, Vaughn, Conrad, or Young on it because it was toxic. The film was directed by George Marshall, a Hollywood veteran in his seventies who had distinguished himself with the likes of Laurel and Hardy, Bob Hope, and Dean Martin and Jerry Lewis, but who was not fully connected to the hip late 1960s. His style of filmmaking and the look of the film, with its limp attempts at comedy, were relics of the '40s and '50s. Sommer was a nonactress who had appeared nude in many of her films as a way of unleashing her thespian gifts. She had graced the pages of *Playboy* magazine, which was why I was personally enthused about visiting the set. The director, the crew, the script, shooting at the nearly shuttered MGM lot, all cried archaic, antiquated, and out of touch. As a last-ditch effort to salvage some kind of box office viability, the producer threw in Werner Klemperer, John Banner, and Leon Askin from *Hogan's* in an effort to inject some lifeblood into an otherwise DOA project.

My dad, playing an American conman in cold war Germany instead of World War II Germany, knew the film was a dinosaur in both method and message. This was 1968, and the *New York Times* made the intriguing choice of feminist author Renata Adler to review the film. She wrote on behalf of her sisters and the changes in the air for women's rights when she pointed out just how old-fashioned, chauvinistic, and downright dreadful the story and depiction of women were and how the film's male characters (specifically my dad) were Neanderthal in their dealings with women. I hurt for my dad, who didn't know Gloria Steinem from Mamie Van Doren. What he did know was that his smile couldn't make up for such a vulgar script. His charm reserve tank had nowhere near the capacity to keep that baby rolling. Colonel Hogan was a winner because solid dialogue and situations propped him up and producer Ed Feldman served as quality-control inspector.

Even with as much skin as Elke Sommer could display, Paula Schulz's wicked dreams turned into a nightmare. United Artists dumped the film out in February, when most feral dogs are released. My dad took his costar billing, his check, and a fistful of bad notices and hightailed it back to his day job.

In spite of the *Paula Schulz* debacle, a year later my dad was offered and accepted the most prestigious role of his career—playing the Cary Grant role in an ABC television production of *Arsenic and Old Lace.* He worked with Helen Hayes, Lillian Gish, David Wayne, and Fred Gwynne. The play was videotaped in front of a live audience in New York. It would be my dad's only project outside of *Hogan's* that had a distinctive level of quality. It also challenged my dad's acting chops. He did a respectable job, but Cary Grant didn't need to come out of retirement to defend his crown. Besides, no one watched the broadcast.

In 1969, what had been our little Tarzana family series was suddenly canceled. Life as my parents, sisters, grandparents, cousins, aunts, and uncles knew it was not being renewed for another season. Dad would never live in our house again. My parents, those rocks of stability, always to be counted on, taken for granted even, just crumbled overnight. Mom and Dad. Together since high school. Married for twenty years. The pioneers who had traveled west in their Oldsmobile Conestoga, braving the

Debbie, Bob, Karen, and Bobby Crane, Tarzana, 1968 (author's collection).

dangers of midwestern food and sleeping rough in Travelodges and Holiday Inns, would never spend another night together. I was seventeen, my sisters eight and nine.

The change came like a tsunami—a warm, comfortable atmosphere one moment, and then in an instant I was underwater, looking for something to keep me afloat. Everything I knew, trusted, and counted on was drowned. Overnight Mom officially became a single parent. Dad was officially gone. Gone with another woman. As blame, anger, mistrust, and confusion permeated the household, I looked at my dad differently from that moment on.

Young people don't like change; they rely on continuity. Still comfortably naïve, I was trying desperately to hold onto something that wasn't there anymore. We had just had our small world rocked by an 8.2 earthquake, and there was no way to prep for the ensuing surge when you didn't know what was coming. It was everyone for himself; just try to keep your head above the rising tide.

I thought what might help me stay afloat was a girlfriend. There with lifesaving water wings was a chipper, freckle-faced redhead who loved politics named Chris Klauser. She and I dutifully played our roles as boyfriend and girlfriend, going to school dances, skiing with her family, making out in my '66 Ford Mustang, which Chris dubbed the White Horse. We would break up, get back together, and ultimately attend the senior prom arm in arm. These were all anxiety-producing, seemingly important moments. In the end, like most high school romances, our relationship wasn't sustainable. There wasn't enough life experience for it to feed off. There's only so long that teenaged hormones can keep a thing alive, but this first serious relationship did serve as a rite of passage, a necessary road for me to take and invaluable life experience in the mysteries of bra hardware.

At the same time I was having profound conversations with Chris about Vietnam, civil rights, and international justice, I found I could also have a pleasant time with a nonpolitical girl named Pam Connell, who had long, dark hair and was two years younger than I, in the tenth grade when I was a senior. We met in photography class. Pam came from a broken home, which I could immediately relate to. She was living with her mother; her dad was gone. She liked Creedence Clearwater Revival. In a lot of ways I could connect with her much more easily than with Chris, who came from a highly educated family stocked with teachers, professors, and principals. In the Klauser household there was always talk of PhDs, theses, and graduate schools, all things that my family had never experienced. Ultimately, I felt I didn't fit in with that family. The Cranes were a circus troupe, a carny family compared to the Klausers. We were freaks. Besides, Pam Connell's bra was a snap to unhook.

The impact on my life of my folks' separation was truly the shattering of a dream. They had always seemed so safe, so certain. Perhaps they had thought so themselves, complacent that they could weather any storm. Hell, they had moved across the country. They had taken creative leaps. They were conservative by nature, politically and in terms of family values. There were no drugs; there was no alcohol. There was no pill-popping craziness, schizophrenia, suicide attempts, physical or mental abuse. We were a small-thinking, small-town family living in a suburban community with a dad who just happened to be on radio and television. However, by the time of the separation and divorce, my dad was a very well-known television star. That fact alone fueled the announcement of the breakup, which begat a raft of rumors and innuendoes: Bob cheated on Anne at work, Anne cheated with her physician on Bob. It was another showbiz family run amok. Former working-class nobodies wrecked by money and fame.

I hated the expressions on the faces of my classmates when I entered a classroom or walked down a hallway. Some were sympathetic, some were smug and smirking, and some were embarrassed for me. I hated the whispers. "That's Hogan's son." I didn't want to be Hogan's son. I cringed at having the same name. I went by Robert Crane to lessen the blowback of Bob Crane. Still, many well-meaning people called me Bob Crane Junior. I would smile and quietly respond, "I'm not a junior; we have different middle names." The well-meaning people didn't care. I wasn't an individual to them. I rose or fell depending on how strangers felt about my dad. I've never been comfortable with that. I didn't enjoy rooms going quiet when I walked in. I didn't want to be the center of attention.

It all became a moot point when I graduated from Taft High School in June 1969 along with a thousand other boomer teenagers. My mom attended the marathon ceremony. My dad did not.

One of my chief motivating factors for going on to college was the simple fact that I wanted to survive past eighteen years of age. Going to college meant a 2-S student deferment from the draft, which equated to not having to draw my last breaths in a Vietnamese rice paddy because that country's people didn't embrace our square peg brand of capitalism and democracy in their round hole. I didn't buy the sleight-of-hand McCarthyesque leftovers being sold by the war industry in Washington, DC, that proclaimed we had to stop the hammer and sickle before it came ashore in Long Beach.

Ours was a nonacademic family. There weren't any parchment degrees and Phi Beta Kappa certificates decorating the walls next to the eight-by-ten glossies at our house. Success in show business didn't require attending great houses of learning or acquiring a string of initials after your name. Still, with the monolithic demon of Vietnam looming over me, I talked to my dad about possibly going to the University of Southern California. USC had a world-class film school, and I wanted to be a filmmaker.

The height of American film—and world film, as far as I'm concerned—occurred during the '60s and '70s. Eagerly anticipated reviews from Charles Champlin and Kevin Thomas in the *L.A. Times* would kick-start boisterous conversations with friends about which film or films to see on the coming Friday and Saturday nights. We would drive over to Westwood and stand in line for an hour or more to get in to see *Easy Rider, Medium Cool, Midnight Cowboy,* or *The Wild Bunch*. Foreign films were at their height of popularity. I knew all the directors: Bergman, Visconti, Truffaut, Antonioni, Fellini. I looked forward to each month's issue of *Cinema* magazine. It was a very exciting time. Looking back now, I know that was partly because of my age and the fact that I was fresh and impressionable, but also it was an era of truly envelope-pushing filmmaking going on right before our eyes. Cassavetes, Costa-Gavras, Schlesinger, Penn, and Russell were just a few of the directors who were making thought-provoking movies. Film was art, and since I couldn't paint, draw, or sculpt, I wanted to go to film school.

In the late '60s there were three choices for film school: NYU, UCLA, and USC. My dad had emceed a few dinners for USC in previous years and happened to know the dean of the cinema school, Bernie Kantor. A phone call was made; I met with Dr. Kantor, filled out an application, and soon thereafter was accepted into the university even with my unexceptional 3.0 grade point average. It was like the Beatles tickets redux. Would I have been accepted at USC without my dad's phone call? I don't know, but since no one in my family had ever attended college, I felt proud of my pioneering soul.

13

Loose Nukes, 1978

On the morning of July 1, I woke with a start. In an instantaneous and regrettable flood of consciousness I realized my dad was still dead and there was a stranger in the next room.

It turned out that the guard hired by my stepmother, Patti, was there because she was paranoid I might clear out the apartment. While there was a lot of equipment there that now technically belonged to her, that wasn't what she was really worried about. Patti was afraid that I would get my hands on video footage and photos that revealed her in some very compromising positions, and the singular fiction she'd been presenting to the court—that my dad was pursuing a life of porn and yet was on the verge of a reconciliation with her—would go up in the toxic fumes of so much unpreserved nitrate film stock. I had seen evidence that proved Patti had a lot to be paranoid about. My dad had shown me photos of Patti and him with a woman they had met at a nightclub engaged in a threesome in the bedroom of their house on Tilden Avenue. The bedroom next to the one where their young son slept. The son Patti was trying to leverage to her advantage when talking to the judge and media jury.

I had tried not to look at the photographs initially, but it was like the irresistible pull you feel passing a car wreck on the highway—my voyeurism got the better of me. It was a looky-lulu moment. How many people ever see their parents or stepparents in carnal bliss? How many want to? Not many would be my guess. I didn't have friends who had seen their stepmother nude, let alone having sex with another woman. Hell, I didn't have any friends who even had a stepmother in the first place. Yet my dad proudly shared these shocking images with me as if he were hawking wares on a card table in Times Square. He behaved like a jock at a fraternity party, oblivious to my uncomfortable reaction. I felt like a cult member witnessing events that would sicken the average person. Nevertheless, I didn't allow in ill feelings because of my belief that life is about processing information to decipher the truth. I felt that recording people and events in my mind's eye always took precedence.

Patti knew my dad had these photos and plenty of other material that ballyhooed her talents as the star of the Midvale Avenue film production center located on our dining room table. She didn't know the extent of my knowledge of her exploits, but she was keenly aware she had to secure the loose nukes that had her empire written on the nosecone. Not that launching her private images would have impacted her inheritance, which was hers alone, but it certainly would have pockmarked the public image she had concocted for the press, the courts, and her son. She was terrified I would back up a moving van to the apartment, sweep everything into it, and disappear, leaving the key in the door with a note reading, "See you in the *Enquirer.*"

The poor schmuck of a guard didn't look like he had gotten much sleep either, and he clearly had no clue why he was in the apartment to begin with since I had returned home. I felt sorry for him. We both made some phone calls, and a short time later he received his marching orders.

Now I was really alone. The seriousness of that aloneness closed around me like the darkness in a theater just before the movie starts. I was in a ghastly horror film, and I already knew the blood-spattered ending. There was no hero coming to save the day, no last-minute intervention by the governor, no swelling of music as the sun slid into a calming ocean. There were only tears. Lots of tears.

At some point on that afternoon of July 1 Patti showed up at the apartment. It was not a condolence call. She offered nothing in the way of sympathy to a son who had just lost his father. She was on a mission. It was a reconnaissance, much like the one I imagine she had done in Scottsdale. She was reconnoitering, mentally inventorying the apartment and its contents. Maybe I was next on her hit list. This was the first time I'd seen or spoken to her since the murder. She was steely, dry-eyed, and cold as a concrete slab. She was not the grieving widow for her prodigal but supposedly reconciling husband. She walked quickly through the apartment, surveying, ticking items off in her head. She knew what she was looking for.

I asked her, innocently enough, "Why did this have to happen?"

"Well," she said as she panned the dining room media center, "I guess your father's lifestyle caught up with him." That was it. One last look around and she was out the door.

I felt as though I were standing naked in the snow. The apartment was a frozen, lifeless place. My dad was no longer part of it. I resolved to move out, pronto. Even if I could have afforded the rent on my own, I would have had to move. All that equipment, the cameras and monitors, the tape decks, editing machine, the wires and cables, had all become just so much steel and plastic. It didn't mean anything without my dad laughing and whistling as he spliced tape together or dubbed in music, entertaining himself with his own ingenuity.

When I did move out, I took a few items that my dad had said were mine. These included a three-quarter-inch videocassette player, a video monitor, and a tape recorder. But I did not take any of his video or photographic archive. I wanted to live to see my twenty-eighth birthday.

I've never been very attached to material possessions because things in and of themselves don't mean much to me without the person they belong to. Clothing, shoes, jewelry, photographs, or other keepsakes just don't resonate unless the person connected to them is still around, not necessarily in the vicinity but still walking the planet somewhere, sharing the air. Otherwise, all that stuff is clutter—dead, inanimate dust collectors. I keep people I love alive in my heart and my mind. I don't need a threadbare sweater or a one-eyed teddy bear to remind me of someone important to me. Besides, I hate dusting.

Even so, I did keep my dad's leather jacket from *Hogan's Heroes,* but I cherished it not just because it was my dad's but also because it was worn by Frank Sinatra in the 1965 film *Von Ryan's Express.* For me, the jacket was as much a piece of cinema memorabilia as it was a family memento. Like a UN peacekeeper I gave Hogan's hat to Patti because she said Scotty always loved seeing his dad in it. Odd, since Scotty wasn't even born until after *Hogan's Heroes'* six seasons were over.

I pulled up in front of my mom and Chuck's house in my four-year-old orange BMW 2002. The usually quiet cul-de-sac was full of cars. I watched as people who had never been to the house before and would never be there again went in the front door. The scene had the appearance of the beginnings of a summer barbeque, albeit without any joviality. I joined the queue. Once inside I immediately spied the father of a friend of mine and some of Chuck's family members, the Worthingtons, making their debut at the house. After my initial question "What are they doing here?" I realized they meant their presence to be consoling, but then I cynically thought, "Were they expecting to see Hollywood stars on the patio overlooking the Valley?"

Entertaining the guests superseded the opportunity to sit down with my mother, sisters, grandmothers, and Chuck to talk about "it"—to cry, hug each other, utter useless platitudes, and rally each other's broken hearts. We were in the middle of a wake—drinks were poured, beers were opened, heads shaking all the while in disbelief. Most of the drop-ins had never met my dad, but they "knew" him.

Afternoon rolled ever so slowly into night, and my family never had that sit-down meeting, that cry fest, that hug-in. Stealing moments, we would catch one another's eye and try to express smatterings of anger, disappointment, embarrassment, what-ifs, and whys. We exchanged comments that were fragments of feelings but never coalesced into a complete picture. It wasn't just the presence of the outsiders. We were not a cohesive unit. We were not the mythical family that I had always fantasized we should be. The family that stands together, finding solace in tragedy.

In any event, I didn't need to cry anymore. I'd done enough of that for now, and I knew there'd be more tears down the road. I also had no need for the hugs and handshakes, the concerned looks from neighbors and parents of friends. They offered up their quasi-religious airy statements meant as comfort, but these rapidly turned mind numbing. What I needed was a dialogue with my immediate family, an acknowledgment between us that some kind of otherworldly, unthinkable abnormality had happened to us. What I needed was for us to develop a mutual plan of attack on how to deal with the emotional fallout. That meeting has never to this day taken place.

On Wednesday, July 5, my dad was remembered by 150 people at St. Paul the Apostle Church in Westwood and buried at the Oakwood Memorial Park Cemetery in Chatsworth (where Fred Astaire and Ginger Rogers rest in peace). Carroll O'Connor, Patty Duke and John Astin, Robert Clary, Larry Hovis, Leon Askin, and Edward H. Feldman were among the attendees. Patti and Scotty avoided my side of the family, but John Carpenter did not. He gave me a warm embrace on the steps leading to the church. Thinking about it now makes me shudder.

Carpenter was always on the top of the Scottsdale Police Department's suspect list. As far as I was concerned, the more I learned about the events of June 28 and 29, 1978, the more the anomalies of this particular trip Carpenter took to see my dad stood out. Carpenter always stayed with my

Pallbearers at Bob Crane's funeral: Robert Clary, Larry Hovis, Edward H. Feldman, and Robert Crane, Westwood, California, 1978 (author's collection).

dad on the road. This time he didn't. Carpenter never called me when he got back from seeing my dad. This time he did. The call itself was innocuous, but the fact that he made it in the first place was bizarre to me.

Eyewitnesses at a nightclub had reported my dad and Carpenter in a heated argument the night of the 28th. There was a video camera tripod missing from the murder scene that the police suspected might be the murder weapon. A section of electrical cord used with the camera had been tied around my dad's neck, although, per the coroner, it was not the cause of death. Recently, my dad had told me that Carpenter was becoming "a pain in the ass," and as part of his changes he was going to end his relationship with him. The police figured that Carpenter, who was bisexual, was perhaps in love with my dad and reacted to this information like a spurned lover.

I also learned that Carpenter had called my dad's apartment and the dinner theater on the 29th from L.A., returning to the scene of the crime, albeit by phone, in the opinion of the Scottsdale police. All of these incidences didn't add up to a conviction of Carpenter, but they certainly gave me pause. Maybe Carpenter was guilty.

It also wasn't out of the realm of possibility in my mind that Patti and

Carpenter were somehow in cahoots—either she had directly put him up to the job or, in a more Machiavellian manipulation of the volatile Carpenter, had stoked him into his own rage. Either way, the result suited her just fine.

The chance that I was ever going to talk to Patti again without lawyers present was virtually nil, but when Carpenter phoned me again over the next couple of weeks I would secretly tape-record those two telephone conversations, though I later inadvertently taped over the first call. I didn't know what I might learn from his calls, but I wanted a record of them nonetheless. The second chat was the last time I would ever have a substantial dialogue with Carpenter, but at least I didn't bungle that taping.*

Weeks after that last recording, I called the AKAI Corporation where Carpenter worked but was unable to get him on the line. He never returned my call, possibly because he had lawyered up by then. The Scottsdale Police Department had leaked Carpenter's name as prime suspect to the press. Carpenter hired Gary Fleischman as his attorney, and they publicly expressed "shock" that Carpenter, Bob Crane's buddy, was even mentioned as a person of interest in the case. Maricopa County district attorney Charles Hyder refused to file charges against Carpenter, citing the less than airtight investigation the Scottsdale Police Department had conducted. "I'm very perturbed about it," Hyder told the *Arizona Republic*. "It's not my policy at all to mention anybody's name until we arrest them or they have been indicted. . . . Certainly not during an investigation. . . . As of right now, I'm sorry to say, there is just insufficient evidence for us to take any action on, I wish it were otherwise."

I decamped from the apartment to my mom and Chuck's house, bivouacking there until I could get my bearings.

---

*See appendix B for the transcript of that call.

14

Love in a Time of War, 1969–1970

The summer of love for the graduates of Taft High School in Woodland Hills was 1969, even though the official Summer of Love was the summer of 1967. That was the year of Haight-Ashbury, Griffith Park love-ins, and the Beatles' "All You Need Is Love." I was still too young, too naïve, and too inexperienced in 1967 to appreciate what that season meant. The highlight of my summer of love in 1969 was our all-night grad party held for L.A. high schools at Disneyland. My girlfriend, Chris Klauser, my friend Chris Fryer, and his date, Sandee Ericsson, and I cut out early from the Disneyland festivities and retreated to a small adobe hideaway that Klauser's family owned in the northern foothills of the San Fernando Valley. We brought food, built a fire in the big stone fireplace, and the four of us spent the night there. I celebrated my graduation by finally getting Chris's damn bra off. Talk about winning a scholarship.

In an eerie footnote to that memorable evening, it just so happened that the Manson family, which we would all hear about later that summer, was not far away from our location at the adobe. Charlie Manson and his clan were living farther up in the hills on an abandoned movie set that had been used in a lot of old-time westerns, such as the Tom Mix movies of the '20s. Manson and his deluded minions were plotting the bloodletting they would perpetrate that August less than a mile from the love nest where the four of us were studying anatomy in our sleeping bags.

On June 27, 1969, I turned eighteen. In a few weeks the dreaded draft lottery for the Vietnam War was to be held. With the war escalating badly, the lottery became a perverse television event. I watched it at home, which by that summer was solely my mom's house, as my parents had separated. The lottery worked by drawing numbers that matched birth dates. There was a big hopper with 366 ping-pong balls, like a Powerball drawing on steroids, except instead of winning a fortune you could win your future. It was a drawing for the rest of your life.

The June 27 ping-pong ball emerged at number 55. That meant two things. The number was, first of all, a guarantee of being drafted. Before the year was out, the military would call numbers 1 through 195 in an attempt to stem the Red tide flowing down the Ho Chi Minh Trail. My immediate reaction when the June 27 ball popped up was a vision of me, scared shitless in the monsoon rain in a Southeast Asian jungle. My body would come home in a box a few weeks later. So, the second and more important meaning of that number 55 ping-pong ball was that I would be the first Crane to go to college. If you stayed in school, you stayed out of Vietnam.

Just when I needed an infusion of character- and confidence-building in my life (and a shorthand education in the world of business, marketing, and selling), in that summer of 1969 between high school and college, Chris Fryer and I created a company called FC Enterprises that designed and manufactured license plate frames for colleges and universities. It was an idea we hatched one summer afternoon on our way home from Zuma Beach. The business model was simple: As an alternative to putting "Fletcher Jones Chevrolet" license plate frames on your car, we would offer USC Trojans frames painted in cardinal and gold. The die-cast frames would have the college's nickname on top, and the school's name would be bookended by its logo on the bottom.

Chris's dad, David, was instrumental in the development of our fledgling enterprise. Dave Fryer's world was retail—furniture, bedding, appliances. Chris and I were proud and excited about our new business. We invited our dads to a lunch meeting, the only time they ever met, at Monty's Steakhouse in Encino to show off our creation and bask in their appreciation of our entrepreneurial spirit and our potential mint. Chris's dad enthusiastically offered advice on building professional relationships; selling, marketing, and advertising the product; and using positive public relations to build the business into something sustainable. My dad listened but had nothing to offer. I was disappointed and a bit embarrassed as I ate my steak sandwich, but later it dawned on me that the only product my dad specialized in was himself. That's all he knew. He didn't have a marketing strategy or ideas for advertising in publications or methods for cold-calling a list of potential customers. He could shake someone's hand, smile, and make a joke. He could stand in front of an audience and talk into a microphone. But he couldn't offer us any business acumen for an inanimate product. That made a big impression on me. His dad, my grandfather, Alfred Crane, would have been more help to us at that meeting because he came from the world of furniture and carpeting and might have supplemented Dave Fryer's ideas. But I was happy, at least, that my dad attended the lunch meeting and listened.

FC Enterprises went on to become something like a dot-com success decades before there were such things. Since our first two accounts were USC and UCLA, it wasn't long before we were spotting our product on a daily basis on the rear end of vehicles speeding along the byways of Los Angeles. Every time I saw the frames on a car, I felt much like what I imagine songwriters feel hearing a song they've written coming out of their dashboard radio. Through direct mail advertising, phone calls, and driving around the country, Chris and I managed to recruit over a hundred colleges and universities to sell school-spirited license plate frames. We expanded the business into service and fraternal groups like the American Legion and the Elks clubs, and ultimately to all the major league sports franchises. So from nothing but a crazy kernel of an idea on the way home from a day at the beach, we nurtured and tended our business into something of a national garden of green. It sure beat flipping burgers.

Chris Fryer and I were both headed to USC, as was Chris Klauser, who had long-range goals for us as a couple. It was pretty heady stuff to be freshmen at a major university, running our own business, making some money, and in our spare time between classes, traveling the country to visit other institutes of higher learning to show them the irrepressible charm of customized license plate frames. From the practical lessons of accounts payable and receivable and the seductive flow of molten metal, I also slid into a slipstream of film studies.

The USC film school in those days was a collection of mismatched and ancient bungalows off to one side of the campus. Some of them looked like Quonset huts left over from a military post, but the dilapidated structures had the charm of a stray dog simply because they were so disheveled. It would be shocking to see those buildings now in contrast to what the USC film school has become, thanks to its many illustrious and monumentally deep-pocketed alumni. Arthur Knight, a celebrated film critic and author of *Playboy*'s Sex in the Cinema series, was a professor at USC then, as were Steve and Eleanor Karpf, who had just written one of Michael Douglas's early films, *Adam at Six A.M.* The film school faculty list was an eclectic and fascinating roster of freethinkers, writers, directors, editors, and producers.

Film school was an oasis from the daily reminder of the Vietnam War, which had infected almost every other aspect of campus life. There were endless classroom discussions, campus protests, and ultimately a shut-down of schools all over the country as students stopped attending classes, swarmed campuses, and in many cases occupied the dean's offices. This was the spring of 1970, and was called the Moratorium. It seemed to me a potent demonstration of the power of the people. We were making a difference. The government was watching. Nixon was watching. Walter Cronkite was watching. The governor of Ohio, James Rhodes, was so attentive he dispatched the National Guard. That little show of executive power resulted in the murder of four students at Kent State that May. The temporary closure of a wealthy, private, and insular school like USC was a barometer of how intrusive and how important the war was to all seg-ments of society. The dean's office may not have been occupied by mem-bers of the SDS (Students for a Democratic Society), but a casting call for Berkeley types apparently had gone out, because there was a bigger influx of hippies and protest bands setting up shop in and around campus during that week than the home of Tommy Trojan had ever witnessed. After the Moratorium was over, that same longhaired invasion disappeared as quickly as it had arrived.

Even though USC is only twenty miles from Tarzana, it might as well have been two thousand. USC was all the things that college is supposed to be—an exposure to ideas, to a broader worldview, to self-sufficiency and personal responsibility. As a result of the country's political and social upheaval, being involved in film at that time felt like being in the center of the universe, or at least in the eye of a hurricane.

Directors seized that moment and became the tuning fork for soci-ety's ills. In one of Arthur Knight's classes we would see yet-to-be-released films and meet their filmmakers. One evening we saw a new film called *Minnie and Moskowitz* directed by John Cassavetes, who was at the height of his fame. He had done important films like *Faces* and *Husbands* and would go on to make the Oscar-nominated *A Woman Under the Influence*. Afterward the students were invited to a pizza parlor called Jacopo's in Beverly Hills, where we shared a couple of pies and pitchers of beer and discussed the impact of film and filmmaking on our turbulent society with Cassavetes and Knight.

Nowadays, I would prefer the slice and brew over meeting most cur-rent filmmakers. While I would have loved to spend time with Mike

Nichols or Francis Ford Coppola or George Lucas early on while devouring a mushroom, onion, and sausage slice, would I want to sit down with Judd Apatow and discuss *You Don't Mess with the Zohan?* Check, please.

When I entered USC in 1969, I had just missed the wave of visionaries who had gone through the film department, including George Lucas, John Milius, who went on to cowrite *Apocalypse Now*, and the amazing film editor and sound artist Walter Murch. The next set would feature such 2-S deferred future superstar directors as Robert Zemeckis, who later made *Back to the Future*, *Roger Rabbit*, and *Forrest Gump*, and Ron Howard of *A Beautiful Mind*, *Frost/Nixon*, *Da Vinci Code*, *Apollo 13*, and Mayberry fame.

It was at this time that I met a bubbly, strawberry-blonde art major named Diane Haas. Her laugh was infectious, and her classical figure would have inspired any Renaissance artist. The first time I laid eyes on Diane I was visiting Chris Klauser at her dorm, the modern block of Birnkrant Hall where Diane also lived. Chris aspired to the world of sororities and the social status that conferred, so it wasn't long before she left dorm life behind and moved onto Sorority Row. That was an alien world to me. I was not interested in the Greek scene, though Fryer and I did go to the sorority house meetings held on Monday nights, ostensibly to flog our license plate frames but really because it was a great way to meet girls and make some money, and it beat the hell out of studying for psychology. Chris Klauser had very different academic interests from mine, and she was much more political than I was. Public office was her calling, whereas I thought I should be wearing a beret and smoking a Cuban cigar while sipping an espresso and talking about the latest issue of the *Cahiers du cinéma*. Our relationship didn't end so much as it evaporated.

I managed to get Diane's phone number and so began hours and hours of conversation in which everything—our personalities and others', our likes and dislikes, the arts, world figures, family dynamics—was explored and dissected. In the dorm she had heard Chris Klauser talking about my dad, the television star. Diane and her family had seen *Hogan's Heroes* a few times during her teenage years, and her father was a television writer, so we were able to compare notes on living through the ups and downs of the business. She demonstrated a natural cool about my "showbiz" family.

For weeks our universe was the telephone, and it focused our attention on our words. It also provided an escape hatch, a way out of this fledgling relationship if either of us heard something we didn't like. But we lived just across campus from each other, and so finally we planned a meeting around our busy freshman schedules. Zero hour was 10:30 on a warm fall evening near Doheny Library. Diane had just finished a painting class and was sporting white paint on her hands and her sleeves. After so many hours of conversation on the phone our face-to-face meeting was a bit awkward. We knew each other pretty well but were strangers in person, so we circled each other like a pair of fencers, ultimately settling on a patchwork brick walkway with a recessed light shining heavenward between us. We talked until the wee hours in that floodlit darkness.

Diane was a beautiful, highly imaginative, creative force with energy and drive. My hand eventually made its way through the beam of light and held her hand. The other hand touched her shoulder or her long hair or cupped the side of her face from time to time. The hours passed in a matter of moments, the night singing of mockingbirds our soundtrack. When it was time to say good-bye, my body blocked the light as I leaned forward and kissed Diane. Her lips were sweet and salty as she kissed then sucked then gently bit my lower lip. Our tongues met in a deep kiss and we held on to each other as if I were shipping out to 'Nam on the dawn transport. We caught our breath, and her hazel eyes absorbed my stare. Then another flow of emotion took over. This was the longest good-bye in my history, possibly in anybody's history. The five-minute walk to Diane's dorm took an hour. With blood raging and hormones and testosterone at dangerous levels, we separated—Lara and Zhivago, Elaine and Benjamin, Katie and Hubbell—and I disappeared back into the darkness. Stopping just short of pinching myself, I excitedly debated under my breath whether this whole evening had actually happened. I didn't even worry about being mugged on the way back to my dorm, where of course I couldn't sleep a wink.

From once or twice a week we started to see each other daily. When we couldn't get together, the world temporarily stopped spinning for me. I went through the motions of life until I could see her again. Accidentally running into Diane during the school day was worse than not seeing her at all. The excitement of being near her without interaction was torture.

Some weekends Diane would go home to Hermosa Beach to see her family. I had gathered that there was still a hopeful suitor from high school standing in the wings, and that they saw each other on Diane's weekends home. I had never felt jealousy like that before. When I bought tickets for an upcoming Crosby, Stills, Nash, and Young concert at the Fabulous Forum, assuming this would be our first concert together, I was wrong. She had already made plans to go to the show with *him*. I spent the evening scanning the seats for Diane and her date. Occasionally, I would watch Stephen Stills and Neil Young jam for a few seconds, but mostly I was preoccupied with crowd surveillance. It was getting to the point where I was no fun anymore.

Chris Fryer and I were roommates in Town & Gown Hall. One of the oldest buildings on campus, it retained as much elegance as a men's dorm could possibly have. (Only UCLA had begun the radical experiment of coed dorms in those days.) Our room was in the front corner on the second floor of the three-story building and had three windows on two sides plus a small landing on the fire escape where I could sit outside in the shade of a magnificent magnolia tree that towered over our corner of the building. As dorm rooms went it was quite spacious and airy.

One night when Chris was on a date and I had the room to myself, I called Diane to invite her over. After an interminable amount of time there was a soft knock at the door. I didn't want to appear too anxious, so I waited until she knocked again. After all, it took me at least half a second to get from anywhere in the room to the door. I prepared the mood lighting—turned off the overhead and switched on a desk lamp—and slowly opened the door. There she stood, backlit by the hallway light, wearing a tight long-sleeved white shirt, jeans, and brown boots. We embraced but out of the corner of my eye I spotted a neighbor coming out of his room. It was Don, one of Diane's fellow art students. It was the first time we had been seen together as a couple, and knowing Don, it would be campus news by daybreak. I was very excited to see Diane on my home turf. I gave her a quick tour of our room—it couldn't be anything but quick—and we sat down on my single bed. We kissed until our lips hurt. Coming up for air, she noticed Fryer's acoustic guitar lying across his bed. She got up, grabbed the guitar, sat down, and strummed a few chords.

"Do you play?" she innocently asked.

I accepted the question as a challenge. "Sure, I was in a band," I answered nonchalantly.

Diane handed me the guitar, and I warmed up with my G-C-D rendition of Cream's "Sitting on Top of the World." Eric Clapton had nothing to worry about, but I was emboldened enough to pull out the heavy artillery. In honor of the CSNY concert we hadn't attended together, I played

"Triad" by David Crosby. I had learned it from Dave Diamond, who had been "my date" at the concert and who is the kind of musician who can watch someone play a song and instantly know the chords.

But Diane's mind was wandering as I plodded through Crosby's ode to a threesome. She leaned into my ear and asked, "Why don't you finish that later?" Gently, she took the guitar from me and leaned it against my desk.

We kissed with a new hyperpassion and soon clothes were flying. I glanced at the clock—Fryer would be away for hours. The last thing I wanted was an audience for the loss of my virginity.

I didn't know if Diane was a virgin, too, but we spent an eternity exploring each other's bodies as though it were all undiscovered territory. Not surprisingly, we finally figured it out. Our bodies were slick with perspiration as we lay in each other's arms in my narrow bed. I was alive with an electric feeling inside my skin. Diane began to cry softly. Were these tears of joy or disappointment? Was she thinking of her CSNY concert date? I didn't have the nerve to ask for answers to either of those questions.

Diane painted large oil-on-canvas images of women, women whose faces were always turned away or in shadow. They were not Playboy Playmate types but nudes of another century. They were, like Diane herself, Rubensesque. We spent hours at Café Figaro on Melrose Avenue in West Hollywood sharing burgers and split pea soup, talking endlessly, and all the while Diane drew ideas for art projects on paper napkins or in her sketch tablet. This was the first time I had been exposed to an artist, and I loved the creative energy that infused the air around her. Romance was in both my head and my heart. We went to museums, galleries, and impromptu art shows in parking garages, restaurants, and apartments. I was a visitor in a foreign world, but Diane made me feel welcomed and a part of the scene. She took my hand and I followed. We went to student protests. We watched John and Yoko pitching peace from a hotel room bed. We saw Elliott Gould as Everyman in every other movie playing in Westwood. It was a poetic, dreamy, and idealistic time, the calm inside the otherwise violent and malevolent Vietnam era. It was what I imagined the Russian Revolution had been like—lofty idealism spinning impotently against a bigger, badder, cynical and corrupt world. Years later when I went to see Warren Beatty's *Reds,* I envisioned Diane and me marching down streets in protest wrapped around hours spent at neighborhood cafés solving the world's problems. We were young and full of ourselves, and she was the ignition for our creativity together.

We hooked up at one point with Ron Heck, the lead guitarist from my long-ago living room band, who was at the University of California, Santa Barbara, majoring in education and surfing. We wrote and recorded songs together at Ron's ad hoc music studio. Diane and I made eight-millimeter films. One was called *25th Street*, an ethereal and cerebral six minutes shot at water's edge in Hermosa Beach near her parents' bunga-low. We added a naturalistic soundtrack of gulls and waves breaking. We were so happy with the outcome that we could have jumped on a jet and taken it to Cannes. We had awarded ourselves the Palme d'Or for work in eight millimeter.

15

Don't Make Waves, 1970–1971

My folks divorced in June 1970, and four months later on the Stalag 13 set my dad and Patti were united in something less than holy matrimony. My dad's parents attended the celebration. Feeling sympathetic toward my brokenhearted mom, my sisters and I did not.

My dad enjoyed Patti as his confidante and the female pal he never had. He felt he could talk to her about anything, and to him that just eradicated the traditional boundaries of "husband" and "wife." From my cynical perspective, I think Patti saw from the outset that my dad was a pliable subject. I never saw their relationship as one of equals. One person had to bend in their relationship, which may be the case in most relationships, but my dad was the one who had to do all the bending.

When my dad and Patti exchanged their vows on the Hogan's soundstage, Fraulein Hilda just happened to have a strudel in the oven. That she was pregnant would not have been remarkable except for the fact that my dad had had a vasectomy in 1968 when he was still married to my mom. He had had the procedure because he knew he didn't want any more kids and also because as a big-time TV star he was having affairs with lots of women, and free love or otherwise, out-of-wedlock children were still a big issue in Hollywood in 1968. Now it's the norm.

I know about the vasectomy because for some reason I never discovered, my dad showed me a document from his doctor confirming the fact he'd had the procedure. A document that doesn't count for much considering the swelling of Patti's midsection. Her pregnancy raised a lot of eyebrows in our family. Maybe the doctor had botched the job. Maybe my dad should have been neutered. That might've helped.

During Christmas break of 1970 my newly married dad thought he would emulate Dr. Joyce Brothers and promote positive relationships and understanding—in other words, he'd turn us into the Brady Bunch. What better way to share the warmth than to take the clan for a weekend to

Mammoth Mountain in California's High Sierras: his new bride, Patti's daughter by a previous marriage, Melissa (known as Mits), and Debbie, Karen, and me. I invited Diane to come along as a kind of buffer, a neutral party in the multifamilial lineup.

We stayed in a rented condo right in the heart of rustic Mammoth Lakes. I was the only skier, so instead of schussing the slopes we spent hours riding plastic saucers at breakneck speed down steep, snow-covered hills. There were laughs and screams as my dad played camp director. He was trying hard to wipe out any lingering ill will harbored by his kids.

Many people love new beginnings and most wish for their happy outcome, but from my corner I felt—I knew—it was only a matter of time before gravity deflated this balloon of bonhomie. I could see that Patti had no use for my sisters, who still felt a guilty sense of betrayal to my mom for spending time with the enemy. Just as Yoko was perceived as the cause of the Beatles' breakup at that time, Patti was fingered by my sisters as the linchpin in the destruction of my parents' marriage. They were too young to understand the underlying circumstances that had led to the dissolution of our folks' marriage.

Diane immediately picked up on a feeling that Patti invested herself most successfully in a male world. Patti's daughter, her husband's daughters, his mother, and ex-wife could only be obstacles to her manifest destiny. Still, Diane and I had fun that weekend: we saucered, hiked, and made love in the back of my dad's frigid station wagon. Our breath and heat fogged the windows, and we loved and laughed until just before the sun came up. My dad liked Diane, and he was really glad that I had a girlfriend. He was enjoying his sex life with his new spouse, and he wanted his only son to also have a berth on the love train. In the past he had shown impatience with my constant self-doubt and analysis. "Damn it, Bobby, jump in and get the good!" was always his fatherly advice.

Diane and I would visit my dad from time to time on various sets. These were opportunities for Diane and my dad to spend time getting to know each other. Since her father was a television writer, "the business" was no big deal except on one unforgettable occasion. My dad was shooting a big, bombastic, flag-waving post–Labor Day special called *Make Mine Red, White and Blue* at NBC in Burbank. I had arranged for Diane and me to spend most of the afternoon visiting the set because unbeknownst to her, Diane's hero, Fred Astaire, was the host of the show. During a break my dad and I introduced her to the iconic dancer. Diane just about levitated as she shook Mr. Astaire's hand and told him what a dedicated fan she was. I watched with glee as her smile virtually lit the set. That brief meeting ranked high on her personal best list for many years, and seeing her reaction made me fall for her harder than ever.

While I was never much into hero worship, John Lennon was one of my guiding lights. I loved his songs and prose, his seductive singing voice, his Rickenbacker rhythm guitar, and his witty, elastic imagination. John and Yoko had really long hair (plus beard for Lennon), and I suspect looked more religious than they wanted to, or maybe not, but being the chameleons they were, they transformed themselves when they decided to cut off all their hair to raise money for their peace project.

With no false courage from drink or drugs, Diane and I talked each other into shearing our own rather bountiful locks in emulation of John and Yoko. So one night in that Town & Gown dorm room I shared with Fryer, who always seemed to be out, Diane and I cut each other's hair off. It was not quite crew-cut length, but it was really short, heretical for 1971. The difference between our appearance earlier in the day and that night was profound. We put our intertwined tresses in a Plexiglas box; we were young and silly, and thought watching our hair cohabiting was exciting. And as I said, all of this was done without any chemical enrichment. There was laughter in the air and sex and wildness and kissing and holding and going to films together on opening day. We were getting high on each other and the life we were sharing.

Whereas Chris Klauser and I had had more of a "like" relationship, the twinges in my stomach I felt with Diane inspired the word *love* from me for the first time. At times I had to see Diane right away or I'd go crazy. We still spent hours on the telephone, often meeting each other at 11:30 at night (not necessarily a wise idea on the USC campus) after studying, attending film classes, making art. I was giddy with a happiness and contentment I'd never known before.

So my first two years at college became a daily regimen of Diane, film, license plate frames, and avoiding Vietnam. My academic life, however, was much too reminiscent of high school. My undergraduate requirements included geology and biology, which had no relevance to life as I knew it. It was like being stuck in thirteenth grade. It was the fear of a Private R. D. Crane body bag that kept me in school.

As 1971 began to unfurl, I couldn't imagine myself with anyone other than Diane for the rest of my life. Our passion was raw, mentally and physically. It was a love riot. We were going to be fueled forever by an intoxicating, highly combustible mix of creativity, art, love, and sex. One night as we were standing in a long Westwood queue waiting to see that great date flick, George Lucas's low-budget futuristic *THX 1138*, we killed time by stealing kisses, holding hands, and whispering "I love you." At one point there was a pronounced silence—the longest dead air we had experienced to date. It wasn't an uncomfortable silence. In fact it was just the opposite. It was a bubble of warmth and serenity that enveloped and protected us from all the turmoil the world was offering on a daily basis.

"Should we get married?" I asked. It was as much a dare as a question.

"Yes," Diane answered immediately, her eyes glistening.

We embraced and shared a long, deep kiss. The line started to move. Since we'd already paid for our tickets, we decided to see the Lucas/Coppola production. Besides, it had been filmed in the San Francisco Bay area, and we had talked about moving north for the next episode of the Bob and Diane Show, so even if the film was awful we might be able to scout locations.

Wanting to go public with our engagement, we decided to take our love on the road. Our first stop was Westwood; my dad and Patti, newlyweds themselves, were soft targets. Of course they liked the idea; they were on their own love high. Patti and I still had a good relationship at the time, but her support of our conjugal scheme seemed like a loan for future repayment.

Next stop on the Love Me Tender Tour was Hermosa Beach, where the plan was presented to Diane's parents, Bob and Betty. Bob was a no-nonsense television writer of shows like *The FBI, Dragnet,* and *Ironside*. Betty was a wonderfully charming, funny, cute-as-a-button mother of three daughters, Diane being the middle child. There were genuine smiles and a group hug. So far, so good.

Then we drove to Tarzana to meet with my mom. This was during the pre-Chuck era. My parents' marriage had always been the support structure for my mom's existence, and with its deterioration and collapse, chaos reigned over the Vanalden homestead. Forty-one years old, my mother was trying to be both parents to my young sisters while coping with her own mother, who did nothing but complain about my mom's poor choice of a husband. Now her oldest child, her only son, was about to embark on a road that she felt could only lead to the cul-de-sac of heartache.

Diane and I laid out our concept of matrimonial bliss. There was a long, very long silence, and then my mom hit the roof. The yelling was volcanic, the contained misery of several years suddenly erupting and flowing like lava down Kilauea. Because her own marriage had ended so badly, mom's feeling was that mine would be the same, if not worse. While she might have been concerned for my best interests, there was also an elephant in the room—an Oedipal elephant. I don't mean to imply there was ever anything other than a mother's love for her first and only son, but from our earliest days in Stamford and Bridgeport, it was always Mom and Bobby, her little man. She loved me so much she didn't want me to be with another woman. She'd already lost one man. Her world was sliding away right before her eyes. She saw my potential marriage only as another divorce, for her and for me.

My mom felt Diane and I were playing dress-up adults. She said we were good at playtime but not so effective at the nuts and bolts of everyday life. Where were we going to live? How were we going to support ourselves? What was I going to do for a living? My mom spoke the unpopular truth about most young courtships. She was the voice of reality, speaking about responsibility, about growing up. She marshaled wisdom in her attempt to talk down two love addicts. I tried to act as referee between the two most important women in my life, but in trying to mediate, to be the negotiator, I never put my arm around Diane and challenged my mom's authority. I never said, "We're doing this whether you like it or not!"

My mom used her emotion and condemnations like a good prosecuting attorney. Hearing this kind of ominous projection of her own future and seeing her mate's inaction, Diane reached her breaking point. "You're not going to fuck up my life!" she yelled back at my mom, index finger pointed menacingly.

"This is going to end badly," my mom replied quietly, taking the air out of not just the room but the bubble that was Diane's and my love.

The drive back to USC was interminable. Diane and I experienced the longest silence of our relationship. I couldn't fathom what she was thinking and feeling. Reflecting on what just happened? Shutting down? Planning her next art project or mulling over a list of potential new suitors? I didn't have the nerve to ask, and I'm not sure I even wanted the answer. The one thing I was sure of, ultimately, was that I trusted my mom's judgment more than my own.

Diane and I had ridden a wave of euphoria for a couple of days, but after the opera at Vanalden we never talked about marriage again. Not once. That was the beginning of the end of my relationship with Diane. She was bitterly disappointed that I hadn't stood up to defend her, our love, our future partnership in life's challenges and rewards. Marriage was to be our next step, and I had hit a wrong note in our relationship that would never go away. We continued to see each other, but there was always a dissonant chord reverberating somewhere in the background.

If the failure of our engagement was the earthquake in our relationship, then I provoked the aftershocks that pretty much wiped out whatever remained standing. It started in a drama class at USC taught by Joan Tewkesbury, aka Joan McGuire, who was a Robert Altman associate. Tewkesbury was a script supervisor by trade who later penned the critically acclaimed *Nashville* for Altman. The class was an easy four credits, but I recognized it more as an opportunity to learn how to communicate with actors since I was still under the impression that I was going to become the next Francis Ford Coppola.

Two of the more interesting students in class were Stephen Randall, whom I would later write for at *Playboy* magazine and who would become deputy editor there, just below Hef on the masthead, and a quietly driven blonde named Laura Ziskin. Laura would much later become best known for producing the *Spiderman* films as well as two Oscar broadcasts, among a long list of other achievements, including the formation of the Stand Up 2 Cancer charity.

One of our acting class exercises included sitting in pairs, closing our eyes, and touching the other "actor's" face. This was frighteningly intimate to me, but it was also thrilling, especially when I finally got to square off with Laura. I wanted to behave like an adult since she was vastly more mature—a year older. As my fingers traced her heavy, half-moon eyelids, which trailed off at the corners, creating a sad, weary, but seductive look, and her thin eyebrows, diminutive nose, and sweet lips, I knew I was falling in love. My feelings were not reciprocated equally, but Laura did take a momentary interest in me, and one night after class we met at the Old World restaurant on Sunset Boulevard in West Hollywood down the Strip from Whisky A Go-Go. In the course of our evening I must have said something worthwhile because she invited me back to her place. I'm sure I had the look of Jean-Pierre Léaud's stock character Antoine Doinel from Truffaut's films, a mix of amazement, trepidation, and surprise, as I followed Laura to her small bungalow rental on Norwich Avenue a few minutes away. She gave me a one-minute tour of the crowded space before leading me to her bedroom. Unfortunately for Laura, I won no Oscar for my performance that night. Not even a nomination. What I lacked in experience and creativity in the sack I made up for in speed.

Now, Diane and I had an open, frank, and sincere relationship. After all, it was the age of honesty, full disclosure. It was the Age of Aquarius, for God's sake. I decided to tell Diane I had slept with Laura. I would display integrity, candor, uprightness. I would behave like an adult. Wrong decision. Fuck integrity. Fuck candor. Fuck uprightness. Fuck being an adult. Diane felt betrayed. We didn't see each other for months after my Honest Abe routine. I had seriously fucked up.

Shortly thereafter Diane left USC for the Art Center College of Design in Pasadena, where she met bright, sexy, worldly art professors and fellow students and formed new relationships. Our pure, raw bond, our sharing of secrets and bodies, was gone. We still loved each other, but the pull of new experiences aggravated the fissure. I was responsible for shattering our marriage dream. I had let down the most important person in the world.

In any event, a new recruit joined the cast in June 1971. Now, my dad was christened Robert Edward Crane, and I am Robert David Crane, so I am not and have never wanted to be a "Junior" although the sobriquet gets pinned on me often. Patti and my dad's new baby boy was named Robert Scott Crane. Who the hell did my dad think he was, George Foreman? When I was told about the name I held my tongue. I didn't raise my voice. I didn't storm out of the room in disgust, in spite of being hurt to the core. The story my dad told me was that Patti, who had had three stepfathers, always felt closest to the one named Robert. I could only shake my head in wounded and pathetic amazement.

"Don't worry, Bobby," my dad said cheerfully, "we're gonna call him Scotty."

I wanted to grab him and scream, "Then why don't you name him Scott Crane? Why didn't you tell Patti you've already got a son named Robert? Why the fuck don't you just call him Ishmael?" I didn't. I couldn't.

My dad's philosophy of "Don't make waves" obviously didn't extend ɔ his firstborn's feelings. I never discussed it with him, but I felt betrayed, e I was being forgotten, erased just like a piece of audiotape. I also felt it was a power play on Patti's part. She wanted what she wanted. There was no regard for my feelings in the equation, and my dad failed miserably to stand up for me. In fact, he just bent over and said, "Thank you. I'll have another."

Basically, Patti hated everyone on my dad's side of the family. That included me, my sisters, my dad's mother, and my mom. None of us could bring anything positive to Patti's life as far as she was concerned. We were a nuisance, an irritant, part of my dad's history that she couldn't wish away. We were all flies in her Cabernet.

16

War Is Over, 1971–1972

In 1971 CBS cleaned house on its primetime schedule, eliminating past favorites like *Green Acres* and *Hogan's Heroes*. Ed Feldman was informed of the cancellation a month before his team was to have started shooting its seventh season. Everyone involved felt there was at least one more season left in the tank. But as a result of CBS's action, *Hogan's* didn't get to make a series' finale episode. Hogan and the POWs could have been liberated and poor Klink and Schultz could have been captured and sent to an Allied forces' POW camp, but we'll never know. Still, as it was, *Hogan's Heroes* lasted longer than World War II.

At this time, Walt Disney Pictures was at its lowest output and quality levels. The studio was undergoing a major transition. It had been almost a decade since *Mary Poppins,* and another decade would pass before the transformation by the Michael Eisner regime. In the meantime, the studio produced tired comedies starring Don Knotts, Tim Conway, and Kurt Russell (still in his cute and goofy mode before his action-hero mode).

Though my dad was famous worldwide as Colonel Hogan, he still admired and wanted to emulate the careers of Jack Lemmon, Gig Young, and Cary Grant. Unfortunately, the acme of my dad's career and fame coincided with the nadir of Disney's creativity, and the result of this unlucky convergence was *Superdad*. The only movie my dad would ever star in was a comedy as out of touch with 1972 contemporary humor as the Elke Sommer skinfest had been with the swinging '60s. It was written and directed by another gaggle of Hollywood veterans who were just going through the motions in the dark at the end of their careers.

The fatigued story of an overly protective father trying to turn back time and delay the development of his teenaged daughter made the viewer wistful for former Disney hit comedies like *The Parent Trap* or *The Absent-minded Professor*. In *Superdad,* Joe Flynn and Dick Van Patten did their predictable comedic turns, and Barbara Rush, who had worked with

Sinatra, looked and behaved more like my dad's mother than his wife. Sensibly, Kurt Russell would bolt the Disney stable after appearing in *Superdad*. Two other castmates who played teenaged hooligans were the actors B. Kirby Jr., later known as Bruno Kirby (who went on to play the young Clemenza in the masterpiece *Godfather 2*), and Ed Begley Jr. (who later appeared in the Christopher Guest films *Best in Show* and *A Mighty Wind*). Interestingly enough, thirty years later, Ed Begley Jr. would also appear in *Auto Focus*, Paul Schrader's Calvinist take on the temptations of Bob Crane and the sexual revolution of the '60s and '70s, a film on which I consulted with Schrader with respect to Michael Gerbosi's script. As it happened, Ed and I were the only two participants in *Auto Focus* who had actually ever met my dad. But I digress.

Disney executives at the time of the making of *Superdad* were not pleased by the rumors circulating around Hollywood suggesting that their new Dean Jones had a penchant for home movies that would make more than Bashful blush. Disney CEO Ron Miller sat on *Superdad* for a year and a half before finally releasing the film during the permafrost season early in 1974. *Superdad*'s quality level can only be described by the title of a hit from another era—*Superbad*. It tanked without even coming up for air once.

It also turned out that showing Polaroids and videotape of naked women to cast and crew was not a good move for a would-be Disney star. The publicity department could handle rumors of Julie Andrews's sexual preferences or Dick Van Dyke's drinking problem, but raw footage of partying females being exhibited on the same lot where Minnie Mouse lived? My dad was not gonna get work cleaning Mary Poppins's chimney doing that. But my dad was clueless in that regard. Film executives, producers, directors, and publicists had lunch together. They talked. My dad believed that his product—his smile, laugh, quickness, volume—would still carry the day regardless of his hobbies. He would sell the charm, the handsome face, the funny cadence of saying words, and those qualities would trump the backstage talk, the gossip, the coworkers going silent when he walked into a room.

Like most men, I've always had a profound interest in the opposite sex, but alongside it I also have a deep-seated respect for women, probably owing to the fact that I was raised by and surrounded by them. Still, I suspect that a large percentage of men, in their private, testosterone-poisoned brains, think about women and sex as much as my dad did. The difference being that my dad stripped the gears of the transmission that engages the thought to the deed. He didn't realize that just because he was on TV not everyone would be interested in him airing his privates. He would have fit right in with the lovefests of the '60s Haight-Ashbury community if he hadn't been a Republican.

As a fringe Hollywood family, we never attended movie premieres. Nowadays, the cast of *Duck Dynasty* or Snooki might show up at a premiere, much to the delight of the fans. Jenny McCarthy smiles her goofy smile, Paula Abdul staggers, Kat Von D. shows off her latest ink, Melissa Rivers whines while keeping a firm grip on her mother's spectral coattails. My family never received an invitation to a big-time Hollywood premiere. Movies were for movie stars. TV stars need not apply.

Instead, my dad and I attended the West Coast premiere of the X-rated *Deep Throat* at the Pussycat Theatre on Santa Monica Boulevard in Hollywood. No limos for this red carpet event. Actually, we lucked out and found a parking space on a side street a couple of blocks away and walked to the box office. In lieu of klieg lights, silver screen luminaries, and adoring fans, the sidewalk throng consisted of a few homeless people, panhandlers, and streetwalkers. The Pussycat Theatre staff ushered us down a soggy red carpet into the hall. My dad stopped to talk with porno producers, actors, distributors, and their polyester-clad publicists. They couldn't believe Colonel Hogan was there, that he might be one of them. But my dad never made class distinctions. He didn't think of himself as a TV star. He thought of himself as the same as everyone else in that theater—paying the rent, having the car repaired, dropping off the dry cleaning, looking for a break. For him it was no different from going to a Disney movie. This just happened to be *The Absent-Minded Pornfessor*.

The premiere of *Deep Throat* was a prime example of a Fellini Excursion. That's a thing my dad and I had, an homage to Federico Fellini and all the bizarre images and people in his films. Whenever we encountered wild, weird, wonderful happenings, we would just look at each other and say, "Fellini Excursion." Here's an example: one time we went to Las Vegas for a bocce ball tournament at Caesar's Palace. This was in the early '70s, before Vegas really became the adult Disneyland. Caesar's was the big hotel of the moment, boasting an enormous enclosed sporting venue where the bocce courts were set up. My dad was there to play for a charity fund-raiser, as was (more of a thrill for me) Joe DiMaggio. DiMaggio was very grumpy. He had one expression for the whole event, and that was "Get me out of this fuckin' place." At one point my dad and I looked at each other as the Yankee Clipper tossed his balls in the sand and said simultaneously, "Fellini Excursion." The significance of Fellini Excursions for me was that I was sharing time with my dad. Just him and me. No matter how bizarre the events, the fact that we were experiencing them together is what I remember and what was important.

Back at the Pussycat, my dad was mingling and signing autographs. I declined to shake anyone's hand. For a brief moment I enjoyed the novelty of my first time in a XXX theater, but sitting in a thinly cushioned seat with my feet on a sticky floor watching some poor young woman bare her talents on the not-so-silver screen quickly lost its allure. After the second or third time Linda Lovelace orally pleasured some slick, greasy-looking guy, I started thinking about the chores I had to do the next day. But *Deep Throat* became a phenomenon, and Linda Lovelace became a "star" in a raincoat-cloaked universe. If Lovelace were alive today, she would be showing up at the same events as Paris Hilton, Kim Kardashian, and Lindsay Lohan, comparing tattoos with the cast of *Jackass*.

Inevitably, it didn't take long until my dad secured his own video copy of *Deep Throat*. He reedited the film, intercutting scenes of Lovelace going down on a nonunion actor while a rocket blasts off with clips of his favorite *Tonight Show* acts appearing with Johnny Carson and Ed McMahon—"Hi-yo!" He did it just to do it, just to enjoy the editing process and technology and, of course, to get a laugh. The next time he and his dinner theater castmates were killing endless days before evening performances in Fort Lauderdale or Traverse City, he could whip out this latest creative effort to delight the crowd. My dad's homespun productions put a new twist on watching television. And viewing the tape once was never enough. My dad was the Pied Piper of Porn, attracting friendly dinner theater employees, stage managers, and makeup artists who would join the cast at my dad's apartment or hotel room for a screening. The state-of-the-art equipment coupled with scenes of the new film icon Lovelace made for a memorable party. Word traveled fast through places like Lake Charles and Jacksonville that Crane's porno palace and laugh salon was the place to be, and an invitation should be had if at all possible while the show was in town. My dad had too much downtime and no structure. He never made the connection that his way of killing time was also killing his career.

My dad and I spent a lot of time together driving around Los Angeles.

He always had a lot of errands. He had to go pick up something for Patti, drop off film for processing, or make a bank deposit. For lunch we often went to a burger joint next to the car wash at the corner of Westwood and Santa Monica boulevards. We'd sit in the car, eat burgers, drink Cokes, and talk. We talked a lot. As I entered my twenties, I became his unofficial junior agent, offering my take on choices relating to his career and the agents, managers, publicists, directors, and actors he dealt with. My dad always listened to me, but he didn't completely trust anyone's judgment and that included mine. I was still a nonprofessional who hadn't opened any doors for anyone.

After *Hogan's*, my dad really lost structure. He missed Edward H. Feldman. He traveled the country appearing in his brisk ninety-minute play cum neo-stand-up routine, *Beginner's Luck*, which he could have performed in his sleep. He was doing his Willy Loman best to pay his alimony and child support to my mom while also sustaining his second wife's real estate hunger. He was to be praised for his financial due diligence, but he was also watering the hillside of his own slippery slope. Outside of a few hours onstage six nights a week at the dinner theater playing himself, the rest of his days were spent like a college freshman who attends all the parties and none of the classes. There was too much free time for the former Catholic altar boy, who was now allowed to be himself. This was where the publicist's dream story of the small-town drummer and radio host who rose to the top of the Nielsen ratings as the All-American highflier the audience rooted for crashed and burned.

*M*A*S*H* star Alan Alda was everything my dad was not. He was an Emmy Award–winning actor on a popular program who expanded his career into writing and directing films. His career seemed to be heading down a road whose on-ramp wasn't even on my dad's map. It might have been easy for me to say, "Hey, Dad, be Alan Alda," but the absence of structure and creative trust in anyone except himself constantly haunted him and held him back. My dad could think brilliantly, a kind of writing on his feet, but he didn't possess the discipline to sit down and put the words on paper, to actually write a script. More important, he lacked the crucial ability to stand back and see the bigger picture and how he might fit into it. He was trapped staring into his own movieola, seeing one disconnected frame at a time.

17

Beacon in the Storm, 1972

Through 1972 Diane and I still dated and even slept together occasionally. I knew she was seeing other men; she knew I was seeing other women. Life was full of possibilities, but she and I still had a connection that didn't exist with other people, at least as far as I was concerned.

One day Diane called me at my apartment. We were cordial, dancing around the heaviness of the recent past. I was anticipating an invitation to her latest school art show. I never expected an announcement that she was pregnant. I couldn't say for sure that I was the father. Nor could Diane. But I was the one she came to for help. It meant Diane still trusted me. I was the beacon in the storm.

Most women knew someone who knew someone who could direct them to a sympathetic physician who would perform a clandestine abortion. We were still a year before *Roe v. Wade*. Diane made several phone calls and through her grapevine found a clinic in South Los Angeles. On a bright Southern California day, I drove her to a dingy, single-story structure that had the look of a temporary office set up on a construction site. The building, the street, the industrial neighborhood were washed out under the relentless sun. The place lacked the open, honest, and unabashed energy of the Free Clinic in Venice where Diane and I had gone in better days for her Pap smears.

Paperwork was signed, and a payment in the amount of $500 cash was made, which was the bulk of my ready capital. Diane was led away. The operation was to take place in a back room, of course. We were strangers in a strange land, in primal circumstances such as these two middle-class young adults had never experienced.

Waiting for Diane's return, I thought of this moment as another big step in my education. I still felt responsible and cowardly for making our marriage disappear, but I was glad Diane had chosen me as her companion on this sordid adventure. My practical assistance—I had a car and an apartment and some cash—eased the situation, yes, but, over and above that, Diane had chosen me to help, knowing not only that she could count on me to provide it but also that it would remain our secret. At least until now. Sitting in that illegal abortion clinic, a gloomy hallway separating me from the woman I still loved and respected, I didn't care whether I was the father or not. I just wanted her to get through this somber affair and get the hell out of this place. Diane was not encouraged to stay for a long recovery period; after what seemed like only a few minutes, I helped her dress and supported her as she walked groggily to my car. I never wanted to see this part of town again. I was relieved to leave the clammy darkness behind us as I drove the sun-bleached streets to the one-bedroom apartment I was renting on Dorothy Street in Brentwood. I kept glancing over at Diane as she slept in the passenger seat to make sure she was alright. We'd decided she would retreat to my apartment for the weekend. No one was to know where she was.

It was Diane's decision alone to abort. I was not consulted. Although we never discussed it, we both knew that motherhood and the pursuit of a career in art didn't mix. At twenty-one, Diane had a greater love for making art than for this unborn child. Her ambition and her ego outweighed her maternal instincts at that point in her life. I would never be comfortable with the abortion, but ultimately it wasn't my body; it wasn't my decision. I helped someone I loved survive a scary, lonely, and very long weekend.

Diane and I would continue to see each other off and on, but now our shared history pulled us apart as much as it brought us together. We were traveling along different paths but—like Gatsby, who could always see the blinking green light at the end of Daisy's dock—I knew Diane and I would have a connection forever.

18

Heeeere's Jackie!!! 1972–1975

In 1972 I was in my third and final year at USC. I was feeling confident that I wasn't going to become GI Bob because the draft was winding down. It ended completely with the close of June 1973. I was still fascinated with film and filmmakers, but I was having problems with my other classes. Basically, I was underperforming in everything but my performing arts curriculum, and the notion that I still had to take a biology course or some kind of math class to graduate made me feel like I was back in high school.

FC Enterprises, my license plate frame business with Chris Fryer, was humming along, and Chris and I had made several road trips that were an important part of my self-discovery. We would get in the car and set out for college towns—Boulder, Colorado; Laramie, Wyoming; Champaign-Urbana, Illinois. I was meeting new people and going to places I never dreamed of visiting. In a weird way I was mirroring my dad's wanderings around the country doing his play. The big difference was that the closest I ever got to getting lucky on the road was chatting up a couple of lookers in the Burger Barn in Beaver, Utah. All Chris and I got, for all our Hollywood magic, were some flirty looks followed by an escort to the county line by four guys in need of some serious acne remediation in a souped-up Camaro. It was a little too reminiscent of *Easy Rider,* and I kept a keen eye in the rearview mirror for some toothless guys with a shotgun in a pickup truck.

What I did learn from these trips was how to deal with rejection, how to overcome objections, and how to walk cold into someone's office and make a pitch, experiences that would help me later in life. But in those early lessons I was guided not by my dad but by Chris's. David Fryer taught me how to pick up a phone and try to sell complete strangers something they had no idea they desperately needed. Attending the University of Dave was a very important part of my education.

So was spending days and days in a car with Chris as we planned how we were going to usher in the next new wave in American cinema. We analyzed films between Madison and Chicago. We tossed around screenplay ideas between Berkeley and Eugene. We made each other laugh till we cried. Our road trips were so much fun I would have done them without a purpose.

During the early 1970s the two of us had also become great observers of the ascendant star of Jack Nicholson. *Easy Rider, Five Easy Pieces,* and *Carnal Knowledge* were big, important films, at least to us. Jack represented an honesty, an abandon that I had seen elsewhere only in old Marlon Brando films. Nicholson crying in front of his paralyzed father in *Five Easy Pieces* was a landmark moment for me. It was a shocking and spellbinding scene. How could you be a man and allow yourself to show emotion like that in front of millions of people? I was stunned by it, but I felt nothing but admiration. Ultimately I wanted to be like that character. I wanted to be that honest and open with other people. That particular scene spoke to me about my relationship with my dad, because except when I was a really young kid I could never cry in front of him. I wouldn't allow myself to be that exposed. Seeing Nicholson do that was a revelation.

The semester after the release of *Five Easy Pieces* Chris and I took a class at USC called The Film Heroes of the '30s and '60s taught by screenwriter Steven Karpf, and we had the idea of teaming up to interview Jack Nicholson as the "antihero" for the ages. It never occurred to us that a couple of tyros from Tarzana and USC film school might not be able to talk to Jack Nicholson for their class project. We just didn't know any better. Hell, we'd been told no by curmudgeonly gift shop buyers in college bookstores all over this great land, but we still managed to sell them license frames. So even though we'd heard the word *no* umpteen times, it just hadn't made that much of an impression. We weren't deterred by the word. We weren't put off by the word. We just stepped around it, coming at the target from a different direction.

I had seen Jack once on a film panel at USC, and at that point in his career he was a great supporter of film, foreign cinema, and up-and-coming filmmakers. He'd been to the Cannes Film Festival with his directorial debut, *Drive, He Said,* but he was still accessible enough that he could be persuaded to make an appearance at a college. This was well before the curtain of opportunity closed for nobodies to get near Jack Nicholson.

Robert Crane and Jack Nicholson, Beverly Hills, 1972 (photo by
Christopher Fryer; author's collection).

Talking to Jack Nicholson was remarkably easy. Through a family
connection of Chris's we got what turned out to be Jack's home phone
number, though we didn't know it at the time. I dialed it, and damned if
the guy himself didn't answer the phone on the second ring. I knew who
it was, but I still asked for Mr. Nicholson just to be polite. He asked,
"Who's calling?" and I introduced myself and launched into my pitch for
an interview. To our incredible surprise and elation, Jack Nicholson agreed
to sit down with us and talk film. It was absolutely unreal. Chris and I
were bouncing off the walls.

Jack invited us up to his house on Mulholland Drive. To illustrate
how different the world was in 1972, there was no gate on the driveway—
the same driveway Jack shared with his next-door neighbor, Marlon
Brando. We rolled up to the open front door and were escorted into the
two-story ranch house as Michelle Phillips, Jack's girlfriend at the time,
passed us in the foyer. Chris and I exchanged looks, trying to be cool, as
we stepped down into the living room. We were in a different world.

There was a large, plush, brown suede couch opposite the wall of windows that overlooked Franklin Canyon and Los Angeles. The house was comfortable, lived-in. I felt pretty much at ease even though I was about to meet one of my film heroes. Jack came down the stairs wearing a navy blue bathrobe with a bat pin on the lapel. He might have just gotten out of bed, although it was well past lunchtime. As I discovered over the next several hours spent talking about film, Jack's upcoming projects, his past experiences, and the future of cinema, Jack wasn't wearing anything under that robe as he inadvertently flashed me several times.

After finally switching off the tape recorder, we took a few commemorative photos—for our benefit, not Jack's—and left the house on cloud 99. We were so juiced that Chris almost killed us, spinning out his Porsche on a Mulholland curve and doing a 360 into a cloud of dust. We came to a stop between a telephone pole and the edge of a cliff. As the dust settled we could hear our pounding hearts, and then laughed like lunatics. Needless to say, we got As in that class.

Serendipitously, after that first interview, Chris and I, separately and together, began bumping into Jack around L.A. I saw him at a Rolling Stones concert, and we exchanged pleasantries. My date, Barbara Stephens, who had been my government teacher at Taft High School, was suitably impressed. Chris ran into Jack at an antiwar/pro-McGovern rally at UCLA. Jack was always where the action was.

Because these chance meetings made us think we were becoming pals, we did the only logical thing—we decided to write a book about our new best friend. There had never been a book about Jack Nicholson, and we felt it was high time and that we were just the guys to do it. Frankly, in 1972 the name Jack Nicholson wasn't yet on the American public's radar screen. On more than one occasion when I mentioned the idea I was told, "Gee, Bobby, I didn't know you were that interested in golf."

Before proceeding we called Jack and asked his permission. Amazingly, he gave us the thumb's up, though to this day I think he felt nothing would ever come of it and he was merely humoring a couple of twenty-year-old film nuts. Chris and I immediately drew up a list of all the people who had worked with Jack whom we were interested in talking to. Everyone from Roger Corman, Bruce Dern, Ann-Margret, and Monte Hellman to Mike Nichols, Robert Evans, Bob Rafelson, and Dennis Hopper was on that list. Then we started making phone calls. A million phone calls to agents, publicists, assistants, anyone with a connection, and if my cold-calling experience ever came in handy, this was the time. Sometimes we failed to secure the subject in question because of time constraints, distance, or just an abiding orneriness, but most of the time when we said Jack had okayed the project those restraints fell away.

Chris and I then spent over two years interviewing writers, actors, directors, and producers, and we even managed to get Jack to sit down for a second long interview. We drove sixteen hours nonstop from L.A. to Taos, New Mexico, to interview Dennis Hopper when we got the call that he had a small opening in his schedule to talk to us. His assistant, Ed Gaultney, met us at the Dennis Hopper Art Gallery in Taos when we raggedly came in off the road. He offered us what he described as "primo grass," but we were really looking for authentic New Mexican cooking, which we found at La Fonda in downtown Taos, where we immediately fell under the spell of homemade sopapillas.

The next day we found ourselves in a small, cozy adobe bungalow, complete with hammocks slung from patio trees, on pueblo land. We were also face-to-face with *Easy Rider*'s Billy. Hopper was soft spoken, calm, and thoughtful, just the opposite of his maniacal image. He even took us on a tour of his home, which he was renting from the Taos Indians. As Hopper led us upstairs into the loftlike bedroom, he quickly ran ahead to fling the covers over the rumpled sheets of his bed. We happened to be doing the interview shortly after Hopper married his third wife, a beautiful but clueless actress, Daria Halprin. That summer Hopper was renting out to college art students a much grander house that he owned, which once had been owned by socialite Mabel Dodge Luhan and been graced by the likes of Georgia O'Keefe, D. H. Lawrence and his wife, Frieda, and Carl Jung.

Another time we had to go zooming up Highway 395 from L.A. to Lake Tahoe because after several weeks of phone calls we were told that we could finally talk to Ann-Margret, who was performing at Harrah's. Unfortunately, that was all the information we had when we arrived at the Sierra resort. Luckily and completely coincidentally, we bumped into Roger Smith and Allan Carr (Ann-Margret's husband and manager respectively) shopping in a sporting goods store near the motel where we had checked in that afternoon. Over a rack of Lacoste tennis shirts we introduced ourselves and arranged to do our interview that night in Ann-Margret's dressing room before her show. After which we were invited to sit front and center for the dynamic song and dance extravaganza.

On top of that we met Mitzi McCall and her husband, Charlie Brill, who were Ann-Margret's opening comedy act. As we made our introductions Mitzi announced, "Oh, I did a movie with Jack Nicholson, too." Our eyes lit up. It turned out she was in Jack's very first film, *The Cry Baby Killer,* so late that night, after the second show, we sat down and Mitzi gave us a short, funny impression about working with the twenty-one-year-old Nicholson.

Only two days after our interview with Ann-Margret she fell from moving scaffolding used in the entrance for her act and was rushed to the ICU unit at UCLA with serious head and face injuries. We sent flowers and talked about sending a card reading, "No, it's 'Break a *leg,*'" but decided in a fit of good taste that that was not appropriate.

During the production of *Chinatown* in 1973 I had found out through my dad's former secretary at KNX, Carole Steller, who worked at Paramount, what Jack's shooting schedule on the Roman Polanski movie was going to be, and I decided to head down to the L.A. City Hall shoot unannounced. I stood in the back of a large room at city hall watching the scene in which a farmer lets his sheep loose into the chamber while Jack's character, J. J. Gittes, watches from the gallery. Polanski yelled, "Cut!" and Jack got up. He was about to light a cigarette when he noticed me standing there and invited me into his dressing room while the crew set up the next shot. It was just Jack and me, sitting in his trailer. He was telling me about having just finished *The Passenger* for Antonioni with costar Maria Schneider.

"I loved her in *Last Tango in Paris,*" I enthused.

"Yeah, I fucked her," he drawled, his trademark eyebrows raised over devilishly twinkling eyes.

I didn't know if Jack was kidding, letting me in on a secret, padding his reputation as a lady-killer, or just testing me for a reaction. I tried to be cool.

All this crazy running around for the book was done completely "on spec," which meant we had no idea whether or not we would ever make a dime from it—we did it purely "on speculation" of selling the finished product. Those are not the ideal conditions under which to write a book, but we would have done it even if we knew it was all going to go for naught. Chris and I were still attending school full-time and running an ever-growing business empire, but at long last we had a presentable manuscript. Yeah, so now what?

Diane's dad, the television writer, put us in touch with his agent in Los Angeles, who directed us to a literary agent in New York, Henry Morrison. Henry sold the book after only a small raftful of rejections to M. Evans/Lippincott, and Chris and I split the royal sum of $4,500 for our more than three years of work. We were making more than that in a couple of months selling license plate frames, but *Jack Nicholson: Face to Face* arrived in bookstores in May 1975, and we were pretty damned excited about it. I asked my dad if it would be possible to hold a book launch party at his Tilden Avenue house. Now, the closest my dad ever came to celebrating one of his own projects was hosting a *Hogan's Heroes* Christmas party once at the Vanalden House.

"Why would you do that?" he asked. "I never do that."

That was the end of the book launch.

It was the first book ever written about Jack, and to this day the only one of more than a dozen to benefit from his amiable participation, his unique voice resonating from the pages. I am particularly proud of that. It was issued simultaneously in both a large hardcover and a softcover format. I never understood the thinking behind that decision. But it was printed exactly the way Chris and I turned it in. There wasn't one change. The photographs and posters are in the positions and order in which we'd laid them out. The words we wrote and the subjects' voices in the interviews are intact. The book features two interviews with Jack, one at the beginning and one at the end, after we'd seen him through the prism of his colleagues.

When we got our advance copies we called Jack to tell him and ask if we could bring him a hardcover copy. We hadn't spoken in over two years, and his first reaction was, "Robert, what is this book?" I jogged his memory about who we were and what we were doing, and he sighed, "Okay, come on up." He was in for a big surprise.

Chris and I drove up to his house with no near-fatal incidents and handed him a book and a T-shirt printed with his face, the photo on the cover of the book, on it. Jack looked genuinely pleased and only slightly bewildered about how, as Bruce Dern kiddingly referred to us, "the two lames from the Texaco station" had managed to produce this beautiful film archive about him. Thirty-five years later Chris and I are still amazed at what we managed to accomplish. To this day we can't have a phone conversation in which one or the other of us doesn't do a bad impersonation of Jack.

The book was published to mild acclaim, including a nice review from Charles Champlin, the film critic of the *Los Angeles Times*. He was someone I greatly admired—not only was his analysis of film intelligent and rational, but he was also a true fan. He was Siskel and Ebert before there was Siskel and Ebert.

The following year Chris was putting together an audiotape as a surprise for the landmark celebration of my first quarter century, my twenty-fifth birthday. He decided to compile salutations from many of my past girlfriends, other friends, USC professors, and naturally, some of the celebrities we had met along the way—Bruce Dern, Sally Struthers, and of course, Jack Nicholson. Chris called Jack to get a comment, a "Happy birthday" to yours truly. Didn't seem like a big deal to Chris, considering we had lived, breathed, and slept the guy for over three years, but when Chris finally got him on the phone Jack reamed him out, telling him how much his time was worth and how everyone always just wanted "two minutes." Chris, unable to comprehend that Jack was saying no, persisted until Jack relented, saying in a snarl he would later use to perfection as Colonel Jessup in *A Few Good Men*, "Okay, turn on the fucking tape, and let's get it on." Jack then delivered an Oscar-worthy performance of a birthday greeting to me. It was astounding. If you heard the tape you'd swear Jack and I are compadres, los dos amigos. We're not, of course. But the tape, which lives on in a box in my closet, says otherwise.

Chris and I did attempt one last connection, showing up unannounced on the set of the Elia Kazan film *The Last Tycoon*, which was shot on location in Hancock Park. The film starred Robert DeNiro, but Jack had a cameo as a union rep meeting DeNiro's Irving Thalberg. When Jack spotted us we said hi and asked if he had any plans for lunch.

"Yeah. No lunch," was the terse reply, and Nicholson retreated as swiftly as possible back to the set.

Chris and I stood awkwardly among the busy crew members preparing the next scene. That signaled the end of our days hanging out with the big boys. On our way out we saw Nicholson having lunch at a table set up under some trees. The "lames from the Texaco station" slunk off into the afternoon, never to see Jack again. Well, not exactly.

19

The Family Photo Album, 1975

Patti was not about to interfere with my dad's seemingly unquenchable thirst for women. In one instance that I was privy to, Patti even acted as pimp for her priapic husband. The setting was a Sunset Boulevard strip club called the Classic Cat, where my dad often sat in and played drums with the jazz combo that accompanied the real entertainment. For him it didn't get much better than beating the skins while simultaneously ogling some. At least not until his forty-seventh birthday.

The headliner at the club was a monumentally well-endowed ecdysiast named Angel Carter. My dad and Patti both had become friendly with her simply by virtue of being at the club so often. So, as any loving wife would do for her husband's birthday, Patti arranged for my dad to have a private little birthday bash with Angel in her dressing room. While my dad beat some skin backstage, Patti sat at her table in the club nursing her red wine. She set it up and stepped aside. My foolish dad jumped in with reckless fervor. Would this later come back and bite him? Like a pit bull.

A few years later when my dad and Patti began divorce proceedings, Patti would cite the birthday bang she herself had organized as an example of my dad being a bad husband and a worse father, not to mention a man obsessed. I'm not saying some of that wasn't the truth, but Patti was the agent, the facilitator of the behavior, at least in that particular case. You can't keep pouring drinks for an alcoholic and then complain when he falls off the stool.

I had been on her good side for a number of years because I was of the male persuasion, a good listener, and interested in her because she had come from a world so different from that of my mom's—modeling, selling cars, and acting. Patti claimed to have slept with Frank Sinatra, Bill Cosby (who, she said, had a preference for zaftig blondes), and *Mannix* star Mike Connors who, while not a great actor, was purported to wield a different kind of huge talent in Hollywood. Patti was worldly and frank with me in revealing her Hollywood escapades as a young starlet. She was a brassy Broadway character, a combination of Gypsy Rose Lee and Auntie Mame. I had never known a woman so intimate and self-assured in her conversation. So the first few years of her marriage to my dad were revelatory for me. She was the older sister I'd never had who had seen and done it all.

Unfortunately, her love of control and her total denigration of the women in my dad's family tilted the seesaw of their marriage into a negative, poisonous angle from which it couldn't be righted. I drew away from her ultimately because any relationship with Patti was a minefield: one day you're minding your own business, and then suddenly your legs are blown off by some form of verbal IED. I was one of the last survivors with my legs still securely attached.

My youngest sister, Karen, was not so fortunate. One afternoon when my dad and I were out together and Patti was inside their house, my then fourteen-year-old sister was charged with minding Scotty on the backyard swing. Scotty flung himself off the seat midswing, and though he seemed okay at first, by the next day it was apparent he had broken his arm.

Patti blamed Karen and demanded that my dad get her back to the house to face Patti's unilateral tribunal. In his best "don't make waves" mode, my dad called my mom to explain that Patti was hopping mad and wanted Karen to come to the house immediately. My mom gave the phone to my stepdad Chuck, and my dad continued, telling Chuck that it was so hot and uncomfortable for him that it was vital for Karen to come and stand before the inquisitor. My dad pleaded, "Chuck, I can't begin to tell you how important this is to my marriage."

I could hear my dad through the phone at Chuck's ear. Chuck stood silently, deep in thought for what seemed like a full minute. Finally, he replied, "Bob, if this is that important to your marriage, you don't have a marriage."

I could feel my dad's immediate deflation. He said, "You're right, Chuck."

So Karen never had to suffer the cat-o'-nine tails or be buried to the waist and stoned, neither of which I would have put past Patti. That incident widened the already uncrossable crevasse between Patti and the rest of my family. It was a pivotal moment. It also showed Chuck at his best.

Luckily, Mary Tyler Moore entered my dad's life again. Her wildly successful production company, MTM Enterprises, specialized in sharply written, three-camera shows filmed in front of a studio audience. These weekly comedy series included her own eponymous show, its spinoffs *Rhoda* and *Phyllis,* and Bob Newhart's show. MTM offered my dad a pilot called *Second Start.* Unfortunately, the one-camera show came with MTM's third-string lineup of creators, writers, and producers. Jackie Cooper, who had directed some *M*A*S*H* episodes, directed the pilot but clearly missed working with Alda. He and my dad demonstrated a total lack of chemistry. Cooper was a bitter, downcast, former child actor who seemed a better fit for a drama series than an MTM comedy. He barked out orders like a compassionless field general out of touch with his soldiers. Perhaps he felt he had better acting chops than my dad. There was no live audience for the pilot, and with a numbing quiet on the set (my dad's drums were nowhere to be found) my dad retreated into his own form of paranoia. Lacking trust in the director was antithetical to producing a successful product for my dad—or any actor. He was lonely and missed the warm joviality of Stalag 13.

Second Start was the story of forty-year-old Bob Wilcox quitting his unfulfilling job in the financial world and going back to his true calling, medical school. The story line had the stagnant feel of a hybrid version of *The Donna Reed Show* and *Superdad. Hogan's Heroes* looked like *M*A*S*H* compared to that drivel. Where was Ed Feldman? Where was Gene Reynolds? Where was *Mary Tyler Moore Show* cocreator James L. Brooks? NBC hated the pilot but liked working with MTM, liked the premise, and liked my dad, in that order. So Jackie Cooper went kaput. The title went kaput. A one-camera shoot went kaput. After a year of (Grant) Tinker-ing (CEO of MTM, husband of MTM), *The Bob Crane Show* became a three-camera comedy series, filmed in front of a studio audience. It made its network debut in March 1975, facing off against *The Waltons.* Do you remember John-Boy? Do you remember Ma and Pa Walton? Goodnight, Bob Wilcox. Goodnight, wife Ellie and daughter Pam. Goodnight, medical school administrator Lyle Ingersoll and Wilcox's goofy buddies Marvin and Jerry. Goodnight, all.

Hogan's Heroes was not a hit because of the talents of any one person. There were scores of actors, writers, camera crew people, set designers, makeup and hair artists, editors, costumers, grips, and special effects artists who all worked together to create a first-class show. The viewers saw the results of the hours of work and years of experience. They didn't see the crew behind, below, and sometimes above the camera. It was a pure collaborative labor, not of one or two people but of eighty. Collaborative heads are always better than one, but since the demise of *Hogan's*, my dad could never trust anyone again. As he got farther and farther away from the sphere of a television or film set, doing his play in a dinner theater in a mall in Paramus, New Jersey, he relied less and less on others. He was in charge of his set, his script, his performance. He was an actor-director trying to survive, which was fine to pay the bills, but in terms of living his life he made all the wrong choices. My dad knew how to sell only one product: Bob Crane. But he never learned or understood the fine line between selling and marketing. He had no trouble selling the quick wit, the charm, the laugh. His problem was he didn't know how to make the suits want to buy the product.

My dad's market had shrunk to cocktail waitresses in places like Scottsdale. His new audience, which was oblivious to the same old stool pigeons with the same old lame pickup lines, perked up when Colonel Hogan entered the room. He created a new small buzz in the space. Even though *Hogan's* had been off the network for four years, the personage of Colonel Robert E. Hogan, grayer, fuller around the middle, a step slower, had arrived, and he could still enlist volunteers for active duty.

While on the road performing his play, my dad began offering video services to cast members fascinated by the new technology. Some of them borrowed the camera and video deck and produced their own cinema verité. Many were enthralled with the instant results of using videotape in the same way we were once fascinated by tearing off the Polaroid and waving it in the air and watching while the image developed. There was an almost childlike preoccupation and obsession with playing back the results. My dad as the video pusher also got to watch. It was the technological advances that he was showing off when he would occasionally share with me footage of nude actresses or waitresses self-consciously adjusting themselves in front of the video camera, not the images themselves. The overwhelming power of the new technology, coupled with my dad's naïveté, self-centered tunnel vision, and desire for instant gratification, took precedence in his mind over how friends and coworkers might react to the bold images. This was All-American Colonel Hogan sharing a family photo album with his costar or director or producer or publicist or agent. Or a family album if your relations happen to be Gypsy Rose Lee, Linda Lovelace, Heidi Fleiss, and the Mayflower Madam.

My dad had no governor in his brain. When he was on the radio the thought—the gag—fired through his brain's synapses and was vocalized into a microphone and sent out through a transmitter on Mount Wilson into the car radio or the transistor radio in the kitchen nook. Except in the case of the radio waves his thoughts and word pictures hadn't been X-rated. He believed that his Polaroids, his black-and-white stills, his half-inch reel-to-reel and three-quarter-inch cassette videotapes were just as cute and funny as his gags on the air. He felt that, because he was the presenter, the viewer would just go with the flow.

His *Beginner's Luck* cast was a traveling troupe, always on the road to El Paso or Columbus. The cast members became their own community. Things got shared. Some people shared their bodies; others shared drugs and alcohol. My dad shared his pornography captured by means of the new hot technology. He was the first kid on his block to have a Sony videotape deck and camera. He was the enthusiastic one saying, "Hey, look at this!" He simply didn't consider that some people wouldn't want to see his "this." Nowadays, we share our new smart phones with our friends— "Wow, it takes photographs, downloads *Lawrence of Arabia,* makes cappuccino." In the '70s, portable video was the new toy, and my dad was more excited about the act of photographing sexy stuff than he was about the sexy stuff itself. He was the Catholic altar boy slugging back the Communion wine and getting a buzz, but it wasn't the blood of Christ getting him high; it was a newfound interest in winemaking.

20

Take the Bunny and Run, 1976–1977

In 1976, I was perusing an issue of *Oui* magazine, which was still part of Playboy and based in Chicago. I found it refreshing in design, international interviewees, out-of-the-mainstream writers, and foreign models, so I picked out a name from the magazine's masthead for a full-frontal assault. John Rezek, senior editor, had an important-sounding name but somehow seemed approachable to me. Using my finely honed cold-calling skills I dialed the 312 area code and number.

"Playboy Enterprises," said the perky voice at 919 North Michigan Avenue in Chicago.

I envisioned a blonde coed with a bunny dip figure. "John Reezik, please," I said, guessing at the pronunciation.

"It's Rez-ek. John Rezek," the future diplomat and centerfold gently corrected. "Just a moment, please."

"John Rezek's office," snapped a new, no-nonsense voice.

"Hi, is Mr. Rezek available?" I went for a familiar but confident tack.

"Who shall I say is calling?"

"Robert Crane from Los Angeles."

There was a long pause as the secretary ran my name through her mental Rolodex. "He's in a meeting," she said in a voice that indicated Mr. Rezek would be in a meeting every time I called.

Well, I'd been put off by more seasoned pros than her. She couldn't hold a candle to the dowager countess of USC's gift store, Helen Trower, who ultimately stocked Trojans license plate frames, having been overwhelmed by the enthusiasm and tenacity of Chris Fryer and yours truly. I immediately wrote John Rezek a letter, enclosing an interview I had conducted with my dad shortly after *The Bob Crane Show* went off the air in

Robert Crane's Temptations interview for *Oui* magazine, 1979 (author's collection).

an attempt to get him some much-needed publicity. The Q&A was titled "Interview with Bob Crane" by David Sloan. I figured a father and son conversation wouldn't attract any interest, so I used my middle name and my stepdad's last name.

As luck would have it, Rezek's father was a huge *Hogan's Heroes* fan, and the piece caught his eye. Now, my dad was nowhere near hip enough to be a *Oui* magazine interview subject, but the interview was a good calling card for me. When John Rezek and I talked on the phone shortly afterward I immediately came out of the footlocker about my subterfuge and revealed the fact that I was Colonel Hogan's son. Thus began a series of conversations in which the young, West Coast, doesn't-take-no-for-an-answer-kid pitched names to the erudite, oenophilic, quick-thinking, big-city, well-traveled magazine editor. I pitched comedians. I pitched athletes. I pitched actors. After half a dozen phone calls and several dozen names, finally one name caught the attention of the bright, pop-culture-observant Rezek. It was the on-the-rise, outspoken Roger Corman alumnus Bruce Dern. Rezek said, "Go."

Since Fryer and I had already interviewed Dern for our book on Nicholson, we joined forces again. Dern was in town filming a Michael Winner loser called *Won Ton Ton, the Dog who Saved Hollywood* at the Harold Lloyd estate in Beverly Hills. Fryer and I visited the set and pitched the idea to Dern. Bruce liked us and trusted us with his words. He also liked the idea of appearing in a well-circulated Hugh Hefner publication. Chris and I discussed possible questions for Dern with Rezek and soon afterward conducted our "Conversation with Bruce Dern." We transcribed and edited the chat, and turned it in to Rezek. Both he and Dern were pleased with the result. In reading the interview one could "hear" Bruce's voice. His words were candid, sometimes wildly outrageous, and very often hilarious. Chris and I received a check for $750. It was our first big-time magazine piece and the beginning of my long association with John Rezek.

The suits at Playboy Enterprises Incorporated in Chicago, which had taken on the French import, soon recognized that *Playboy*'s ooh-la-la sibling didn't quite fit in with the mahogany décor at 919 North Michigan Avenue. Hugh Hefner and his board decided that *Oui* reflected a Los Angeles sensibility and moved operations to the Playboy building on Sunset Boulevard. The official press release stated something about Hefner wanting each magazine to retain its unique role in men's magazines. There was no going-away party.

The new West Coast *Oui* occupied spacious, sun-drenched offices in the heart of the Sunset Strip and featured a freewheeling roster of editors, including Jan Golab, Stewart Weiner, Richard Cramer, Sharon O'Hara,

La-La Land: Traffic Jam in the Fast Lane

by Robert Crane, Jr.

hings to do today
shower
shave
shit?
call people
eat lunch
decide I'll exercise tomorrow, instead
drive around
watch early-evening news on TV
eat dinner (Mexican)
get my BMW filled with gas
watch late-evening news on TV
play new Weather Report album
call people
go to bed
get head
play dead

Veteran actor Robert Crane (right) relaxing with son Robert, Jr., on the set of Hogan's Heroes. The elder Crane was murdered last year.

This ain't makin' it. Getting up mid-morning, only to remember I'm still unemployed (I want to make movies; doesn't everybody?); driving in to the inner city from the Valley (main difference: red lights closer together in town) to check out the new stacks o' wax at Tower Records on da Strip; cruise Rodeo Drive (I don't know why); look at new Fiorucci's on Beverly Drive (it works in Milan and New York City, but it's gonna die of neglect out here); get a falafel or a Fatburger; go home; use the telephone; have a beer and just die—fuckin' die.

The palm trees are dying, too. Can air pollution cause skin cancer? Does the mayor of Los Angeles have a job? One of these days I'm gonna vomit on Cal Worthington's dog. Spot. Or his hippo, Spot. Or his ox. Spot. Shit, who can tell the difference? Yeah, I know I sound pissed off. My father, who was an actor on TV and in real life, was murdered last year, two days after my 27th birthday. (Really, you chuckling shits.) I'm not gonna use it as a crutch, though. This is Southern California. I'm much too mellow (comatose?) to shout about it.

Fuck.

Fuck.

Making a living in La-La Land is tough, unless you've passed the bar (I've passed a lot of them in this turn-out-the-lights-by-eleven hick town), or you've got your M.A. or your M.D. or your CLU or your D.D.S. or your M.D. or your CPA or, the most important one in this town, your B.S. (I've left by myself from a lot of bars in this turn-out-the-lights-by-eleven hick town.)

It's not easy being single in La-La Land. You don't pick and choose. You cruise. You zap. You enlighten someone's life. You pervade. You run out of extraordinary things to say. Fast. You get tired. You quit. You sulk. You grow weak. You need help.

Fuck.

Fuck.

Wait. Wait. Here it comes. No, no. You grow weak. You sulk. You need help. Fast, fast. I spell relief f-u-c-k.

Saturday night in La-La Land. Gettin' it up for your younger sister's 19-year-old girlfriend, who asks, "Did you know Paul McCartney was in a band before Wings?" Christ. Intellectual giants live here in La-La Land.

Hey, let's drive to Rosemead today. No, really. La Cañada, Montrose, Gardena, Hawaiian Gardens. Pass the Ripple and give me a handgun, Carlos. Shit, you know my 19-year-old fast, fast, fast relief? She

thought Al Pacino was a way to cook spaghetti, before I took her to see Bobby Deerfield in Westwood. Movies. The social event in La-La Land. She still doesn't know who Al Pacino is.

My car is bitchin'. No, you don't understand. I said, My car is bitchin'. In La-La Land you need a bitchin' car to get around. Valley—Beverly Hills. Beverly Hills—Hollywood. Hollywood—zip zip bang! I'm outta here. Ain't ever gonna find me in Redlands, chump. Or West Covina. No way, baby. It's strict confines for me. Only place east of La-La is Morocco. Sorry, I love New York. I love New York. You know the "in" place in New York? The toughest place to get into? No, not Studio 54. Jackie O's asshole. Nobody gets in there.

Fast, fast, fast relief.

You've got to be self-assured in La-La Land, like all the bitches at the Polo Lounge or struttin' down Rodeo Drive, shoppin' and struttin', spendin' money and spendin' time. They all have bitchin' cars. But so do I. But I'm not makin' it in La-La Land. My tank's always empty. Zip zip bang! I'm outta here.

133

Robert Crane's article on Bob Crane for *Oui* magazine, 1979 (author's collection).

and Toy Gibson. The building also housed the studios where Playboy Playmates were photographed, so I always planned on taking half a dozen elevator rides during a visit in hopes of sharing a few floors with Miss October. There was a lofty, sophisticated attitude about the models and employees of Playboy that trumped the louche, counterculture look of *Oui*. The editorial offices resembled a dean's office full of occupying students. Hefner made it clear that *Playboy* magazine was and always would be number one in his heart. The *Oui* staff relished its position as the black sheep of the family.

I conducted interviews with Dern, Karen Black, Fred Willard, and the Temptations (with Dave Diamond), contributed to a "How I Learned about Sex" survey by the children of celebrities, and wrote a rock 'n' roll bubble gum–blowing contest fluff piece featuring Joan Jett, Alice Cooper, and Debbie Harry. Later I was also given an assignment by Golab that resulted in a wee hours one-draft ramble about my dad's death. With vivid memories of enjoying my dad's stack of *Playboys* in the back room, I thought I was as close as I would ever be to the big bunny.

21

Scottsdale Redux, 1978

On the afternoon of June 29, 1978, at approximately 2:00, after my dad's
Beginner's Luck costar Victoria Berry ran screaming from unit 132A, the
Windmill Dinner Theatre's "star apartment" at the Winfield Apartments
in Scottsdale, Arizona, the Scottsdale Police Department was called.
Investigators entered the dark dwelling and in one of the two small bedrooms, atop a queen-size bed, found a body lying on its right side, right
arm straight out, perpendicular to the body, left arm bent, left hand
tucked under the chin. The body was clad in boxer shorts and wore a
watch on the left wrist. There was an electrical cord fastened tightly
around the neck. A pillow stood almost vertically, not flat, at the top of
the head. An opened duffel bag sat on top of the bed near the feet of the
body.

Upon closer inspection, investigators noticed two almost parallel
gashes slightly above and behind the left ear. Blood droplets fanned the
ceiling, the wall at the head of the bed, and the nightstand lamp. There
was human tissue on the wall. The bedsheet and pillowcase were soaked
with blood. There was a brief trail of blood indicating that the weapon
had possibly been wiped toward the foot of the sheet. The blood flow
originating from the two gashes by the left ear cascaded across the body's
face, resembling a Rorschach test or a map of some untraveled territory.
The head's thick, graying hair was matted. There were dried bloodlines
weaving across the shoulders and back as if the person had lain down
naked in a field of tumbleweed. There was semen or a sexual-aid gel on
the left thigh. Later, at the autopsy, Scottsdale Police Department detective Dennis Borkenhagen asked the assistant to the medical examiner,
Eloy Ysasi, to collect the specimen, only to be told, "What's that going to
tell you besides he had a piece of ass?"

The medical examiner, Dr. Heinz Karnitschnig, locally referred to as
Dr. K, had, in an unorthodox manner, begun his preautopsy at the crime

scene, shaving a portion of the head around the strike zone (in the process other hairs on the bed mixed with the decedent's), cutting the electrical cord and a portion of the sheet where the presumed weapon had been wiped, and examining a flaky substance resembling semen in the groin area. Technician Ernie Cole caught all of this out-of-the-ordinary behavior on videotape. It could have been titled *How Not to Process a Crime Scene*. When the police established that the apartment was rented by the Windmill Dinner Theatre, the theater's manager, Ed Beck, was called in to ID the body. Beck told investigators, "There was no way I could identify him from one side; the other side—yes."

Later, Lieutenant Ron Dean of the Scottsdale Police Department spoke to the assembling members of the press outside the crime scene and updated them in vague terms. He was followed by Dr. Karnitschnig and his assistant Eloy Ysasi; the latter, in a terrible breach of protocol, mentioned the electrical cord that had been placed around the victim's neck. Later, Dean identified that bit of unprofessional disclosure as ground zero in the blossoming distrust between the police, medical, and legal departments assigned to the case. On average two murders a year occurred in Scottsdale, which didn't help matters. The Scottsdale Police Department even lacked a separate homicide unit.

The only name the Scottsdale Police Department divulged to the press was that of one John Henry Carpenter. Dean and Borkenhagen theorized that their prime suspect, Carpenter, unable to handle the bad news that my dad was making changes in his life, had blown his "short fuse" and made some changes of his own—he killed his best friend. Charles Hyder, presiding over the Maricopa County Attorney's Office at the time of my dad's murder, felt it was premature to mention anyone as a suspect or even a person of interest.

The police refrained from discussing matters they'd screwed up, like not searching Carpenter's room at the Sunburst Motel in a timely fashion. They had let too many hours pass after Carpenter's hasty departure the morning of the murder, time for the maids to deploy their solvents and vacuum cleaners on all the awaiting fabric in the room. That Carpenter was even staying at the Sunburst stood out as odd from the beginning. Witnesses of the Crane/Carpenter dynamic, like Patti, frequent *Beginner's Luck* actress Ronnie Richards, and I, knew that when he was on the road Carpenter always settled into my dad's hotel suite or apartment for a few days of R & R in Cincinnati, Dallas, or Scottsdale, to name just a few of the cities where they frolicked. Carpenter didn't go into his own pocket for accommodation if he didn't have to.

The SPD continued giving Hyder agita by discussing possible murder weapons with the press. Blunt instruments of destruction—tire irons, golf clubs, fireplace pokers—were mentioned. The police also leaked information about one of the crime scene's only missing items, an album containing Polaroids of women displaying their bodies for Dr. Land's invention.

The police investigators maintained that my dad had had two tripods set up in the apartment's living room for video, still, and, possibly, eight-millimeter cameras, to photograph posing Playmate wannabes and close encounters of the cocktail waitress kind. Only one tripod was found at the murder scene, and it was not the weapon used in the crime. A Phoenix Police Department criminologist inspected a bedsheet from the crime scene and figured that a bloody mark on it had been made by a tripod, not a tire iron, golf club, or fireplace poker.

In the days following the killing, a thin, three-inch smear of blood was collected from the padding near the top of the passenger door of Carpenter's Chrysler Cordoba rental. A lab determined the blood sample was type B, my dad's blood type, which only one in seven people have. Carpenter was not one of those seven. Police also determined that no one had bled in the car. In addition, a one-sixteenth-inch speck of fatty tissue or brain matter was also visible on the same door panel near the blood sample. With today's forensics the case would likely have been solved in less than twenty-four hours, and it probably would have been "Turn out the lights, the party's over" for John Henry Carpenter.

Police interviews with family, friends, coworkers, and business associates began in earnest. I was interviewed that summer by Borkenhagen and Dean of the Scottsdale Police Department, Larry Turoff and Ron Little of the Maricopa County Attorney's Office, and by the DA himself, Charles Hyder. Hyder called me on the phone at my apartment in Los Angeles. He asked, "Excluding Mr. Carpenter for the time being, do you know of anybody that might have had a motive to kill your dad?"

My reply, recorded in police transcripts, was immediate. "Patti, my stepmom, because of their [Patti and dad's] situation . . . the will . . . is clearly one sided and cuts everybody else out of the thing except her. And according to Carpenter, Patti and my dad had a fight on the telephone at approximately eleven o'clock the night before the murder, and it would not be unlike Patti to fly into Phoenix unannounced. Or, any city unannounced. She had just flown into Phoenix two weeks before his death unannounced."

That thread of Patti's spontaneous appearances was picked up by Maricopa County deputy attorney Turoff during an interview he conducted shortly thereafter in the Beverly Hills office of Lloyd Vaughn with Vaughn, Bill Goldstein, Chuck, and me. The married Vaughn mostly kept mum on the subject of the second Mrs. Crane, since he was the only one at that table who had spent many evenings squiring her around town.

"Some years earlier didn't Patti come in cold turkey to California [from another vacation in Seattle], too?" Turoff asked the group.

Goldstein, talking to me, said, "Remember when your dad was here [Los Angeles], and Patti found out that he left your sister Karen at the Tilden house unsupervised?" He turned to address Turoff and continued, "Patti was in Seattle, jumped on a plane, flew down here. Hung out in town for two days, and then went to the house and confronted Bob."

Turoff was a bit baffled. "She hightailed it here from Seattle in the middle of the night, and then didn't confront him immediately?" he asked.

"No, she waited," Goldstein replied. "She was hanging around town for two days." Goldstein was trying to illustrate to Turoff the cunning and calculating nature of Patricia Crane.

I added, "Our family was divided in two halves. Patti hated my grandmother, my dad's mom. She hated my two sisters. She accused my older sister [Debbie] of streetwalking in Westwood. She accused Karen of breaking Scotty's arm three or four years ago. Patti also accused Karen of sleeping with my father. Patti is insanely jealous of other females." I continued my mini-rant: "I just recently found out about my dad's will. It's totally one-sided in favor of Patti, Melissa, her daughter, and Scotty, my half-brother."

"When was this will made?" Turoff asked.

"The main portion of the will was done in January '75," I said, "but the codicil, which completely cut my two sisters and me out of any kind of inheritance, was done shortly before the murder."

"Who drew up the will?" Turoff followed up.

I looked at Lloyd Vaughn, who sat grim and poker faced. "Lloyd did," I said, continuing, "Patti saw the end in sight. My dad was not going to get back with her; he had in fact bought a house of his own. He had asked me if I wanted to move in with him again in the new house in

Sherman Oaks. I told my dad he was a slave in terms of his own marriage. He was the one making all the money. Patti never worked again after *Hogan's Heroes*."

Turoff was turning off. I could tell he wasn't really listening to what I was saying. He said, "We need to wind it up; we've got another appointment."

But I wasn't quite finished. "Look," I said. "My dad, from everything I could tell in the last couple of months was a new guy, optimistic, new directions, just didn't want to be part of that whole kind of slavery trip that he had been into in terms of Patti running the show. The other thing was that according to Carpenter, my dad called Patti in the Seattle area [Bainbridge Island] on the final night at eleven—"

Turoff interrupted, "Yeah, we know about that. We're starting to run a little short on time and we have another interview."

I just kept talking, "They were on the phone, and got into a big argument. They hung up. Patti tried to call him back later, according to what she told me, but there was no answer. Carpenter, who had been in the other room listening to the argument, and my dad had left the apartment. It's conceivable to me that she would, she could, hop on a jet and fly into Phoenix—it only takes two and a half hours—knocks on the door. My dad answers. They either make it or they don't. He knows her obviously, and eventually he goes to sleep. She gets up and lets him have it. There's really nothing at this point to be lost, and a lot to be gained financially."

Chuck added his two cents. "One other time we [Dad and Chuck] had talked about burglaries and Bob related a situation, it may have been in Chicago, where Bobby and Karen were with him, and someone had come into the room and rifled their wallets and taken some money. As a result of that incident he always locked his doors."

"Again, and this is according to Carpenter," I added, "my dad positively dead bolted the front door every time. I assume the person at the door he readily let in. It was obviously somebody he was comfortable with."

Turoff and Little packed up their gear and left us then, but reconvened the meeting a day or two later with more questions. They wanted to know if Bill Goldstein had contacted Patti after initially hearing about the incident involving my dad.

Goldstein told him, "Immediately upon getting my call from Lloyd

Vaughn that there was a rumor out that something is going on at Bob's apartment [in Scottsdale], I felt that it was important to call her [Patti's] attorney."

"Now this was between 3:00 p.m. and 5:00 p.m. on the day of the murder?" Turoff asked.

"It was between 3:30 and 4:30," Vaughn volunteered.

Goldstein elaborated. "I know for a fact he [Patti's attorney] couldn't reach her right away. He finally did, but it was substantially later. She was not to be found, though she did finally get back to him after 7:30 that night."

I chimed in, "Don't forget that Patti had dropped into town [Scottsdale] a couple of weeks before the death, so obviously her finger-prints are going to be there. She knows where the apartment is. In past history, my dad had told me she had hit him with coffee cups, drinking glasses. She threw a videotape box at him once, hitting him in the lip, and opening a big cut."

Ron Little asked me, "When was the last time you spoke to your father previous to his death?"

"I spoke with him on my birthday, Tuesday, June 27th."

"Did he indicate who was with him?"

"Yes, John Carpenter."

"Did he say when John had come into Phoenix?"

"He had in a previous phone conversation the week before. He said Carpenter would be coming into town, I believe, on that Saturday, which was the 24th."

"What percentage of time would Carpenter actually live in the same apartment that your father did?"

"I assumed it was a hundred percent of the time," I said. "Every time my dad called me, and Carpenter was in town with him it always seemed to me that Carpenter was in the background."

"Were you ever specifically told that by either your father or by Carpenter?"

"I was told that by my father."

Bill Goldstein added, "I asked that same question of Patti, and she said to the best of her knowledge Carpenter always did stay with Bob."

"Know any reason why Carpenter had rented the hotel room at the Sunburst?" Turoff asked.

"I didn't even know that he had rented a motel room," I responded. "I just assumed he was staying with my dad."

Turoff continued, "Your father never indicated to you that they had an argument of any type, so that he told him to get out or you can't stay with me or anything like that?"

"There was an indication before Phoenix," I told him. "In a conversation I had with my dad regarding Carpenter coming into town, he said that Carpenter was getting to be a pain in the ass. He said he just didn't need Carpenter hanging around him anymore."

Then Turoff subtly put the spotlight on me, asking, "Now Bobby, I saw you the Sunday after your father was killed, right?"

"It was Friday," Goldstein corrected.

"It would have been the 30th," Ron Little added.

"You had just come in from L.A., I gather," Turoff continued.

"We had come in Thursday night," I said.

"Were you in L.A. Thursday morning?" Turoff asked.

"Yes."

"And Wednesday evening?"

"Yes."

"Where were you?"

"I was at the apartment on Midvale." Had I become a suspect? I wondered. "I was home all that week up until Thursday night transcribing an interview with Chevy Chase because I had an assignment with a magazine."

Turoff continued, "We know your dad was alive somewhere in the early morning about 2:00 a.m. He was killed somewhere between 2:00 a.m. and 2:30 p.m. on the 29th. Where were you at that time?"

"I was at my father's apartment, my apartment, our apartment at 634 Midvale Avenue, West Los Angeles, probably fast asleep at that point."

"Were you by yourself?"

"Yes," I said, and that was that. I guess I was never a serious suspect because no one ever asked me again about my movements or whereabouts.

The DA's office always thought that Carpenter was the killer, but just didn't have enough evidence to pin the murder on him. This was well before DNA testing. The police had the blood sample from Carpenter's rental car, which he returned on the day of the murder, but although it was the same blood type as my dad's, they couldn't say conclusively that it was my dad's blood. They also had a few other suspects who may have had motives: some faceless Mafiosi from Chicago, a couple of irate husbands and boyfriends of strippers and cocktail waitresses in different cities. And, of course, there was Patti.

In that summer of 1978 Lloyd Vaughn had told me, "You're going to see some money out of this," meaning my dad's death. Possibly that was supposed to be a very lame attempt to console me. I recognized that people are uncomfortable with death, and maybe even more so with grieving survivors, but the notion that money would be a palliative to me seemed insensitive, even considered in the best light.

Vaughn, who was my dad's business manager, already knew that my sisters and I had been cut out of my dad's will by virtue of the codicil that he had drawn up, supposedly for my dad and Patti. The cynical conspiracy theorist in me questions the authenticity of that codicil, especially since Patti and Lloyd were on exceedingly friendly terms, particularly when my dad was out of town. Maybe my dad never even saw the codicil, let alone signed it. Maybe Patti had an inkling that something bad might befall my dad. The codicil was her way of protecting her interests, since she alone benefited from his death. Maybe she made a few phone calls to contacts she might have had from her days with the rat pack and arranged for some heavy-handed gorilla to slip into my dad's apartment, with a key she might have provided, while he was sleeping. Who knows? Maybe Patti was also on the grassy knoll.

It turned out the money I received was an insurance policy that my folks had set up for me at Mass Mutual when I was a little kid. After my dad's death it was cashed out for $6,000. That money and a couple of pieces of electronics from the apartment were the sum total of my inheritance.

I took that money and immediately invested it in making a short film called *The Second Morning After,* which was written by Chris Fryer. I wanted to direct. I wanted to expose film. I had made movies in eight millimeter, Super 8, and sixteen millimeter, but it was time to play with the big boys and shoot in thirty-five millimeter. So with that $6,000 I rented a thirty-five-millimeter Mitchell camera, dolly, a bank of lights, and some sound equipment. I hired Ray Nankey, a cameraman who also doubled as editor. I also hired a soundman, a couple of actors. It was "Lights, camera, action."

The Second Morning After is an eight-minute comedy about a middle-aged couple on the honeymoon morning of what is the second marriage for both. The shoot went well, though Shepard Menken, the actor play-

Second Morning After set, Casa Serena Hotel, Oxnard, California, 1978:
Carole Cohen, Shepard Menken (back to camera), Ray Nankey (behind
camera), and Robert Crane (photo by Christopher Fryer; author's
collection).

ing the husband, broke his leg a few days before we started. We had to
reblock all the scenes to keep his thigh-high cast out of the frame. Even
eight-minute films are not without their challenges.

   In the fall of 1978, *The Second Morning After* opened at the United
Artists theater in Westwood, on the bill with *The Big Fix,* which was the
latest star vehicle for Richard Dreyfuss. As I had done with an earlier short
I'd made with Rick Decker called *Mirage,* which played at Westwood's
National Theatre with *Dog Day Afternoon,* I would often go to the theater and just stand in the back, listening for the laughs, and then leave the
cinema before the feature film began. *Second Morning After* was up for
Live Action Short Oscar consideration but didn't make the final list of
nominees.

   In a way my dad had made the production possible, and I think he
would've gotten a couple of laughs out of the film. But if I'd bought six
grand worth of Disney stock in 1978 I'd be a millionaire today. That's life.

As my friend Dave Diamond always says, "If I had some ham, I could have ham and eggs, if I had some eggs."

I was just trying to get a handle on where the hell I was headed. I knew I didn't want to be an actor or in any public aspect of show business. I knew I wanted to write. I wanted to be behind the scenes. I wanted to create stuff, provided I wasn't seen or known visually. I never wanted to be recognized on the street because of all the experiences I'd had with my dad and how uncomfortable it had always made me feel.

Even the most well-meaning fans—and there are a lot of good people out there—interfere with the living of life. I didn't want any of that. Dad was always comfortable with his celebrity. He enjoyed it. At a ballgame, I'd seen him set down his "Dodger dog," wipe the mustard from his hands, and miss a great catch while he cheerily autographed a fan's program. The same program that probably went out with the next week's trash.

22

Heeeere's Bobby!!! 1979

A year after my dad's murder, I attempted to do something I'd never had the cajones to do while he was alive—host my own radio show. Operating under the one star per family theory, and with fear of my dad's criticism and skepticism now out of the equation, it was time, not to be a star—I had no interest in that—but to reexperience the creative outlet I had enjoyed as a kid, being on the radio, being in a windowless room with a microphone and nobody looking at you. I set myself the challenge to produce, book the guests, sell advertising time, and front a show on a Los Angeles outlet. FM was out of the question as most stations were still musically oriented—rock or easy listening. AM was an uphill battle because it fell into two major categories—talk and all news. Talk was ruled by KABC, with the white Michael Jackson as its leader, and the 24/7 (though no one said 24/7 yet) news was led by my dad's former station, KNX, which previously had been all entertainment. My dad and I shared a love of extracting information from people, of interviewing celebrities. I did it for magazines—why not do it over the airwaves?

Since I was a no-name radio entity with a short interview résumé, I lowered my sights considerably and found a mom-and-pop station called KIEV (which decades later assumed the call letters of L.A.'s rock 'n' roll dinosaur KRLA) in Glendale, east of the San Fernando Valley. The sad-sack stucco, single-story office complex on San Fernando Boulevard housed a five-thousand-watt station that played a hodgepodge of entertainment programs along with a bit of news and talk. I approached the hardened station manager, who had heard and seen every two-bit "artist" walk through his dirt-streaked glass front door. I did my pitch of why Robert Crane would be an asset to the station. I could offer my vast stable of celebrity "pals" from my magazine Q&As who would like nothing more than to spend their afternoons in Glendale. I did not mention my dad. The outcome was I was allowed to rent an hour of airtime on Sunday afternoons. It was quite possibly the worst timeslot on the worst radio station in Southern California, but it was a win-win for KIEV: the station was earning money for an hour of dead zone. I had to come up with $400 a week for at least the next four weeks, at which time, if my head was above water, I would continue with my exercise in vanity.

The one problem I might not be able to overcome was how to get Angelenos, who on Sunday afternoons are out at sporting events, the beach, or in the backyard barbequing, to tune their car or transistor radio dials in on a station with about as much pop as stale Rice Krispies. The prospects reminded me of my dad's old joke: "My show got a minus two rating—no one listened, and two people knocked it." Nonetheless, I welcomed my own challenge, recalling stories from my dad about "just doing it," initiating the momentum and not waiting for the phone to ring. It might never ring. No one helped my dad get work on the radio. In fact, his family discouraged it. "Get a real job, Bob" was the cry of his father and brother, the Willy and Biff Loman of Stamford.

As long as I didn't scream obscenities over the airwaves, the station was fine with whatever I wanted to do. As far as it was concerned, the KIEV ledger showed plus $400 even if the only people in L.A. listening were shut-ins and illegals peeling onions in restaurant kitchens.

My girlfriend at the time, Lori Otelsberg, hit the pavement with her youthful enthusiasm and sex appeal, and enticed several owners of small businesses to buy commercial time on the show. I also got a tip and branded a steakhouse on Beverly Drive in Beverly Hills for a few sixty-second spots at seventy-five bucks a shot. I was almost three-quarters of the way to covering my nut for the first week.

The next step in my Sisyphean labor was to book guest number one. Who was one of the hottest stars in show business? Chevy Chase. He also happened to be the *Oui* magazine interview subject I'd been working on at the time of my dad's murder, so it seemed appropriate that he be my first celebrity guest. It kind of closed a circle for me.

The *Oui* interview had hit the newsstands in early 1979. Chevy became the first star of *Saturday Night Live*, bolted after just one season, had his own special for NBC, and costarred with Goldie Hawn in his first studio hit, *Foul Play*. Everything he touched turned to gold. How about lending his Midas touch to Sunday afternoon radio, being a non-prime-time player for an hour? I called his publicist, Jasper Vance, and made my plea. Chevy and Vance had been pleased with the magazine piece because

A CONVERSATION WITH

CHEVY CHASE

He stumbled into America's heart by falling on his face, and it's been clumsy going ever since. A pullout from the show that made him famous. A jerky plunge into movies. And a head-on collision with the word "sellout." Life is lonely near the top.

Cornelius Crane Chase was hard to figure from the beginning. A funny writer who wasn't ugly as sin. An Eastern WASP crashing on the Lower East Side. A preppie who couldn't keep his finger out of his nose.

So, when he made the world's fastest leap into stardom, anchoring "Weekend Update" on Lorne Michaels' *Saturday Night Live*, he was as surprised as everybody else. And what followed was pure soap opera.

Successful comic faces tough career choices. Grabs megabucks. Leaves nest. Goes Hollywood. Makes nice. Loses wife and "perspective." Becomes superstar.

Sort of. Chase is too intelligent and self-conscious to lie down that comfortably in the mold. His movie experience consists of a starring role in the hit *Foul Play* but, as he says, "I want to do everything." He'll have his chance soon enough: Currently he's working with Michael O'Donoghue on a screenplay, *Saturday Matinee*, and will also write and star in more NBC specials.

OUI correspondent Robert Crane conducted the interview at Chase's Emmy-laden office in the MGM Studios. As you'll see, Chevy may have lost his perspective, but his madness is still intact.

OUI: You've become quite a celebrity since you came to Hollywood. How do you handle all the women who constantly seem to accost you in public?

CHASE: Between the two big toes. Normally, I would just say between the toes, but for the purposes of this interview I'll say the two big ones. I'm very flattered by it, actually. I love it. But there's a way you can be polite and say, "Excuse me, I really have to be going"; and there's a way to say, "Look, I *really* have to be going," and then push a little harder. Recently, one pack of girls actually wanted me to go watch them play volleyball. I really did have to be going, and as I walked away one of them yelled, "Faggot!" as loud as she could. So I figure the next time I'm accosted by a group of women, I'm going to make all of them pregnant.

OUI: What is it in a woman that turns you on?

CHASE: What magazine is this for?

OUI: OUI.

CHASE: That's funny. My publicist told me it was for *NON* magazine—*N-O-N*. Well, it figures that OUI would want to know what kind of woman I like. Actually, I like very, very overweight Japanese women—short, overweight Japanese women who cannot speak Japanese.

OUI: What about Goldie Hawn?

CHASE: She's not short enough. She's not Japanese enough. But, yeah, she's a very lovely woman. She's just what you see there on the screen—a little deeper, actually. She's bright and she's very clever. She

was a delight to do that love scene with. We worked it out ourselves. We wrote it. [Chevy answers his buzzing telephone Radner.] Gilda? You're calling me from New York? Yes, I have your laundry. I burned your shirts and we lost the rest of it. Should I send you the burned shirts? I'm having an interview even as you speak to me. . . . Yes . . . you're very sweet to say that, Gilda. . . . Yeah . . . you like that, huh? . . . I'm still here. I just think it's so sweet of you to call and tell me that billions of women all over the country love me. Actually, I'm in the middle of an interview with OUI magazine . . . OK, you finish. . . . [Chevy puts the receiver up to our microphone and continues to talk with Gilda.]

RADNER: . . . Stick it up your bum!

CHASE: I can't hear you!

RADNER: Don't let them hear me.

CHASE: What?

RADNER: Have you got me on a loud-speaker?

CHASE: No. Do you have a loudspeaker?

RADNER: No, but I mean, am I, like can they hear me?

CHASE: Oh, no, they can't hear you.

RADNER: OK, Chev?

CHASE: Yeah.

RADNER: My favorite moment [referring to *Foul Play*], when you two were gonna kiss. That's what people really say. They say, "What'd you think of me the first time?" That was wonderful.

CHASE: We were just talking about that

scene when you called.

RADNER: Oh, Chevy, it was wonderful.

CHASE: We wrote that scene.

RADNER: You did?

CHASE: Uh, Gil—uh, Goldie and I—I get you and Goldie mixed up

RADNER: I get it all the time. yeah. Everyone calls me Goldie, and when I go up to Harlem they yell, "Oh, there's the girl on *Laugh-In*!"

CHASE: Oh, those silly black people. [He takes the receiver away from the microphone.] Yeah . . . no, I know; I really am in the middle of an interview. I love it that you're calling . . . When are you coming out? . . . Thank you . . . no . . . oh, Gilda . . . is it a simple D and C? No, nothing. I'm kidding. I'm coming to New York on Tuesday. Can I see you? . . . OK, so long as you have something. . . . OK, I'll hang up on you now. . . . I love you . . . I can't wait to see your little face . . . gesundheit. [Chevy hangs up.]

OUI: You were talking about that love scene with Goldie . . .

CHASE: Gilda was calling me about *that* love scene. Isn't that amazing? The first time Goldie and I met we read that scene. Finally I said, "Let's throw the script away and do it this way." It felt very natural. It's easy to play a love scene with her. There's no reason why you wouldn't want to kiss her. The only thing I didn't like was that little dog. The idea that I would have a little dog! I would have shot that dog if there were one more day of shooting.

OUI: In your own love life, what time have

ILLUSTRATION BY STAN WATTS   71

Robert Crane's Chevy Chase interview for *Oui* magazine, 1979 (author's collection).

Chevy felt that it was the first interview that not only got his words right but accurately translated his brand of humor ("I'm Chevy Chase and you're not!") to print, which was not an easy undertaking. He had thanked me for holding up my end of that job. Plus, his given name was Cornelius

Crane Chase. How weird was that? Was this six degrees of separation? Who knew? Who cared? He hadn't even worked with Kevin Bacon. Chevy agreed to be on the first segment of *The Robert Crane Show*, set to debut July 1, 1979.

Bobby was back behind a microphone after a twenty-year hiatus. I had an engineer who played the prerecorded commercials, reviewers, comedy bits, and our upbeat theme "Teen Town" by Jaco Pastorius and Weather Report. Although we were light years from NPR, I was shooting for an arts and interview program, a kind of *Time Out America* live from Glendale.

Chevy, behind the wheel of a black Porsche 911, pulled into the weedy, empty parking lot accompanied by Brian Doyle-Murray, older brother of Bill, who was a writer-performer on *Saturday Night Live* at the time. Also in tow was Doug Kenney, who was instrumental in the development of *National Lampoon* magazine and one of the writers of the ridiculously successful *Animal House*. I saw that film a month after my dad's death with Diane's younger sister, Kris, who was trying to lighten things up for me by providing a dose of John Belushi, reigning king of all media that summer.* The reason Chevy was with Murray and Kenney was that they had just finished a round of golf in preparation for their film *Caddyshack*, which has become iconic not because it's that great a film but because of the cast, which includes Chevy, Bill Murray, and Rodney Dangerfield. It was *Animal House* on the links.

The theme kicked in, and it was immediately three against one. I thought I would have enough problems just going one-on-one live with Chevy, but Doug Kenney severely challenged my concentration as he tossed a plastic bag of marijuana onto the table where the microphones stood. He rolled a spliff the size of a Louisville Slugger, leaned into his microphone, took a deep hit, and blew the smoke across the cramped studio, offering me a toke just seconds into my brand-spanking-new, uphill-battle, off-hours attempt at emulating my dad. I declined on-air—"No, thank you"—failing to disclose to the tens of listeners that chaos had overtaken my program and I was already losing control. Chevy was having fun listening to a couple of his best sketches from *SNL*, including the

---

*Belushi had the number one film, *Animal House;* the number one late-night TV series, *SNL;* and, with Dan Aykroyd, the number one album, *The Blues Brothers.*

Doug Kenney (back to camera), Robert Crane, and Chevy Chase, KIEV
Radio studio, Glendale, California, 1979 (photo by Meris Powell; author's
collection).

classic with Richard Pryor where he interviewed Pryor for a sanitation
worker position using word association. He read the commercial for my
Beverly Hills steakhouse, stretching the succinct sixty-second copy into
three minutes, injecting myriad ways to prepare meat and baked potatoes.

The spot has to rank as the cheapest and most hilarious celebrity ad of all time.

I introduced the program's two regulars: movie reviewer Desly Movius, who did a sardonic take on *Alien,* talking about Sigourney Weaver running around in her knickers, and Diane Haas (yes, my Diane Haas, now living in New York), who filled in ex–New Yorkers, traveling New Yorkers, and wannabe New Yorkers on what was happening in the Big Apple. The hour zipped by. There were tons of laughs. Brian Doyle-Murray threw in the occasional barb while a stoned Doug Kenney giggled and Chevy rained hilarity. All I had to do was hit the cues and get out of the way.

Even after that first hour with Chevy it was still a constant battle to enlist sponsors. No one listened to a program in that ungodly timeslot. Even the steakhouse in Beverly Hills sizzled out after two weeks. *The Robert Crane Show* died as quietly as it had been born. I don't know who took my place the Sunday after the fourth week. Probably the station manager's mother humming show tunes. We were not missed.

I'm glad I did it, though, for all the hats that I wore on it. Most of the ventures in my life were either created or cocreated by me. And because those phone calls offering you your dream job don't actually come, I had to create my own product and my own market. I never got that phone call from Sony. I never got that phone call from Paramount. Michael Ovitz never called saying he had to have me to package his next big project. Bob Evans never called to say he wanted to make *Second Morning After* into a sidesplitting hour and a half. I'm sure he just misplaced my phone number and has been kicking himself ever since.

23

There Ain't No Stinkin' Closure!
1979–1980

As the '70s drew to a close, the interest in my dad's murder case seemed to diminish exponentially. As far as district attorney Charles Hyder was concerned, the Scottsdale Police Department investigation led by Ron Dean and Dennis Borkenhagen had failed to produce enough compelling evidence to lead to an arrest and trial of John Henry Carpenter—or anyone else, for that matter.

It was just a pity there was no Columbo to winkle out the facts, no Barnaby Jones to put two and two together, no Joe Mannix to swoop in in his Olds Toronado and save the day. The Scottsdale Police Department didn't even have an Andy of Mayberry to piece together the puzzle. What they did have was lots of Barney Fifes.

Tom Collins would assume the role of district attorney in Maricopa County during the inauguration of the Reagan '80s, but by then the case was colder than a morgue slab. Officers, detectives, investigators, and medical examiners had moved on. The Scottsdale PD was anxious to put this blighted case behind it. One investigator who hadn't moved on was county deputy attorney Larry Turoff. Although he proclaimed that the attorney's office, in its latest review of the case, couldn't find "anything new that could lead to an arrest," he stressed that the case was not closed. But there wasn't much optimism about a break in the case. I had about as much expectation that the Scottsdale Police Department would solve my dad's murder as I did that the Beatles would get back together.

I was still stumbling emotionally. As far as the public was concerned, my dad was ancient history, but I was still having moments when I thought I'd pick up the phone to call him, only to be shocked to remember he was dead.

Nowadays when tragedy is still warm people talk about "closure." I haven't got any idea what that means, thirty-seven years on. If you lose someone you love, you never have closure. You keep him alive in your mind and your heart. His spirit ignites every time you think of his smile, his laugh, or his hand on the back of your neck. His existence has meaning because you make it meaningful with your own existence. There's a grave marker on Page and Eloise Smith's grave in northern California that reads, "It is a fearful thing to love what death can touch." Loving mortal things is what makes us human. I don't think we ever "close" that door.

Many of my evenings were spent sitting by the Jacuzzi at my mom and Chuck's house in an old terrycloth bathrobe watching the lights come up in the Valley as the sun slipped behind the Santa Monica Mountains. Never much of a social animal, I had become all the more reclusive because I felt myself to be a drag on any kind of gaiety and an easy target for cheap attempts at humor. Once, handing my credit card to a waiter at a local restaurant, I was heckled with "You're Bob Crane? I thought you were dead." I also had an old acquaintance sidle up to me and ask out of the blue, "Your dad took care of you, right? You get *Hogan's* rerun money, don't you?" Even worse, a bar patron, overhearing me talking about my dad to a friend, butted in, with no mock shock, "You mean Colonel Hogan's dead?"

To which the bartender replied, "Wasn't he a TV guy or something?"

And even the bar back joined in: "Yeah, what was the name of that show he was on?"

I said loudly, "Can I get another beer?"

Twenty-nine years old and my dad, my dear dead dad, was still making it hard for me to walk into or out of rooms. Then again, maybe it was just my own paranoia. Looking back on it now, it seems a bit solipsistic to think that people would be so focused on me. From my vantage point now, I want to tell my twenty-nine-year-old self to get off his ass. And I did try, giving myself a change of venue.

After Playboy had produced *Oui* for a few years, the magazine's monthly sales numbers were nowhere near those of the company's flagship publication, and Hefner's lieutenants stoked doubt about the whole venture. Hefner caved and off-loaded *Oui* to a New York consortium, which moved the operation from the glitz of La-La Land to the grit of Eighth Avenue in Manhattan.

144

The new editor was Dian Hanson, late of *Puritan* and *Juggs* magazines, who could have, and should have, been the star of a European film about the sexual revolution. She was a free spirit, so open about all matters carnal that the only person I could compare her to was my dad. What a couple they would have made. Hanson was from Seattle, my age but decades older in life experience, living with a biker/tattoo artist and now overseeing the Playboy cast-off. As the sale and transfer between the two companies was occurring, Hanson visited Los Angeles to clean up some of the loose ends. She had read and liked my interviews and articles in the magazine, caught wind that my dad was the murdered actor Bob Crane, and gave me a call to ask for a meeting. The rendezvous was in her motel room on Franklin Avenue near the Hollywood Freeway on-ramp. We talked about the new direction *Oui* would be taking; she thought Hefner was a fossil. Within minutes of saying hello, Hanson asked me to be a contributing editor. My writing career was taking a giant leap forward. To seal the deal, she propositioned me and we jumped into the sagging bed. I felt as if I were making love with an uninhibited pleasure seeker, but Hanson was just the new-age '80s professional woman—fucking and working was the same release. No need to sign on the dotted line. Sex was the new handshake, and I knew she and I would never make love again.

I was one of the few writers to make the hump from Hefner-era to post-Hefner *Oui*. *Oui* magazine instantly became a dim memory to the board of directors at Playboy. I didn't care. I was moving to the Big Apple. "Hey, Ed Koch, how'm I doin'?"

I bought a trunk, loaded up some clothing and my trusty tape recorder, and moved in with newlyweds Chris Fryer and Desly Movius at their one-bedroom apartment on West Seventy-first Street off Central Park. I was one block from John Lennon and Yoko Ono's Dakota enclave. Chris and Desly graciously allowed me to sleep on their rollout couch while I acclimated.

My first day on the job I took the subway south from Seventy-second Street and Central Park West to the *Oui* offices at Forty-third Street and Eighth Avenue. With no Miss Any Month in sight, I shared the one grimy elevator with characters that made Ratzo Rizzo look like an aristocrat. At the magazine's fifth-floor office I stepped through the door into a poorly lit and unkempt atmosphere featuring a small ensemble of art and copy editors working alongside advertising personnel, who all talked out of the sides of their mouths like Buddy Hackett. All that was missing was a troupe of grizzled men hovering over a fire in an open oil drum. Yet another Fellini Excursion. People moved between offices, doors closing ominously behind them. I immediately got the impression that activities way beyond the production of a men's magazine were taking place behind those doors. Hanson greeted me out of the gloom and introduced me to some of the resident troglodytes. She proudly handed me the first issue of the new *Oui*.

When Playboy owned the publication, the paper quality and color separation were top notch. It was slick. The magazine I now held in my hands was a piss-poor relative—the photographs were grainy, the color separation bled, it was badly printed on subpar stock. In my mind I could hear the former Los Angeles staffers erupting in laughter, thankful that they hadn't moved a trunkful of clothes to sleep on a hide-a-bed and work in the publishing equivalent of a roach motel. I studied one nude layout and stopped short of asking Hanson for a pair of 3-D glasses. And yet, the magazine was still a viable publication. People were buying it—and I had a job.

Regardless of the sales figures, the publicists for the Bruce Derns, Chevy Chases, and Karen Blacks kept turning us down because of the atrocious look of the book. Whoever said, "Any publicity is good publicity" hadn't seen the new *Oui*. My office space was perfectly in keeping with the look of the magazine. It was grim. There was no privacy. There were refugees from the parole board moving about the space doing god knows what. I was now fielding calls from representatives of "celebrities" like Louisa Moritz and Pamela Sue Martin. The magazine was becoming a joke, not even a shadow of its former self. As much as I enjoyed being in New York, after a couple of weeks I knew this enterprise was doomed. I had made a terrible mistake. I loathed spending time at *Oui*'s hellhole offices.

I approached Dian and shared the news that I was not meant to be a full-time employee in an office situation. I was a freelancer at heart and much more comfortable in the field. She expressed disappointment but said she understood. So after an educational two weeks, I abandoned Chris and Desly's couch and hauled my trunk and my ass back to Southern California. On the flight home I was already rehearsing comeback lines to the inevitable razzing I would receive from my sisters about not being able to keep a job. But I still continued to write for *Oui*. I contributed pieces like an exposé on the rampant lesbianism among female golf profes-

Pete Best autographed this "Silver Beatles" poster (Liverpool, early 1960s) in 1983 (author's collection).

sionals called "Ladies to a Tee" and an interview with '50s survivor Terry Moore regarding her relationship with Howard Hughes. I'd turn in the work and patiently wait to get paid. I could never guess when the check would arrive, or if it did, if it would even be good. Once, after I'd made numerous requests to be paid for an article, I received a check written on an automotive shocks and transmission company check. I'm not kidding.

My personal highlight of that time with *Oui* was an opportunity to spend some time with the man who missed out on the greatest show business phenomenon ever. I was assigned to interview Pete Best, the Beatles' first drummer, who was hawking a book and a vinyl record of some leftover tracks by the pre-Ringo Silver Beatles. I spent two hours with him in his modest hotel room on Pico Boulevard in West Los Angeles absorbing how bleak and depressing it was to have been on the Beatle float and then to have been coldly cast off, not by his bandmates but by Brian Epstein, who was doing the dirty work for Lennon, McCartney, and Harrison. Best had continued to drum for a while, but then chucked it all and found

147

steady employment as a mailman. Pension aside, the inner turmoil of missing out on the plunder of superstardom had taken its toll. Like the rest of us, he couldn't live a day without hearing a Beatles song played somewhere. He lived in an internal prison called "What if?"

And I thought I had suffered disappointment, going from the Sunset Strip *Oui* to the Sun Has Set *Oui*. Life never ceases to give you perspective. Still, for my part, Dian and the thugs at *Oui* had allowed me to talk to a Beatle, albeit a former one. Years earlier, I'd recognized the importance of the Beatles when my dad acknowledged he hadn't seen or heard anything like them since Frank Sinatra. He was respectful of their place in music, which made me feel good on the father-son bond level even though on TV's *Pat Boone Show* my dad once referred to one of the Beatles as "Paul Lennon." That embarrassed me to no end.

As if I wasn't melancholy enough in 1980, on December 8 I was watching Monday Night Football with Chuck when Howard Cosell made the announcement that John Lennon had been shot in New York City. A couple of hours later it was reported that he was dead. I thought of all the Beatles as my "friends," but John in particular. I never met him. The closest I ever got was sitting behind the visitors' dugout at Dodger Stadium in 1966 while he and the other lads performed at second base. The Beatles were and still are a theme in my life, providing me with listening and viewing pleasure over hundreds, if not thousands, of hours. Lennon's death was a four-alarm blaze in my head to get focused, get going, and try to appreciate every day I still had a pulse.

So it was in that spirit of carpe diem that I accepted an invitation to a *Seems Like Old Times* party at a private home in Beverly Hills. *Seems Like Old Times* was a Neil Simon comedy starring Chevy Chase and Goldie Hawn, who were riding the moneymaking wave of their *Foul Play* collaboration. Chevy's publicist, Jasper Vance, invited me because Chevy had so liked our interview work together. I took as my date a woman who had always held a kind of fantasy role in my head. Diana Menken was the younger sister of a friend of a friend. She was wildly attractive, frighteningly intelligent, and obviously unhinged because she agreed to go out with Mr. Morose. I picked her up at her parents' home in Malibu, and we drove into Beverly Hills. We walked into the New England–style house, and there was Neil Simon. I didn't introduce myself but watched him from a safe distance. I tried to figure out if comedic genius gave off an aura or a force field or even some kind of smell.

Goldie was there. Chevy was there. I introduced Diana to the bold-faced names, but I felt like this freelancer was in over his head, so I threw back a couple of beverages and got just enough buzz to relax a little bit. Diana was having a good time. Her dad was an actor and voice-over specialist. Though she hadn't really been exposed to lights this bright before, she handled it all with aplomb, just as I'd imagined she would.

I wandered off, observing everyone and everything, as a good fly on the wall does. I eventually found myself in a room with a piano, a bass, and a drum kit set up in the corner. I went over and sat at the drums, looking around the big, quiet room. Suddenly, Chevy Chase appeared from god knows where. "Do you play?"

"Well, you know," I said, noncommittally.

Chevy, who is a pretty fair pianist, went over and sat down at the keyboard. He had played with Donald Fagen, later of Steely Dan, when they were both at Bard College together years before. Chevy started noodling some little jazzy number. I followed, lightly applying brushes to the snare drum. Somebody else wandered in and picked up the bass, joining the jam. I wasn't doing anything complicated, just keeping the beat, but I was having an out-of-body experience watching myself making music with the Chevy Chase Trio. We kicked it along for quite a while, and to my ear it sounded pretty good. When we finished I just got up and left the room. It wasn't until an hour later that I got nervous, thinking what an idiot I was to do that.

It was moderately late when I dropped Diana back in Malibu. We had a splendid goodnight kiss on her doorstep, which fueled me back to the Valley, but that was our one and only date. I don't remember if we ever even spoke again. To this day, though, I still haven't seen *Seems Like Old Times*.

24

For Members Only, 1981–1982

Before *Oui* magazine started hopscotching around the country, my original editor there, John Rezek, had seized the opportunity to jump from Hefner's rowboat (*Oui*) to his yacht and moneymaker, *Playboy*. Even though circulation was down a bit from its peak of 7 million copies a month in the '60s, the bunny was still moving upward of 5 million units a month in the early '80s.

While everyone's first thoughts about *Playboy* are almost always centered on the centerfold, *Playboy* has always offered long interviews with newsmakers like Martin Luther King, Fidel Castro, and Malcolm X, musicians including the Beatles, Sinatra, and Miles Davis, actors like Marcello Mastroianni, Marlon Brando, and Jack Nicholson, filmmakers Ingmar Bergman, Fellini, and Kubrick, and writers Vladimir Nabokov, Ayn Rand, and Norman Mailer. The interviewers themselves have included notables like Alex Haley and Alvin Toffler.

Since there were only twelve interview slots available every year, a kissin' cousin to the *Playboy* interview was created, dubbed "20 Questions." Obviously shorter than the feature interview, the "20Q" nonetheless had subjects who were readily recognizable, distinguished even, if not of Muhammad Ali or Johnny Carson greatness. The occasional exception would be someone like Jack Lemmon, Truman Capote, or John Kenneth Galbraith, who had already done the main interview but was promoting a film or book and got placed in the "20Q" hopper instead. "20 Questions" was John Rezek's domain from its debut in the October 1978 issue of *Playboy*. The prototype was model Cheryl Tiegs, interviewed by future writer-director John Hughes. Though irregular the first couple of years after its inception, the "20Q" became a popular monthly fixture beginning in 1982.

During my tenure writing for *Oui* after it was cut loose from the SS *Playboy* (employment I kept close to the breast), I continued to call Rezek and pitch him "20Q" subjects. On a whim, I pitched Joan Rivers, who was not exactly a new comedienne at the time, but she was riding a renewed career wave thanks to multiple appearances on Johnny Carson's *Tonight Show.* Rivers was perfect "20Q" material—well known but not big enough for the main interview (that would come a few years later when Joan became Johnny's permanent guest host). Rezek gave me the green light.

Publicity stands for one thing—control. From the large firms like PMK to the single-occupant offices on Van Nuys Boulevard in the Valley, publicists guard, protect, and build bomb-resistant walls between their clients and magazine, newspaper, and nowadays Internet writers. If the publicists could conduct the interview themselves and eliminate the middleman—writers like me—that would be their utopia. The interview would also be fluff. All parties concerned need people like me to ask penetrating, quirky, or funny questions to produce a readable and memorable interview, and since creative, insightful, and funny editors, like Rezek, find themselves mostly stuck behind their desks, the role of Hollywood trench reporter fell to writers like David Rensin, Warren Kalbacker, Bill Zehme, and me, who would assume Rezek's alter ego in the field.

I called Joan Rivers's publicist and did my pitch with as much enthusiasm as I could muster, stressing that the interview was fun, fun, fun, wouldn't take too much of Joan's time, and on a separate date would include a photo session with the photographer of Ms. Rivers's choice, resulting in a full-page original shot facing the first page of the interview. Joan's publicist liked the idea of *Playboy,* but would, of course, have to discuss the matter with her client and get back to me. The five most dreaded words anyone in Hollywood can hear are "I'll get back to you," but amazingly enough, less than twenty-four hours later, I received the go-ahead with a date, time, and Joan Rivers's home address in a tony West L.A. neighborhood where the interview would be conducted.

I immediately called Rezek with the good news. He expected a lively and funny interview. I anticipated a job well done and looked forward to a Playboy Enterprises Incorporated check signed by one Christie Hefner.

The day before an interview was the most crucial, amusing, loose, and sometimes depraved part of the whole job. It was the final compilation of questions for the interview, some mine alone, others hybrids, and many pure and direct from the wickedly funny mind of John Rezek. Nothing was out of bounds. Rezek was a musician riffing on a couple of notes I threw down. I would offer one question, and he would follow with a dozen, including new areas of inquiry that I hadn't even considered. He was the urbane, steadfast professor who went wild every once in a while at the local pub. I would scribble madly, and generally by the forty-five-minute mark I had dozens and dozens of questions written down.

My actual interviews were usually sixty or seventy questions. I would then transcribe the audiotape, tidy up the answers, and send everything to Rezek. He would then choose his favorite twenty Q&As. Although pitching scores of potential subjects was always tiresome, the rest of the process became automatic—a well-oiled production line delivering goods that Rezek could always work with. After its initial sporadic appearances, "20 Questions" became the cheeky alternative to the monolithic *Playboy* interview. If all went well, Joan Rivers would be positioned as the eleventh "20Q" following Jack Lemmon (who had also been the May 1964 *Playboy* feature interview).

I arrived at Rivers's palatial estate in Bel Air and was ushered into the library by someone approximating a butler. I plugged in my trusty Panasonic cassette recorder, readied my questions, and anxiously waited. All at once, the entire family entered—Joan, instantly recognizable and way more attractive in person; her husband, manager, and minder, Edgar Rosenberg, who would sit in during the interview; and Melissa, her teen-aged daughter and future costar.

I mentioned that my dad had appeared with Joan (and drummer Buddy Rich) on a *Mike Douglas Show* episode many years ago. Joan said she was sorry about his death and that she had liked him. I thanked her for doing the interview and explained the stockpile of questions ("Yes, I have more than twenty"). With our introductions and small talk completed, Melissa left the room, I placed the tape recorder as close to Rivers as possible without distracting her, pressed the record button, glanced over at Rosenberg, who had his dark eyes trained on me, and we began.

I would often preface a question with a reference to "my editor and I" as a cushion to suggest that the *Playboy* magazine brain trust was behind this effort, so if interviewees were put off, repulsed, or felt the question was an invasion of their privacy I had some deniability. Hey, don't shoot the messenger!

Joan was ready. We called her "the sexiest comedienne working today," to which she replied, "I was asked to pose nude, but then I took a look at my Jewish thighs." She talked about being turned on by "situations like being stuck for days after an earthquake with a handsome Italian guy." She described her husband Edgar being romantic: "The nicest thing he says is 'You don't look bad.'" Of her first sexual experience, she said, "It took longer to pick the dress for the date than the whole sexual act." Joan and I laughed a lot. Edgar never cracked a smile.

I guess Rivers enjoyed the experience because she invited me to the Desert Inn in Las Vegas to see her show. I took Diane Haas's good friend Dana Bieber along just for the Fellini Excursion, and she and I wound up "babysitting" Melissa while Mom was on stage and Dad hovered somewhere behind the curtain. Melissa was bright, quick, and loud like her mom. They acted more like sisters than mother and daughter. On the other hand, I felt no connection between father and daughter.

Rezek was pleased with my results. He chose the twenty most revealing, diverting, and funny question and answer combinations for the magazine. I agreed with his choices. There were times when I might fight for a question here or an answer there, cut because of flow, repetition, or space, but Rezek was always 95 percent spot on.

I heard through Joan's office that she wanted to be photographed by Hollywood veteran Harry Langdon, and, this being my inaugural "20Q," I thought I would see the assignment through and "hang" at the photo session. I contributed nothing to Langdon's couple of hours with Joan, but I got the chance to see two accomplished artists in their respective fields trade ideas, cajole, and compromise to get the job done. Joan looked beautiful in the photograph that accompanied the interview, revealing the wise, elegant New Yorker that she was before she became obsessed by cosmetic surgery.

"20 Questions with Joan Rivers" appeared in the August 1981 *Playboy.* Team Rivers was pleased with the result, as was Rezek and the silk pajamas he reported to. I was also happy, especially when I tore open the envelope with the bunny head and Chicago return address and stared at a check for $1,750. Nice work if I could keep getting it.

I felt as though freelancing was in my veins—the uncertainty, the stress, the unknown, all rewarded by a sit-down with a boldfaced name for an hour, working a tape recorder, typing two-fingered, and all of it capped off with the receipt of a check payable in U.S. dollars. I thought I'd strike while I was hot. I called Rezek's office and launched my best shot. "My favorite television show featuring the funniest cast on the tube, taped in Canada starring mostly Canadian performers and alumni of Second City who skewer the phoniness of television programs and the insincerity of celebrities." I took a breath. Rezek was still listening. "*SCTV. Second City Television.* It's on NBC Friday nights after Johnny Carson."

There was a long pause. Then, "Call me tomorrow," Rezek said.

One of the impressive things about John as an editor was that although he didn't strike me as a television watcher or a movie attendee (I always pictured him in his leisure time playing a game of chess or opening a cherished bottle of La Mission Haut Brion), he was aware of who and what was out there in the pop culture miasma. He had to be. I doubted he had ever seen an *SCTV* episode at 12:30 in the morning or had even set up his VHS recorder to tape one, but he probably knew about John Candy, Catherine O'Hara, and Eugene Levy, or, if not, he would certainly ask around the *Playboy* offices before the next time we spoke.

I had discovered *SCTV* through my dad. Besides taping *Carson* every night, he had begun to tape a half-hour, low-budget comedy show with a cast I had never heard of. It aired at the deadly time of 7:00 Saturday evenings on L.A.'s local channel 9. He told me *SCTV* was a show I "had to watch." NBC's *Saturday Night Live* had been on the air a year (1975–1976) capturing ratings and Emmys for the talented cast, which included Second City alums John Belushi, Dan Aykroyd, Gilda Radner, and, in the second season, Bill Murray. Andrew Alexander, the co-owner of Second City, didn't want to lose any more talent to *SNL,* so he helped create *SCTV* in 1976.

The next day I nervously dialed Rezek. The leap—opening myself to acceptance or rejection—has always been exhilarating, even with its downside.

"Mr. Rezek's just stepped out," his assistant said, and my heart plunged, "but let me go see if I can find him." She put me on hold. After an excruciating sixty seconds or so, John came on the line. "Good news. We think *SCTV* is perfect for '20Q.' Go ahead. Keep me updated."

Now came the hard part. I actually had to wrangle an interview of the entire cast for the piece. I knew the Canadian Second City stage was in Toronto, so I started there. Another cold phone call (thank you, David Fryer), this time to the Great White North.

"Second City," answered the clean, crisp voice. I explained that I was a writer from *Playboy* and needed to contact the *SCTV* publicist about an interview. The voice passed me to someone who knew something about something. Sally Cochran was her name. She ran Second City stage in

Toronto and happened to be married to the coproducer of *SCTV,* Patrick Whitley. I did my pitch on how *Playboy* would be conducive to translating the show's humor to the printed page and how we were all big fans at the magazine. Sally was pleasant and seemed semiexcited that someone from a big U.S. publication wanted to focus on their farm club. Doing the interview was not going to be without pitfalls, she warned me. "You're going to have to go to Edmonton. That's where they're shooting this season." Cochran's voice expressed dread, as if the shoot were taking place at the Molokai leper colony.

"No problem," I reassured her.

I had never been to Canada. I got out a map to find Edmonton. In the minute or so between my hanging up with Sally and calling the *SCTV* office in Edmonton, she must have alerted the troops that they would be receiving a call from a *Playboy* scribe. When associate producer Jason Schub answered the phone, there was a distinct air of nonchalance, as if the interview were a matter of when, not if. Schub said that cast, writers, and crew were practically working seven-day weeks because NBC wanted ninety minutes a week instead of the show's previously syndicated thirty-minute version. All work and no play would pay off in back-to-back Emmys for Best Writing for a Variety Series in 1982–1983. Plus, there wasn't much to do in Edmonton except attend Oiler hockey games.

Executive producer Andrew Alexander and his partner Len Stuart, producer Whitley, the writing staff, and, of course, the cast—Candy, Levy, O'Hara, Dave Thomas, Joe Flaherty, Andrea Martin, and Rick Moranis—had debated and voted that appearing in *Playboy* magazine was better than not appearing in *Playboy* magazine. There must have been at least one call made to Belushi, Aykroyd, or Murray about how *SNL* had been treated by the magazine in its *Playboy* interview. Anyway, we had liftoff.

As the Air Canada flight made its approach to Edmonton and I was directed to stow my tray table and raise my seat back in both English and French, I looked out the window and saw miles and miles of wheat fields and farmland. This was a comedy hub? Oy, Canada!

I rented a car, drove to the Four Seasons downtown, checked in, and then sped out to the ITV Studios in the 'burbs, which began in Edmonton after what seemed like a couple of highway minutes. I wanted to be on the set pronto. I wanted to hang out with Guy Caballero, Edith Prickley, Johnny LaRue, Bob and Doug McKenzie, and Lola Heatherton.

SCTV was sharing stages and offices with "the regulars" who were producing news and other "real" programs for the local market. When I arrived at the studio, a collection of nondescript buildings in an industrial park, I was escorted onto the soundstage, where John Candy, playing Gil Fisher, the Fishin' Musician, was interviewing punk rockers Wendy O. Williams and the Plasmatics. Wendy was decked out in a platinum Mohawk and ripped tights, her prominent breasts adorned only with electrical tape Xs over her nipples. The NBC censor on set was having conniptions. Phone calls were made to 30 Rock in New York City. Pixilation was discussed. Tighter camera angles were considered. Cancellation of the segment was threatened. John Candy wanted her on the show because Williams as the *SCTV* musical guest would stand in stark contrast to *SNL*'s usual acts, more conventional ones like Paul Simon and James Taylor. Levy and Moranis were adamantly opposed to her being there, but Candy won out. The series belonged to the cast, writers, producers, directors, and the hair, makeup, and wardrobe personnel, but this segment was Candy's baby.

As I met each cast member in a hallway, office, or dressing room, I jotted down notes: "Creative chaos; the energy from the cast could light up much of Canada; they tape in Canada because they don't want to be part of the scene in New York or Los Angeles, where the *SNL* rip-off called *Fridays* was taped. These were the very places where the shows they satirized were made." As I interviewed each cast member, I wrote down brief impressions: "John Candy—lovable bear, a warm, funny man; Andrea Martin—least inhibited, most accommodating; Eugene Levy—careful, most precise; Rick Moranis—best impressionist; Dave Thomas—most opinionated and thought-provoking; Joe Flaherty—most shy and introverted off-camera; Catherine O'Hara—most changeable in appearance and the best figure."

During the week, I would interview them all one-on-one, occasionally in pairs, and sometimes in tag teams. They answered every question I asked—involving television, drugs, group dynamics, sex, censorship, words you can't say on TV (which, oddly, included *breast-feeding* and *turd*), and comparisons with *SNL*—with gusto and candor. These people were smart and needed constant challenges.

Somehow, word had gotten out at the *SCTV* offices that Colonel Hogan's son was the writer on scene for *Playboy*. I had never mentioned it. But when I stepped through their asylum door, there were never any sideways glances or rooms getting quiet. John Candy would later tell me that everyone immediately felt more comfortable with me because I had been around the business for years and obviously appreciated comedy. Of course, the fact that I told the cast and writing staff that *SCTV* was my favorite television program didn't hurt either.

There is what I call the show business club. It's been there for as long as film, television, radio, stage, music have existed. Its members are performers, writers, directors, producers. They enter a room, glance at one another, and give the all-knowing nod. As in most professions, performers have their own language, their own shorthand. With a look, a word, or a phrase they can communicate volumes to each other. They acknowledge that they are different from the masses. For better or worse, they occupy a different orbit because they have talents most people don't. The club doesn't differentiate between those talents. If you're one of those rare people who as a profession stand in front of a camera or an audience and make people laugh or cry or cower in fear, then that's the ticket of admission to the club. My dad was never more comfortable than when he was in front of a microphone, a camera, or a live audience. The club creates, however temporarily, a warm cocoon, nurturing among its members the shedding of inhibitions.

I received a guest pass (issued primarily by Candy and Thomas) to the *SCTV* chapter of the club. I sat in on script meetings, discussions with producers, chats among cast members, engagements with business managers, attorneys, and agents. I was more than a fly on the wall. Thomas invited me to watch him film a segment called "Power Play" on location in which he played William Shatner portraying a hockey coach as Captain Kirk. I felt included, honored. When he asked me to put on a sweater and play the coach's assistant standing next to him for one shot, I felt like Mal Evans doing the audible countdown to the orchestra crescendo on the Beatles' "A Day in the Life." The *SCTV* "20 Questions" appeared in the May 1982 issue. Billy Joel was the feature interview, though I thought they should have been reversed. My piece received good notices from *Playboy* staff and readers alike, and as a result, the editor's door was cracked open: I had become a member of Rezek's club.

25

Kari, 1982–1985

I had become a peripatetic freelance writer, scratching out what I called a living. Most of my possessions were left in trunks and boxes, safely stored in my mom and Chuck's garage. I lacked a steady enough income to rent my own apartment, so I lived at my mom and Chuck's, ready and available to serve as somebody's house sitter at a moment's notice.

Through Diane during our days at USC, I had gotten to know a wonderful figurative painter named D. J. Hall and her husband, Toby Watson, a modernist architect. During that very dark summer of 1978, Diane had invited me to a party at D. J.'s studio in Culver City. Diane and I were a million light years apart by then, but she thought of me for the gathering and kindly asked me to accompany her. The star of that evening—and every evening where she was in attendance—was Debra Jane Hall. She is an attractive, athletic blonde who is alternately outrageous, funny, and obsessively creative. Toby, taking the permanent backseat, tolerated her many male fans. That night I joined the queue. Visiting this foreign world of "artistes" spieling on about the lackluster condition of the art world in minor league Los Angeles temporarily took my mind off the all-pervading, humorless wag called Death, who was my constant companion.

Venice Beach, California, was home to D. J. and Toby. When they took off to Hawaii for a couple of weeks they asked me to house-sit their 1920s Carroll Canal cottage and look after their black cat Mies (after Mies van der Rohe). I jumped at the opportunity for two reasons: I knew nothing about Venice and therefore my stay would be my own exploratory vacation, and second, my mom and Chuck would get a break from my long face.

I settled easily into the world of aging hippies and quacking ducks. Lots of duck shit covered the heaving, narrow walkways around the maze of canals. I played the house music chez Hall/Watson, which included

Steely Dan, but I passed on D. J. and Toby's Tom Waits albums. I listened to the radio, which was always tuned to the Santa Monica–based National Public Radio station, KCRW. I looked through D. J.'s books on still-life and figurative artists Pierre Bonnard, Mary Cassatt, and Cecilia Beaux. I never turned on their elderly television. I also stayed away from the phone for the first few days, so at first I didn't see the note D. J. had left on a torn piece of graph paper next to the black rotary dial phone. D .J. explained that their friends Bruce Everett and Kari Hildebrand had broken up after having lived together for five years. I had met Bruce once at an art opening. He was a talented plein air painter who taught art at Cal State Northridge. Kari, a former student of Bruce's, was a professional landscape designer. D. J. suggested I give Kari a call during my stay. I trusted D. J.'s taste. I waited until late in the afternoon, and the passing hours gave me an opportunity to conjure up the nerve and contrive some warm dialogue for the cold phone call.

When Kari answered from her home in the San Fernando Valley, I introduced myself and lamely giggled as I mentioned that D. J. had left her phone number for me. Kari said D. J. had told her about me. She was working on a xeriscape design for a home in Calabasas. I asked what xeriscape was, and she explained that in the desert region we called Los Angeles it was worthwhile, if not necessary, to install drought-tolerant native plants that didn't require much water. Kari said she despised lawns. She sounded like she was keenly aware of the environment, bright, and creative.

The conversation swung in my direction. "I do interviews with celebrities for magazines," I explained when she asked what I did.

"Such as?" she probed.

"Well, *Playboy* is the big one. They're the premier market for Q&A interviews."

There was an uncomfortable silence, so I continued. "My friend and I wrote a book about Jack Nicholson. We interviewed him a couple of times."

"Oh, I like some of his films," Kari said, breaking her silence.

"Yeah, Chris almost drove us off a cliff after our first interview session, we were so excited." I punctuated the rest of the call with nervous laughter.

Kari said she had to complete a blueprint over the next couple of days, but the weekend would work for us to get together. She said she'd come to Venice and we could figure out what to do from there.

Late Saturday afternoon, after feeding Mies, I watched through the front window as an aged beige Volkswagen Bug parked on the one-way single-lane road opposite Carroll Canal. A slim woman wearing glasses, her dark hair longer than shoulder length, emerged from the car and focused her gaze on D. J. and Toby's house. I ducked out of view and crawled into D. J.'s tight studio space, where a large, light-filled, vibrant canvas of two women in a swimming pool dominated the room. There was a knock at the front door. I counted to three, fixed a smile to my face, and approached the door.

"Hi, Kari." I pronounced it *Carrie,* as in the Stephen King novel, with bubbling enthusiasm as I swung the door open. Several years later Kari decided to change the pronunciation of her name to *Kăr ee,* which she felt was more in keeping with her Scandinavian lineage.

"Bob?" She correctly pronounced my name.

"Come on in," the consummate host said.

My immediate impression was that Kari was much younger than I— say, a college student—though it would be revealed later that we were only a year apart in age. She wore boots, tight jeans, and a colorful tie-dyed blouse. She didn't possess the usual Rubensesque figure that I was accustomed to think of as my "type," but she struck me as sexy, as if she could take off her glasses and shake out her thick hair and drop the librarian look at any moment. We shook hands, and I thought of my dad's advice: always make physical contact with a woman as soon as possible.

Since Kari knew D. J. and Toby's house well, I didn't have to take her on a tour. She did ask to look at what D. J. was working on. As we studied the blitzkrieg of color on the canvas, I asked Kari whether she found time to do art. She did smallish pencil drawings that played off what she referred to as her "out of the mainstream" sense of humor. I told her I would love to see some of her work. I have always enjoyed quirky.

Kari said she had heard a good review on KCRW for a new documentary called *The Atomic Café* and had checked the *L.A. Times* to find it was playing at the nearby Fox Theatre on Lincoln Boulevard. The film was about nuclear war and the cold war scare of the '60s when we were grade-schoolers practicing drop drills and learning to "duck and cover." The film was well made, intercutting good news footage that took us back to a frightful time in our young lives.

Considering that Westwood was chock-full of movie theaters showing big studio films with big stars, this small, independent documentary was an interesting choice for us to make on our first date, perhaps a good introduction to what our relationship would be—a mostly serious, art-infused life, with occasional doses of humor. Kari felt art and life were serious business. Kari wasn't a flaky actress type or the next comedienne hopeful taking the stage at Laugh Your Ass Off on open-mike night.

We had a vegetarian dinner afterward, also a preview of things to come. We talked about everything—the Southern California art scene, her drawings and the juried shows her work had appeared in, my magazine work, traveling, friends, family. I found out Kari was involved in feminist issues—marches, writing pamphlets, the Women's Building downtown—and that her art subtly commented on society's ills. Kari had started her own landscape design business, competing in what was then a very male world. For her, being a landscape designer meant control, precision, tightness. I found that attractive at that time in my life because I needed structure. I wasn't out of control, but I lacked my own plan. I was bouncing around, making a few dollars here and there, but I had no kind of blueprint for my future.

My first love, Diane, had gotten married in 1980 to a younger man involved in advertising. Then my best friend, Chris Fryer, had married a beautiful, globetrotting woman named Desly. My other longtime friend, Dave Diamond, had married a woman whose large family came from Utah. My cohorts were out in the world behaving like adults, working and sharing life with another person, paying rent, paying bills, trying to save money, putting a future together. This was big stuff to me. It was grown-up stuff. And yet here I was, a struggling freelance writer, still living at home with no major direction.

Kari represented a framework—she had steady work that she was good at, and she knew what she was doing. She introduced me to the world of plants and all things flora. Kari was also a fine artist with a wacky, understated sense of humor who would draw a half chicken/half cat posing seductively. The sum of these parts was pretty attractive to me. Not to mention she was a handsome woman with an air of elegance in her understated manner. She was my polar opposite.

Back at Carroll Canal, we said goodnight with a quick, businesslike kiss. Kari got in her Bug and proceeded to back into a telephone pole. We both pretended she hadn't as she pulled away into the night. I was intrigued by Kari, but it was hard to reconcile this new multidimensional woman with what I saw as my dismal living situation. Kari seemed to have everything going in the right direction. What could I possibly offer her? To wait a week was a less than gentlemanly thing to do, but I did eventually call her again, and we started going out.

Kari never got to meet my dad, of course, but she took notice of the showbiz factor in my family, however slight, which was new to her. Ultimately, like Chuck, Kari paid little attention to the film and television business and was, perhaps, even repelled by it. But like Diane and I, Kari and I enjoyed going to films. We liked live theater as well.

Kari also took me to art galleries, juried shows, and museums on a major scale. That was still a foreign world that I found interesting and mysterious. My first impression of Kari had been that of a college student, and indeed she behaved as if she were a student with a zealous, constant craving for information. I found that challenging and attractive. A friendly competition was in the air between us, but much of the time Kari's outward confidence dictated it had to be her way or the 405 back to Mom's.

Kari was renting a tumbledown house in Canoga Park built in the '60s that was fronted, ironically, with a browned-out, weed-infested lawn. We'd been dating for several months when Kari, whose roommate was vacating her digs, put the offer out for me to move in with her. I felt as if I were standing at the end of a long pier staring at the vast ocean. Kari presented me with a life-altering choice: turn around and run back to the safety of Mom and Chuck's or, as my friends had done, take a chance and leap into the unfathomable depths. I jumped with glee.

After our first week of cohabitation, it dawned on me that this was the first time I had gone to bed and woken up with a woman for more than one weekend at a stretch. There was a gentle learning curve, a daily sorting out of what was important from what wasn't in our relationship; how to keep the relationship fresh; and, most important, how to maintain a sense of humor. Kari was the straight man for the most part while I offered up goofiness and tried to lessen the everyday pull of gravity. My dad, the great philosopher, often said when it came to relationships, "Don't sweat the small stuff."

I learned to prioritize in our early days together, concentrating on stepping out of myself and taking care of another person. Living with Kari was my first time experiencing that daily life wasn't all about me—my goals, my work, my pleasure. I offered my thoughts, opinions, and assistance to a person who had learned early in her life that she was on her own. Kari's parents were divorced. She felt her father was weak and removed as a parent, and her mother behaved as if she were Kari's younger sister.

Respect became part of my new daily bread as well as liking and loving. This was an everyday relationship. The small stuff fell by the wayside and a bigger picture loomed: caring about someone, taking care of her, trusting her, putting our two heads together to come up with decisions. This was very new stuff for me.

Money decisions rose rapidly to the surface. Things got serious at times because day-to-day survival was often tricky. Kari got steady work as a landscape designer because she was creative, talented, and cheap. She worked on her own, a one-person business. But she never knew when the next job would be coming or where it would be, the same scenario for me as a freelancer. So, as in many relationships, money matters took precedence, like when we had to get Kari a newer car because her work took her on the road all across Southern California. For Master Bobby, it wasn't 100 percent playtime anymore, as my relationship with Diane had been: a steady diet of film, music, and art. The biggest financial difficulty Diane and I ever had was scraping together some cash for dinner and a movie. Now, for the first time, someone was depending on me to produce an income to help with monthly rent and put gasoline in the cars and food on the table.

Kari and I were a team taking on the world, losing our self-centered personalities, working toward common goals. I felt as if I were finally growing up, putting my trust and faith in another person and behaving like an adult. Kari, though a year younger than I, was already a grown-up, serious, dedicated to her designs, art, and life. With Diane, it had all been about laughter and the pursuit of happiness. Kari's sense of humor was sporadic, unexpectedly careening from the sedate to the wonderfully silly. We would laugh together at *Late Night with David Letterman, SCTV,* and Monty Python, but laughter wasn't priority one. I didn't see this alteration with Kari as a bad thing.

I pitched a set-visit piece to editor Irv Letofsky at the *L.A. Times's* "Sunday Calendar." Dave Thomas and Rick Moranis were writing, directing, and starring as the McKenzie brothers in the MGM film *Strange Brew.* Riding the crest of their monstrously successful comedy album, they took a Cheech and Chong–like path to the movies. Kari and I spent a few days in Toronto visiting a former psychiatric hospital where they were filming. I jotted notes and interviewed Thomas and Moranis in their trailers between setups. The coup for me was meeting and interviewing Max Von Sydow, who took a supporting role in the film because his children were avid *SCTV* fans, loved the Bob and Doug McKenzie characters, and threatened to disown him as a father if he declined the role.

The highlight of anything I ever did involving show business was watching Kari's face explode with delight and awe as she shook hands with the towering Von Sydow. This wasn't some comedic mug; this was Ingmar Bergman's leading man. This was as important a moment for Kari as meeting Fred Astaire had been for Diane. When Von Sydow was called by the assistant director back to the set for rehearsal, the elated Kari returned to her stoic self.

Letofsky liked the piece and gave it three pages in the all-important "Sunday Calendar" section. I had grown up reading the calendar, anxiously waiting for and then devouring the film reviews and articles by Charles Champlin and Kevin Thomas. To join their ranks with my own article gave me a real sense of fulfillment. Thomas, Moranis, and MGM were pleased with the press attention, Kari met Max Von Sydow, and I was in the *Los Angeles Times*.

After we'd resided in Canoga Park for six months, an apartment became available at Chuck's twelve-unit, single-story, '50s-style complex in a leafy section of Van Nuys. The wood floors, fireplace, patio, pool, and the huge savings in rent closed the deal for us. We could save money and live in a villagelike environment where Marilyn Monroe and Carl Sandburg had been visitors decades earlier. We now shared our second place together, but the first that was uniquely ours.

This was a huge commitment, at least on my part. We had been together approximately a year. The word *marriage* kept finding its way into our conversations. Internally, I had kicked and screamed for years against growing up even as my best friends, Fryer and Diamond, had transformed their lives and embraced adulthood. Their former selves had receded, and their commitment to a new life shocked, scared, and impressed the hell out of me. I was thirty-one years old, and I wanted to emulate my closest pals, and Kari was the right person to do it with. I got serious about everything. I figured I had to act seriously to be serious about initiating change and growth. Marriage was the next logical step.

Kari and I tied the knot on June 25, 1983. We produced our own event as if we were the first two people ever to marry. For a location we chose the El Encanto Hotel in the green hills above Santa Barbara. The hotel was an alluring collection of 1920s bungalows set amid lush foliage. The El Encanto had hosted hundreds of weddings and I'm sure a multitude of midafternoon honeymoons. It had an old Hollywood feel, and I could easily imagine the glamorous set ensconced there for the weekend.

Fifty friends and family made the seventy-five-minute drive from Los Angeles and gathered by the fishpond surrounded by an arbored courtyard as we exchanged our nonsectarian vows. Kari wore a smart white lace dress—no train—and I sported a tan three-piece suit. We found our simply designed rings—reminding me of twisted metal rope now—for under $100 at a Native American shop in Burbank. Our guests looked on under a lightly falling mist as Kari and I exchanged those rings and a few humble words of devotion. We nervously looked into each other's eyes, understanding that we were not the couple made in heaven but looking forward to linking our disparate talents and problems and trying to create a new identity together. We trusted that the sum of our whole was greater than our individual parts. We would work with each other's weaknesses and try to turn them into strengths. We were scared, but the idea of change for me was exhilarating. I was the ultimate design project for Kari, a young Frankenstein's monster with thinning hair, and she was the monster's bride, a challenging, self-reliant force that never totally trusted men.

Our green partnership had immediately declared its independence by scraping together the few thousand dollars we needed to bankroll the afternoon. We wanted no parental patronage. We paid for the hotel; the talent—Dave Diamond's brother, Bryan, looking like a young Paul Simon, on guitar; the cake—a beautiful sheet from Anderson's Bakery on State Street; and the catering—healthy salmon and chicken, veggies, salad, and delicious champagne served by the hotel's culinary staff. Our wedding was our first coproduction, held two days before my thirty-second birthday and four days before the fifth anniversary of my dad's murder. (As revolutionary as Kari and I thought our mating was, we did succumb to the lure of the traditional June wedding.) The good time continued as Kari and I honeymooned, though we called it vacationing, in the Canadian Rockies in Alberta. Chris and Desly joined us in progress as we all hiked, took photographs, and shared laughter. We liked the mountains and in the future would backpack in Yosemite and ski downhill and cross-country at Mammoth and Mount Pinos. It was a good start.

When I first met Kari I read some nice short stories she had written. In addition to her fine arts and landscaping design skills, Kari could turn a phrase. She was a genuine woman of the arts, and that added literary dimension was just another reason I loved her. We collaborated to make a short film in 1984 called *She'll Never Make It to the Olympics*. There was no dialogue. Just a gardener, me, clipping away at a hedge while a woman, Kari, gets into the pool on the other side of the hedge to do some laps. We were never in the same shot, so we filmed each other. After establishing the woman swimming, we see a shark fin coming up behind her in the pool, though the gardener doesn't see this. He looks over after a beat to see an empty pool, though the woman's towel and lemonade remain on a table. Assuming the swimmer has temporarily left the poolside area, the gardener drinks the lemonade and then goes back to clipping the hedge. The whole film was only a couple of minutes. We were delighted because we made it for a hundred bucks. We literally cut the film in the camera. Kari had storyboarded it, so we knew exactly what we wanted and how to shoot it. We added the sound of the pool and the clippers in postproduction, along with the credits. We got it booked on some paid cable outlets and made a few hundred dollars, but the main point for me was just doing it. We planned it, we executed it, we got it shown. To me, that made it a rousing success.

Now, I had first heard the word *feminism* during my run at university life in the early '70s. I had grown up around strong women who took control of everyday life because they had no choice. They didn't have to announce their roles on a placard or in a book. Theirs was a situation that just was. But with Vietnam protests came equal rights protests as well, and I was all for it. I had just never lived with a protester until Kari. I soon met many of her feminist artist friends, attended feminist art shows at places like the Women's Building in downtown L.A., and stopped thinking John Lennon's quote—"Women should be obscene and not heard"—was funny.

Art and landscaping were still male-dominated worlds, but Kari was enjoying success in both endeavors. Diane had also been a surviving artist in a male art world, but although I always saw her as brave and admirable, I never affixed the tag "feminist" to her. As with my mom and grandmother, it was implied, if not stated—they just got on with it. But American society was going through a tumultuous upheaval in the early '80s, and the key word was *serious*. The women I met through Kari were largely doubtful that men could contribute anything of value to society. Many of them were utterly humorless. I noticed looks of tired skepticism

Robert Crane and Kari Hildebrand, Los Angeles, mid-1980s (author's collection).

on their faces whenever I was included in their gatherings. Men were in the way for them.

One afternoon the telephone rang at our apartment and I picked up. A grave female voice asked for Kari. I said, "Just a moment. Who's calling?" The solemn voice on the line snapped, "That's none of your damned business." I was so taken aback by the woman's rudeness that I couldn't even muster a comeback. I set the phone down. Fuming, I stomped into Kari's workroom and exclaimed, "I don't know who the hell this is but somebody wants to talk to you." Kari's expression said to me, "Now, you know how I feel when a man treats me badly." I had been swept into a wave of social sobriety. Luckily, I think my maternal grandmother's

Scandinavian heritage helped a portion of my DNA prep for these frigid elements of life.

Kari always breathed a small sigh of relief when I received a check in the mail for a job, but unfortunately a large, black embossed bunny appeared on the upper corner of the envelope above the Chicago return address. While Kari appreciated the fact that Christie Hefner had signed the check for $2,500 that would pay our bills, ranking high on the feminist movement's archenemy list was my "real boss," Hugh Hefner. The problem for Kari wasn't Hef per se, but the objectification of women. But I also felt Kari had some jealousy and self-worth issues that arose in the presence of those air-brushed heads (and other parts) of the Playmates. It was all just entertainment to me, prose and photography. Kari enjoyed reading interviews in *People*, *Architectural Digest*, or *Art in America*, just not in *Playboy* or *Oui*. I often reasoned with her that the men's magazines allowed for a freer, wider-ranging interview; the results were more likely to be out of the ordinary and unexpected. I didn't have the same latitude in *Disney's Adventures* magazine, where I published a bland John Candy interview.

Kari put up with my situation because she loved me and it was how I earned my living, but it was not ideal. She tried to accept it, but my working for *Playboy* was like a little splinter she just couldn't get out. When her friends asked what Comrade Bob did for a living, I'm sure *Playboy* was never mentioned because her oh, so serious friends would disapprove. Kari was always encouraging me to do something else. She was trying to light a fire under my ass to challenge me to be a "serious writer" because writing for *Playboy* and its ilk could not be taken seriously. One day during the first years of our marriage, a conversation that began genially, placidly, rapidly ran off the rails. Kari was becoming unhappy with the direction her project (me) was taking.

She started delicately. "Why do you have to write for *Playboy?*"

"They pay well and they're one of the only magazines that actually print Q&As. You know how much I admire the format. They're the purest form of interview," I explained.

"But those magazines are embarrassing. Why can't you try somewhere else?"

"I am. In addition to the monthly men's stuff, I've sent out query letters to a dozen magazines and the *L.A. Times*, *L.A. Reader*, *L.A. Weekly*, *TV Guide*." My defense rested.

"But nothing is happening. I'm working everyday, sometimes seven days a week, and you're just sitting around," Kari said with hints of anger, frustration, and resentment in her voice. "Why can't you write for *People?*" She was amping it up.

"Oh, yeah, that's the answer." The volume in my voice was rising, too. "You sound like my mother," I said, knowing full well how much women like to be compared to their mothers-in-law.

"Yeah, well, she doesn't have to live with you," Kari volleyed.

"Kari, look, every magazine is a club. *People* is not only a club but one with a restricted membership. It's a very tough nut to crack, and to be perfectly honest, I'm not sure I'd even want to."

"Because you're doing so well?"

I looked around for some sandbags to crawl behind. The shrapnel was coming. "Freelance writing is not the easiest profession in the world," I countered.

"And being a female in the landscaping business is?"

I could visualize Kari's friends circling the wagons around her, with the telephone woman bugling the battle cry. "It may appear as if I'm not doing enough for your satisfaction, but I am trying," I said sincerely.

"I have clients waiting for me everyday," she said. "I don't have time to sit around and wait." Kari's eyes narrowed. "You're not trying hard enough. I think you're lazy." She waited a beat for the final fusillade. "You're a failure."

That word cut right to the bone. I explained to her that a failure doesn't try. I was trying. What had precipitated this combat was a series of setbacks for me at magazines like *Los Angeles*—I couldn't crack the editorial team and place any articles or interviews. As rejection letters piled up, I kept returning to *Playboy* because I had a solid relationship with John Rezek, the subjects for my interviews were pleasurable, the work was fun, and the money was good. Not to mention millions of people read the damned magazine. I was in a groove that I had carved out for myself, and it was tough to just give it up. Kari hurling the word *failure* at me was meant to be a wake-up, a shake-up, but it hurt like hell because I *was* trying, and I applaud anybody who tries. No matter how bad a project turns out or even if it doesn't come to fruition at all, I feel you can't fault someone who is trying. That person will always have my respect. I always rate the worst Netflix rentals at least one star because the damn thing got made. Knowing Hollywood as I do, I know that in itself is an amazing achievement, and I celebrate that. In today's world, every child receives a trophy, but I believe in winning and losing. Sometimes you win; sometimes you lose. But that word *failure* still hurts like hell.

My easygoing personality accentuated Kari's black-and-white view of the world. Her parents had divorced when she was in high school, and she often had to act as mother to her two younger sisters when their actual mother did not. Generally, men seemed to let her down, starting with her father and moving through relationships with high school boyfriends and later with a ten-year-older art professor. Kari wanted to control our marriage the way she controlled the rest of her landscape, and yet my writing for *Playboy* was way out of her control. I was at risk of becoming just another of Kari's disappointing knuckle-draggers, but I was not about to let that happen.

When Kari would ask, "Why can't you fix the sink?" I would respond to her in my best HAL 9000 voice from *2001: A Space Odyssey:* "I'm sorry, Kari, your project will go 100 percent failure in thirty seconds," and I would make light of the situation, though that voice could infuriate her if I kept the bit up too long. Like my dad, I took a "don't make waves" position. I pointed out that I enthusiastically mowed the pathetic lawn of the rental house. I could caulk and paint. Make coffee. Clean toilets. Vacuum. Not to mention what seemed like the most challenging job of all—provoking a smile or laughter out of my sometimes humorless mate. I would follow Kari into her makeshift work area and joke about a rejection I had just received from a magazine. My telling of the lame reason behind the spurn would make us both laugh. She herself was not used to rejection. She either took on a design job or she didn't. On rare occasions, property owners might change their minds and opt not to install her landscaping plan, but she got paid for the plan nonetheless. In contrast, I could do an untold amount of research, pitches, and sending of samples— a process that could take weeks—and yet still be turned down and not make a dime for my efforts. Kari couldn't comprehend doing work for nothing.

These occasional rumbles notwithstanding, I felt a texture in my life that I had never felt before. I was growing up, finally shedding my youth, and being adult with a living, breathing female as my wife, and we were mostly happy.

26

Bobby Ten Hats, 1986

The first time I met and interviewed John Candy for *Playboy* he told me he was a *Hogan's Heroes* fan. He was fourteen when *Hogan's* debuted, the prime demographic. John was a fan of my dad, and I was a fan of *SCTV*, which I had discovered thanks to my dad. Since that first meeting in Edmonton on the set of *SCTV* I had met with and interviewed John in Toronto, New York, and Los Angeles. I used the material like a fine, creative chef, not wanting to waste any of the wonderful product. As a result, one interview might be sliced and diced into several paychecks by going out in different portions to those who dined on celebrity interviews. The filet mignon went to *Playboy*, but other tasty morsels might be served up to *USA Today*, *Oui*, *Video Review*, *Los Angeles* magazine, the *L.A. Daily News*, or even *Disney's Adventures*.

Only once did I find myself in the stew pot: when I sold an interview with Candy to *Playboy*'s chief rival, *Penthouse*. I was paid $2,000 for a week's work, which I thought was a small fortune, considering I had made barely that much for my share of the Jack Nicholson book, which took three years. Unfortunately, shortly after the *Penthouse* piece appeared I got a call from John Rezek. He made it abundantly clear that even freelancing for *Penthouse* was a poison carrot for a writer who wanted to keep his career at Bunny Headquarters. I tried to justify my treason by explaining that Candy had made three appearances in short succession in *Playboy* in various formats, including a pictorial in which he was made up as Boy George for the *Playboy* music issue. I went on to say there was a scene in his new film, *Splash*, where he was reading a *Penthouse* magazine, as if that justified everything. There was a long, uncomfortable silence on the Chicago end of that line. I pleaded that the interview was a one-off and promised I would never write for or even read a *Penthouse* again—which I haven't. Such was the rivalry between the two magazines, even though I was strictly freelance and unsigned to any exclusivity deal by Mr. Hefner.

There could be no divided loyalties. The choice was an easy one for me, and I was grateful to Rezek for welcoming me back into the hutch.

In July 1986 I was summoned to John Candy's homestead in woodsy Mandeville Canyon in Brentwood. The spread was three acres of precious Los Angeles real estate. There was a four-bedroom mock-Tudor home, a swimming pool, a tennis court, and two guesthouses—one for living and one that doubled as pottery studio and workout room. Standing resolutely by the swimming pool was a seven-foot replica of the Statue of Liberty.

John and I met in his small office upstairs in the main house. He sat behind his desk playing the role of the executive. I was unsure why I was there. Did he want me to do another article, coordinate some live event, or maybe just walk his dogs?

John had an old-time, old-school publicist named Paul Flaherty (no relation to his *SCTV* colleague Joe Flaherty), who had been around Hollywood for decades. He expended minimal effort on John's career while maximizing time on the links at the Bel-Air Country Club. John and Paul were a mismatch—the old 9-to-5 Hollywood versus the new 24/7 Hollywood. They were, at the very least, a generation apart, whereas only a year separated John and me. For quite some time I had been arranging way more publicity for John than his salaried publicist had.

John came straight to the point. "Would you handle publicity for me on a tour I'm going to be doing in August?"

My face flushed. I had visions of Derek Taylor, who handled PR for the Beatles. I didn't want to appear too eager. I was going to milk the moment. After all, I had a busy writing schedule. I would also have to check with Kari. "Yes," I answered in about two seconds, ever the master negotiator.

"It'll be two weeks in New York, Toronto, and British Columbia," said Candy in his most businesslike manner, with not a hint of Johnny LaRue.

I would be John's lean, mean, publicity machine. Okay, not so lean, but I would be the guy who ran interference for, and stood between, the "talent" and the world at large.

"It's for a movie called *Armed and Dangerous*," John continued. "Eugene [Levy] is in it with me and he's going to join us in New York and Toronto." He stared at me. "Seventy-five hundred okay?"

"For two weeks? Yeah," I said, with as much reserve as I could muster. "Thanks for thinking of me, John. This will be fun."

I drove home and excitedly detailed the arrangement without mentioning my new pay scale to Kari. She took it all in, then asked, "How much are you being paid, or are you doing this as a favor to John?" She was sure this was pro bono work.

I gave her my best poker face. "Seventy-five hundred," I answered, suppressing a Jack Nicholson–sized smile.

I could see her brain immediately tallying up all the bills that would be paid. She smiled as big a smile as I had. For her I knew it was a win-win. We could catch up on some outstanding debts, and she could have two calm weeks in the house by herself. I pointed out that if all went well this could be the start of a new career that involved something as novel as a regular paycheck.

But first things first. We had to go see the epic. Kari and I attended a screening of *Armed and Dangerous* at the Burbank Studios. The film starred John, Eugene Levy, and a pert newcomer named Meg Ryan. The script, written by Harold Ramis of *Animal House, Caddyshack,* and *Stripes* fame together with Second City's Peter Torokvei, was originally destined to be a vehicle for John Belushi and Dan Aykroyd. After Belushi's untimely death, Aykroyd tried to hook up with Bill Murray for the film, but instead they made *Ghostbusters.* As the script gathered dust, other actors like Jim Belushi came and went. It wasn't until Ron Howard's *Splash* with Tom Hanks, Candy, and Levy made sizable waves that Columbia Pictures declared "Surf's up" to *Armed and Dangerous.* The studio hoped the *SCTV* and *Splash* juju would generate enough interest in B-listers Candy and Levy to ride the curl to a big payday. When the lights came up in the screening room, I squeezed Kari's hand as we silently exchanged looks. The movie was not funny. Even John Candy's genial personality was unable to save the sophomoric script and idiotic plot—*Armed and Dangerous* was a total wipeout.

Nonetheless, I waxed up my enthusiasm as point man for John. In my initial conversations with the Columbia Pictures publicity department, I quickly understood why I was onboard the SS *Candy.* The studio's department consisted of a crash of crusty publicists from the '50s and '60s who didn't know what to do with a commodity like John Candy. Their reference points were Gary Cooper and Barbara Stanwyck. They had no idea what John could bring to the publicity table and seemingly had no interest in trying to find out. I had the feeling that the old-wave veterans I spoke to didn't know about or couldn't be bothered with *SCTV.* John, who always had a good sense of the room, lost his patience very quickly in this case. Columbia was running the show, but it was my job to shield John from the uncreative, antiquated ideas of publicity that were being pushed in his direction. The Columbia flacks pitched inappropriate or worn-out newspaper, magazine, and radio reporters. These were people who were used to making a call to Walter Winchell or Louella Parsons for an interview with their star, then retiring to their three-martini lunches. *Saturday Night Live, Rolling Stone,* and *David Letterman* were alien to them. I quickly earned Columbia's enmity as I turned down one lame venue after another. I felt I should be wearing Kevlar when moving John from point A to B. I arranged MTV, *Spin* magazine, and *Late Night with David Letterman* interviews and appearances.

Sometimes after a writer had interviewed John, I would call him or her to politely clarify a point or to ask for a deletion. Often, in an effort to massage the situation, I would offer some unique piece of information or extend an invitation to a party or screening that involved John. I knew what kind of perks would be persuasive or soothing to writers, and John always appreciated that my dad had been an actor and that I had grown up around the business. He liked that I had been on the other side of the table asking the questions. He trusted me to look out for his best interests, which I always did.

The studio desperately wanted John to appear on one of the big morning television programs, *Today* or *Good Morning America.* I explained that he would not be at his best at those ungodly early hours, and that John felt late night was where his audience was anyway. He loved Johnny Carson but was absolutely petrified at the notion of appearing on *The Tonight Show.* He felt comfortable with David Letterman, who admired *SCTV* and its cast. I liaised with Columbia Pictures regarding which venues were compatible with Mr. Candy's performing sensibilities, which fit and which didn't. Those in the publicity department couldn't go over my head because John didn't want to talk to them. That only increased Columbia's animosity toward me, but at the same time it increased my leverage. I dug in my heels to assure that John would be in his comfort zone. I reasoned that it was John who would be on camera or in front of the microphone, not some nitwit publicist who had once lunched with Hedda Hopper. If John were uncomfortable, the interview he did wouldn't be worth the tape that recorded it.

While I wasn't responsible for moving amplifiers and guitars around,

I was in charge of safely transferring a larger-than-life, rock 'n' roll–like persona from home to limousine, limo to plane, plane to limo, and limo to hotel. Everyone seemed to recognize and love John Candy. Camouflage was out of the question. We checked into Le Parker Meridien on West Fifty-sixth and met up with Eugene Levy. He was as unsure of the Columbia publicity team as we were.

My first piece of business was to get John together with *Spin* writer Glenn O'Brien. Then Eugene and John went to MTV, where the studio was abuzz with excitement. John and Eugene were hilarious together, playing off their Second City improvisational skills. Their promo appearances were much funnier than the actual movie was. They deserved better. I kept the New York minions of Columbia Pictures at arm's length, and I knew full well that in their field reports they would take credit for all of the arranged press. I didn't care. I was making money for hanging out with two *SCTV* stars in New York City.

The next night, Candy, Levy, and I were chauffeured from the hotel to the NBC Studios at Rockefeller Plaza, home of *Saturday Night Live* and *Today* and the former location of *Tomorrow* with Tom Snyder and the legendary *Tonight Show* with Messrs. Allen, Paar, and Carson. Normal folk could have walked the six short blocks in a third of the time it took to go in the town car. Walking into 30 Rock, I was struck by the astounding memory of my dad filling in as guest host for Johnny Carson on *The Tonight Show*. He occupied Johnny's chair for three nights in 1968 while Johnny staged a contract negotiation sickout. My dad loved being king of New York for the few nights he spent in the number one media hub of the planet, and while he may have had the notion that taking over Carson's desk might not be a bad permanent gig, he knew Johnny had no intention of leaving *The Tonight Show* and CBS was not about to cut Colonel Hogan loose. Not at that point, anyway.

Kari and I were big fans of David Letterman's show, and our favorite moment, hands down, was an appearance by John Candy entering stage right with his hair done up ridiculously like Dave's preceding guest, actress Nastassja Kinski. No one made reference to it. Not Dave, not John, not Dave's number two, Paul Shaffer, and it made the segment increasingly silly and hilarious as the interview progressed. Paul Shaffer, John's fellow Canadian, was not only old friends with many of the cast members of *SCTV* but had worked with Eugene Levy in a Toronto production of *Godspell* years earlier. When we entered Studio 6A, we were taken directly to Shaffer's dressing room. Lit joint in hand, he welcomed us with a wide grin. Paul, John, and Eugene immediately fell into reminiscences of Toronto while the joint circumnavigated the room. I now understood why Paul was so goofily funny night after night.

The next morning, John and Eugene were interviewed together by a couple of New York newspapers. They behaved like musicians, riffing off each other, filling in when one or the other temporarily ran out of bits. They were quite capable of performing solo, but they preferred a group dynamic. They enjoyed the give-and-take, the improv, and they especially liked making each other laugh. We blew out of New York before Columbia Pictures publicity department could again raise the specter of appearing on morning television. John and Eugene were night people, a product of all those years doing two shows a night on the Second City stage.

There was a collective sigh of relief aboard our Air Canada shuttle to Toronto, the capital of Candy and Levy's beginnings and numerous triumphs. Once in the air neckties were loosened, cigarettes lit, cocktails ordered. These guys felt they were going home. While the intense media heat of New York was behind them, the home fires presented their own dangers. The locals expected, almost demanded, face time with their native sons and national heroes. When John and Eugene walked through the lobby of the Four Seasons Hotel in Yorkville, people literally screamed with delight. *SCTV* catchphrases were yelled out, and cameras flashed as I herded them into an elevator for a ride up to meet the press. Local radio, the *Sun* and *Star* newspapers, and yes, AM Canada, all wanted time with Harry the Guy with the Snake on his Face and Earl Camembert. John was more accommodating with media requests in Toronto because of the wild reverence he felt from his fellow Canadians. He tolerated people and situations that were much more intrusive than he would have in the States. This place, these people, even the oxygen were different. Maybe this was how the Beatles felt about Liverpool.

As a favor to a local producer John had worked with, he accepted a guest appearance on a low-budget, single-camera fishing-show television pilot that was to be shot on Vancouver Island. The host of the show was a National Hockey League beast named Tiger Williams. He had amassed the most penalty minutes in history over the course of his bruised and bruising career. John figured it wasn't too far out of our way home, and it would be a relaxing end to our whirlwind publicity tour to chill out for a few days in beautiful British Columbia. I thought of my dad and our Fellini Excursions. This would be my first with John.

We said good-bye to Eugene Levy and flew ("Did you drove or did you flew?") to Vancouver, where we exchanged an Air Canada jet for a four-seat puddle jumper to Nanaimo on Vancouver Island. I felt like one of the *Apocalypse Now* team heading deep into unknown territory to find Brando's lost waistline. We were collected at the landing strip and driven to a remote fishing lodge. Tiger and the small crew expressed amazement that a heavy-weight movie star was appearing in their flyweight production.

During the next day's shoot, things went swimmingly; John and Tiger swapped stories and spent hours together in a motorboat pursuing the big catch while being videotaped. This was an *SCTV*'s Gil Fisher, the Fishin' Musician segment but without the irony. At night, with the cameras off and nothing but crickets for entertainment, the booze flowed like Niagara Falls. Celebrating the first day of filming, Tiger drank a couple of fish tank's worth and went berserk swinging a hockey stick at a crew member with whom he'd had a difference of opinion. John and I kept our distance, but the next night John also got royally tanked and started beating himself up for ever accepting the invitation to this land that time forgot. I sensed John had trouble saying no, especially north of the 49th parallel.

The next morning at 6:00, I had the delicate and unenviable assignment of waking the slumbering bear. I had made an executive decision. We were getting the hell out of there! As far as I was concerned, the producer had two days of footage in the can and was trying to power-play John into a third day of shooting, which would have meant a third night of god knows what. I told the producer he had plenty to work with—the shoot had gone well—and John was in no shape to spend the day out on a fishing vessel. In addition to which Columbia needed him back in Los Angeles. The producer valiantly attempted an end run but I blocked him, quietly procuring a car, throwing John's bags in the back, and loading John inside. John's head was hurting, and the bumpy ride back to the landing strip where our aircraft awaited seemed as though it took hours, if not days. The producer was pissed at me but I took the hit. It was all part of the job. When John stopped seeing triple, he thanked me for getting him safely out of Tigerland. The fishing show pilot was never sold.

As far as I was concerned, I had passed the job audition. I had been responsible for John Candy for two weeks on two coasts in two countries and he was none the worse for it. *Armed and Dangerous* was launched to a mediocre box office tally and lukewarm reviews. Columbia Pictures was on to its next wave of releases, and I was but a dimly remembered nuisance.

John's number one publicist, Paul Flaherty, was soon knocking at the door. He wasn't giving up a television and possible movie star account to some young nobody without a fight. John Candy, like many savvy businesses, often worked both sides from the middle. He always had a plan B, and in terms of publicity the B stood for Bob. Boss Candy would observe who did the best, fastest, and most complete work for the right price, and who presented the image most aligned to the company—him. And, maybe most important, who was the most fun to hang with. Flaherty would show up at the Frostbacks office on his way back from the golf course and swap golf stories with John over a cocktail. I don't play golf, but Flaherty always watched me out of the corner of his eye because he felt the breeze of a well-struck Titleist heading in his general direction.

27

Crane in the Hutch, 1986

Despite Kari's protestations, I continued to write for *Playboy*. At least I could count on a semiregular paycheck (I was competing with at least a half dozen other Q&A monkeys jockeying for the twelve "20Q" slots a year). From her workroom, Kari could hear me lowering the volume on my phone voice as I pitched names to Rezek. The giveaway was when I periodically exploded into hysterical laughter as John weighed in on my proposals. Anything even remotely related to scantily clad Playmates always brought a frown to Kari's otherwise wrinkleless face.

"How about Jamie Lee Curtis?" was my first fastball to Rezek.

"[David] Rensin did her already."

"Sigourney Weaver has two big films coming out."

"She's in the works."

"Chevy?" I waited. "Chase?" There was a deafening silence.

"Tom Hanks? He did *Splash* and has a few films coming out."

"Too soon," Rezek countered. "Let's see what develops."

"How about Kathleen Turner from *Body Heat* and *Prizzi's Honor?*"

"[David] Sheff did her for an upcoming interview."

"Martin Short?"

"Refresh my memory."

"Late of *SCTV* and now a regular on *Saturday Night Live*."

"Let's wait."

"George Harrison? His company is producing films now with the Monty Python guys, among others."

"We did Lennon and McCartney already."

"Tommy Lasorda? Outspoken manager of the Dodgers."

I could hear the wheels grinding. "No."

"Tom Cruise? A bunch of movies coming out."

"In next month's issue."

"Julia Louis-Dreyfus? Very cute, funny performer from *Saturday Night Live.*"

"What does she have coming up?"

"Making the transition from television to movies," I said, trying to make that transition sound irresistible.

"Let's wait," Rezek resisted.

"Well," I sighed, figuring next month's rent would be late, "how about Koko?"

"Who?"

"Koko, the cat-cradling, American Sign Language–communicating gorilla."

This time the wheels were whirring. "Look into that one. Let me know what you find out."

"Thanks, John."

"We'll talk soon."

Like most people who had read Dian Fossey's courageous and moving memoir, *Gorillas in the Mist,* the closest I'd ever been to a real gorilla was sitting in a movie theater watching Sigourney Weaver's inspired performance in the film of Fossey's life in the Virunga Mountains. But now I was proposing a sit-down, face-to-face interview with a gorilla for the world's leading men's magazine. How would Hefner react to having an ape, *gorilla gorilla graueri,* grace the pages of *Playboy?* Rezek, shockingly, gave me the go-ahead. He was clearly taking a chance, but a successful roll of the dice could pay off big in terms of publicity for *Playboy.*

Dr. Penny Patterson was the director of the Gorilla Foundation in Woodside, California, and it sounded like she dropped the phone when I requested an interview with Koko, not for *Scientific American* but for the legendary publication with a bunny for a logo. "Are you serious?"

"Absolutely," I answered. "This piece will introduce Koko to a whole new audience. An audience with lots of disposable income for donations to research foundations."

"You know we're located in the mountains west of Palo Alto."

"I do. In fact, I think one of your neighbors is Neil Young," I said, showing my fondness for research.

"Yes," said the slightly befuddled Patterson. "How much time would you need? We're trying to mate Koko with Michael and it's not going well, so I don't want to bother her for too long."

"An hour and half, tops," I said, adding, "Koko will enjoy the challenge of the questions. We'll need an original photo of her, but nothing too racy."

"Let me run this by my partner." Dr. Patterson sounded both surprised and intrigued by my proposal. She would discuss the matter with fellow gorilla researcher Dr. Ron Cohn, who, it turned out, also happened to be her mate.

The mountainous terrain and heavy forest of Woodside made me feel as though I'd somehow crossed into equatorial Africa as I approached an unmarked chain-link gate. I rolled down the window of my rental car and was immediately assaulted by a pungent odor, neither aromatic nor foul, just a unique smell of animal. I remembered my friends Chris and Desly Fryer, who had been to Rwanda a couple of times, telling me how they could smell the mountain gorillas long before they could see them. A Gorilla Foundation staffer opened the gate, and I drove very slowly down a dirt road toward a small cluster of temporary-looking structures. Dr. Patterson, a handsome woman reminiscent of a young Jane Goodall, greeted me cordially and took me on a brief tour of the foundation's offices, introducing other staff and Dr. Ron Cohn, her co-everything. Ron also happened to be a skillful photographer who had recorded innumerable images of Koko over the years. I kept that in mind since *Playboy* would need an original image of our subject to accompany the interview, and it was unlikely Koko would be traveling to Hollywood any time soon to pose for Randee St. Nicholas, Antoine Verglas, or Peggy Sirota.

Penny Patterson was Koko's teacher and interpreter in American Sign Language, and that aspect of the study was going quite well. Koko was the most celebrated gorilla in the world because she was the first to use any kind of human language. The interview would go like this: I would ask a question, and Dr. Patterson, using ASL, would sign it to Koko, who would then ponder the question for a bit and sign an answer back to the doctor, who would translate it for me.

In my introduction to the piece in the magazine I described the scene: "Koko, 15 years old and 230 pounds, sat poised and ready in her open-air living area. She looked me in the eye and, using American Sign Language, commanded, 'Show me your teeth,' which I respectfully did. She was delighted by the enormous amount of gold and silver in my mouth. Her mate, Michael, 13 and 350 pounds, who shares quarters with her, never looked me in the eye—something to do with the fact that I was a stranger and a male." During the questioning, I would occasionally glance at

Michael, who would instantly look away. At other times, when I looked away, I could feel Michael's stare boring a hole in me. I asked Koko about her boyfriend.

"Koko, do you think Michael is cute?"

Koko responded, signing with both hands for emphasis. "Cute, sweet good."

"What's the difference between boys and girls?" I asked.

"Corn there good," Koko replied, meaning she gets a corn treat because her floor is clean, whereas Michael doesn't because his is dirty. She added, "Girl people," since she thought of herself as a person and Michael as an animal.

"Girl girl" was Koko's retort to "Which sex smells better?" I was sure *Playboy* readers would agree with that.

"Koko, what do you want for your birthday?"

"Earrings. Cookie."

My time with Koko flew by. I asked her about being interviewed. "What do you say when you're tired of being asked questions?"

"Gorilla teeth. Finished."

The interview was over. I thanked Koko for her well-thought-out responses and for her time. I looked at Michael once more, and he quickly turned away.

It was a wonderful experience: a brilliant day in that mountain community, replete with new smells, serious behavioral researchers, and a delightful ape who thought enough of our kind to give us a glimpse into the mind of a gorilla. On my flight back to Los Angeles, I smiled with amazement and elation as I relived having been in such close proximity to such an intelligent and majestic animal. At the same time it was all a bit melancholy knowing that Koko, as pampered as her world was, would never spend two minutes in her wild, natural habitat.

Weeks later, Dr. Cohn shot a glamorous Koko against a red background for the interview's accompanying full-page illustration. Oh, and for those with a more prurient interest in gorilla hookups, Koko and Michael never did successfully get together.

Sometimes the questions Rezek and I devised were more outrageous than the responses they elicited. When I interviewed the sexy golf pro Jan Stephenson at her home in Ft. Worth, I asked, "Do your breasts ever get in the way of your swing?" and her response was, "No, I never notice them at all." And when I asked *Star Wars* icon Carrie Fisher at her log cabin in Laurel Canyon, "With whom would you want to spend your life, Yoda or E.T.?" Fisher responded, "E.T., because he's so much more popular, though I like Yoda because he's smaller than I am." When I asked actress Marg Helgenberger to describe the Marg Helgen "Burger," she playfully offered, "Cheeseburger, pickles and ketchup. On a toasted sesame seed bun. Rare to medium rare. I don't like it to be dry. It's got to be moist inside. Moist and juicy."

I interviewed beautiful and talented women like Lucy Liu, Carol Alt, and Sela Ward; funny people like Ben Stiller, Phil Hartman, and Jimmy Kimmel; sexiness personified with Traci Lords, Catherine Bell, and Tori Spelling; and quirky or weird subjects like Nicolas Cage, Juliette Lewis, and Milla Jovovich. Taking silver and gold, respectively, in the peculiar division were Amanda Peet and Teri Garr. I met Peet at the Coffee House on Sunset Boulevard across from Chateau Marmont. I asked her about her Quaker education, maintaining firearm safety while topless (*The Whole Nine Yards*), and speaking while belching. I thought I had her attention and she was enjoying our exercise, but she suddenly laid her upper body across the table next to my tape recorder. She closed her eyes and I think took a short nap. This interview was obviously a commitment to a publicist for promotion of her new film, and she wanted to make it very clear she didn't want to be there. My instinct was to be a wiseass and ask, "Am I keeping you awake?" but I didn't. I wanted to finish the job, type it up, turn it in, and get paid. Peet's terse answers meant the "20Q" would take up only a page and a half in the magazine. At least there would be a stunning Firooz Zahedi photograph of her accompanying the piece.

The Teri Garr episode was both odder and more nerve-wracking. She was a big comedy star from several Mel Brooks films, including *Young Frankenstein,* and multiple appearances on David Letterman's program, and was also a fine actress, as she showed in one of my favorite films, Francis Ford Coppola's *The Conversation.* We met at her office in Hollywood with no representation of any kind present. The interview was going swimmingly. Here was Garr describing men (either "burger and fries" or "slow, nice gourmet food"); her chief neurosis ("relationships with men"); her dream guy ("Robert Redford is in my dreams a lot"); and David Letterman persuading her to take a shower on his show ("David Letterman browbeat me into doing it . . . must have been some kind of a sexual conquering"). Garr was funny, candid, playful, and sexy, and then just as suddenly as Amanda Peet's bout of narcolepsy, Teri asked me to turn off the tape recorder. I thought she needed a bathroom break or had to call her agent. It was much worse.

She faced me. "Why am I doing this?" asked Garr.

My eyes panned the room seeking a camera. Was this a gag for the *Letterman* show? "What do you mean?" I asked.

"Why am I doing a *Playboy* interview?" Garr was all business. "I hate *Playboy*. I hate Hefner. I hate everything *Playboy* stands for."

Oh, shit, I thought. There goes my pitch to Rezek, hours working on questions, research, and background. Not to mention my paycheck. Damn it. Channeling David Fryer, I looked Garr in the eyes. "Well, first of all, you're doing a great job. Great answers." I was being totally sincere. "Secondly, this interview is about you. The venue just happens to be *Playboy*. A lot of diverse people have been interviewed for *Playboy*—world leaders, politicians, athletes, actors, writers. Hell, Fidel Castro was in *Playboy*. Your interview is going to be great."

There was a long moment while Garr processed my words. I still wasn't sure if this was a put-on or a kind of Living Theatre exercise. "All right. Turn the machine on," she instructed.

I pushed the record button on the Panasonic and asked the remaining dozens of Rezek/Crane queries. Garr finished in fine form, insecurities blazing, self-deprecating and cute. The session was a huge success. Garr was calm as we finished, and I thanked her for doing the interview. I slowly backed out of the room, gently closing the door behind me, then sprinted toward my car. At least my part of the job was finished. An original, full-page photograph of Teri would be needed by the editors (Shelley Long was the only subject who refused a photo) to accompany the Q&A. Good luck with that, I thought. Weeks later, the photo session was booked and I was secretly relieved. I chose to stay away so as not to conjure up any unpleasant memories for Ms. Garr. Rezek and company were well satisfied with my efforts, I received my check with Christie Hefner's autograph, and I moved on, another "20Q" under my belt.

One small perk of writing for *Playboy* was being on the magazine's comp list. When the mail arrived one day, I immediately noticed the distinctive black cellophane that hardly camouflaged each monthly issue. I ripped it apart like some human Fido, and when I saw Teri Garr's name on the contents page, I journeyed through the silky paper with trepidation. Would the photograph page facing the interview be blank? Or would it depict Garr destroying a poster of our leader, Comrade Hefner? I arrived at "20Q." What I saw shook me to my toes. A dripping-wet Garr stood in all her naked glory, exposing all but the nasty bits while coquettishly smiling from behind a shower curtain in an old-fashioned bathtub. Just a few months earlier, she had berated me about what a dreadful enterprise *Playboy* was, proclaiming Hefner to be the enemy. And now here she was, gracing those very pages not with a conservative headshot but a full-blown attempt at foldout fame, a photograph by Bonnie Schiffman that must have passed muster with Hef.

In what I would call a full-circle event, I interviewed television star Mariska Hargitay. Decades earlier, my dad had interviewed Mariska's mother, Jayne Mansfield, at her Beverly Hills estate. Now I was meeting Hargitay in the cozy confines of the Mercer Kitchen in New York City's Soho District. There we sat, the two of us, children of long-gone celebrities (one killed in a horrific automobile accident, the other murdered), and I showed her a photograph of my dad, pant legs rolled up, bare feet in a heart-shaped swimming pool, sticking a KNX radio microphone in the face of a bikini-clad Mansfield. The photo represented an era when Hollywood was a carefree, never-ending search for fun and frivolity. That opening connection was a good icebreaker and led to a fun and enjoyable interview.

The best of all possible scenarios for me was traveling to a film location shoot, doing my "20 Questions" interview with someone I really wanted to spend time with, meeting filmmakers I admired as a bonus, staying at a first-class hotel, discovering a new restaurant in town, and at the end of all that fun having *Playboy* send me a check. A perfect example of that was going to Vancouver, talking to Ashley Judd, meeting director Bruce Beresford, staying at the Sutton Place Hotel, enjoying an Asian fusion dinner, and then getting $3,500 for my troubles.

Those troubles included what happened on the set. I walked onto the location. I saw Ashley. She saw me. Our eyes locked.

"Mr. Crane," she said, extending her hand.

"Ms. Judd," I responded with my best ad-lib.

She grabbed two director's chairs and positioned them right in the middle of the set, with the crew working around us. With our knees touching, I faced the comely actress and the interview began. Her devotion to her craft, her stamina reminiscent of the energizer bunny, and her fearlessness were rapidly apparent. She told me she had been shooting a chase scene on foot all evening and her long khaki pants kept getting dirty, which was why wardrobe maintained a dozen backups nearby. Director and crew were about to film another take, so Judd excused herself and promptly dropped trou in front of me and everyone else, so we could continue talking and not keep Beresford waiting. I noted both her dedication to her job and the more interesting fact that she was not wearing any underwear.

As a dedicated journalist reacting to the moment, I followed with an improvised line of questioning. "What's so bad about underwear?"

"It's uncomfortable. My mother remarked in public that I don't wear underwear, and it's followed me ever since."

For the next ninety minutes, Judd filmed, answered questions with razor-sharp wit, and changed her khakis over and over. I probably should've asked Rezek for hazard pay.

John Candy had so many fans at *Playboy* headquarters that even though he'd appeared in the magazine several times Rezek still threw me an assignment for a Candy solo "20 Questions" interview. John and Steve Martin were shooting interior scenes for John Hughes's *Planes, Trains and Automobiles* at the MGM Studios in Culver City just minutes from 40 Acres, the former home of Stalag 13. John had invited me out to the old lot to watch some filming and make arrangements for our upcoming "20Q." I was a big Steve Martin fan and also was intrigued to observe writer-director Hughes in action. As I sauntered around the MGM lot, passing soundstages that had seen the glory days of Hollywood stars like Tracy and Hepburn, Gable and Lombard and had housed sets from film works like *Wizard of Oz* and *Gone with the Wind* as well as television stalwarts like *Combat!* and *The Man from U.N.C.L.E.,* I rounded a corner and spied a large man in complete devil regalia—horns, red cape and tights, red makeup—having a smoke outside the soundstage. This image of John Candy is forever burned into my brain. John was waiting for the blinking red light at the stage door signifying that filming was in progress to turn off. Studio employees walked by, some yelping with glee when they recognized John.

"Hey, Satan, how's it going?" called out a passing grip from another production.

John saw me suppressing a laugh. "Could you have caught me on a worse day?" he asked sheepishly.

"No, you look good. Very natural." I was laughing out loud now.

I followed John onto the stage, where they were filming the scene in

John Candy and team for *Playboy* photo shoot: (standing) Ben Nye Jr., Clair Burrill, Robert Crane, Dione Taylor, Sharon Nye; (seated) Jeff Cohen, John Candy, George Hurrell, Los Angeles, 1989 (author's collection).

which he drives the wrong way between two eighteen-wheelers. In the scene Martin looks over at Candy as they are about to meet their maker, and John appears to him as a devil. The shot would be on the screen for fewer than three seconds, but it took hours to film. I was enthralled watching Hughes, Candy, and Martin work, but the process is mind-numbingly boring to most detached observers.

During a break, I met both Martin and Hughes. This was one of the few times John ever introduced me. Steve remarked, "I recognize that name." That was the extent of our interaction. Hughes was in the process of consuming his fifteenth cup of coffee and twenty-fifth cigarette of the day. He was the author of the screenplay, but he behaved on set as if the whole thing was being made up as they went along. He also gave Kubrick a run for the title of "exposed film king," tweaking each take with a note to his costars as if the scene were the most important in the film, not just three seconds' worth.

The solemnity of the process aside, the trio worked well together and produced what would turn out to be my favorite John Candy film. John was much funnier off camera than most of the kings and queens of humor I was meeting and interviewing. He enjoyed a good time while being self-deprecating and making light of public situations where he was often the object of worship. He completely understood the Fellini Excursion thing, recognizing that much of show business was silly and unimportant.

After completing work on *Planes, Trains and Automobiles,* John was going to spend a few weeks at his farm north of Toronto. He was going to be flying from L.A. to Toronto on Air Canada, and I managed to coerce *Playboy* into purchasing a first-class ticket for me to accompany him. That gave me five hours of downtime with John, and I took full advantage of it. He was my captive interviewee, and I was happily his captive audience. In between bites of hors d'oeuvres and flowing rum and Cokes, John gave me one of the funniest Q&A's ever.

"For what food product would you consider being a spokesman?" I asked.

"Brussels sprouts," was John's reply. "Sure, they give you gas, but they're good for you. Nobody pushes Brussels sprouts. They're forgotten."

"How do you juggle being a father and a party monster?"

"You've got to teach your kids when they're young. Show them how to mix that drink and work that blender. How to keep things real cool on ice. Keep that fridge stocked. How to use a credit card."

That was the shortest five-hour flight I ever took.

28

Going to War, 1986–1988

After three years paying the reduced apartment rent, thanks to Chuck, and scraping together some savings, Kari and I approached our bank's loan officer with the intent of chasing the American Dream. We were going to purchase our first home. Suits behind desks scrutinized the assets and salaries of these two questionable, freelancing, high-risk citizens as if we were trying to obtain papers to travel out of East Germany during the cold war. My mom and Chuck pushed the Sisyphean down payment over the top when they loaned us some money to complete the $30,000 down on a fourteen-hundred-square-foot, three-bedroom, one-and-a-half bath, 1951-built bungalow five minutes from our apartment in a section of Van Nuys where the sidewalks were engraved with a 1926 date of pour.

Our home to be had simple front and back yards with lawns that would become Kari's open-air landscaping laboratory. I was thirty-five, married, with a house and a cat. Just a few years earlier, I could never have imagined putting enough money together to leave my mom and Chuck's house, let alone being married or owning a home. I hadn't ever even considered not being a lifelong renter and not being involved in sporadic, infatuated relationships of no real consequence. Instead, I now had the empowering feeling that I was not little Bobby anymore. Grown-ups owned stuff, and Kari and I owned a house just like my mom and Chuck did, or my dad and Patti had. I felt as though I had entered the mature arena, and while I may have had bad seats, I was in and I could appreciate what the ticket holders had achieved to get here. I will always have Kari to thank for that.

In the first year of our pride of ownership, Kari and I went room by room ripping out the remnants of the Segals, the old couple who had previously kept the key to our castle. Green carpet—gone. Natural wood floors exposed, sanded, and polyurethaned. Light fixtures resembling a 1890s San Francisco bordello—gone. New, hip, track and bare metallic

lighting, in. Bathroom fixtures and toilets from a Romanian prison—
gone. American Standard and Kohler, in. But the most revolutionary
change came to the grounds of our kingdom. Front and back lawns—
gone. Kari had an aversion to water-sucking sod and set about transforming our yard into a lush and wild mosaic of lantana, Mexican and aromatic
sage, rosemary, statice, and several crepe myrtle trees. There was society
garlic and tall wild grasses whose gold and maroon heads waved seductively in the wind. A flagstone walkway wove through the greenery, replacing a straight concrete approach to the front door. Kari's laboratory was
distinctive. When you rounded the corner of our sedate little cul-de-sac
you saw mirror-image rows of manicured suburban sprawl with the kalei-
doscopic exception, halfway down the block, of the oasis that was the
botanical riot of our yard. Hummingbirds zoomed, butterflies flitted, and
bees worked the never-ending parade of blooms industriously, their pol-
len sacs filled to bursting. Our yard was tinglingly alive.

Kari and I enjoyed being a married couple, faced with daily decisions,
working together, solving problems, making love, feeding the cat, working in our garden, reading the newspaper. Together. And while we did not
inhabit a million-dollar piece of art in Venice or a trendy loft downtown,
it was our world and it was almost perfect.

One hot summer San Fernando Valley night, Kari woke me up and
said, "Feel this." I thought, "Fun, mischievous bedroom games on a sul-
try night." She had awakened out of a dream in which she'd visited
James Garner in the hospital. We loved James Garner. I don't know
whether "Rockford" had put his hand on her breast, but something
woke her out of that hospital-room dream. I put my hand on her left
breast and felt a small, well-defined lump. If life is one big roller coaster
ride, we had chugged to the top of the first big hill and were about to
plunge headlong into a stomach-churning descent. We didn't sleep the
rest of that night.

Because all this was pre-Internet and pre–cell phone, Kari and I,
working from our two landline telephones in our spare bedrooms cum
offices, took turns contacting anyone we knew in the medical field or who
could connect us to someone who could connect us to someone with
knowledge, an opinion or, at the very least, another telephone number in
an attempt to find the appropriate doctor. Sometimes while Kari was talking to someone about the lump I would sneak down the hallway to peek
at her as she struggled to maintain her businesslike demeanor in this new

medical whirlpool. It was especially challenging to Kari because this was about her body and for the first time she didn't have control over her own life. How could she have a lump in her breast? Yes, it was probably just a benign cyst that we were hyperventilating over. Benign. The word *cancer* was never mentioned by either of us. Kari was a physically active, diet-conscious, hard-working thirty-five-year-old woman who didn't have time to deal with lumps, cysts, or any other time wasters. She only had time for making yards look beautiful; creating odd, whimsical art; over-seeing her mother's erratic life; and loving, being frustrated with, and guiding her malleable husband.

A friend of Kari's recommended a clinic that served as a one-stop surgical and treatment superstore aptly named the Breast Center. The facility occupied several floors of a hospital ten minutes from our home. Twenty-four hours after Kari's James Garner dream, we sat in the crowded waiting room watching women of all ages take their turns receiving diagnoses that would, one way or another, permanently alter their lives, with either relief or dread. Whatever the outcome, I was con-vinced every woman in that center was currently going through her own personal hell. The title of art critic Robert Hughes's book *The Shock of the New* applied to Kari and me as our brains processed all the new informa-tion, hope, and fear in a kind of hyperdrive. As Kari filled out multiple pages of new-patient information, I watched many women who were waiting alone. I wanted to ask them, "Are you here alone by design or because a mate couldn't get off work, or worse, couldn't handle the situ-ation and just jumped ship?" Before long, Kari Hildebrand (never Kari Crane) was called. "Good luck," I whispered to Kari as well as myself as she was led away to an examination room.

I stayed behind because those were still days before I felt welcomed in that private eddy occupied by Kari and the doctors. I do have a sneaking suspicion, however, that most men, if they show up at all, prefer reading magazines or watching television in the waiting room rather than partici-pating in the frank, life-changing dialogue being exchanged behind those exam rooms' closed doors. The minutes limped by as the Breast Center's well-trained staff took care of a never-ending flow of incoming patients. I was amazed at this supermarket of all things breast: women checked in at the front desk for mammograms, checkups, follow-ups, surgery, and chemo. The doctors and staff clearly were making a conscientious effort to present themselves as more than just medical workers. Instead, they appeared to be caring souls watching over and guiding sisters in distress. There was a projected warmth in this facility, which was at the time unique. Kari emerged after an exam, mammogram, and biopsy and gave me two thumbs up for everything about the center: its staff, technology, goals, and purposes. All that was left for us to do was go home to wait for the results of the biopsy.

Two days dragged by. Neither Kari nor I mentioned what was hanging in the house like radioactive fog. Kari kept busy working out details of her latest landscaping plan, and I wrote questions for an upcoming "20Q" interview with the pouty *Family Ties* star Justine Bateman.

Every story has a before and after. I wished that the one we were in the middle of might have a never, but eventually the phone call came. The doctor announced that the lump in Kari's breast was malignant, but he was upbeat. He said they had caught it early. He said that with surgical removal of the fingernail-sized tumor and follow-up treatment, the prognosis was good. After relaying the conversation, Kari stoically looked at me for a moment, then fell into my arms, sobbing. This was the first time since her tween years that Kari was feeling dependent and unable to control her own life. She was justifiably anxious and scared. I could only hold her.

In the mid-1980s, MTV was a big deal, a television groundbreaker. A publicist I knew had been pitching me her clients for magazine interviews, and as a small incentive she sent me two tickets to the annual video awards show being held at the Universal Amphitheater. Kari and I were going to be rock 'n' rollers for a night, have a bit of mindless, big-haired (for Kari) fun. This was something we never did in our straight and narrow life together. The night of the award show turned out to be the same day we got Kari's breast cancer diagnosis. "Life is what happens when you're busy making other plans," as John Lennon said, so a lump in Kari's breast cancelled our walk down the red carpet.

In the deserted waiting room on the morning of Kari's lumpectomy, I put my arms around her and kissed her face, but I could feel her absence. Kari was already retreating, facing her call to arms on her own. Cancer was frightening and humiliating, an unplanned detour from her work, family, and friends. Now she had an additional job on her docket: ridding herself of an invasive plant. "I love you," I whispered, though there was no one nearby. "Don't worry about anything. These people are good. They'll take care of you. This operation will be a success, and we'll get this terrible thing over with." I kissed her again, holding her close.

She pulled away and strode purposefully toward a prep room. There was no pause, no sentimental look back over her shoulder. No doe-eyed look like Diane on the way to her abortion. I again whispered, "Good luck." I don't know if Kari heard me.

I read months-old, torn magazines about parenting and real estate and world events. I got a cup of coffee from a machine. I watched people awaiting developments for themselves, family members, or friends. For some there would be relief, for some heartbreak, but for all of us who paced that room it was a period of hours and minutes spent in a community of sympathy and utter anxiety.

Finally Kari's surgeon came to tell me the lumpectomy had been successful and Kari was doing well. The surgeon said his team also took a few lymph nodes as samples for analysis, but the good news was there appeared to be clear margins adjacent to the breast lump. These "clear margins," I learned later, were vital for a more optimistic prognosis. After another couple of hours, Kari was wheelchaired out of recovery and loaded into our car. We headed home. End of story, we thought.

A few days later we returned to the Breast Center for postsurgery follow-up. In the physician's examination room, where I was now an active participant, Kari opened her gown to reveal the tape and gauze wrapped around her chest. The doctor carefully unspooled the mummy-like covering, looked at and delicately palpated the sutured breast, and smiled. "How're you feeling?" he asked.

"Sore, but otherwise okay," Kari answered, putting on her business voice and, in effect, declaring victory for the home team.

There was an insidious asterisk to the exam, however. Because of Kari's age—thirty-five—and the aggressive nature of the cancer cells they'd biopsied, the doctor felt that both chemotherapy and radiation were called for. Kari was just too young, had too much life ahead of her, not to be militant about her treatment. Chemo would be administered at the Breast Center, radiation at a facility nearby.

As we maneuvered through the crowded waiting room, I looked at Kari with love and relief and said, "Let's get the hell out of here!"

We walked to the car. I opened the passenger door and helped Kari gingerly lower her body into the seat. I closed her door, and by the time I walked around the car and opened the driver's door, she was weeping with such force that intermittently she couldn't catch her breath. In the car I couldn't position myself to hold her, but I put my right arm across her shoulder. Goddammit, I thought, cancer's black flag is not going to be a shroud for Kari or for our life together.

Kari had a horrible time with chemo. The sessions were set up for every third Friday because, in theory, that would give her the weekend to recover. What it really did was allow her two days to literally camp out in the bathroom and vomit. The vomiting was followed by more vomiting. I stood outside the bathroom door, feeling helpless, my own guts knotted. I was useless. There was nothing I could do to help Kari through her misery except keep pushing fluids for hydration and help her crisscross the hallway back to the bedroom for some rest before her next wave of nausea.

The first week after her chemo sessions was always an unsteady one as Kari tried to regain her strength and appetite. Week 2 almost resembled real life, with work, food, laughter, and movies our main focus. Then the dreaded third week approached. I could see the storm building off in the distance, thunderheads of anxiety that never varied their direction. And then it was Friday at the Breast Center, with Kari attached to an IV dripping poison from a plastic bag into her arm while I scoured more dated, torn magazines. I don't know why I never brought material from home to read. After another wobbly walk to the car, we went home, where our tortoiseshell cat, Nutmeg, watched as Kari slowly teetered to the bedroom. Kari tried to get comfortable but the nausea came on rapidly, and another weekend was spent mostly sitting on the cold black-and-white tile floor of the bathroom.

The absolute worst times occurred on those Fridays when Kari's blood was drawn and her white cell count was so low the clinic couldn't administer her treatment. Then the dread of anticipation would be held over for another week.

After twenty-six weeks, half a year, Kari had had seven treatments. She was bald as an egg but wore bright-colored scarves or a wig, which didn't begin to approximate her own luxuriant hair. To complete her course of thirteen treatments she would have to endure at least another half a year of periods of unbearable sickness bracketed by weeks of anxiety that were nearly as intolerable. Kari couldn't continue. She elected to quit her chemo, over the protestations of the Breast Center physicians. She and I had hours of discussions about the pros and cons and the unknown. Kari talked to her doctors at length. Of course, they wanted her to do the full regimen. She was young, an otherwise healthy woman of childbearing age. Kari preferred to just wipe her hands of the anticipation, the dread, the weakness, and the days in the bathroom. Most important for Kari, I think the decision was based on her desire to regain control of her life. Cancer was not going to tell her what to do and how to do it. She researched homeopathic remedies. Her chum Linda, the good witch of the West Valley, started chanting ceremonies with candles and incense. Kari's diet grew stricter. No more Wendy's burgers and fries as the occasional treat for us. The sandbags were filled, the Kevlar vests strapped on, ammo stocked, troops at the ready. We were going to fight this enemy Kari's way.

So Kari went AWOL from further chemo, but she did take up the banner for radiation treatment five days a week for six weeks at a facility minutes from the Breast Center. It took us longer to drive there than it did for the daily scattershot of rays. No angst, no dread, no storm clouds approaching, no sickly weekends, just a precise daily drill for a month and a half. Kari was into precise. Her landscape designs and blueprints reflected her precision. This she could do. This was a walk in the garden.

At the conclusion of radiation, the physicians at the Breast Center were still pushing for Kari to finish the chemotherapy. Their mission was to eradicate her cancer with extreme prejudice, but after yet more hours of discussion with family and friends, Kari decided the ordeal was over. After all, there was no history of cancer in her family. Kari had never been a smoker (except for the rare marijuana hit), and her idea of drinking was, at most, two glasses of wine with dinner. We researched the chemicals in blueprints. We researched the compounds in Round-up, an herbicide used voraciously by landscape installers to exterminate weeds. If Kari's cancer had resulted from an environmental quirk, it was a one-off. She was young, strong, and determined. As far as Kari was concerned, it was "Adios, cancer!" The protocol now became simply a checkup every three months at the Breast Center—blood work, X-rays, scans, meetings with doctors.

Kari's brush with mortality accelerated her desire to accomplish things. Our life had been shaken at the foundation, but we were still standing. I tried to bring some levity to our daily life, but dark, crazy thoughts played with my head. I had watched my wife absorb XXX poison into her system. I had picked up her thick, raven hair from the furniture and the pillowcases and the shower drain. Each day was still a roller coaster ride because we didn't know what was coming around the next bend.

"Why Kari?" I thought. "What did this model citizen of our sick world ever do to deserve this?" Then I'd get pissed off for feeling sorry for myself, for thinking cancer might make me a widower, put me on my own again when I was just getting the hang of being a couple. What had *I* done to deserve this, other than be a semimodel citizen of our sick world? Hadn't I already sacrificed one family member? Were the gods not appeased? I was in my midthirties, finally behaving like a mature adult, and cancer was trying to face me down, daring me to keep my wits and integrity intact. I accepted the challenge. That was part of my responsibility. That was part of being grown-up. Hell, I had looked and smelled and memorized my dad's murder scene. That blood-splattered wall had my DNA on it. I had been in the Scottsdale morgue with my dad laid bare on the slab. Did those evil gods think a little cancer was gonna scare me now? Fuck them.

Kari and I had tried to have children before her cancer. She would have given structure to a youngster's life as she had given it to me. But now a pregnancy would push her estrogen to an unsafe level and possibly lead to cancer's return, so we decided against it. We thought about adopting and found an attorney specializing in it. For several months we were keen on the idea, but it gradually lost steam. Our priority was Kari. We concentrated on her care. We weren't in the clear. I don't think cancer survivors ever consider themselves in the clear. There's always an anticipation of another summons being slapped against the chest.

The cost of Kari's surgery, hospital stays, outpatient visits, consultations, checkups, blood work, chemo, and radiation eventually exceeded $200,000. Although we had good medical insurance through Blue Cross, we were freelancers without employee-subsidized insurance, and we still owed an enormous amount of out-of-pocket expenses to the Breast Center. It would take us a few years to pay off the bill, but I always felt that if we showed we were trying, that we weren't running from the invoices, then no doctor's office or surgeon or hospital would come after us. We sent in a monthly check in the amount we could afford. I continued to write for magazines as well as receive a few bumps from John Candy and Dave Thomas for publicity services rendered pertaining to promotion of their films and personal appearances. Those generous checks helped pay off our medical bills.

The experience had rocked Kari and me, but we tried to be optimistic about the future. We convinced ourselves that our engagement with cancer had been a one-time skirmish. We fought the fight, crossed the battlefield, and emerged from the irradiated fog of war slightly scarred but confident the hostilities were behind us forever.

29

Full-Fledged Chongo, 1989

Kari's spirits rebounded. She was back at work, in control, designing land-scapes, transforming mundane yards into visually exciting environments where families, hummingbirds, butterflies, and bees could all thrive.

One afternoon I got a phone call from John Candy. Fresh on the heels of the success of *Planes, Trains and Automobiles* and *The Great Outdoors,* John was about to star in another John Hughes film, *Uncle Buck,* which was to be filmed on Hughes's home turf in Chicago. John wanted me to reprise my role as protector of publicity and to liaise with the Universal Pictures publicity department and the eager Chicago press. He also wanted me to wear the tour manager hat. Those responsibilities included getting John from one point to the next. This wasn't always easy because John was often incapable of saying no to fans, newspaper columnists, or studio types in black towers. So I was to become the buffer, the obstacle, the doorman and bouncer that the great unwashed had to get past if they wanted to get to the goods. Almost every performer has at least one gatekeeper. Some posses consist of a small army of deterrents.

"Can you get on a plane tomorrow?" John asked, mission at hand.

"Of course."

I hung up the phone and instantly saw the world from a different vantage point. I was now working for a movie star who was appearing in a big studio film written and directed by arguably the hottest hyphenate behind the camera. Then I realized I had also swapped tracks with Paul Flaherty, John's golfing PR veteran. I was now on the A train bound for the Second City, and he was in the rough looking for a scalded ball.

The night I landed in Chicago I headed directly for the Ritz Carlton where John was staying. I found him in the hotel bar where he had just spent a delightful hour with Julian Lennon, son of John and now himself a rock star. Like me, John was a Beatles fan—he had seen them at Toronto's

Maple Leaf Gardens in 1964—so meeting and spending time with a Beatle's son was still a momentous occasion even at his lofty perch. John had had a few rum and Cokes, and he welcomed me to his beloved Chicago—a city where he had spent innumerable hours performing on Second City's stage on North Wells.

We had the big-picture talk, John laying out the plans for his future work, the kind of publicity opportunities he was looking for, what he thought I could bring to the mix, and a rundown of Team Candy's personnel. I had my last Heineken at 3:00 in the morning and took a cab to the Talbot, a boutique hotel a few blocks west of the Ritz, where the rest of John's posse was ensconced. John had a 6:30 a.m. makeup call to transform him into America's favorite uncle, Buck.

A few hours later that morning, John told me he had had another drink after I left him at the bar, which I soon learned meant two or three more, so while I had caught a couple of hours' shuteye, John had had none at all. Even so, he went through a full day of makeup, rehearsal, and filming with maximum energy and nary a complaint. Whereas I was trashed by 10:00 in the morning. As I looked for a quiet place to nap, Hughes enthusiastically mapped out the next scene with John, who was alert and funny, had no bags under his eyes, and had every line of dialogue memorized. He had the strength of a Brahma bull, and I noticed the performer's adrenaline kicking in before each take.

Though they were of different generations and followed dissimilar paths, John and my dad shared that adrenaline, that rush that transported them to an altogether other place to achieve the comedic goal of a scene for film or videotape or to persuade a live audience to let its guard down. John and Dad didn't drink coffee or do drugs, though I did see John smoke grass once or twice. But at 6:00 in the morning, you couldn't find two more alive humans whose mission was to elicit laughter, whether at KNX Radio, Stalag 13, or a closed-down high school north of Chicago being used as the set for *Uncle Buck*.

Of course there were also a couple of major differences between these two actors: one could drink all night and smoke cigarettes all day, while the other preferred to tirelessly photograph women until they achieved a sort of monotonously naked blur. But because I was close to my dad and I became close to John, I also knew they shared the most important similarity—a yawning gap separated them from the nonperforming world. Just as brain surgeons and plumbers perform a range of tasks beyond the ken of most of us, standing in front of a camera and crew or live in front of an audience while assuming another identity requires traits that most of us don't have and probably don't want. I knew these guys were different. I could never do what they did. I could share a camera frame with my dad in the opening credits of *The Bob Crane Show* where I didn't utter a sound. I could even walk by John in an office shot in *Delirious* and say, "Hi, Jack" (a cameo role that still pays me an annual residual of as much as ten bucks, I might add), but to actually walk and talk while hitting a mark with the weight of a film or television production sitting squarely on my shoulders requires an alienlike quality I could never imagine possessing.

There was always a moat. John and my dad occupied the castles while the rest of us inhabited land on the other side of the drawbridges. We could meet halfway or I could visit the castle, but we would always return to our respective sides. Those living in the castle had the same set of responsibilities the rest of us do, such as being careful and taking care of oneself, but it was up to the kings or queens to recognize that for themselves. If one of us knaves dared to suggest a change in behavior or lifestyle, well, then "Off with his head!" I once witnessed two "old friends" of John's from Toronto seriously confront him about his weight. That was the last time I ever saw or heard about them. In my dad's case, I was never aware of an agent, publicist, or friend confronting my dad about his homemade porn and the impact it was having on his career. I wasn't secure enough myself—meaning simply that I didn't have the stones—to discuss and suggest lifestyle changes with him.

Uncle Buck was a big-time Hollywood studio movie. This was not *Superdad* or *Gus* or *The Wicked Dreams of Paula Schultz*. This was the work of legendary entertainment honchos Lew Wasserman and Sid Sheinberg, Midas-touch writer/director John Hughes, and the Canadian comedy actor who didn't realize he was the hippest guy in the room, John Candy. It was fifteen-hour days and a million feet of exposed film. Hughes was allowed that kind of indulgence because he had had a string of box office hits and the executives in the Black Tower knew he would find just the right moment for his actors, so Universal paid to let him keep shooting. Hughes pushed John hard, never settling, always striving for the perfect take, when John would come as close as possible to expressing Hughes's words as Hughes had originally heard them in his head sitting at the typewriter. Amy Madigan brought authenticity to her role, and because a young Macaulay Culkin worked a funny, staccato, *Dragnet*-like interrogation scene with John in *Uncle Buck,* he was rewarded with another script Hughes had in development. That was *Home Alone.*

John's personal team had decades of experience in film and television production. Teamster driver Frank Hernandez didn't actually drive John. Another Teamster did that, but Hernandez took care of John's trailer, his home away from home, where more hours were spent than in John's hotel room. Frankie kept the trailer stocked with beverages and snacks and, more important, kept an eye on John's wad of per diem cash, which was money over and above his salary. He kept the $3,000 that was delivered to the trailer every week safe and neatly stacked, ready to be spent on a John whim. Back in the early '80s, Frankie had taken the green, wide-eyed kid from Toronto under his wing and showed him the ropes of film production. Size mattered in Hollywood, Frankie had explained, as in the dimensions of an actor's trailer. On their first film together (*Going Berserk*), Frankie had taken John out of a honey wagon dressing room, which was the size of a closet, and repositioned him in a trailer worthy of the star of the film. It was always good to know someone like Frankie Hernandez in Hollywood.

Then there was a dapper professional named Silvio Scarano, John's personal wardrobe man. Frankie and Silvio were opposites, but they respected and trusted each other like an old married couple. Ben Nye Jr., the son of a famous makeup artist, handled all non–special effects makeup for John. He was efficient and patient. Dione Taylor did hair, making John look suitably lead actorish before he actually was a movie star. John's stand-in/stunt double was a guy named Bob Elmore, who was always trying to figure out why he wasn't John Candy and not just some guy from Riverside, California, who stood under hot lights with a setup crew hitting the marks that John would eventually hit. As John's fame and fortune grew, so did the list of demands written into his movie contracts. The list included the above-mentioned personnel, who all came along on the production company's dime.

Team Candy, dubbed "the Chongos" (monkeys) by Frankie, had taken the ride on any number of Candy films. I was the new guy and therefore was being watched and broken in, sanctioned by the leader but kept on a short leash with the posse just to make sure I would have the leader's back at all times. When, during a break in the filming, John and the Chongos took to the sky on Super Bowl weekend to see the game in Miami, I took the opportunity to migrate west to spend time with my wife.

I had been gone over a month, but it seemed much longer, at least to me, because the days were so long—endless shoots followed by John's need to relax at a bar, a club, or back at the Ritz-Carlton. I felt as though I had been gone closer to three months. Kari was pleased that I was bringing in a steady $750 a week and, though I didn't know how long this would last, I was satisfied with my move from freelance writer to publicist-tour manager-babysitter for the rock 'n' roll group called John Candy. I felt the experience would loom large on my résumé.

Kari was still working. She was in remission and feeling better, running her own life. But when I got home there was tension in the air. The kisses and embraces I had expected were not forthcoming. It took time that we didn't have, on my short R & R visit, to settle back in and feel as if we fit together. The temporary nature of my return didn't do anything to diminish the uneasiness.

On Super Bowl Sunday Kari and I watched the game for a quarter while Candy, Frankie, and a few others stood on the sidelines at Joe Robbie Stadium in Miami and watched the San Francisco 49ers do battle with the Cincinnati Bengals. When the Niners were attempting to retake the lead from the Bengals, Niners quarterback and MVP Joe Montana was so relaxed on the field that he is reported to have said, while in a huddle calling an important play, "Here's the play, and hey, look, there's John Candy."

After a too-short few days I was back on a plane to O'Hare. To avoid another long separation, Kari rearranged her work schedule and, two weeks later, flew to the Windy City for the first time. This created a different kind of dilemma for me. On the one hand, I wanted to be part of John's club. After all, I was the new guy and wanted to fit in. Yet on the other, I wanted to spend time with Kari, showing her the sights and sounds of Chicago. So while Kari visited, I had to take a hiatus from hanging out with the guys at clubs and bars after work. Instead, Kari and I took in the symphony, the art institute, and a number of terrific north side restaurants. While we enjoyed sharing a "Windy City Things to Do" list, I still missed the boy's club and felt guilty when I spent time away from John and the rest of the Chongos. If only there had been a way to be in both places simultaneously. The club was a place where men left the daily grind behind. They swore and belched and told inappropriate jokes with the only goal that of making the boss happy. It was a locker room atmosphere that Kari and the other wives had little interest in joining. Kari enjoyed meeting everyone, but her brain would have gone numb after an hour of the survival tactics deployed by this small group of men enduring long hours on the road. We all served at John's pleasure during the day and many a night, because all we had was each other to share a beer, a laugh, or a gripe with. We took everybody on and had John's back at all times. Loyalty was the coin of our realm.

John was an oversized personality in every sense, and I dealt with many overzealous fans and well-wishers: women who wanted hugs and kisses, men who wanted to share a beer. John was a rock star. We even started making each publicity tour into something like a rock 'n' roll tour, complete with hats and other imprint gear. We had the Guns 'n' Snakes tour, the Just the Fax tour, and the Dangerous Times tour. It was all just an inside joke for us, but all the fun and laughter it provoked was medicinal. I don't think Kari ever understood that aspect of my job. She saw me as an extremely well-compensated babysitter, and while I admit there was an element of truth to that, I do believe that being adored by the public at large puts an enormous amount of pressure on the adoree, and I was there to help alleviate that.

Try to imagine what it would be like if every time you went out people started yelling your name or making references to jobs you'd done.

"Yo, emergency room nurse, wanna check my swelling?"

"Look everybody, it's the H&R Block guy. Woo-hoo!"

"Hey, bank teller girl, got change for this?"

It wouldn't take long before most of us would start packing heat. John never lost his cool even when it was warranted. Except once. After putting a day's filming in the can, John, off-duty Chicago Police Department detective Tim O'Meara of the Bomb and Arson section, and I headed to a blues bar on the north side of Chicago. If there was ever a guy who would have your back 24/7, be your right arm or point man, it was the salt-of-the-earth O'Meara. He liked to have fun, but he didn't take shit from anyone. We pulled up to the subterranean club and got out of the town car. Belushi and Aykroyd had spent hours at this place after a day's filming of *The Blues Brothers*. There were fans and celebrity watchers hovering near the entrance. When they spotted John, a collective shriek went up, women clamoring for a photo op with the cuddly big man, and guys wanting to shake hands with Johnny LaRue, Del Griffith, and Ox. John, as always, was gracious with his time, attending to everyone's needs—these were the people who bought movie tickets. He signed autographs, posed for photos, and tolerated hugs and kisses. As we descended the stairs to the club's entrance, we heard someone yell, "John Candy sucks!"

We had heard negative things said before and even had objects like batteries thrown at us during sporting events, but the posse always stayed together, kept moving, and laughed. Not that night. John stopped, looked up, spotted the wiseass, and returned to street level. "What's your problem?" John growled, getting in the retreating weasel's face.

The guy said something under his breath while trying to leave, but John's arm shot out, grabbed the guy by the throat and pinned him up against the brick wall, cartoonlike, the man's feet dangling a couple of inches off the pavement. I stood there, shocked. I had never seen John react like this.

"John, let him go, let him go, it's not worth it!" O'Meara and I yelled.

John stared into the man's eyes and slowly released him. The heckler slid slowly down the wall to the ground as O'Meara and I shepherded John toward the club entrance.

Twenty minutes later, as John and I imbibed (O'Meara did not) and listened to the music in the club, the guy from outside reappeared, walking toward John with his right hand tucked inside the left breast of his jacket. O'Meara's radar immediately went off. The man produced his right hand in a revolver simulation, pointing his finger at John and pulling an invisible trigger. "I could've got you," said the smirking Travis Bickle wannabe.

O'Meara jumped up, grabbed the guy by the collar, and shouted, "We're going upstairs!"

By the time John and I followed, O'Meara had the man cuffed and up against the wall on street level. He had also called in a favor from his Chicago PD buddies. A paddy wagon appeared within ten minutes and the man, despite his protests and profuse apologies, was whisked away to be booked for disturbing the peace and to reap the pleasure of spending an all-expense-paid evening in the Cook County Jail. That scumbag could brag to his cellmates that he had scared the shit out of the big man, the movie star, but he still had to spend the night with at least one eye open. In today's Twitter/iPhone/YouTube/TMZ society, cell phone footage of "Comedian John Candy on a rampage attacking a fan during a wild night clubbing in Chicago" would have instantly gone viral. I'm pleased that that footage doesn't exist.

30

Groundhog Day, Scottsdale, 1990

Chinese and Jewish calendars notwithstanding, Planet Earth was now in the 1990s. Richard Romley came to bat as the third Maricopa County district attorney since my dad's murder. On January 30, 1990, Romley declared that a new team of investigators and prosecutors as well as an appointed review panel would reexamine the many volumes of files pertaining to the unsolved case. My new best friends became Jim Raines, an investigator with the Maricopa County Attorney's Office, and Barry Vassall of the Scottsdale Police Department's Criminal Investigations Bureau. This was the very same Barry Vassall who on June 29 twelve years earlier had turned around in his seat in the unmarked police cruiser and told me my dad was dead.

Raines and Vassall conducted multiple telephone and in-person interviews with my stepdad, Chuck, and me during 1990. We turned over the audiocassette recording of a telephone conversation I'd had with Carpenter in the weeks following the murder. I told Raines and Vassall that at the time Chuck and I had mentioned the recording to police detectives Dennis Borkenhagen and Ron Dean and to Larry Turoff of the Maricopa County Attorney's Office, but they weren't interested.

Raines, Vassall, and Captain Page Decker of the Scottsdale Police Department were encouraged by a new laboratory technique using deoxyribonucleic acid, or DNA. The Scottsdale PD sent the small blood sample found in John Carpenter's rental car and a more substantial sample of my dad's blood to Cellmark Diagnostic Lab* in Maryland for comparison. They were hoping to conclusively connect the two blood samples to the same human being, my dad.

Unfortunately, the minute size and comparatively old age of the sample taken from the car prevented Cellmark from making a definitive pro-

---

*The Cellmark Lab was made famous by the O. J. Simpson trial.

nouncement; the new DNA technology couldn't prove conclusively that the specimen was my dad's blood. DA Romley refused to speculate whether a blood match would have led to the arrest of Carpenter, but he continued to be encouraged by all the newfangled science and his modern investigatory team. He was determined to finally solve the crime, to disperse the dark cloud that had been hovering over his office for more than a decade. To that end, he laid the Crane case in the lap of the incident review board he had assembled months earlier. The board, consisting of fifteen prosecutors and investigators, had already discovered fresh findings in two other unsolved murders in Maricopa County.

Every investigation requires a bloodhound—someone with a tireless motivation to endure and to overcome missteps, false leads, dead ends, lies and deceptions. Someone able to keep his or her nose to the trail and follow the real scent. County investigator Jim Raines was the alpha dog of the new team assembled when Richard Romley assumed the DA's role in 1989. Perennial prime suspect John Henry Carpenter's Beverly Hills attorney, Gary Fleischman, could not imagine what new evidence they'd have after so many years. "There must be a statute of limitations somewhere in this case," he commented to the press. There wasn't. The crime of murder has no such statutes.

Through dogged tenacity and a quirk of blind luck, Raines unearthed long-forgotten color photographs of the interior of Carpenter's rental car from 1978. They were found in a box in a storage room in the Maricopa County Courthouse. Besides the three-inch trail of type B blood near the top of the padding on the passenger door, there was a one-sixteenth-inch speck of what was possibly human tissue visible on the same door panel. The Department of Public Safety, whose photographer had documented Carpenter's car on film, hadn't preserved that speck, didn't possess the film negatives, couldn't recall the photographer's name, and was unable to produce any records that noted the possible tissue because, in 1988, all of its reports regarding Carpenter's rental car had been destroyed. Public safety indeed.

31

Bob's Candy Shoppe, 1990

With the Two Johns (Candy and Hughes) enjoying another box office hit with *Uncle Buck* (which would turn out to be their last film together as actor and director), John envisioned big things for his Frostbacks Production. The rapidly filling slate of projects necessitated a move out of a two-bedroom condo cum office in Brentwood into a real working space. John's attorney/business manager at the time, Clair Burrill, informed the landlord, actress Shelley Fabares, that Frostbacks was on the move. That was the same Shelley Fabares who had worked with my dad on *The Donna Reed Show*. Frostbacks moved its shingle less than a mile away, morphing at the same time from a minor league production company to a major boutique production house. Candy would now pay $10,000 a month to his new Japanese landlord, Brentwood Pictures (a company that never produced a film while we were in residence in its building), to occupy the ground floor of a two-story 1960s building on San Vicente Boulevard across the street from the antediluvian Veterans Administration complex.

Frostbacks was at least five thousand square feet. From the broad reception foyer the hallway described a rectangle around the interior of the building with offices on either side; John's was in the back corner and big enough for the king of the castle to feel comfortable. There was a con-ference room, a kitchen, bathrooms, of course, a fully equipped recording studio, and, when the hallway made the last turn back to the entry, the bar room.

The landlord never quite understood the significance of his tenant's company name, Frostbacks Production. John Candy, born and raised in Toronto, traveled the tundra to make his way to the US of A, where for-tune and renown awaited. He thought of himself as the northern version of a wetback. Frostbacks was also a tongue-in-cheek salute to his fellow expats Eugene Levy, Dave Thomas, Martin Short, Dan Aykroyd, Paul Shaffer, Catherine O'Hara, and Rick Moranis, who had also crossed the border to make more money than they could ever have imagined growing up in Hamilton or Thunder Bay, Ontario.

I became John's in-house publicist. I coordinated campaigns for his films with counterparts at Universal and 20th Century Fox. I arranged interviews with television and radio-segment producers, articles with newspaper and magazine editors. My medium-sized office housed shelf upon shelf of stills, posters, promotional kits, lobby displays, hats, bags, and buttons from many of John's films. I could have dubbed my office Bob's Candy Shoppe. The *Uncle Buck* kit included pancake mix, a spatula, oven mitt, and apron, devised for the sake of nudging media scribes and critics to write and speak about this latest product. I read and organized thousands of autograph requests sent in by fans and by collectors who were trying to make a different uncle buck. I noticed that most of the mail was from the U.S. Midwest, Australia, and Germany. John always took an interest in the return addresses and dutifully signed every request himself—either a still from a film (predominantly *Stripes, The Great Outdoors,* or *Planes, Trains and Automobiles*), his own headshot from the *Armed and Dangerous* period, or a new full-length shot from a Harry Langdon photo session, reminiscent of Carol Reed's *The Third Man* in its style and slightly skewed angle. I was the Frostbacks' gatekeeper nearly everyone had to talk to before reaching John. John, on the other hand, just had to yell down the hall to get my attention.

Saturday morning television programming has always been the provenance of children, and John wanted to participate in that, not only for the sake of his kids, Jennifer and Christopher, but also for the Frostbacks coffers via the swift-flowing revenue stream that sponsors for kid products produced. NBC was happy to work with John again after the *SCTV* days of the early '80s, so the network brought in two major animation houses, Saban and DiC, to work with Frostbacks to create a series called *Camp Candy*. The scripts revolved around themes of friendship, telling the truth, and the principles of right and wrong, topics John thought important for preteens. The light comedy also gave camp counselor John an opportunity to perform vocal work with mates like Eugene Levy, Dave Thomas, Valri Bromfield, and Bob Costas. The Frostbacks' sound studio was the weekly location for laughter and fun as vocal director Ginny McSwain led her cast through the pages, some of which were provided by the Beatles' *Yellow Submarine* cowriter Jack Mendelsohn. I became John's voice outside the studio. I read all the *Camp Candy* scripts, made notes and suggestions, kept John in the loop, and made sure he was pleased with the direction of the show. I was becoming his Neil Aspinall, the Beatles' right arm, the guy who wound up running their company, Apple. I was becoming the person I had always wanted to be. Instead of being the eyes and ears of everything good and bad regarding the Fab Four, I was working for the Fab One.

John continued his multimedia blitz with a syndicated radio show, *Radio Kandy*. Doug Thompson, a radiophile from Toronto, put that deal together. John would host a weekly two-hour program with guests and music that would air over three hundred stations across North America. Thompson produced, wrote, and directed the project, booking guest musicians like Clarence Clemens and Levon Helm.

So Frostbacks Production, employing ten people, served as Candy's tax shelter on movies while actually generating weekly television and radio product and revenue. The in-house recording studio was also rented out for commercials and creative endeavors like Rabbit Ears Radio, the children's storytelling company from Connecticut, which recorded John narrating "Stormalong" with music by NRBQ. Disney producer Thomas Schumacher moved in for weeks and recorded John as Wilbur the Albatross for *The Rescuers Down Under*. On any given day, the likes of Mel Gibson, Michael Keaton, Whoopi Goldberg, Elizabeth Taylor, or Harry Nilsson might walk through Frostbacks' front door headed for the recording studio.

One day it occurred to me that my steady employment meant the "A" publicist, Paul Flaherty, was on his way out. The youthful vibe at Frostbacks better suited Candy's personality. Except for Burrill, we were all under forty, with John being the oldest of us youngsters. After a round of golf Flaherty would often show up at Frostbacks to throw back a few while trying to capture an hour or two of Candy's time. The old duffer didn't bother with me anymore. He was a relic of the old studio system like those publicists I'd dealt with at Columbia, and his ship was sailing into the sunset.

There was no comparison necessary since I was performing his duties in addition to wearing multiple hats at the company. John recognized my value and, appropriately, gave me a raise. I brought enthusiasm to my work while becoming a set of rabbit ears to John's ups and downs, professionally and personally. It was at this time that he appeared in a spate of loser films like *Who's Harry Crumb?* and *Speed Zone*. John performed nobly and gladly accepted the multiplying zeroes on his paycheck to support his family in Los Angeles, a nonworking farm north of Toronto, and various relatives who needed a handout. His brother, Jim, two years older and unemployed, was set up in a small house in East York, Ontario, across the street from his and John's mother and aunt, ostensibly to keep an eye on them. John's father, Sidney, had died at thirty-five of a heart attack and John, since the age of five, had been variously playing the roles of son, brother, and breadwinner to his side of the family.

While my extended work and play schedule meant a nice salary bump, the downside of it was spending more and more time away from home and Kari, even when I was at Frostbacks' office in Los Angeles. Our workday and wind-down time usually translated into fifteen-hour days. Luckily, the after-work retreat was just down the hall. It was John's proudest creation, jokingly called the Frostbacks Bar and Grill, a place to unwind and meet with agents, hangers-on, L.A. Kings' players, and team executives as well as film and television personnel working on projects that often had Frostbacks' participation. John's accountant, Gary Kress, found a seventy-year-old curved mahogany bar, complete with brass footrests and glass shelving for bottles and drink ware in an old St. Louis joint gone bust that truly became the centerpiece of the Frostbacks' office space. There was a jukebox, pinball machines, air hockey, TV—it was the first modern man cave. When the day's work was finished we migrated to the bar where, with music blaring and Heinekens in hand, we watched the world go by on San Vicente Boulevard from behind our pub's one-way glass. It was John's infinitely superior rendition of Belushi and Aykroyd's Blues Brothers Bar from *Saturday Night Live* days. It was a place where he could fire up a Marlboro, enjoy a rum and Coke, and delay going home. He could play air guitar to a Rolling Stones tune, pretend he was Bob Costas announcing a sporting event, or recite Gary Oldman's dialogue as Sid Vicious in *Sid and Nancy*. It was John's personal playground, and he felt safe there.

I could feel the emotional pulls—Rose and the kids awaiting their dad and Kari expecting her husband. Many of the Frostbacks employees discovered it was difficult, if not impossible, to punch the clock at 6:00 and say, "Goodnight, see you tomorrow." Our jobs didn't work like that. At 11454 San Vicente Boulevard there was no 6:00. Our day was as long as John wanted or needed it to be, and that sometimes included time for the boss to have multiple drinks. John was never a sloppy drunk, and he always had the good sense to know that a celebrity under the influence can never drive. So the employees developed a rotation system whereby some would leave early and enjoy their own lives while others worked the late shift and drove the boss home. The next night, the dance cards would reverse. There often came a point in the evening when, the work, discussion, and analysis of the day completed and the imbibing dialed up to eleven, the fun and good cheer dissolved into babysitting. For my part, on most nights after a couple of beers, I was ready to say, "Good work, everybody. See you in the morning." We all wanted to go home. There wasn't anything else to do except consume more alcohol. For John's part, though, as much as he loved Rose and his kids, he was so used to being on the road and on his own that when he sat at the bar at Frostbacks, he could have been in Chicago, New York, or Toronto.

Now, my dad never corralled the horsepower of John Candy, but he did as much as he could with his own celebrity to make people feel good, forget their problems for a few minutes. In the '60s and '70s, he always showed up on telethons: Jerry Lewis's annual; fund-raisers for polio, arthritis, jock itch, you name it; channels 5, 9, 11, 13 in Los Angeles, answering phones, talking with the host, playing drums. He never turned down anybody asking for an autograph. He would stand in a dinner theater lobby and sign programs and photographs until every last customer was satisfied. But John Candy had real power; he was a "movie star."

To better illustrate the use of that high voltage there's this: I fielded a call from Sharon Monsky, founder of the Scleroderma Foundation. I had no idea what scleroderma was as I listened to Monsky make her pitch. Later in my research I found out that, put simply, scleroderma is a hardening of the skin and arteries. It breaks down and makes brittle all the body's soft tissue both internally and externally. Scleroderma was a medical mystery that needed wealth and publicity to help solve it. Monsky told me that the Scleroderma Foundation was hosting its annual golf tournament and dinner at a country club in South San Francisco in the coming weeks and would love to have John Candy's participation. A successful attorney, wife, and mother of two young kids in her midthirties, Monsky never mentioned in our conversation that she herself was suffering from scleroderma's debilitating effects. I asked her for some written information to show John. I thanked her for her work and congratulated her on being the bellwether for an enormously tough uphill battle.

John would often decline an interview or appearance that I would have bet money was a sure thing, like an interview with NBC's Maria Shriver. Then he would turn around and approve an invitation that was problematic to attend due to time or travel constraints. The Scleroderma Foundation event was such an occasion—as I reminded him, he was scheduled to be in Toronto for an appearance, followed by downtime at his farm. But the plight of this young, sturdy woman who was making a stand for a cause appealed to John. He had been raised by a grounded single mother who stood up to the world. "No problem," he said, dismissing the scheduling conflict. We would cut the farm R & R and swing by San Francisco on the way back to Los Angeles.

John was a left-handed golfer. He didn't hit long but he hit straight, and he spent an enjoyable afternoon with the likes of Willie Mays (I loved watching John watch the "Say Hey Kid" in awe), Willie McCovey, and other retired greats of the Giants baseball team as well as an impressive lineup of 49ers football players and other local celebrities and politicians. All were drawn there by Sharon Monsky's conviction and positivism.

After the golf, the first notable whom Monsky wanted to greet was John. When I saw her approach, my jaw dropped. She was almost unrecognizable from the photographs we had seen earlier, which had shown her as the young beauty she was before scleroderma's ravages. She had become skeletal, her skin stretched to the max, her lips pulled into a frightful rictus. It was not easy to look at her face without feeling her pain. She was slight as a dandelion, obviously in pain, and had almost no movement in her face. Speaking was a chore. Her one facial expression was of fright. The hundred-pound Monsky walked right up to John and disappeared into his three-hundred-pound hug. The world was right and safe for that moment.

A segment producer for the television program *PM Magazine* sidled up to me with a request for an interview with John. I took John aside and relayed the request. "Fine. I'll do it with Sharon," he said. When I conveyed the good news to the producer, her face took on a pain of its own. No penny needed for her thoughts. She glanced at John and Sharon, undoubtedly wondering how she was going to sell this to her executive producer.

The new best friends were led into a nearby sitting room with a sofa and chairs. The segment producer immediately tried to separate them, placing John on the couch solo and Sharon in a chair, conveniently out of the shot. John Candy had invisible sensors. He was a satellite dish listening to what was going on behind him, in front of him, to the side of him. He heard every conversation in the room, paying special attention to the segment producer talking with her sound and camera crew. John knew one thing for sure; he was there for Sharon Monsky and scleroderma, not for any publicity for himself. At first he watched quietly as the segment producer tried to position Sharon out of the television screen frame, out of the room, out of the building. Finally, John announced firmly, "No, that's not how it works. Sharon sits next to me on this couch or I don't do it."

I watched the panicked exchange of looks between the segment producer and her cameraman as if to say, "How are we going to show this?" John knew showing it was exactly the point. It was why everyone had schlepped to the South San Francisco event in the first place. The room got very quiet.

The producer's call was simple: Candy or no Candy? Segment or no segment? John didn't care. Of course the *PM Magazine* team acquiesced. I stood still and fought back tears as I witnessed the power of celebritydom at its best and most effective. *PM Magazine* would promote the hell out of its exclusive interview with funnyman John Candy, but because Sharon was practically sitting on his lap, there was no way the camera could shoot around her, and John knew it. Sharon's lipless, ravaged face was in every shot as the program was broadcast into living rooms across North America. John at first attempted to speak about scleroderma, but then just graciously turned it over to the expert, founder of the foundation, and sufferer of scleroderma, Sharon Monsky.

This moment was worth all the hours of babysitting John during late nights at Frostback. I was intensely proud of him. If they gave Oscars for humanity, John would have a shelf full of them.

32

John, John, Jack, and Johnny, 1990–1991

The closest John Candy ever got to an Academy Award was handing one out in 1990.* Bruce Vilanch and his staff of edgy writers came up with the idea of Candy presenting the Best Live Action Short Film. A big fat man presenting an award in the shorts category? Funny stuff, no? John, instinctively, sidestepped that bomb of a joke and said he would present with former *SCTV* mate Rick Moranis, who was also to be on the telecast. He had just starred in the remake of *The Little Shop of Horrors*. Working together created a comfort zone for both Candy and Moranis; they shared a shorthand whereby each knew exactly what they were going to do, starting with the rewrite of the inane patter provided them by Vilanch and company.

That Oscar broadcast, hosted for the first time by Billy Crystal, was scheduled for a Monday. The rehearsal spanned the preceding weekend. All presenters and talent went through their motions for a few minutes as they found their marks and read the half-witty TelePrompTer–provided repartee. John and Rick had rehearsed and run lines a million times for *SCTV* so this practice session was standard stuff. They did their shtick a couple of times and knew without nervousness that the next time would be on Monday night, live in front of a billion people worldwide.

After the run-through John needed a Marlboro. As we approached the exit door, we heard a cry of "Hey, Johnny!" echo down the hallway. It sounded so like Jack Nicholson's character Jack Torrance saying, "Heeeere's Johnny" in *The Shining* that I started to laugh. We stopped,

---

*Although he won Emmys in 1982 and 1983 for "Outstanding Writing in a Variety or Music Program" for *SCTV*.

turned, and watched in amazement as Nicholson himself and Warren Beatty rapidly caught up with us. They were presenting the Best Picture award that year. John, Jack, and Warren shook hands and made small talk—"How have you been?" "What are you presenting?" The four of us stood in a circle, though I was given neither an introduction nor a hand-shake. I was invisible, having a Fellini Excursion all by myself. Jack gave his full attention to John, never once looking in my direction, which was incredible, really, since Chris Fryer and I had spent many hours in the intimacy of his living room talking about film and creating the first ever book about him.

I smiled to myself, hoping my dad, wherever he was, was tuned in to this bizarre quartet, though he was probably still trying to figure out why his son and Fryer chose Nicholson over Jack Lemmon or Gig Young. My dad's own close encounter with Jack Nicholson happened when he, Patti, and I had attended the opening of the Palm West Hollywood in 1976. I spotted Jack and his then girlfriend, Anjelica Huston, come in, and I went over to say hello. The Nicholson book had just been published the year before. We exchanged pleasantries, but the crowded restaurant and Nicholson's handler didn't permit my calling my dad over for an intro-duction. I would have loved seeing the interaction between Colonel Hogan and Billy "Bad Ass" Buddusky.

Returning to the tableau of the moment, I panned left to right: Candy, Nicholson (facing me), and Beatty, who impressed me with his height, at least six two, on my right. Beatty was literally looking down his nose at me, trying to figure out who the hell I was and why the hell I was sharing the same oxygen with greatness. His stare made me feel as if I were some kind of smear on a laboratory slide. Jack's eyes never met mine. The three pros cracked jokes and were having one hell of a time. John was so caught up in the moment it never occurred to him to intro-duce his publicist. Frankly, I was enjoying my cloak of invisibility. Both Jack and Warren were charming to John. I was impressed that Jack had called out to John in the first place. I wondered what was his favorite John Candy film and if Beatty had ever even seen a John Candy film. The three of them had certainly never spent time together before, but the actors' club was in session. I, not being a member of that elite club, was relegated to the sidelines, but I was satisfied with my dugout box seat. The thespians shook hands, said good-bye, and John finally got to have his cigarette.

When game day arrived, John didn't feel comfortable walking the Red Carpet. He didn't want to pull up in a limousine in front of the Dorothy Chandler Pavilion and make small talk with Mary Hart of *Entertainment Tonight* or tell Joan Rivers whose tux he was wearing or kibbutz with decorated stars and producers who, he felt, would be asking themselves, "What is Candy doing here?" John just wanted to do his thing with Moranis and beat it out of there. So he decided no limo, no Red Carpet. We were going commando through the loading dock. John wore his tuxedo because all male presenters and indeed any male backstage (including all the television personnel) had to wear one. I was also suitably attired: "Yes, Joan, I'm wearing a Gary's rent-a-tux." We found an exit door that John could crack open to have a smoke while he waited for a stage manager to take him to the green room. John and Chevy Chase, Dan Aykroyd, Steve Martin, Tom Hanks, Daryl Hannah, Robert De Niro, and Martin Scorsese all swapped small talk as they headed toward the stage. The call came for Moranis and Candy. They got a couple of laughs, and the whole megillah was over in three and a half minutes. *Work Experience,* produced by James Hendrie, won Best Live Action Short. Backstage, Rick and John said their farewells. I walked with John back through the Dorothy Chandler Pavilion loading dock, jumped in the idling town car, and lit out for the territories. We sped down Interstate 10 to the Frostbacks office, where I swapped horses and hightailed it to the Valley. Kari was still watching the broadcast as I walked in the front door, dressed to the eight and a halfs. John and I had spent an hour backstage, then traveled halfway across Los Angeles, and I had still gotten home with over an hour of airtime left. Crystal was hilarious in his debut.

In many instances, John took on roles for all the wrong reasons. Sometimes, I think, he didn't even bother reading the script. *Delirious* was a perfect example. He trusted the director (and script doctor), Tom Mankiewicz, to overcome a mediocre text by Fred Freeman and Lawrence Cohen through sheer energy and will. The script had made the rounds in Hollywood for years, and the studio involved was MGM, a mere shell of what it had been in its glory days. That said, John thought Mankiewicz was smart, and costars Emma Samms and Mariel Hemingway were beautiful and delightful, respectively. Stir those elements with the chance to work with a legend like Raymond Burr and comedy actors Charlie Rocket and David Rasche and voilà, all systems go. In fact, it was a love-in for everyone involved for the three months of filming, which included an on-

Delirious set: Robert Stevens (partially hidden), Robert Crane, John Candy, and Tom Mankiewicz, West Fifty-seventh Street, New York, 1990 (courtesy of MGM; author's collection).

set visit in New York City by Tom's father, Oscar-winning writer/director Joseph L. Mankiewicz. There was constant laughter on set, and Tom told wonderful stories of the film business everyday after the wrap. Drinks were poured, cigarettes lit. No one wanted to go home. It was the best time John ever had on a set, but he was deflated by the film's eventual lackluster release by a bankrupt studio. John even made an offer to MGM to pay for the film's promotional posters, but CEO Alan Ladd Jr. told John to save his money because he couldn't guarantee his contribution would be spent for that purpose.

John worked with fellow Second City alumnus Dan Aykroyd in Steven Spielberg's first bomb, *1941,* John Landis's *The Blues Brothers,* and the perennial cable television favorite *The Great Outdoors,* which Annette Bening no doubt wishes she could remove from her distinguished résumé. When Aykroyd called John asking for a big favor, Candy's automatic response was, "When and where?" Again, John didn't bother to actually read the many-drafted "Valkenvania." He simply wanted to lend a hand with friend Dan's directorial debut. He joined Chevy Chase, Demi Moore, and Aykroyd in the cast, taking on dual roles as a brother and sister.* The shoot was interminable, the budget bloated to $40 million, Chevy intentionally farted in front of the cast and crew, and Demi sulked. Aykroyd was overwhelmed, and John was busting his ass with constant wardrobe, hair, makeup, and gender changes. John Hughes and Tom Mankiewicz visited the set with script inserts and practical ideas like doing away with the playback monitors for each actor, which promoted the notion that everyone was the director. Someone at Warner Brothers sadistically renamed the film *Nothing but Trouble,* and when it was finally released, it was skewered by critics and roasted to cinders. Aykroyd never called John for another favor.

John Candy's friendship and working relationship with John Hughes was different, however, and did pay dividends. Hughes was producing and Chris Columbus was writing and directing a dramedy for 20th Century Fox called *Only the Lonely.* It was an opportunity for Candy to work again with wunderkind Columbus after their twenty-two-hour marathon shoot on *Home Alone.* John had taken the Screen Actors Guild minimum for that extended day's work, turning down Hughes's offer of 1 percent of the gross. John never attached a price tag to a favor. *Home Alone* became the highest-grossing comedy ever at that time, with over $500 million in the till. Fox, Hughes, and Columbus knew they owed John a $5 million dollar favor. I read the beautifully written original screenplay by Columbus. Hughes Entertainment cast Anthony Quinn, Jim Belushi, and Bert Remsen in supporting roles, with Ally Sheedy as the love interest, and topped it all off with Maureen O'Hara, who came out of a twenty-year retirement to play John's bigoted mother. O'Hara, who was both John Wayne and John Ford's favorite actress, represented everything about movies that Candy loved—a sassy, funny, beautiful legend of the silver screen who was as quick and clever as he was.

The first day on the set, John found his doublewide, a movie star trailer that expanded to almost the size of my house, but he also found a problem: Maureen O'Hara had been tucked into a pitiful little dressing room that was normally used by a day player, not a living, breathing film icon. John thought it was insulting and imploded. There were no histrionics, just John politely knocking on Ms. O'Hara's tiny trailer door.

---

*John was nominated for a 1992 Razzie award for Worst Supporting Actress for his efforts.

"Hi, John," said Ms. O'Hara cheerfully, as she pulled the tinny hatch open. She was excited about working with him.

"Maureen, you're taking my trailer. Get your stuff out," John said sternly but with great respect.

The Chongos went to work, switching out Candy's clothing and duffle bags with Ms. O'Hara's wardrobe and makeup. Ms. O'Hara didn't know what had hit her, but she enjoyed her new digs. John, on the other hand, looked like André the Giant sitting inside a walnut shell.

John knew only too well how the show business chess game was played. He dealt with nonverbal insults, false promises, and flat-out lies from producers, assistant directors, production assistants, and production managers, who always played on the side of the cheap better than anyone. He knew they figured they were going to save a little money, and what the hell, Maureen O'Hara had been away from films for such a long time she wouldn't know the difference between a doublewide and a double espresso. So instead of going to the production office and throwing some kind of star tantrum, John very quietly took care of what he saw as a problem by himself. When people in the front office heard what their star had done, they went into freak-out mode. Within an hour another doublewide was pulled up next to Miss O'Hara's. The Chongos then moved John's gear for the second time that day. Checkmate.

Like millions of other late-night television viewers, John was a huge fan of Johnny Carson, but he was so intimidated by Carson that he'd never been on his show. 20th Century Fox persuaded John to make his only *Tonight Show* appearance escorting Maureen O'Hara on behalf of *Only the Lonely.* Surprisingly for an actor who had attended major award shows, met and done business with sports and Hollywood legends, John was a nervous wreck. He paced backstage at NBC Burbank, muttering to himself that appearing with Letterman was easy—Letterman was a goof. But Carson, the King of Late Night? John felt unworthy. For all his bluster and assuredness, the thought of sharing a stage with Johnny Carson turned him to jelly, the armpits of his shirt soaked through, which was odd because John, like my dad, never perspired. His brain was firing escape plots at warp speed, which included one where he would sneak down the hallway, go out the exit into his black Mercedes sedan, and disappear into the night. I reminded him that it was too late to be Houdini, and besides, he couldn't let Maureen O'Hara down, could he?

Doc Severinsen and the *Tonight Show* orchestra played the costars on, Carson guiding Ms. O'Hara to the freestanding chair closest to his desk. John relaxed a bit, a pressure valve opened by sharing the couch with Ed McMahon. Ms. O'Hara laughed easily and graciously as Carson made it clear that he considered her one of the great actresses of film and an idol of a bygone era. John mumbled a few partial answers to Carson, only too glad to throw it back to the lovefest happening between the film and television legends. Ed told John how much he had enjoyed meeting him. John, for his part, never wore that shirt again.

Unfortunately, *Only the Lonely* was one of the few ventures in which Hughes and Columbus stubbed their toes. The film was released in May, even though it was a fall picture, and did only fair box office business. It did, however, represent the first time John really looked like a star and leading man onscreen.

One morning in the midst of a busy year for John, in which he filmed *Home Alone, Delirious, Nothing but Trouble,* and *Only the Lonely,* and while also hosting his weekly syndicated radio program, *Radio Kandy,* and supplying the voice of camp counselor John for NBC's Saturday morning animated series *Camp Candy,* we sat in John's office going through the mail stacked atop the well-worn trunk used by his character Del Griffith in *Planes, Trains and Automobiles.* As usual I was prodding him to respond to requests for autographed photographs when an envelope from Universal Studios caught his eye. He opened it with the serene expression of the Cheshire Cat and sniffed at the innards. "Mmmmmm," he purred. "I love the smell of surrender in the morning."

John handed me the contents of the envelope. It was a check. It was a check from Universal Studios. It was a check from Universal Studios signaling that its chief executives Lew Wasserman and Sid Sheinberg and their raft of lawyers and accountants had given in, finally admitting that *Uncle Buck* had turned a profit. The pencil-pushing, ledger-thumping suits in the Black Tower of the Universal lot had waited as long as they possibly could to issue the check before John's pit bull Century City attorney, Skip Brittenham, unleashed enough special effects for another Universal Studios Tour ride. The cause of John's delight, the reason this would be a beautiful day in Brentwood, was his profit participation—a percentage of the net profits—from the exploits of every family's nightmare relative, Uncle Buck. I knew everything would be good for at least the rest of the afternoon. It was a check for the largest amount of money I'd ever seen: half a million dollars. "Pretty nice," I said with a smile.

"Well, that's as good as waving a white flag from the Black Tower," John said gleefully. He was pleased with his victory in *Man v. Universal Bean Counters*, and I was happy he chose to share that pleasure with me.

"Lunch is on you," I said.

33

Murder Cases Never Close, 1991

In June 1991, I received a telephone call from Maricopa County investigator Jim Raines asking about my awareness of "an eight-millimeter camera and tripod that was owned by the victim." In 1978, eight millimeter meant film, not video, and I told Raines about my dad's various video cameras and recorders but also that he hadn't used movie film, to my knowledge, since we had produced our home movie classic, *I Was a Teenager for the FBI*, in the '60s or, perhaps, at my sisters' high school graduations in the '70s. I told Raines about his Nikon still camera as well as his Polaroid. I explained that in my possession were a three-quarter-inch videocassette recorder and monitor that I had secured from the apartment I shared with "the victim." Patti had everything else.

Two months later, in the midst of another scorching Phoenix summer, Maricopa County district attorney Romley announced to the local press that within the next "three or four months, we will either have someone or say there isn't enough evidence to go on." Romley continued that his panel of reviewers had spent the previous few months surveying evidence, including interviews with subjects who had observed my dad and Carpenter having an argument at a night spot just days before the murder, and established "a couple of pieces of significant information" that could be heading toward an arrest. "John Carpenter is still the prime suspect, as far as I know, unless somebody has come up with something else," said Romley. Even if there were no arrest at this time, Romley assured the public that the case would not be closed because "murder cases are never closed."

Gary Fleischman in Beverly Hills jumped into the fray on behalf of his client Carpenter: "They're barking up the wrong tree since day one with John Carpenter," Fleischman said, repeating his client's long-standing denial of wrongdoing.

Richard Romley had assumed control of the Maricopa County district attorney's chair in 1989, but with ongoing media criticism of what was so plainly an inept investigation at an all-time high, the heat on the "new" discovery team was ratcheted up. The *Arizona Republic* and the *Los Angeles Times* lavished scores of column inches retracing the developments over the past decade while soliciting remarks from Fleischman and Carpenter, who continued to maintain that Carpenter had been made a scapegoat for the Scottsdale Police Department's shoddy work.

34

Planes, Cars, and Roller Coasters, 1991

In 1991, Kari developed a rash that resembled sandpaper on an area three inches long by two inches wide at the top of her forehead just past her hairline and into her scalp. We both inspected the peculiar-looking eruption and figured it was some kind of dermatological problem, a bodily backlash to all the chemo and radiation she had endured. We went to the dermatologist who, upon examination and review of Kari's chart, said very sympathetically, "This isn't a dermatological matter. I wish it were. You've got to see your oncologist."

Kari and I were immediately choked with fear. The Breast Center got her in quickly and did a biopsy. We waited. The next day the call came from Kari's oncologist. He wanted to see her as soon as possible. The air was sucked out of our house. We were boarding the roller coaster again.

Later that afternoon, we stood with the oncologist. "This is cancer, I'm afraid."

I looked at Kari, who drifted into an unfocused gaze then caught herself and concentrated on the doctor. Another surgical procedure would be performed—a scraping of the scalp where the cancer had surfaced. The roller coaster jerked as it built up speed. Kari and I were holding on again for dear life.

No sooner had the procedure been successfully executed than Kari developed pulmonary edema, which caused her great difficulty in breathing. We could both hear the wheezing in her lungs. Kari said she felt like she was trying to breathe through a water-filled snorkel. We made another visit to the Breast Center, and I watched as a physician delicately punctured her skin with a ten-inch needle, entering through her back and working the needle into her left lung. A viscous fluid made its way out into a plastic bag, allowing Kari to feel almost instant relief. She gave me a little smile, but we both knew this episode was not a good omen.

Kari started chemo and radiation again, with a renewed resolve to endure the full regimen. I didn't know which was harder for her—cancer's return or surrendering control of her life. Weekends were again designated for camping out in the bathroom, but Kari had set her mind on obliterating the errant cells this time around. Her beautiful thick hair began falling like dandelion seeds, and her spirit also seemed to be cast adrift.

Kari became a student of New Age remedial alternatives, homeopathic medicines, cures, potions, lotions, and juices. She went to a Native American sweat lodge in Lancaster one weekend. That was followed by a visit to a curative diet clinic and health spa in San Diego. Kari had embarked on a body makeover, using diet, mega vitamin doses, and macrobiotics. I spent a lot of time praying—to Jesus and Allah and Yahweh and Buddha and Krishna, shooting stars, lucky pennies—to anything and everything that may have the power to control the universe, or at least some diabolical cells in Kari's body. I was just throwing up a Hail Mary pass and hoping something caught that sucker in the end zone.

I am a skeptic by nature, but I am especially leery when it comes to nontraditional, non-Western medicine. I don't know much about it, and I don't trust any so-called experts. They're all snake oil salesmen to me, and even Kari's friend Linda, who was all for chanting and incense, thought the San Diego adventure would be a waste of time and money. But Kari wanted to do it, and if Kari wanted it, I was going to get it for her. If any of it could help, then great, as long as it couldn't do any harm.

She went through the program and her always-conscientious diet was now even more refined with the addition of rounds of vitamin shots, oral vitamins, rectal vitamins, pills, juices, seaweed concoctions, you name it. None of these curatives kept her left lung from refilling with fluid, and her gurgling snorkel returned. So it was back to the world of real medicine to have the lung drained again, which stemmed her bubbling wheeze. I could only imagine how awful that lack of oxygen felt. All I could compare it to was my own experience as an inept snorkeler whose misadventures ended in coughing, choking fits as I tried to get a good part of the ocean out of my lungs. Still, not much of a comparison.

While Kari's medical issues continued, I was juggling my full-time jobs as husband, support, and driver for Kari with in-house publicist and handler for John Candy. For the first time in our lives together we were unencumbered financially, but now we were overwhelmed emotionally.

John was set to do a new ensemble comedy called *Once upon a Crime* for the financially crippled MGM. It was going to be shot at the world-famous Cinecitta Studio in Rome. Over the decades, its soundstages had been graced by the likes of Fellini, Bertolucci, and Visconti, just to name a few. William Wyler had shot *Ben-Hur* there, and Joe Mankiewicz had settled in on the lot for years making *Cleopatra*. Presently, it was the studio of choice for veteran producer Dino DeLaurentiis and his rookie director Eugene Levy, Candy's fellow *SCTV* alum.

My job was to accompany John to Rome. We boarded the Alitalia 747 out of LAX and had the entire first-class section in the upper deck to ourselves. I was laughing at John's stories and sipping champagne, but I was thinking about my wife being ferried to chemo by her mother, Loretta.

When we landed at Roma-Fiumicino airport, we cleared customs, walked past Italian soldiers toting machine guns to a waiting curbside limousine, and navigated the wild Roman traffic to the Hotel Hassler, located above the Spanish Steps. As we settled in, I thought, my god, I'm in Rome. It could be like *Roman Holiday*. I was excited—thrilled, really—to be in this beautiful place. The only problem was that my princess, unlike Gregory Peck's, was in Los Angeles, probably heaving her guts out at that very moment. I felt unrelentingly guilty for even being there.

My days were spent solving minor problems for John, walking the grounds of Cinecitta, watching John, Ornella Muti, Jim Belushi, and Cybill Shepherd film an absolutely witless Charles Shyer/Nancy Meyers script. I ate pasta and drank wine for lunch, and fell asleep at 3:00 in the afternoon. I talked to Kari every night when it was morning in Los Angeles. I felt like I was a million miles away from her. It felt so wrong to be in Italy having an almost good time while she was in California going through hell.

At the end of our second week away, I was sitting with John on his patio overlooking Rome. The burnt-orange glow of the city was breathtaking. I explained my guilty feelings to John. I was in a total quandary: working for him, making my money, but at the same time wanting desperately to be by my wife's side. His powers of observation had already informed him that Crane hadn't been behaving like Crane over the past two weeks. John stopped me as I fumbled for the right words to explain my dilemma. "You're out of here," he said. "You can't be in two places at once and being with Kari is more important right now." He knew the making of a silly movie was way down the priority list. Human beings were always the first of Candy's Commandments. "Get on the next flight. You're covered here," John said, wrapping me in a bear hug.

The next morning, feeling guilty about leaving my responsibilities (I couldn't win) and already missing Rome, I caught a ride with a production driver to the airport. I had missed one of Kari's chemo treatments, and I didn't want to be absent for another. I needed to be with her, driving her, taking care of her.

Back in Los Angeles, I spent time with Kari and took care of Candy business at the office. After weeks of blood work, checkups, and chemo, Kari announced that she was at a point where the worst was behind her. She had the routine down. Her mother and sister would alternate shifts helping her. She knew I was torn, wanting to be with her and wanting to be with John in Rome. "I'll be okay," she said, her tired eyes watching me as she made her pitch. "You only have two more weeks on the movie. Go and enjoy Rome. I'm feeling better. In fact, I'm going to work on our script while you're gone."

I was happy to hear that Kari was going to write again. She had taken short story–writing classes at our local city college, and she had a knack for crisp, economical dialogue. Over a decade earlier, Chris Fryer and I had written the first draft of a film script entitled "Easy Money," about a poor slob who takes himself hostage to get out of his unhappy marriage. I wrote another few drafts over the years. Then Kari became interested and we worked on it, together and separately, and the script became "Suburbia Blues," a Sidney Lumetesque drama with humor, a *Dog Day Afternoon*–flavored piece. The fact that she felt well enough to write, or at least said she did, convinced me I could return to Italy to help John as he wrapped up his work on the film.

The highlight of those two weeks had nothing really to do with the film, just an evening at dinner with John and a group of people from the cast, including Lina Wertmuller's favorite, Giancarlo Giannini. I was living my version of *La Dolce Vita*.

Out of the blue, while John was filming *Once upon a Crime,* aka "Troublemakers," aka "Criminals" in Italy, his legend-worthy longtime agent, John Gaines of Agency for the Performing Arts, fielded a call from Ixtlan Productions' A. Kitman Ho asking about Candy's availability in

June for an Oliver Stone project called *JFK* being shot in New Orleans. An inquiry for a project like this was so far removed from the usual kind of John Hughes, Dan Aykroyd, Chevy Chase, or Jim Belushi vehicle that landed on John's desk that he said yes without even seeing a script. It was a serious, important film involving an Academy Award–winning writer/director who wanted to do a bit of stunt casting by using funnyman Candy in a straight role opposite Kevin Costner and Gary Oldman. John was shaken by the opportunity. He liked Stone's work, particularly *Platoon*. The idea of sharing a credit crawl with a star-studded cast that also included Sissy Spacek, Ed Asner, Jack Lemmon, Walter Matthau, Joe Pesci, and Tommy Lee Jones validated all John's acting aspirations.

I had been to New Orleans several times, the first time accompanying my dad and Patti in the mid-'70s, then with John during Mardi Gras 1984, and with Dave Thomas during Mardi Gras 1986. John and I checked into the Windsor Court Hotel off Canal Street a few blocks from the Mississippi River.

We stayed focused on John's big scene with Costner, where John's character, the New Orleans bottom feeder Dean Andrews, who knows all the wrong people, has lunch with Costner's character, local attorney Jim Garrison, who is in charge of the definitive report on the assassination of John Kennedy. The scene was eight solid pages of dialogue. There was no partying for John on this trip. He was in his dedicated actor mode. Over the course of three days, we ran the dialogue a hundred times, John as Andrews, me as Garrison. During the first day of our rehearsals in a secure conference room at the five-star hotel, a cold sore resembling Mount St. Helens broke out near John's mouth. I felt really bad for him as I tried to keep the cheerleader aspect of my job alive. Although John would appear onscreen only for a few minutes, this was an important job for him. It was arguably the most prestigious production of which he had ever been a part. He was working beside Oscar-winning filmmakers Costner and Stone, not Bobcat Goldthwait. These were A-listers, and John wanted to prove to all of them, Costner, Stone, Warner Brothers, and the moviegoing public, that he was a much better actor than most of the material he had appeared in. In the meantime, the cold sore had doubled in size, and I bought bags of creams and ointments in an attempt to mitigate the burgeoning volcano on John's lip. And poor me, I was jonesing for a beignet from Café du Monde.

As a warm-up to John's big scene with Costner, one afternoon John was called out to a courthouse in town where his character, Dean Andrews, was on the witness stand being questioned by Costner as Garrison. This was just a brief scene—half a script page—but a nice way for John and Costner to meet.

The schedule was fluid because the temperamental New Orleans weather continually caused shooting changes. The exterior scenes would have to be scrubbed because of rain, and as a result of one such cloudburst, John's interior shoot came up at the last minute.

John went into makeup, and the crack team went into high gear camouflaging the Etna on his lip. We picked up a vibe that the set was tense at the moment because of a verbal skirmish between Stone and Tommy Lee Jones. It was whispered that director Stone had to remind Mr. Jones how many Oscars he had on his mantelpiece. So into that atmosphere walked Mr. Candy, who possessed no Oscars, but did have something almost as big ready to explode on his face.

Stone shot the scene in a few short takes. He knew he had a great script (by Zachary Sklar and himself), a fine cinematographer in Robert Richardson, and the ace editing team of Joe Hutshing and Pietro Scalia. John's scene was finished in no time, and he was placed on call for the next day for his eight-page restaurant scene, subject to the weather report, of course.

I watched John immediately relax, having gotten his toes wet, cracking the seal on his participation in this big studio Christmas release. Even his facial eruption started to retreat. We retired to the hotel, John and I having cocktails for the first time in a few days. We read through the restaurant scene dialogue a dozen more times.

The next morning, with New Orleans anticipating a considerable amount of rain, the production moved indoors for John's star turn. The scene between Dean Andrews and Jim Garrison took place during lunch at a French Quarter restaurant, the actors facing each other, spewing their pages and pages of dialogue as they devoured a platter of crab. John lit a cigarette and pretended to imbibe. Stone and his actors rehearsed the scene a few times and were ready to try a take. I positioned myself directly behind Stone who, like most contemporary directors, faced a video monitor and wore a headset. I was excited for John, rooting for him to do well, and interested to watch and hear Costner, a real actor, perform the part of Jim Garrison, though I have to say the real Garrison would have been pleased by all the nuances I had brought to the role back in the hotel conference room over the previous several days.

During the many takes John and Costner kept pushing the scene, making each other better with each ensuing take. The rapid-fire dialogue was covered in a variety of camera angles—stationary and handheld, close-up and extreme close-up, though not too close on John's lip. As the crew readied for yet another take, I was so focused I stepped closer to the video monitor, my head positioned just above and behind Stone's left shoulder. Suddenly, Stone spun around, looking past me, and exclaimed to all set workers and watchers, "I hate when people look over my shoulder!"

I, of course, spun around as well, looking behind me, trying to locate the asshole who was interrupting the maestro's train of thought. L'asshole, c'est moi.

I snuck a look at the always-aware-of-his-surroundings Candy, who was convulsing with laughter at my miscue. Even filming the heaviest scene of his career, John could appreciate me gettin' blowed up real good in front of a hundred dedicated artistes. Having a clown on set is always a good tension destroyer. I always enjoyed making John laugh because, of course, most of the time he was in charge of the laughter department. I backed slowly away from Stone and never again even looked him in the eye.

Later, between camera setups, I felt someone sidle up to me. I glanced over. It was Kevin Costner. He was sucking on the pipe his character carries through most of the film. "So, what do you think?" he asked, sotto voce.

I studied his face. "About what?"

There was a prolonged silence. I waited.

"The scene," Costner clarified.

"Oh, the scene. Yeah, the scene."

Costner waited.

"Are you kidding?" I asked, looking around to see whether Stone was nearby. "It's terrific. You guys are doing a great job."

Costner nodded as he was called back to the set. That was the first and last time I ever spoke with him. Later, I told John about my encounter and facetiously described how Costner, by consulting me, obviously felt my opinion ranked with the likes of Pauline Kael and Siskel and Ebert. John and I shared a good laugh.

A few weeks later, John was called back to New Orleans to film a short interior scene with Tommy Lee Jones and one of John's favorite actors, Gary Oldman, who was playing Lee Harvey Oswald. Over the years, John had watched his laser disc copy of the cult classic *Sid and Nancy*, with Oldman playing punk rocker Sid Vicious, at least a dozen times. He'd marveled at Oldman's performance, and now he found himself working with him, albeit in only another half-page scene.

When shooting began, Stone took less than an hour to get what he wanted from John and company. He signaled the end of John's participation on the project by thanking him for his work on the film. John shook hands with the cranky Tommy Lee Jones and with Oldman, who mentioned he had a week off and was headed to Los Angeles. John said that he was headed there as well and suggested Oldman travel as his guest on the private jet hired for the trip.

I sat quietly in the back of the plane watching Oldman and Candy, long-standing members of the actors' club, become fast friends with each refill of their Waterford crystal glasses. They sat side by side in the empty (except for me) Gulfstream. Oldman was making short work of the Scotch, while John had his usual rum and Cokes. The hours flew by, so to speak. With the alcohol on continuous flow, as we neared Los Angeles Gary and John had formulated a plan to create a production company for serious films and live Shakespeare in the park, with John as Falstaff and Gary doing Macbeth. Alas, Uncle Buck and Sid Vicious no more forever!

After we landed at Van Nuys Airport, the new best friends were poured into their respective limousines and headed off, each in his own direction, into the Southern California summer night. John never saw or spoke to Gary Oldman again.

In addition to his full schedule as movie star, John added a new role as a minority co-owner, along with hockey great Wayne Gretzky and L.A. Kings' king Bruce McNall, of the Toronto Argonauts, his hometown's Canadian Football League team. Aside from his million-dollar investment in the team, John took it upon himself to promote and resuscitate the ailing CFL, which boasted eight clubs, two of them unimaginatively nicknamed Roughriders. John made personal appearances across Canada from Vancouver to Ottawa. His investment of time and legwork began to pay off. Attendance at CFL games picked up ("Hey, there's Uncle Buck!"), and aside from an occasional D battery hurled his way, the self-styled CFL ambassador felt like a kid again.

During the middle week between Kari's chemo installments, the "normal" week, if Kari had the strength and felt well enough, she would join John and me in Winnipeg or Calgary or Toronto. But for the first and third weeks of the cycle, she was benched. So while I was in Regina or Edmonton holding John's hand, I had very mixed feelings. I was away from my ailing wife, but I was holding down the fort financially. My employment with John freed Kari from working unless she wanted to. The downside was the many days we spent apart. At least Kari never called me a failure again.

Canadian football consumed the rest of 1991. John was enjoying his role as CFL ambassador. It was a Cinderella year for his Argonauts. They went on to win the Grey Cup, the Great White North's version of the Super Bowl's Lombardi Trophy. John seemed to make his million-dollar investment back many fold in terms of fan excitement and the smiles he generated on the faces of locals, who enjoyed John's presence at all the games.

It was also in 1991 that John left his agent, John Gaines, and APA, and hitched his wagon to another Hollywood icon, former Rat Pack publicist turned agent Guy McElwaine at ICM.

With *Camp Candy* canceled and *Radio Kandy*'s plug pulled after proving to be an expensive hobby for John, Frostbacks' employees began to fall by the wayside. The few of us who remained metaphorically set up sandbags in the Frostbacks Bar and Grill, trying to protect our leader while watching for friend or foe to enter through the main doors. Mostly we watched McElwaine, on his way home from somewhere, draining the bar's beverages with John, weaving tales of Old Hollywood, promising work, and delivering none.

35

Just a Speck, 1992

On May 29, 1992, deputy county attorney Myrna J. Parker, one of Richard Romley's top lieutenants, filed a complaint signed by Judge David R. Cole of Maricopa County Superior Court charging John Henry Carpenter with first-degree murder. The trigger for the indictment was the photographs of Carpenter's rental car's interior passenger door. These, long forgotten by police, investigators, and prosecutors until Jim Raines rescued them from a county courthouse storage room, provided medical experts in Texas and New Mexico with a glimpse of a one-sixteenth-inch speck of human tissue that they determined to be brain matter.

At 6:10 a.m. on Monday, June 1, 1992, Carpenter was arrested in Carson, California, on his way to work and held without bail at a downtown Los Angeles jail. Later that morning, Romley announced, "We will be presenting some new evidence that maybe [Hyder and Collins] did not have the opportunity to present." Carpenter's attorney, Fleischman, told the *Arizona Republic* and the *Los Angeles Times* that he was "shocked [again] at the paucity of evidence," calling the details outlined in the complaint filed against his client "old soup." Romley refused to speak about specifics in his team's findings and conclusions, while Fleischman was already testing his personal wiggle room with "How can you [the D.A.'s office] sit on this for fourteen years and expect this man [Carpenter] to defend himself?" Carpenter's wife of thirty-seven years, Diana, weighed in with the press as well: "It's only because Bob Crane was a TV star that this whole business has dragged on." She very well might have been right. In the meantime, Fleischman had some other pressing problems to contend with. His "wrongly suspected" client in a homicide case had waived extradition to Arizona, but before he could take his free trip to the desert Southwest there was one other little matter that had to be cleared up. John Henry Carpenter was also the defendant in a child molestation

Suspect Charged in 1978 Death of Actor Bob Crane

■ Crime: The South Bay man was an acquaintance of the 'Hogan's Heroes' star who was killed in Arizona.

By LESLIE BERGER
and LAURA LAUGHLIN
SPECIAL TO THE TIMES

One of show business's most provocative murder mysteries took a new twist Monday when a long-time suspect was arrested nearly 14 years after "Hogan's Heroes" star Bob Crane was found bludgeoned to death in his Scottsdale, Ariz., apartment.

John Henry Carpenter, 64, was arrested by Los Angeles County sheriff's deputies in Carson. Carpenter, who lives in an undisclosed South Bay community, was charged with first-degree murder by Arizona prosecutors, who offered no motive but say they have linked him to the case through blood and tissue samples.

The electronics company employee, who authorities say had visited Crane in Scottsdale during the days before his death, has long been under scrutiny in connection with the case. But two previous prosecuting attorneys declined to file charges against him and he has consistently maintained his innocence.

Last week, however, Maricopa County (Arizona) Atty. Richard Romley filed a sealed murder charge after experts said blood and tissue found in Carpenter's rental car and on Crane's pillowcase most likely were produced by the same fatal blows.

"This is an important statement

Please see CRANE, A3

Front page of the *Los Angeles Times*, 1992 (author's collection).

case in Long Beach, California. He was ordered held until that case was resolved.

On the peaceful morning of June 1, 1992, I was staying with John at his farm in Queensville, forty-five minutes north of Toronto. The fresh country air was intoxicating as I sipped my coffee on the patio. John was in the middle of an unplanned hiatus. His agent, Guy McElwaine, had not been able to find work for him. The film industry was going through yet another upheaval, sifting through its roster of actors and actresses, embracing the up-and-comers, deciding what to do with the ones who didn't do

233

boffo biz every time out. John loved to work. He had always worked. Inactivity brought out his insecurities.

Into that climate we received a phone call from Arlene Brownstein back at the Frostbacks office that there was a breaking story on the front page of the *L.A. Times*. Brownstein read aloud that the new district attorney of Maricopa County, Arizona, Richard Romley, had decided to finally arrest and arraign John Henry Carpenter for my dad's murder—fourteen years after the crime. Reporters were calling the office, and Brownstein wanted to know how to handle them. I was baffled that anyone knew Bob Crane's son worked for John Candy. John's insecurities vanished instantly because he now had a project: protecting me. He told Brownstein, "Tell anyone who calls to contact Skip Brittenham." Ziffren, Brittenham & Branca, attorneys at law in Century City, handled clients on the magnitude of Michael Jackson. Brittenham put together rapacious contracts for superstar performers, producers, and directors. I doubt he was in the habit of taking phone calls on behalf of the likes of me, slain *Hogan's Heroes* star Bob Crane's kid. Nonetheless, Brittenham's office would be acting as my surrogate for a while because his client had asked a favor. It was another case of John empathizing with the little guy, me in this case, and taking immediate action to solve a problem and make the unfair world right again.

From June 2 forward, the "Man Held in Crane's Death Was a Suspect from Day 1" (*Los Angeles Times*), and my dad's case occupied print space in newspapers from the *New York Post* to the *Chicago Tribune* to the *San Francisco Chronicle* and air time from *Entertainment Tonight* to KNXT 2 News in Los Angeles, but it was the so-called supermarket tabloids, "the rags," that really had fun with the breaking developments—the *National Enquirer* ("*Hogan's Heroes* Fans Help Cops Solve 14-Year Murder Mystery"), the *Star* ("*Hogan's Heroes* Murder: Shocking Inside Story—Tragic TV Good Guy Bob Crane"), and the *Globe* ("At Last! Police Zero in on Murderer of *Hogan's Heroes* Star"). The *Arizona Republic* brought levity to the indictment, the positives and negatives of the charge condensed into a headline—"Key to Crane Case Just a Speck."

36

Go and Stop, 1992

One of the more important lessons in work ethic I learned from John was to follow up and follow through. When he got an idea, he'd start calling actors, writers, and producers to help him make it a reality. John would act like the project was a "go" from its inception. The project might be anything, from a script like "Hauling Ashes" with *Cops* producer John Langley to an *SCTV* one-off special for NBC. John would move on the idea with such conviction that anyone on the other end of the phone would already be checking *TV Guide* or *Entertainment Weekly* for the release date. He liked self-generated movement, not wanting to wait for a producer to call. Initiating his own material equated work with the enjoyable task of bringing creative artists together for a common goal. He was good at that. For every ten strikes, maybe one would catch fire. That positive stance greatly influenced me, the freelancer at the mercy of editors deciding when, where, or if an article would appear.

Kari and I had a finished draft of "Suburbia Blues," and I worked up the courage to show John the script. Kari and I thought he would be hilarious as the put-upon loser husband. I handed the folder to John, who looked at the title page. "Hey, when did you guys do this?" John asked.

"We've been working on it for years," I said, looking at the ground. "We think you'd be great for the lead role."

John set the folder on a mile-high stack of scripts. That was the end of it. At that moment it dawned on me that giving John Candy homegrown scripts was not part of my job description. I was there to perform many functions, for which I was being paid, and paid well, but script development was not one of them. I vowed not to forget that, and I promised myself I wouldn't bother John about the script again.

That was until the day I was talking on the phone to his television agent, Alan Berger, at ICM, regarding John narrating an episode of *Shelley Duvall's Bedtime Stories* ("Blumpoe the Grumpoe Meets Arnold the

Cat"). With that bit of business taken care of, I got a bolt of testosterone-enriched lightning that strikes occasionally and asked Berger, "Alan, may I show you a script? I think it would be perfect for Frostbacks." I pitched it not as a John Candy lead role but as production fodder for Candy's company.

Alan said, "Yeah, send it over."

I felt a bit guilty about pursuing this particular Hollywood Dream behind John's back, but I was certain John and Frostbacks Production would be the chief benefactors.

A day later, I received a call from Berger's office. "Bob, we love the script. What do you want to do?" Alan asked.

He was nowhere near as excited as I was. I said, "John's got a copy. It would be great if he could be in it, but that's between you guys. I've always thought it was a project for John to be involved in."

I transferred Berger's call to John's office, and then I quietly called Kari to let her know that, at least, we were at bat. I hovered in the hallway outside John's office while Berger repeated what he had told me—a couple of people at ICM had read the script and loved it. I peeked around the corner and saw John frantically searching his desk for such a hot property. After a few minutes, I got the gist of their conversation—"Suburbia Blues" was not big-screen material, but it would be perfect for a TV movie.

In those early '90s, CBS and NBC both had a movie of the week. John had a relationship with NBC because of *SCTV* and appearances on *Saturday Night Live, The New Show,* and David Letterman, who was still at 30 Rock at the time. Berger pitched NBC on a John Candy movie of the week, and NBC jumped on it like a hanging curveball. The only problem, and it was no small hurdle, was that John was not convinced that he wanted to be in a TV movie. Television movies of the week were for Barbara Eden or Robert Urich or Richard Chamberlain, not someone starring in Hollywood multiplex fare directed by A-listers like John Hughes, Chris Columbus, and Oliver Stone. John had served his time on the small box and wasn't of a mind to go back to it.

Then I had another flash of inspiration. "John, why don't you direct it?" I suggested.

John swished that idea around like a fine pinot noir. He'd never directed before. But every actor wants to direct. He loved the idea.

There was a flurry of meetings at NBC Burbank. We acquired a new production partner in Stan Brooks, a veteran television movie producer.

There were rewrites. Then there were more meetings. Then some more rewrites. Kari and I thought we were the new Joan Didion and John Gregory Dunne. After six months, the person at NBC in charge of TV movies was fired, and that had an immediate trickle-down effect on us. The new regime had a different focus on what they wanted to do with their movies. They wanted important, Emmy-nominated products—not John Candy goofiness. We were cast adrift. But not for long.

At that same time, the upstart Fox Network ("with the Fox attitude") had started a movie night on Tuesdays to compete with NBC and CBS. Berger, Candy, Brooks, and Kari and I took the project to Fox, which wanted to work with John Candy real bad. Plus, 20th Century Fox had a retainer deal with John, through which it tried to find film projects for him. This was payback for his appearance in Fox's *Home Alone* at the Screen Actors Guild day rate—for a film that grossed a mere half billion dollars. The Fox Network went along with Candy making his directorial debut as long as he showed his face in a cameo role.

George Wendt from *Cheers* was cast in what would've been the John Candy role. Wendt was the small-screen Candy. Oh, yeah, and everyone involved except the screenwriters wanted the script to be funnier. It was adios, Crane and Hildebrand, hello, Second City alumnus (like Candy and Wendt) Peter Torokvei. His brief was to punch up the words. That included the new title, *Hostage for a Day*. Upon receiving the news of our untimely demise, Kari and I looked at each other with disappointment, but we still felt pride and a sense of achievement, tempered by Hollywood war weariness. Our tour of duty was finished. We were being furloughed.

Our home front went through an upheaval as well. Like the iconic actress Greta Garbo, Kari announced, "I want to be alone." Although she was surrounded and supported by family and friends, she had come to feel that facing cancer was a one-on-one fight. After all the Hallmark cards, the flower arrangements, the candles, and weekend retreats, it came down to something like a Vincent Price/Boris Karloff standoff from a bad AIP horror film of the 1960s. Kari wanted no dance partner for this routine. I was hoping death wasn't part of this pas de deux. I dislike the phrase, but Kari "needed space." The intellectual side of me got it, but my emotional side took her announcement as pure rejection.

Kari's comfort zone was our house and yard, so the only civilized thing for me to do was to pack up and move. Luckily, my stepdad Chuck had a vacancy at his twelve-unit complex where Kari and I had previously lived. I settled into a one-bedroom that, coincidentally, was where Chuck lived during his divorce from his first wife, Virginia, but Kari and I were not talking divorce. We were five minutes apart. We talked on the phone. We went to movies together. We had dinners together. But at the end of the evening, after a goodnight kiss and hug, she would go into our house and I would drive back to the apartment. I would "give her her space."

My own ego screamed, "My wife doesn't want me by her side while she's going through hell!"

Her friend Linda tried to soften the hurt with "Kari is seeing certain things for the first time." Was this the equivalent of my dad discovering the color orange?

Kari was taking a creative writing class at Valley College during this period. After a few months of separation, I got wind that there was an attraction between Kari and one of her classmates. Now, during our occasional "date nights," she was preoccupied, distant. During the course of her treatment she had told me how she felt so unattractive. She had a skin rash, her hair had fallen out again, and she had lost a lot of weight. She felt old. She was only in her late thirties, but her body felt beaten up, exhausted. I felt in my rational self that if, indeed, she had an admirer, a fan, even a lover from her writing class, someone other than her husband who was making her feel beautiful, inside and out, I couldn't argue with the end result. If the newness of a man, the excitement of an unexplored relationship, made her rise above the gravitational pull of illness and what she saw as a stale relationship, and if it made her feel like an alive, vital woman, I could only wish her well. If our separation was the beginning of the end of us as a couple, then so be it. I tried. I did my best. I loved her. She had pushed me away. There was no pushing back. This infatuation, or whatever it was, was completely out of my control. If someone else was making her feel good, excited about being alive, then I was all for it. The bottom line was that she felt something other than feeling like shit.

Kari and I had had no sex life for quite a while. Getting her better was my priority. Sex didn't seem important in the overall struggle between life and death. Kari was such a great person, such an asset to the world that, ultimately, her existence was way more important than our union. Though our relationship had started in a very serious and almost businesslike manner, through all our hardships and enjoyments, we had come to love and respect each other in the deepest possible way.

37

The Beat Goes On, 1992–1993

In October 1992 I received a letter from deputy county attorney Myrna J. Parker: Re: ROBERT CRANE MURDER INVESTIGATION *STATE V. CARPENTER*, CR 92-04718. Having been interviewed by the police and county investigators, I was a potential witness for the prosecution, and my name and address would be shared with the defense, which had the right to speak to anyone on the prosecution's list. I never heard from any of John Carpenter's representatives.

By mid-November Carpenter was still in California. As the jury selection process began in his molestation case, Carpenter wangled a plea bargain down to one count of sexual battery. In December Los Angeles Superior Court judge James Pierce sentenced Carpenter to three years' probation, thus clearing the way for the Pied Piper of Home Video's return to Arizona to stand trial in the murder of his friend, a man, Carpenter had told me, "I've never said a bad word to . . . in the twelve . . . or thirteen years that I've known him."

On Tuesday, February 16, 1993, a hearing began in Phoenix's Maricopa County Superior Court, Judge Gregory Martin presiding, to determine whether there was enough evidence to try John Henry Carpenter for first-degree murder. Carpenter sat quietly as the prosecution presented color photographs of my dad's lifeless body and the clinical appearance of Winfield Apartments' Unit 132A on Chaparral Road in Scottsdale.

On March 11, after a three-week evidentiary hearing, Judge Martin commented to the court that all the law enforcement personnel originally involved in the almost fifteen-year-old case performed "sloppy work." Despite his stinging remarks, Martin then ruled that "probable cause has been shown that the crime of murder . . . was committed." He went on to state in a three-page finding that the blood and tissue (the speck) found on the passenger door of Carpenter's rented Chrysler Cordoba created the "only reasonable inference . . . that the blood is that of the victim and the tissue is body tissue of the victim transferred from the scene of the crime to the defendant's rental car." A May 26 trial date was set. Until that time, Carpenter was free on $98,000 bail. His new attorney, public defender Stephen Avilla, told the press that he would appeal Judge Martin's ruling to another judge and, possibly, all the way to the Arizona Court of Appeals.

38

Hostage No More, 1993

As a lark, I threw a surprise party for Kari at Marix, a Mexican restaurant in Encino, inviting twenty friends and family members. We gathered to celebrate, to separate the hell of the recent past from the wishful anticipation of a healthy future. We all crossed our fingers, no one knowing what was going to happen, purely enjoying the moment. John, Rose, Jennifer, and Christopher were part of the observance, clearly at ease and happy as they talked with everybody in the room. We had a great evening. John and Kari talked and shared a lot of laughs together, and I watched them with a feeling of warmth and calm. John's presence was more than I expected, and his making the effort to be there meant a lot to Kari.

While Kari was in the midst of chemo and radiation and the Maricopa County Attorney's Office was in the process of finally building its case against Carpenter, Frostbacks was running short on cash and employees when John Candy got a call from his latest new agent, Michael Menchel at Creative Artists Agency. Walt Disney Studios and former film executive turned producer Dawn Steel were offering John a supporting role in *Cool Runnings*, the inspiring true tale of four Jamaican bobsledders participating in the 1988 Winter Olympics. John would play the over-the-hill coach, an ex-Olympian who had hit rock bottom. It was a semiserious role. The project reminded me of my dad and *Hogan's Heroes*. It was an out-of-the-ordinary, off-balance idea with great potential.

In no time I was back on the road in Calgary, Alberta, with the Candy posse. Chuck joined me for a week at the eighty-year-old Canadian National–built Palliser Hotel, during which time we observed filming at various Calgary Winter Games locations. In typical Hollywood fashion, the second half of the movie was being shot first.

John was the heaviest I had ever seen him, and he adopted a grizzled, weary appearance to help sell the coach as having lost his way. He spent many of his off hours with actors Leon, Doug E. Doug, Malik Yoba, and

Rawle Lewis in an "us against them" stance, just as the true Jamaicans and their coach had experienced. There are many actors who do their lines, film their scenes, and disappear back into their trailers. John wanted these unknown actors to trust him, know that he believed in them. He took the young actors playing the disorganized, inept sledders under his wing off-screen just as Coach Irv Blitzer did with them onscreen.

Everyone in Hollywood has a Dawn Steel story. Allegedly, when she ran Columbia Pictures, she called her female staff "cunts and bitches" and proved to have bigger balls than most male executives and producers in town. Now she was an independent producer, teaming up with her husband, Charles Roven, and a newbie director, Jon Turteltaub. Everyone benefited from being under her enormous, bullshit-proof wing.

Her reputation had preceded her to the set, and the Chongos anticipated fireworks when Candy met Steel. The day of the first script read-through, John, almost always in the moment, walked in the rehearsal room, cracked a joke to Steel that made her laugh, and then hugged her, Steel's tiny frame disappearing into the six-foot-two, three-hundred-pound-plus of Candy. All the buildup about the Steel legend didn't mean anything to John's work technique and demeanor. He had taken the bull by the horns and diffused any potential producer-actor bullshit in two seconds. I smiled at this proof that no challenge, human or otherwise, was too large for John. He set his priorities, and doing good work was at the top of the list. He wanted, needed, to get his career back on track.

I always tried to emulate John's "in the moment" existence, and I had an unsettling test of my progress shortly after the *Cool Runnings* shooting began. Laura Ziskin, my college heartthrob, now a successful producer of films like *Pretty Woman, No Way Out,* and *What About Bob?* flew into town to visit the executive producer of *Cool Runnings,* Susan Landau. I was immediately reminded of my inadequacies, not only in my one and only sexual encounter with Laura but in the show business arena in general. Laura, Susan Landau, John, and I had lunch on one of John's days off. Here was Laura, star of the USC Cinema Department, who had given me a one-night audition over twenty years ago, then worked her way through menial television jobs, rising through the film ranks to now stand proudly and assuredly alongside Steel, Sherry Lansing, and Amy Pascal as a leader in the motion picture industry. I was a minion in the Candy camp, feeling awkward and a bit embarrassed. I was proud of Laura, in awe of her, really, and slightly scared of her. I tortured myself with this comparison while she enjoyed her lunch with her friend and her new acquaintance John. There was much laughter and no apparent unease on her side of the table, and the afternoon played out as if Laura Ziskin were meeting me for the first time. She was, as always, bright, gracious, and beautiful.

John was going to need living quarters in Jamaica, so after Chuck and I returned to Los Angeles, I was dispatched to Montego Bay. I met with the Jamaican Film Commission personnel, who were excited about Disney, producer Dawn Steel, John Candy, and millions of dollars coming to their island. For John and the Candy clan's housing needs, I was sent to the private enclave of Round Hill, west of the airport. There, individual homes and a hotel sat on beautifully manicured grounds facing the ocean. William Paley, Ralph Lauren, Truman Capote, and director Robert Zemeckis were just a few of the boldfaced names connected to the gated facility's history. I found an open-air house with jaw-dropping views of the bay, a swimming pool, a full-time cook, and wait and cleaning staff on call. I was told Paul McCartney and family had just ended a monthlong stay. The tab for this tropical paradise was $1,000 a day. I called John in Calgary. He sounded pleased. Then I called my mom and Chuck in Los Angeles to say I was coming home. I saved Kari for last. As I looked out on a Caribbean Eden, I listened to my wife describe how awful she felt. The chemo and radiation were kicking her ass. She said she felt like a tackling dummy for the Chicago Bears' Refrigerator Perry. I told her I had one meeting in the morning with the *Cool Runnings* Jamaican office, and then I'd be on a flight back to L.A. I told her I missed and loved her. I hung up the phone, sipped a Red Stripe beer, and watched one of the most breathtaking sunsets I'd ever seen. I was the loneliest guy in the world.

Kari and I were in our ninth month of separation. I was beginning to wonder if we would ever get together again. She called me one day, sounding hesitant. I thought, "Oh, shit, here comes more bad news."

"I'd like you to move back," she said in a low voice. "Do you want to come home?"

My cynical, sarcastic side wondered whether the relationship with the man in the writing class hadn't worked out. Had Kari rejected him? Was the cancer too much for him to handle? Ultimately, it didn't matter. "Of course I do. Are you sure about this?" I asked, not certain I wanted the answer.

"Yes."

I collected my clothing, futon, portable television, meager kitchen items, and books, and made the five-minute move back home.

Perhaps Kari had initiated our separation because she had just tired of her whole lot, which included me. Perhaps she felt she was preparing me for a life after Kari. Perhaps she had chemo brain and just wasn't thinking clearly. What had happened? Why was it over now? Analysis was irrelevant. I was home with my wife. We never talked about it.

Kari completed her chemo treatments and continued her radiation. Team Kari had done research locating homeopathics, alternative medicines, diets, sweat lodges, and just about everything but a flying swami. She was weak, her weight down to under a hundred pounds. She was hairless, suffering from pulmonary edema, and now came a new announcement from the Breast Center—the cancer was on the move again. It had traveled not back onto her scalp but into her brain.

We all wanted to keep things as positive as possible, even though standing in the corner of the oncologist's office there was a pink-ribboned elephant that would not be denied. I was sitting there holding the hand of the most important person in the world to me, and neither of us would say, "This looks pretty bad."

If you're religious, faith should kick in about now. If you're a skeptic, cynicism should take the lead. If you cry easily, sobbing was the order of the day. Kari was living in a shit storm I hoped like hell I would never encounter. I'd seen her wheeled into surgery, watched IVs of poisonous chemicals dripped into her arm, heard her wheezing lungs struggling for oxygen in the middle of the night, observed giant needles enter her back on their way to her liquid-filled lungs, listened to her being sick over and over again, smelled vomit on her clothing, carried her slim body through our house, brought her pills and glasses of water. But even with all of that, it wasn't as though I had been through it firsthand, and I don't think anyone can make an assessment about what it's like to have cancer without actually having cancer. We were still a million miles apart on that front.

When we were told the cancer cells had migrated to her brain, Kari, without appearing to give up, began pulling away. She was rundown, frustrated, and disappointed. Her competitive streak was really pissed off that something might be going to defeat her. In that summer of 1993 at Century City Hospital in Los Angeles, the radiologist informed us that Kari had maxed out on radiation. There is only so much a body can absorb without creating more damage than benefit. We were at the outer limits. Chemo was over. Radiation was over. The cancer had metastasized and further surgery was futile.

Kari's homeopathic remedies hadn't worked. Diet change hadn't changed anything. Chanting, lighting candles, and a visit to a sweat lodge hadn't altered the dismal accounting. There were no other protocols to follow, no new doctors, experts, or philosophers to consult. Sitting in the radiologist's office, Kari and I exchanged that shorthand look that, I hope, everyone can experience with one other person during his or her lifetime. We said a million words to each other without uttering one. It was resolved. We knew.

We drove from the hospital to John and Rose Candy's house in Brentwood. John was home alone; Rose and the kids were in Toronto. The three of us sat in the den, Kari and John sharing a couch. I watched them as I blurted out the announcement that Kari was out of moves, out of time. Kari sat quietly, embarrassed at being the center of attention.

John, gracious as ever, asked, "What can I do?"

"Nothing. Thanks. We just wanted to share the developments with you."

We were all lost.

Next we drove to Mom and Chuck's house in Tarzana and told them. There were tears from Mom and bravery, as always, from Chuck. "What can we do?" they asked.

More nothing, we answered.

We told Kari's mom. Her eyes watered, but she kept her emotions in check. She would cry later on her own time. Kari called her father, with whom she had a semi-estranged relationship. She couldn't forgive his alcoholism and had been disappointed by his lack of strength and reluctance to behave as she felt a traditional father should. Men always seemed to let Kari down. I felt I was another body on a stack of underperforming males. Kari always depended on herself first, then her female friends, and then, to a lesser degree, her sisters and mother. Then she might get to me.

In an uncharacteristic fit of sentimentality, I called the El Encanto Hotel in Santa Barbara and booked the Presidential Suite for the upcoming weekend. Kari and I would return to the scene of our wedding and spend a quiet if not quite honeymoonlike few days there. We visited one of Kari's favorite public gardens, the Santa Barbara Botanic Garden. Kari was weak, severely underweight. She appeared ten to fifteen years older than her forty-one years. She was having problems walking, so we got her a wheelchair and a walker. She was humiliated but knew it was necessary. At least we were fortunate to have the means to spend time together in beautiful Santa Barbara.

In the midst of all this sadness and exhausted hope, Kari's and my screenplay, *Hostage for a Day,* was finally coming to fruition. We received a green light from the Fox Network. Shooting was to begin in early October in Toronto. Candy was directing and doing a cameo. George Wendt, John Vernon, Robin Duke, Don Lake, and Christopher Templeton would costar. Peter Torokvei had extensively rewritten our script. Because of the direction John wanted to take the material, the words had become much sillier. Kari and I knew this was not going to be the next *Dog Day Afternoon,* the great Sidney Lumet hostage situation story with a documentary feel. We resigned ourselves to that fact, but we were elated the film was finally getting made. It had taken a decade of work.

As first timers, we got the Screen Writers Guild minimum, which at that time was around $30,000. But Alan Berger's office got two bumps written into our contract. One was that Hildebrand and Crane would share a producers' credit. However, because the twenty-day shoot was taking place in Canada, the production company could only have so many U.S. personnel in key positions. Thus we became "supervising production consultants." That's a title that translates from the Canadian into "Stay the fuck out of the way, eh." So we got $10,000 for making ourselves scarce. Then we got an additional ten grand from the "if the picture gets made" clause. All told, our work on the script and our nonwork on the production brought home some $50,000. We were thrilled. We would happily watch from the sidelines while all the Second City alumni—Candy, Wendt, Duke, Torokvei, Lake, and John Hemphill—went to work.

Kari's treatments had concluded. The medical establishment said nothing else could be done. There were still hundreds of alternative options, but Kari and I had agreed that we were folding up the Red Cross tent. If Kari bade a last farewell to our house, her garden, or her cat Nutmeg, she did it privately. We were still looking forward. We were going to Toronto to see our film get made.

I had hundreds of thousands of miles logged on Air Canada. I redeemed some of them for three first-class tickets from L.A. to Toronto on a jumbo 747. Kari, her mother, Loretta, and I sat in the first row behind the nose of the aircraft. Kari mentioned that this was the first time in her life she'd ever flown first class. That made me feel good. Mother and daughter gabbed while I read and thought about what would happen next.

At Pearson International Airport in Toronto, we were picked up by the Prestige Limousine Service and driven out to the Candy's property in Queensville. John and Rose had graciously opened their rustic, two-story guesthouse overlooking acres and acres of golden farmland just for us. I knew getting Kari up and down the stairs was going to be problematic. She was very frail. We were not going to be taking walks through the cornfields. In fact, the truth of the moment was that Kari was bed bound. She was never even going to make the visit out to the film set.

Each morning I drove with John to the production office. Everyone on the office staff and production crew was excited about working with one of Canada's favorite sons. I pinched myself each time I read Kari's and my name on the script's title page. The hell with Sidney Lumet, we were the authors of a big-time movie. We were in Toronto in the beautiful autumn making a film.

Loretta spent the first week with Kari but then had to go back to her job in Los Angeles, so I dipped into my Air Canada Aeroplan miles basket and exchanged Loretta for Kari's middle sister, Deborah. During the day, I would check in with Kari and her minders. As Kari was becoming less and less verbal, Deborah mostly provided me with the patient updates. Deborah's week sped by and then she, too, had to get back to work. Air Canada's next guest was Kari's best friend, Linda, who was still holding out hope for some kind of supernatural or Wiccan intervention. Linda chanted and prayed a lot during that third week at the farm, but Kari was declining rapidly. Her speech and appetite were almost gone.

One evening Kari tried to speak. I was dreading what I thought I was going to hear, that she was in extreme pain, that she needed more meds or, worst of all, that she was ready to say good-bye. She whispered a few words, and to my great relief, I finally understood what she was trying to say—she wanted French fries and a chocolate shake. I didn't know whether to laugh or cry. This was way out of the bounds of Kari's normal comestibles. She had always avoided fast food like some people shun Woody Allen movies, but we both knew it didn't matter anymore, and I was just happy she wanted to eat anything. I went to a Harvey's a few miles away and picked up her order. This was a big treat, and she delighted in every fry and every sip of her shake.

As the days went by, Kari began withdrawing from the world. Linda or I would ask her a question regarding her comfort or whether she wanted something to eat or drink, and we were not sure our words were getting through. I did things by rote, just moving ahead. Kari hadn't bathed in a few days so I carried her ninety-pound frame into the bathroom and carefully placed her in a warm bath. She didn't speak but her face broke into a beatific smile.

On Friday night, October 1, John and I drove into Toronto to do a live remote interview for *Larry King Live*. John was promoting the opening day of *Cool Runnings*, his best work in years. Larry asked John inane questions that had nothing to do with the film. After the broadcast, John and I noted that Larry was losing it. *Cool Runnings* turned out to be a big hit for Disney, Dawn Steel, and John Candy, reviving John's somewhat sagging film career.

I arrived back at the guesthouse around midnight, quietly got undressed, and slipped into bed next to my sleeping wife. I stared into the blackness. My boss was on top of the world, my wife at the bottom of the sea. I listened to Kari's light breathing and wondered where she was, dreaming on the edge of two worlds. I could feel the warmth of her body. I knew I couldn't do anything for her except make her as comfortable as possible.

The next morning I awoke to a scene out of *The Godfather*. I felt wet and sticky like the character played by John Marley. As Kari slept, I slowly pulled my side of the covers down and discovered not a horse's head but a mattress and sheets soaked with urine. Kari's body was on its way to a total shutdown. When Linda woke up, I told her what had happened. We moved Kari into another bed and began cleaning up the mess. We concluded it was time for yet another indignity for Kari, diapers.

All day Saturday, Linda and I spoke to Kari individually and together. We both knew the situation was not going to improve. I whispered to Kari, "It's okay, baby. You can let go."

I watched as my wife, my love, my partner, my teacher lay not speaking, not eating, just staring into space. I was there talking, reading out loud, being present all day and night. I couldn't eat and barely got myself to the bathroom. I didn't want Kari to embark on her last journey without seeing her off.

Early Sunday morning, I woke for no apparent reason and looked at the clock. It was 2:30. I lay there in the dark. I listened for Kari's breathing. The room was silent. I turned on the lamp on the nightstand and looked over at Kari. Her eyes were open. I felt the top of her head. She was warm. I looked at her again, listening and watching for any sound, any movement. She was gone. Typical of Kari, she had departed on her own terms. I kissed her lightly and put my head on her thin, soundless chest. I thought my own heart would burst.

After composing myself I padded down the hallway to Linda's room. I tapped on the door and announced with resignation and a perverse sense of relief, "Linda, Kari's gone." I returned to Kari's side. I told her I loved her and missed her already as Linda entered the room. She had just lost her best friend, but she had been preparing for this moment for a long time. We tried to close Kari's eyes but they refused, not like my dad's when I had viewed his body at the Scottsdale Police Department morgue fifteen years earlier. "Still stubborn," I said, and Linda and I laughed.

We held our own wake, sharing stories that produced both tears and laughter. We stood on either side of the bed looking at Kari and talking in reverential tones until the sun came up.

This was to be day one of life without Kari. We had shared eleven years. As I looked at her prematurely aged but now restful face, I thanked her for teaching me responsibility, work ethic, and precision of craft. I thanked her for showing me what a grown-up relationship looked like. Although I had matured I still apologized to her for my many mistakes and the numerous silly and stupid things I had said and done during our life together. I thought of all the changes over those years. I had full-time work with John. I was making steady money. I owned a house. I tried to imagine what my life was to become without her calming adult wisdom. The last two years of her life had been anything but calm. I had filled numerous roles: husband, lover, friend, admirer, cheerleader, and finally caretaker. Kari was a selfless, gracious citizen who would be missed by many. She was also very competitive. She could be a two-headed monster. Sometimes her competitive nature was good for me, and sometimes it was just a pain in the ass. Sometimes I felt as if we were competitors when we were supposed to be on the same team.

Linda and I made the necessary phone calls to family and friends. There were tears and gasps followed by a gaping silence as the news was processed. Everyone had expected it, of course, but still the passing sent a shockwave through Kari's community. It was just the exclamation point on a life much too short.

Around 8:00 in the morning, Linda took charge and called the local coroner, Dr. J. D. Fearon, and the mortuary, Roadhouse and Rose. I called John and Rose Candy. Soon John pulled up to the guesthouse in his truck as Chris Fryer arrived from New York. We had a meeting of the minds in the living room—Chris, Linda, John (wearing an Irish wake pin), and me. We talked for an hour about Kari. Dr. Fearon arrived. He did a double take when he saw John Candy sitting there, but quickly gathered himself and went about his examination of Kari's body. He filled in the death certificate, the ultimate in unbiased existentialism. Cause of death: metastatic carcinoma of breast. By what means: natural.

I spent a final moment with Kari. I removed her diaper, straightened her *Seinfeld* T-shirt and cotton workout pants, kissed her one last time, and said good-bye to Kari's physical self. Per her wish, she was to be cremated. Kari was placed in a body bag and loaded into the mortuary vehicle for the short trip to Highland Memory Gardens and Crematorium.

John faced me and said, "Go back to L.A."

"I will briefly," I said, "but I'm coming back."

"No, no, no, no. Just go back. We've got it covered here," John insisted.

"You think I'm gonna miss *Hostage for a Day* now after all this, and how much Kari put into it? Not a chance. I'm coming back. I can't do anything else for Kari. Besides, I want to see if you're any good as a director."

That last remark made John smile.

The next day, Linda and I returned to Los Angeles with Kari's ashes. Thank god, this was before 9/11, before the TSA. Nowadays, I can imagine the container being X-rayed and examined and Kari's ashes flying all over the Air Canada terminal at Toronto's Pearson International.

The following Sunday, October 10, I hosted a memorial for Kari at our house. Close to one hundred people attended—friends and family, neighbors, landscaping associates, artists, teachers, feminists. I laid out Kari's office with her short stories, our *Hostage for a Day* script, her artwork, blueprints of landscaping jobs, and photographs covering her all too brief life. We had a bar and finger food, and everyone shared their favorite Kari stories. After most of the guests had left, Kari's family and closest friends spread her ashes throughout the garden she had worked so hard to nurture into our own little Eden.

Kari's youngest sister, Mindy, approached me. She was worried about how dry it had been in Los Angeles. "Her ashes are gonna blow all over the place," said Mindy. "She's gonna be sitting out here on leaves and shrubs for weeks. She might end up in the street."

The fact that Kari was eternally ensconced in her leafy creations was all I cared about. "Don't worry about it. It'll be okay," I said, trying to reassure Mindy.

Late that evening, Desly and Chris Fryer, my friend Janet Spiegel, and I were all who remained of the mourners. I told them about Kari's sister's comment. There were smiles and head shaking since Mindy's concern ranked pretty low on our list of concerns, but just at that moment we heard the nearby rumbling. Then we saw the lightning. Suddenly the sky opened up and rain poured for twenty minutes. Then it slowed and stopped. Kari's ashes were now completely at one with the backyard flora. As Angelenos will tell you, it almost never rains in October. I felt Kari had something to do with that oddity. It was her statement from beyond declaring that everything was okay and that no one, not Mindy, not any of us, should be worried. Kari had solved another problem. She had taken control, just as she had all her life.

39

Adios, Amigo, 1993–1994

The year slipped by, and during my first Christmas without Kari, I received a letter from prosecuting attorney Robert J. Shutts of the Maricopa County Attorney's Office announcing that he was assigned the Crane case "due to the unforeseen illness of K. C. Scull." The trial of John Henry Carpenter was scheduled for March 21, 1994. Happy New Year.

On the Frostbacks front, John relented to fulfill a long-standing commitment he had with Carolco Pictures. Once a fresh-faced darling of a company with hits like *Rambo* and *Terminator 2,* Carolco was now a bruised has-been bleeding too much money on mediocre projects. The company had tried to ignite a project with its *Rambo* star, Sylvester Stallone, and "Uncle Buck" John Candy, in a new John Hughes comedy called "Bartholomew vs. Neff," but it never caught fire. As a result John still owed the company a film. A lame script called *Wagons East!* that had been making the rounds was sent to Michael Menchel at CAA. It was a different kind of role for John. He'd never done a western. The role would fulfill his Carolco obligation and, oh, by the way, put $3 million in his wallet, but it meant working with an unknown commodity, director Peter Markle, and a cast that included Richard Lewis and Ellen Greene. John wanted to keep working after the pleasant *Cool Runnings* and *Hostage for a Day* experiences, the unpleasant memory of a year sitting on the bench still fresh. Not to mention Frostbacks Production was hemorrhaging cash even as it was being downsized. John was also out $1 million on the money-losing but fun Toronto Argonauts adventure. He needed to work, and his favorite situation was being on the road earning money, away from the stresses of home life and the celebrity magnifying glass of Los Angeles. John and my dad shared the feeling that life on the road was simpler. You focused on the work, and when the work was finished you could play. So we were heading for Durango, Mexico, altitude seven thousand feet, locale of numerous John Wayne westerns and a favorite film of mine, *Kid Blue*, with Dennis Hopper.

One of the more enjoyable aspects of working for John was taking Chuck (and sometimes my mom, too) on trips where they could explore a new city for a few days without my having to babysit them, and I could just get on with my job. We had had great times in Toronto, Chicago, and Calgary. It was a small repayment to Chuck for his fatherly wisdom and guidance through the years. Now we were off to Durango on a fact-finding mission that included securing a private home for John to use for twelve weeks, locking in suitable accommodations for the Chongos, and meeting and greeting the production personnel.

With no direct flights, Chuck and I flew through scenic Puerto Vallarta to get to dusty, reportedly scorpion-ridden Durango. We were picked up at the airport by a production vehicle and taken to an ancient motel where the Duke and company stayed decades ago. This Old West relic was production manager Ted Parvin's number one recommendation in town. We went in to check out the digs proposed for John. Chuck was immediately taken back to his air force days by the distinct aroma of fresh lye in the bathroom. "Oh, my god, I don't know what just happened here," Chuck said, "but this place smells awful. John is definitely not going to stay in this dump."

Parvin, who was always keeping an eye on the bottom line for his bosses at Carolco, feigned shock. This place might have been good enough for Mr. John Wayne a thousand years ago, but Señor Juan Dulce wouldn't be spending even one night in this hellhole. Chuck and I hired a taxi. The decrepit beast listed to the driver's side and had a blanket on the backseat to prevent the aggressive seat springs that had punctured the original upholstery from skewering the unlucky passenger's backside. We arrived at the *Wagons East!* production office, which was guarded by two local "security agents" brandishing automatic weapons. I mentioned to Chuck that Carolco was taking this *Rambo* thing a bit too seriously, but then we spied a floor-to-ceiling safe containing, we later learned, millions of U.S. dollars in cash. Our scouting trip was fast becoming a Fellini Excursion.

We updated John periodically using the Frostbacks' brick-shaped cell phone. Frankie Hernandez had taught John to be wary of all production managers. Their only concern was coming in under budget, saving the producers money, and thereby securing a position on their next movie.

We found the "best" hotel in town, the El Presidente, which featured clean rooms and beautiful local women lunching everyday in its restaurant. It was good enough for the Chongos, but John would want more privacy and more space, so Chuck and I looked at the house where Paul Newman stayed when he was filming *Fat Man and Little Boy*—about Robert Oppenheimer, Los Alamos, and the atomic bomb—but it was a two-story affair with narrow hallways, unsuitable for John because of his smoking habit and general physique. Climbing stairs at seven thousand feet probably wasn't too good an idea, either. Chuck and I settled on a single-story circular home featuring a large living room and satellite bedrooms and baths. It was located in the "nice section" of Durango, next to a public park that featured only occasional gunfire at night. The house came with a swimming pool and a Volkswagen Bug that had two usable gears. The place fit John's needs and was priced at the take-it-or-leave-it price of US$10,000 a month. We took it. It was obviously the best Durango had to offer. Assignment completed, Chuck and I flew home to Los Angeles.

Just after New Year's Day, 1994, John and a truncated posse—Frank Hernandez, Silvio Scarano, former Argonaut lineman turned John's personal trainer Kelvin Pruenster, and I traveled via private jet to Durango. I delighted in watching everyone's eyes grow large as we were driven into the city.

Here we were, six years short of a new century: John, my friend and employer, was getting physically larger by the day, while his career was becoming more uncertain. Frostbacks was getting smaller, my job more tenuous, and all the while my personal life was a disaster. I was missing, aching for, Kari and all that she and our life together had been.

Filming proceeded slowly. Director Markle seemed intimidated by and unsure of how to use his big star. My days were broken up by visits to the torta truck and cell phone calls to the Frostbacks office. The weeks crawled like desert tortoises. Most evenings were spent at John's casa, watching movie videos, drinking, and listening for the intermittent rounds of gunfire in the park. Some nights, at 3:00 or 4:00 in the morning, I would drive the dilapidated Beetle home past the park, through the residential streets that narrowed as I approached downtown Durango and the El Presidente. My senses were on full alert, but I was not really scared. These were the days before drug cartel assassinations and kidnappings took over so much of Mexico.

The shoot was a disaster; uncleared hurdles included an unfunny script, a total lack of chemistry between John, Richard Lewis, and Ellen Greene, and John missing home. What was really missing was John Hughes. John didn't want to be in Mexico and was especially unhappy appearing in yet another piece of dreck. As miserable as he was, John was always thinking of others, and so he hired a local priest to come on set during Ash Wednesday to perform rites for the many Catholic crew members. Perhaps John had him perform a novena for a hit film.

While John most influenced me by teaching me about follow-through, my biggest impact on him was organization. John was a guy who would write down ideas for *SCTV* sketches on drink napkins at the bar, coming in the next day to the writers' meeting fumbling through rum-soaked pieces of paper as he presented possible sketches. He was a volcano of ideas but a lava flow of disorganization. The essence of my work for him was always to look forward. We had to get from point A to B, and no one else thought about that process. Then what would happen when we get to point B? Where would we be, who would be there, where would we have to go next? Working out all those logistics was my responsibility. Everyone else at Frostbacks and in the Chongos kept their noses to the road trying to keep pace with their leader. I looked at the horizon. I kept it level. I opened John's eyes a bit in terms of managing each day: what we had to accomplish, who was involved, and how and where it would get done. He was the talent, the brain trust, the guy on camera. He didn't need to be concerned with minutiae involving location, time, and personnel. That was my job. John's mantra was, "Don't second-guess, just anticipate."

I did second-guess him once and failed miserably. While he was shooting *Wagons East!* in Durango, he wanted to film a commercial promoting the upcoming season's ticket sales for his Toronto Argonauts. The sixty-second spot called for a TelePrompTer, a scrolling video cue card from which John could read the prepared message. It was very difficult getting anything other than tequila and tortas down in Durango. I didn't consult John about the prompter as he was busy filming, so I did the best I could under the circumstances. A playback monitor looking like something out of 1950s Tajikistan was delivered. The screen was set up, and John tried to work with it. The miserable quality of the picture made it next to impossible to read. Frustrated with the reality of twelve weeks in Durango and dealing with a television set that would have been thrown out the window in the *SCTV* opening credits, John shot me a look that said, "What the fuck were you thinking?" Words were not necessary. I felt like an idiot thirteen-year-old again. John turned and walked back to the set. Instead of settling for an electronic device from Manuel's TV and Volkswagen Repair, I should have called Los Angeles and secured a state-of-the-art monitor with an operator and told John that we'd have to wait a day to get exactly what he wanted. I went for speed and ease, not satisfaction, and it backfired. Never again, I vowed. From that day forward, I kept John informed of the trajectory of an item or a person needed for his next plan. I could have gotten a job with UPS. I bored him with details to the point that he acknowledged there was life outside of his insolated bubble.

"John, I spoke with half a dozen prompting systems companies in L.A. and the best one is called QTV," I explained during a break in filming. "QTV's best operator is named Lynette, and she will fly to Durango with the equipment."

"Fine," John said. He was running dialogue in his head.

"She has to fly commercial," I continued.

"Fine."

"The earliest she can be here is the day after tomorrow. She'll rework her schedule just for you."

"Okay." He was miles away.

An assistant director approached.

"It won't be cheap," I droned. "Should she send the bill to the Argonauts?"

"I'll handle it," John said as he started back to the set.

"You'll be happy this time," I said, following him. "Shall I give her the go-ahead?"

"Yeah, fine."

"It'll be worth it." Now I was really overselling. John was disappearing into a tribe of Hollywood Indians.

"You're killing me, Bob," John joked over his shoulder.

"Lynette only works in Farsi and Cajun," I yelled after him, relieving my tension. I don't think he heard me.

John was going to finish the dismal *Wagons East!* sometime in March, and I was planning to fly directly to Phoenix from the film set for the start of Carpenter's trial. John was threatening to attend it with me. He wanted to lend his support and get a close look at the suspect. John's presence would have shaken the courtroom. "Will it be *Cool Runnings* for murder suspect John Henry Carpenter?" one of *Court TV*'s talking heads might have asked, giving the trial a few minutes of airtime.

In the midst of John's cinematic unpleasantries in Durango he received some very unwelcome news about his beloved Toronto Argonauts. Candy and Gretzky may have been the public faces of the franchise, but they were just minority stakeholders in the team. The real say-so rested with L.A. Kings and Argos majority owner Bruce McNall. He had gone into the Argos strictly as an investment. John was in it for different reasons. He was the local kid who'd made good, the Neil McNeil High School lineman turned movie star, who was now an owner of the centerpiece of Toronto sports. John was on the field, in the dressing room, hanging out with the players, traveling across Canada promoting the product, getting would-be fans off their duffs and into the stadiums. He was living his Canadian Dream.

John's personal glory aside, at the end of three seasons in the red, in spite of the first season of sellouts and the Grey Cup Championship, the always-looking-over-his-shoulder McNall and his soulless chief financial officer, Suzan Waks, dumped the team without even a courtesy call to his minority partner. John found out about the sale during a phone call from his Los Angeles–based accountant, Gary Kress. His childhood team, his first sporting love, had been sold behind his back. It was crushing. I'd never seen John more depressed during the entire time I'd known him. He felt utterly betrayed. All the goodwill he had sold to the people of Toronto and across Canada during those three seasons now appeared like a complete sham. He was angry, disheartened, and embarrassed. He felt as though he were just another Hollywood weasel, a con man. If John had had more power than that of a minority owner, he would surely have voted to maintain ownership, continue to sell seats, packages, and good times to his fellow Torontonians. McNall, an L.A. boy with no commitments to anyone, was gone in an Inglewood minute.

After hearing of the sale, John went on a two-day tequila bender. I'd never seen him drink tequila in the thirteen years I'd known him. He was seriously in the dumps. The Chongos took turns sitting Shiva with him as he mourned the loss of his baby, but it wasn't long before we were all burned out. Considering all the alcohol that had been consumed over the years since our initial meeting, it was a shock to see John put an ice bag on top of his hurting head. But then if I'd drunk half the tequila John had, I would've been six feet under a Boot Hill cross.

John had a few weeks remaining on the shoot. He knew that I had been organizing a posthumous Kari Hildebrand art show at the Orlando Gallery in Los Angeles. It would stand as her only solo exhibition and was going to benefit the Wellness Community in Santa Monica, which offered free support and counseling to cancer patients and their families and friends. Gallery owner Bob Gino donated his space for two weeks starting on Friday, March 4, and he and the Wellness Community would split the proceeds. I wasn't taking a dime. I was just happy to make this happen for Kari. I only wish I could have seen her smile of satisfaction.

I said good-bye to John and the Chongos at the end of February and flew back to Los Angeles. While my work was done in Durango except for hand-holding sessions, I was still busy organizing upcoming publicity for John's directorial debut, *Hostage for a Day*, which was to air on the Fox Network in March. I also had other Frostbacks business to handle and still had to collect Kari's work for her show. John and I decided I should stay in Los Angeles.

At 10:00 on the eve of Kari's opening, I checked in with John in Durango. "Helloo," he answered in his signature way.

"Hey, John, it's Bob. How'd it go today?"

"It went well." He sounded tired and as though he had had a few rum and Cokes. "I was happy with the scene I did today with Richard Lewis."

"That's great," I said, feeling guilty for not being in Durango, but secure knowing I was where I should be. "You've only got twelve days left."

"Yeah, a couple of weeks. I can't wait to get out of here," John said wistfully.

It felt like a prisoner/visitor exchange through that bulletproof glass. I continued my cheerleader role. "You'll be back in Brentwood in no time, amigo. We all miss you. I wish you could be at Kari's show tomorrow night," I said, trying to pump the energy up a notch.

"Me, too," John sighed. "I'm sorry I can't be there. Good luck with the show. Give me a call and let me know how the opening went." John was clearly trying his damnedest, but he sounded as if the governor had just denied his plea for clemency.

"Hang in there, John," I said. "I'll give you a call about this time tomorrow night and give you a complete update."

"Okay, Bob. Say hi to everybody," John said with a tinge of the gallows.

"Talk to you tomorrow." I hung up the telephone.

My house was quiet, still. My mind was not. I was one of the last standing employees of Frostbacks Production. I had worked steadily alongside John for six years. What began as a two-week tryout on the *Armed and Dangerous* publicity tour had evolved into full-time employment as publicist, road manager, consultant, psychiatrist, and friend. I was always true to his words in the interviews and articles I had written about him. Celebrities like John, Chevy Chase, and all the others who'd been burned by writers appreciated the fact that I'd printed their words just the way they'd said them. And John had been there for me through the years of Kari's illness and after her death as a friend first. I didn't want anything from John. We had seen people come and go—professionals, so-called friends, acquaintances, a parade that ultimately wanted to tap into the Candy bank, the Candy favor wagon, the Candy good time—everybody wanted something. I had proved that I was there for him all the time, doing my jobs and watching his back, no strings attached. John and Rose Candy trusted me, and Rose's circle of family and friends was even tighter and smaller than John's.

The next morning, the telephone rang at 7:00.

"Hello?" I croaked.

"Bob?"

"Yeah."

"It's Frankie."

"Hey, Frankie. What's up?"

"I don't know how to say this . . ."

Why the hell was Frankie Hernandez calling me at 7:00 in the morning? I waited, a million scenarios ricocheting through my brain.

"John's dead."

Make that a million and one. Was this a sick joke courtesy of the bored Chongos?

Frankie continued. "We went to his house to pick him up to go out to location. There was no answer so we busted the door open and found him in the bedroom."

Frankie wasn't bored; he was in shock. Now so was I. "What happened?"

"It looks like a heart attack," said Frankie. "He must have been sitting on the edge of the bed putting his shoes on. It looked like he'd just fallen backward onto the bed. His feet were on the floor. This is unfuckingbelievable, Bob." He sounded like he might cry.

"It sure is, Frankie. Listen, I've got to tell Rose before she hears it on the news. Thanks, Frankie. I'll call you back in a little bit."

Although family and friends had feared this moment for years—the result of John's excessive drinking, smoking, weight, high cholesterol, and family history (his father had succumbed to a heart attack at a young age)—still, I was paralyzed with shock. I stood for a moment in a haze until the images of Rose, Jennifer, and Christopher became crystal clear. I picked up the phone and called Chuck. As I never called him this early in the day, he immediately anticipated the worst when he heard my voice. I explained what had happened according to Frankie. Chuck and I knew what we had to do.

This was 1994, well before tweeting and texting and viral video. CNN was the only twenty-four-hour news service, but all of the network morning programs were broadcasting. I didn't want Rose to get the bad news from Katie Couric or Charles Gibson. I couldn't imagine a worse scenario than receiving life-altering news from a media outlet as millions of strangers heard it simultaneously. When my dad was killed I was glad I didn't hear about it from traffic and weather on the eights.

Chuck and I met near the San Diego Freeway in Sherman Oaks and drove together out of the Valley to the Westside. We made good time, getting to John's house in Mandeville Canyon in twenty minutes. My worst fears of pulling up to the house and seeing local television news trunks blocking the driveway happily didn't come to pass. It was quiet up and down the block as we buzzed the electric gate. One of the housekeepers answered.

"Hi, it's Bob Crane and Chuck Sloan to see Mrs. Candy," I said in my most emotionless voice.

We parked, got out of the car, and went to the front door. Chuck and I looked at each other. I rang the bell. We stood there like a couple of glum missionaries. It was 8:06. Lives were about to be altered forever.

Rose opened the door. Chuck and I didn't say a word. She looked at Chuck, trying to figure out why he was there with me. Then she looked at me. It took her only a few seconds to work it out. No one said a word.

Rose let out the loudest shriek I've ever heard. Chuck and I surrounded her, worried she was going to pass out. We took her back inside, and when she calmed down enough to make sense of it, we told her what Frankie had told us.

By 8:30, the breaking news was on CNN. Rose's telephone was ring-ing, and friends of the family were showing up at the front gate. Chuck stayed at the house while I accompanied Rose to St. Martin of Tours, the Catholic school that Jennifer, fourteen, and Christopher, nine, attended. Rose and I stood in the principal's office and watched as two assistants pulled the Candy kids out of their classes and walked them toward us. They were about to find out that their father would never hug, play, or laugh with them again. Even though I had been in their position, I had no words of wisdom that would lessen the body blow they were about to receive. I felt hopeless and heartbroken: for them, for me.

The *Wagons East!* production was rocked. It had lost its star and leader. The producers, Gary Goodman and Bobby Newmyer, shut down production while they, director Markle, the assistant directors, and production manager Parvin figured out how many scenes were left to be filmed involving their departed number one on the call sheet and how they would deal with this gaping hole.

Frankie Hernandez had to deal with the transportation of John's body back to Los Angeles. Rose faxed a letter to the local authorities stating there was to be no autopsy in Durango. Her instructions were to just ship her husband home. The Chongos had their final mission accompanying their fallen commander.

By early afternoon the dazed and mourning were arriving by the busloads at the Candy home. Chuck and I fielded calls, attended to Rose's needs, and greeted visitors. It occurred to me that there wasn't much else I could do for John and his family at this point and that Kari was having an art show opening that night. I had a vision of Kari and John sitting side by side on the Candys' couch less than six months earlier when Kari and I announced her dismal prognosis.

I received a phone call from Janet Spiegel, who had helped me organize Kari's exhibition. She admired John but had already decided to "get with what is," as Jack Nicholson once told me. "Kari's show is still on for tonight, right?" she asked.

"You're damned right it is," I said defiantly. I was sick of death. "The show must go on, and you can quote me." We both mustered a less than heartfelt laugh.

That evening the Orlando Gallery was packed with several hundred fans of Kari's work. The Wellness Community, the gallery, and people who knew me all wanted a reaction to the day's upheaval. My emotions were sadness for Rose, Jennifer, Christopher, John's mother, aunt, and brother (Van, Fran, and Jim, respectively), John's friends, and his fans around the world. I felt joy and happiness for Kari, who was having her first full-blown solo art show, and for the attending supporters, who could see dozens of her idiosyncratic and humorous pieces in one location. Disbelief was the other consuming sentiment: my career as a publicist and bob-of-all-trades had just imploded. I had lost my wife, I had lost my boss and friend, and I assumed I'd be losing my job, all in the last six months. Could it get any worse?

The opening was a huge success. I had the pleasure of writing out a check to the Wellness Community for several thousand dollars, the proceeds from Kari's sold artwork, but I never got to make that phone call to John to tell him how well it went.

I'd been Kari's husband in a marriage not without its issues: disagreements, ego problems, Kari's basic mistrust of men, and my basic mistrust of marriage stemming from my dad's poor behavior toward women in general and my mom specifically. And I'd been a foot soldier for John, watching his back, guarding him as much as I could. With both their deaths, I felt as if I were the civilian equivalent of the military messenger, the person who makes the phone calls reporting death, transports the ashes, informs the widow, arranges the memorial, makes sure the ashes get spread or the burial is undertaken without a hitch. I was becoming Charon, the ferryman on the River Styx.

John's memorial at St. Martin of Tours in Brentwood and funeral at Holy Cross Cemetery in Culver City were star-studded events. The *Los Angeles Times, People* magazine, the *National Enquirer,* and *Entertainment Tonight* were among the news organizations that sent reporters and photographers to scan the hundreds of attendees looking for familiar faces. *SCTV* was well represented by Martin Short, Dave Thomas, Eugene Levy, Joe Flaherty, and producer Andrew Alexander. John's *Splash* and *Volunteers* costar Tom Hanks was there, as were *National Lampoon's Vacation* cohort Chevy Chase and *Stripes* buddy Bill Murray. Jeff Bridges also attended, though I wasn't aware that John and Bridges had ever even met. Perhaps Jeff was a fan just paying his respects. Wayne and Janet Jones Gretzky were there.

I was stationed at the front door of the church along with some of the other Chongos, making sure that the paparazzi and funeral crashers were kept out. Frankie Hernandez, Silvio Scarano, Kelvin Pruenster, and I were still guarding John, still watching his back. Also walking the parapet with us was the sad sack Bret Gallagher, a new recruit to Frostbacks who had joined the ranks barely a week before John died. For his short tour of duty he received three months' severance pay.

The hearse arrived bearing John's coffin and was transferred to a gurneylike cart to be taken into the church. As John was rolled down the aisle of the full house of silent mourners, one of the wheels on the gurney squeaked loudly with every rotation. John would have gotten a huge kick out of that.

John's *The Great Outdoors* costar Dan Aykroyd gave an emotional, Sunday-go-to-meetin' eulogy. He bolstered Christopher and Jennifer, telling them how lucky they were to have John as their dad and letting them know that we were all going to watch out for them in their fatherless future. One person who truly did was Jim Belushi, who later took young Jennifer under his wing to work on several television and film projects.

The Candy posse had one final assignment—ensuring John's safe arrival at his final resting spot, a crypt above that of actor Fred MacMurray at the Holy Cross Mausoleum in Culver City. The seventy-car procession left the St. Martin's grounds and headed east on Sunset Boulevard and then south on the 405, the San Diego Freeway. On any typical Wednesday at noon in L.A., that seven- or eight-mile trip could easily take forty-five minutes, but this was not a normal Wednesday. The Los Angeles Police Department in tandem with the California Highway Patrol escorted the procession to the freeway; unbeknownst to us, they had closed off all the on-ramps along the route. I looked through the rear window of the car I was riding in and noticed that, aside from the cortege and the motorcycle cops, the entire southbound side of the freeway, all five lanes, one of the most heavily traveled roads in the world, was empty. A CHP car had all traffic stopped on the freeway under the Sunset Boulevard overpass. Cars were backed up in a standstill all the way to the Sepulveda Pass. Dozens of cars idled on the on-ramps waiting for the CHP officers on motorcycles to give them the go-ahead. I witnessed one irate driver looking for a reason for the delay. The officer mouthed, "John Candy," and the driver's frustration immediately dissipated. It was a show of love and respect by Southern California law enforcement for a man who had always acted as if he were a typical working guy, just like them. The sight of an empty freeway, midday, midweek, in the land of the car, brought chills to all of us. This freeway detail was the ultimate gift from the LAPD and CHP. Rose Candy was just as surprised and touched by the actions of the good officers bidding farewell to their friend as were the rest of us. Gazing out the car window, I felt a kinship with the motorcycle cop holding off traffic for John right up to the end.

The morning after John's funeral, I opened the front door at Frostbacks at 9:30. The space sat quietly, as if waiting for something to happen. The Frostbacks Bar and Grill was holding its breath. John's mother, aunt, and brother were in town for the funeral, and they wanted to have a look around the offices. I watched John's older brother, Jim, walk into John's office and sit down in his chair behind his immense wood desk. He fingered the stacks of scripts, the letters and notes, as if trying to receive a message from his little brother. If a picture tells a story, this image was of a man searching for clues, for directions, from a brother he never connected with in life. Jim was jealous of my relationship with John, a friendship with no conditions. The Candy brothers had erected barriers between each other decades earlier, and I could see those memories playing out in Jim's head now. Jim never had power or fame or even individuality. He was John Candy's brother, subsidized by John, the caretaker of their mother and aunt. Jim sat in John's swivel chair grasping for any signs of a common ground, but the gulf between them had no crossing. Van, John's mother, led her sister, Fran, and her brother, Ken, on a walk-through of her son's playground for the last time. The once-vibrant space felt like a museum on a Monday. Frostbacks' cavernous office complex was now lifeless.

I felt as remote as Keir Dullea's astronaut character in *2001: A Space Odyssey*. Every afternoon when I left the empty office, which reminded me of John every second I was there, I returned to my empty house, which reminded me of Kari even before I got out of the car. Her death replayed in my mind as I walked through the tall, wild grasses she planted, the rosemary she nurtured, the lantana and sages and lavender she babied. Kari was all around me, blooming, scenting the air, feeding the bees and the butterflies and the hummingbirds. When I got in the door I would listen to Sarah McLachlan's "Fumbling towards Ecstasy" and James Taylor's "Secret of Life." I could see Kari's untouchable face while I sobbed. Crying came easily and became a necessary therapy for me. Weeping at night was a way to dump all the emotion I controlled during the day. I cried more over Kari's death than I did over my dad's or anything else in my life. When the tears want out, you can't keep 'em in. Kari's death is the saddest moment of my life. I still love "Secret of Life," but even now I can't listen to it without welling up.

When you're sick, it's hard to talk to people who are well. I didn't want to burden friends and family members with my dark, claustrophobic thoughts. I never looked for an escape or a crutch. I didn't turn to religion. I didn't turn to drugs. I have little patience for the latest celebrity or child of one who has died of an overdose or is habitually entering rehab. I didn't have to turn to heroin, I didn't have to turn to coke or prescription drugs or alcohol. I tapped into the inner strength that my mom and Chuck demonstrated everyday. My mom never crumbled, and Chuck had created his own blueprint for life—no one helped him. He built it himself, moved in, and lived it everyday. I followed their examples. I took care of what had to be done each day and didn't rely on other people. I had to face myself. I had to do it alone. I derived satisfaction and strength from relying on myself. The more I did it, the easier it became.

In the mornings I would drive to John's shrine and begin yet another day of sorting through the offerings. I was constantly receiving calls from the press asking questions about one of Canada's fallen heroes. Plans were already being made for John's playful face to adorn a Canadian 51¢ stamp and for his name to be chiseled into Toronto's Walk of Fame, not far from Neil Young's.

I also strapped myself in for another roller coaster ride, the television debut of *Hostage for a Day*. What would have prompted a raucous and celebratory viewing party in the Frostbacks Bar and Grill instead became a wake attended by a few former Frostbacks employees and the *Hostage* rewriter Peter Torokvei. I hoped Kari, John, and my dad were having their own party. The film was dedicated to Kari. Unfortunately, all the credits were locked in, so another dedication—to John—couldn't be added. The few of us stood at the bar and watched the movie, knowing that this was the last social event that would ever take place at Frostbacks Production. Bittersweet didn't half cover it.

After everyone left and I was closing up the office, I began to think of all the work John and Kari had accomplished, professionally and personally, helping people get through the private hell of their own days. I missed dealing with daily problems by sharing a laugh with John. I missed his thoughtfulness, generosity, and courtesy toward humanity. I smiled, knowing John's tender and madcap performances would provoke laughter forever. I missed Kari's resplendent ideas and visions for a better place in which to live. How many beautiful, colorful, climate-appropriate gardens will bloom year after year with the life Kari imbued in them? In John and Kari there was light and warmth and a humanity that seemed to me to be in very short supply. My life was forever enriched for their presence and now irrevocably diminished with their passing. Friends and family all craved their company, but over time we'd reconcile ourselves to the harrowing reality that they had left our world. A search for substitutes would be futile.

40

Judgment at Scottsdale, 1994

In May, Maricopa County Superior Court judge Gregory Martin ruled that videotaped sexual encounters involving my dad, Carpenter, and various women, shot in different *Beginner's Luck* tour cities, could be shown to jurors during the trial. Martin said, "They are relevant because they establish the relationship defendant John Carpenter had with Crane." I shuddered at what was coming.

On June 1, two years after Carpenter was first arrested and charged with my dad's murder, I, still referred to as "Mr. Robert Crane Jr.," received a subpoena ordering my appearance on June 20 "to give testimony on behalf of the State of Arizona."

On June 16, I received a letter from legal assistant Dick Strobel informing me that the defense "has filed a Motion to Continue the trial until late August of 1994, and the judge has granted that motion."

On August 15, I received a subpoena "for your testimony at trial" re: *State of Arizona v. John Carpenter,* CR 92-04718, for September 6.

After the jury selection process was completed, the trial finally got under way. Judge Martin read the Willits instruction to the jurors which, in a nutshell, states that "any evidence lost or destroyed by the State of Arizona can be looked on by the jurors as a weakness in the prosecution's case." Court-appointed public defender Stephen Avilla planned to focus on "the slim physical evidence," raising the notion that "Crane's active sex life" gave "perhaps a jealous husband or boyfriend . . . or even the women involved" the motive for murder. Carpenter told the *New Times,* an alternative publication: "I never even had a fight with Bob. He was my friend. And he was the goose who laid the golden egg for me, in terms of meeting ladies." Robert J. Shutts and the prosecution team would illustrate that fact by showing the court videotapes containing images of "Crane and Carpenter simultaneously having sex with the same woman." They would concentrate their case on the point that my dad was ending

Robert J. Shutts
Deputy County Attorney
Bar ID #: 003469
301 West Jefferson Suite 800
Phoenix, AZ   85003
Telephone: 602 506-5780
Attorney for Plaintiff

IN THE SUPERIOR COURT OF THE STATE OF ARIZONA
IN AND FOR THE COUNTY OF MARICOPA

The State of Arizona,	)	NO. CR 92-04718
	)	
Plaintiff,	)	CRIMINAL SUBPOENA
	)	
vs.	)	
	)	MURDER FIRST DEGREE
JOHN CARPENTER,	)	Victim: Bob Crane
	)	
Defendant.	)	

THE STATE OF ARIZONA, to:

Mr. Robert Crane Jr.

Van Nuys, CA   90049

YOU ARE HEREBY ORDERED TO APPEAR AT 1:30 p.m. on SEPTEMBER 6, 1994, at the Superior Court of Arizona for Maricopa County (report to the Honorable Gregory Martin, Central Court Building, 201 West Jefferson, Room 6A, Phoenix, Arizona) and remain there until excused by the judge conducting the proceedings or otherwise discharged, to give testimony on behalf of the State of Arizona.

IF YOU FAIL TO APPEAR AS ORDERED, A WARRANT WILL BE ISSUED FOR YOUR ARREST.

DATED at Phoenix, Arizona, August 15, 1994.

Our office will contact   RICHARD M. ROMLEY
you with the exact date   MARICOPA COUNTY ATTORNEY
and time your testimony
will be needed.
                                By _Robert J Shutts_
                                   Robert J. Shutts
                                   Deputy County Attorney

CERTIFICATE OF SERVICE
The undersigned swears (or affirms) that he/she is qualified to serve this subpoena and did so by showing the original to and informing the witness of its contents and by delivering a copy thereof to him/her at _____a.m./p.m. on _____, 19____, at _____, Arizona.

_____
Person serving subpoena

Superior Court subpoena, Maricopa County, Arizona, August 15, 1994 (author's collection).

the friendship "that gave Carpenter access to women attracted by the actor's fame . . . women that [defendant John Henry Carpenter] could never obtain for himself." They would argue that Carpenter killed my dad with two blows from the missing camera tripod (and strangulation from an electrical cord). As evidence they had a three-inch blood trace in Carpenter's rental car along with a "dark, irregularly shaped" one-sixteenth-inch speck of brain tissue.

Shutts argued that Carpenter "returned" to the scene of the crime by telephone, calling the afternoon of June 29 asking for my dad, but never asking why the phone was answered by a police detective instead. Carpenter also called the Windmill Dinner Theatre and spoke with employees Jenny Brown and Linda Hinshaw, asking where my dad was and if he would be in that night. Then Carpenter made the strange, almost noncall to me, followed by another call to my dad's Scottsdale apartment.

Victoria Berry took the stand, the second of a hundred witnesses for the prosecution. She described her costar, my dad, as a "vain, sexually obsessed man" who "memorialized his sexual escapades" on videotape. She told the courtroom that "shortly after 2 p.m." on June 29, 1978, she entered my dad's apartment through the unlocked front door, walked through the dark hallway calling out my dad's name, looked in a bedroom, and saw a person in the bed with "the head all smashed in . . . blood all over." She said she was there to meet my dad to overdub dialogue on a videotape that "John Carpenter recorded three days earlier of Bob and I rehearsing our scene in the play."

Next, Patricia Olson Ateyeh Crane took the stand. She told the courtroom that her husband's extramarital sexual behavior never bothered her ("He often slept with and videotaped women he met while touring"), that their marriage never created "missed opportunities" for the "hobby" that "consumed him" ("He often filmed family events . . . as well as his sex acts with women"), that her husband's video equipment ("including several camera tripods") always went on the road with him, that his pornographic video library "was never an issue" in their marriage. Always the manipulator, Patti didn't mind the jury thinking of her as compliant, just not complicit. She was playing the role of the good little hausfrau who couldn't control the ravenous appetites of her colonel, not the scheming puppet master holding all the strings.

September 6, my testimony date, came and went, but I wasn't called to the stand. Weeks went by before I received a call from Strobel. That evening, Chuck and I flew to Phoenix, checking into the downtown Holiday Inn Crowne Plaza. I had not attended any of the proceedings up to that point because I was still busy boxing up Frostbacks. A few days passed as we awaited instructions from Shutts and company. But life was not without its small pleasures, as we had one of the best hamburgers ever one afternoon at the hotel. That evening, Shutts dropped by, explaining

269

that the next day appeared to be a choice one for me to take the stand. Shutts knew in his heart that Carpenter was guilty, but with a sixteen-year lag between crime and trial, and the lackluster performance by most of the county servants in pursuit of gathering and preserving elements at the crime scene, he also knew that this trial was definitely taking an uphill route.

The next day at noon, I put on my best suit and Chuck and I walked through downtown Phoenix past tall commercial buildings to the Central Court Building on West Jefferson. With the temperature over one hundred degrees, I was a sweaty, nervous mess when I met with Shutts during the court's lunch break. He was not pleased with what he saw. I had to come off as cool and calm on the stand, not someone reminiscent of Peter Lorre in *M*. Wisely, he delayed my appearance.

Meanwhile, Carpenter's long-estranged son, John Merrill, described his father as having "had a violent problem in the past and he called it tunnel vision." Merrill told the silenced courtroom that the "tunnel vision" would occur when his father got into inflamed arguments with other men. "He told me he took karate classes to gain self-control," said Merrill. (An earlier witness from the Winfield Apartments had testified that Carpenter had told her he was a karate expert and had even demonstrated how to deliver a lethal blow.)

Thomas Jarvis, the medical examiner who performed my dad's autopsy, said to Shutts and the jury that my dad had died within a minute after being struck by a "rounded blunt instrument." The electrical cord, in his opinion, didn't play a role in the death.

Consultant Rod Englert, a homicide investigator from the Multnomah County Sheriff's Office in Portland, Oregon, testified that the murder weapon was a camera tripod; this was consistent with bloodstains on the bedsheet that formed a V. There were also "hand smear marks" on my dad's upper back. Englert remarked that the initial blow was dealt with "medium velocity," and it was the subsequent, harder hit that delivered the blood splatter.

The prosecution also made good on its offer of homemade porno, shot with a video camera atop a tripod, the tripod used to kill the victim. Public defender Avilla objected to the video of buddies Crane and Carpenter having sex with a woman being shown in court because the images would "inflame the passions of the jury," but the judge allowed it. Shutts attempted to show that the tripod that helped deliver the XXX-rated pictures costarring Carpenter was the same tripod that accomplished the murderous assault and was then carried away in Carpenter's rental vehicle to be disposed of.

By the time I took the stand, I could sense that the prosecution's case had slipped away. I attempted to make eye contact with the jurors who, for the most part, declined, possibly out of either embarrassment or disgust at having just seen my dad, All-American hero Colonel Hogan, father and husband, engaged in low-grade, black-and-white, three-way sex recorded by a video camera possibly attached to the blunt instrument that ended his life. It was autoerotic decadent misbehavior, costarring a fallen television actor, his "best friend," a woman who didn't know any better, and presented by the New Technology at its instantaneous best. I sat in the witness chair, looked to my left at Judge Martin, who seemed preoccupied or bored, looked to my right at the middle-American jurors, who looked away, looked straight ahead at prosecutor Shutts, who knew he had a failure on his hands after sixteen years of Scottsdale Police Department fuck-ups. I looked back to my right—the collective look in the jury box was one of wanting to get the hell out of that courtroom and into a long, hot shower. I glanced at public defender Avilla, who had victory in his eyes.

Finally, I stared at video equipment salesperson John Henry Carpenter who, no matter the outcome of the trial, would no longer be Hollywood's favorite sidekick, the guy who took the modern electric gizmos out of their cardboard boxes in upscale living rooms. We hadn't spoken since the summer of 1978. He looked at me with dead shark eyes, not allowing himself to feel the connection between the witness and the victim. I felt like Tom Sawyer looking out into the crowded courtroom at Injun Joe. My main bit of testimony was supposed to drive home to the jurors that my dad had grown tired of his relationship with the defendant and that he was making changes in his life ("seeing orange for the first time") that would affect Carpenter. I don't know if it made any impression at all.

Prosecutor Shutts made his closing arguments to the jury on October 26. He reinforced that there had been no break-in to the apartment and that Carpenter had easy access to the crime scene. He reiterated that my dad wanted to end their friendship and that Carpenter retaliated with two blows to his friend's head with a camera tripod that was now missing but that had left a blood trail to Carpenter's rental car. "John Carpenter needs to be told that you don't kill your friends even if you're told that they don't want you hanging around," said Shutts.

Public defender Avilla faced the jury and said that the state of Arizona had "failed to prove its case," berating the prosecution's lack of hard evidence—like a murder weapon, for example ("the tripod theory is absurd," said Avilla, citing the opinion of a forensics expert who favored a tire iron or crowbar)— and accusing the prosecution of hiding behind "sex, sex, sex," referring to the videotape shown in the courtroom. "There are two things sex can't replace," explained Avilla. "One is chocolate, the other is hard evidence."

So ended the eight-week trial. The jury spent two and a half days deliberating and returned to the courtroom on October 31. The jury foreman, Marine sergeant Michael Lake, referring to the "speck," the dark mass on the Department of Public Safety's lost and found photographs, later explained to the media, "Nobody knows what it was, not even the doctors. . . . There wasn't any proof. You can't prove someone guilty on speculation." The verdict was "not guilty." Happy Halloween.

John Carpenter was, naturally, elated. As his wife, Diana, sobbed, "It's over, it's over" to the press, he proclaimed, "My life is back together again after sixteen years."

That's more than I could say for my dad. Carpenter outlived him by twenty years, dying of a heart attack on September 4, 1998.

41

Ninety to Zero, 1994–1995

Much to my surprise, Rose Candy kept me on through 1994, breaking down the Frostbacks offices, packing up and sorting the paperwork. The bar went to a restaurant on Navy Pier in Chicago, and the sound studio was donated to UCLA's communication department. I sent out eight-by-ten photographs of John without autographs to fans whose requests arrived too late for a signature, and I hosted several of John's friends and colleagues on a final walkabout through his workspace. The hours, days, months, and years of John's life and creative output were reflected in the photographs, movie posters, jukebox, bank of chairs from the demolished Comiskey Park in Chicago, boxes of hats, jackets, T-shirts, "Valkenvania" (*Nothing but Trouble*) police badges, *Uncle Buck* and *Only the Lonely* duffel bags, theater lobby displays, videocassettes, and laser discs, now lined up in neat rows for transfer and storage in a cool, dark, quiet, unfriendly location. John's road trip was over—from ninety miles an hour to zero in an instant.

My relatively brief tour of duty as a publicist for John Candy came to an unceremonious end. I had come to disdain publicists. The film and television industries were changing rapidly, and I couldn't care less about playing the role of protector of and buffer for most working actors and actresses. Dealing with Jim Belushi? No thanks. Watching over Bonnie Hunt? Who cares? My heroes were spoken for: Jack Nicholson had had the same publicist for years; Marlon Brando didn't want one. I would have derived more pleasure taking care of writers, directors, and producers, but for the most part, their needs didn't include handholders. Besides, Stanley Kubrick wasn't looking for help.

After conducting several interviews with Candy cronies for an A&E *Biography* on John for executive producers Andrew Alexander and Rose Candy, I was out of work. Although I never thought I would say this, I missed freelancing. I missed mining information from the interview subject. I missed editing. I missed John Rezek and *Playboy* magazine.

I hadn't spoken with Rezek in a few years, and phoning him I felt as if I were making that cold call to him back in 1976 when he was an editor at *Oui* magazine. This time around, though, was a lot less stressful. I brought him up to speed on what was happening in my life. He updated me on his second wife and kids. We shared a few laughs. I pitched names. He gave me an assignment. Ex–studio head, now independent producer, Hollywood legend in her own time: Dawn Steel. I was back in Rezek's club.

42

Yet Another Cold Call, 1996

A year had passed, but my house still radiated Kari. Her spirit imbued the interior and exterior design, creating an aura unwelcoming to the few female visitors who dared cross her threshold. Kari's essence, her scent, permeated, intimidated, and spooked them all. Diane Haas, rock manager Lori Otelsberg, and actress Christopher Templeton never came over more than once. I had visions of having to tear down the structure and install Astroturf in the yard before I could go on with the rest of my life. That all changed one morning when I was anchored in my dentist's chair.

I had known Dr. Jeri Munn for many years. Kari had designed a landscape plan for her and her husband, Tom, also a dentist. Together they shared their kids, laughter, good times, love, and their dental practice. When my longtime dentist retired, Kari had sent me to Jeri. I trusted Dr. Munn with my mouth and my life. The Munns had watched helplessly as their friend Kari went through the ravages of cancer.

Now, Jeri was working on a nasty cavity in my molar. "How is the world at large? Working?" she asked.

My mouth was numb, a suction tube in one corner and a high-powered drill at the other. This was not a Q&A moment. I touched my thumb and two fingers together and raised the other two on my right hand.

"Animal?"

I wiggled the two raised fingers.

"Bird? Bunny! You're writing for *Playboy* again," deduced Jeri. "Are you dating?"

I held up two fingers.

"You've gone out on two dates? Anyone promising?"

I carefully shook my head minimally. I didn't want any accidents.

"I may have someone for you to go out with if you're up to it."

I gave Dr. Jeri a thumbs-up.

275

"Let me talk to this person, and I will call you back and let you know what it looks like," said Jeri.

I smiled, looking like Jaws, the villain from the James Bond movie.

Dr. Munn stopped drilling for a moment and stared at my well-worn Nikes. "In the meantime, you have to get some new shoes and try to look a little better."

I could feel my face flush with embarrassment. Jeri was right. I had to get my act together and face the real world. If I hadn't had a dozen implements in my mouth I would have asked when she branched out into fashion advice.

When Jeri called a few days later, I sensed her excitement over the phone. I could imagine the matchmaker song from *Fiddler on the Roof* playing somewhere in the background. I was secretly hoping Jeri was going to tell me that she and Tom had broken up and announce her own availability. Every man who met Jeri fell in love with her. But no. "Her name is Leslie Bertram and she works in television and is interested in talking to you," said Jeri, her smile beaming through the landline. She gave me Leslie's telephone number. I thanked her and promised to call back with the play-by-play.

The cold phone call. I had made so many of these frosty outreaches over the years it was becoming second nature, but I still thought of Dave Fryer, Chris, Chuck, my dad—all doing their spiel. Like my dad, I was going to be selling myself. I worked up the nerve and made the call. What was there to lose? Besides my trusty old Nikes, nothing at all.

Leslie picked up the phone after a few rings. I heard a barking dog and a young girl's voice in the background. Leslie seemed a little distracted by the raucous Jack, her German shepherd, and five-year-old Meagan, her daughter. Leslie mentioned she was working two jobs as, for lack of a better title, a switcher, on the popular television series *Murphy Brown* and *The Drew Carey Show*. Both shows were filmed in front of audiences with multiple cameras, and Leslie selected the shots that were shown on the overhead monitors in the studio. She was basically editing the episode for the editor. I was impressed.

When I called, Leslie was in the middle of prepping dinner for herself and Meagan, so we decided to continue the conversation the following day during her break on stage. I smiled as I hung up the phone. Dogs, children, a sweet voice—no cancer, no death. These were new lives and there was hope for a future.

I waited for Leslie's phone call with great anticipation. I was hoping that Leslie might be the one to take me by the hand and pull this wooly mammoth from the tar pit I had allowed myself to be mired in since the deaths of Kari and John and the reliving of my dad's death through the John Carpenter trial. Where were the fields of poppies? Maybe Leslie knew.

I allowed the phone to ring a few times before I picked up. It was Leslie, on a dinner break from the *Murphy Brown* stage at Warner Brothers. She explained that she worked the Candice Bergen series on Mondays and Tuesdays and Drew Carey on Thursdays and Fridays. Wednesday was her day off. "I hear you're in the business," Leslie said innocently.

I cringed. I have always disliked the phrase "in the business." Hell, everybody in Los Angeles—pool cleaners, car wash attendants, bartenders, waiters, realtors—is just waiting to be discovered. Leslie's estranged husband, Mark, was in the business—a producer of reality-based television programs. Everyone had a hand in. I was just a freelance hack. I immediately went on the defensive and became a wiseass. "We're all in the business out here, aren't we?"

Well, that was a conversation ender. After a few uncomfortable seconds, Leslie poked through the dead air and suggested we get together the following Wednesday. I recovered, dusting off the layer of inferiority that had settled on me, and enthusiastically exclaimed, "I'd love to meet you for dinner. Looking forward to it."

The following week I sped north on Interstate 5 to Santa Clarita, the newer, more upscale version of the San Fernando Valley. I pulled my beige Mazda pickup truck into the driveway of Leslie's rented house. My well-traveled Audi 5000 looked nicer but had become nerve-rackingly unreliable, and I didn't want to have to call AAA on our first date. I sat in the driveway for a minute with the hope that tonight I could shed a skin and begin anew. I was a forty-four-year-old widower with a tortoiseshell cat named Nutmeg and nothing to lose.

"Happy Valentine's Day," said Leslie as she opened the front door—cheerily, but with a touch of playful sarcasm that I admired. I also admired her shapely legs and her smart skirt. I rarely saw women contemporaries in anything but pants. This was already something new and exciting.

"I would have brought you flowers, but I don't know you," I said, drawing a laugh from her.

The petite Leslie introduced me to Jack the dog and took me on a short tour of a well-worn living space. Jack was very happy to have a new creature to sniff.

"Where's your daughter?"

Leslie explained that both Meagan and Jack went back and forth between their father and mother.

"Shall we go eat?" I asked.

We drove for hours, repeatedly checking in with hostess desks all over Santa Clarita. An hour wait here, ninety minutes there. In our relationship positions, estranged and postmortem, respectively, Leslie and I had both forgotten how important Valentine's Day is to the eatery economy. We talked nonstop and easily broke the seal on the relaxation phase of our fresh encounter. Leslie's sweetness and good nature made me want to forget all the recent years of hyper-gravity that had flattened my life. I wanted to feel good again, with something, someone, to look forward to.

Finally, we found an open table for two in the bar area of a TGI Fridays. Not exactly the culinary experience we had hoped for, but we didn't care. After two hours we were hungry and wanted to continue our talkathon face-to-face. I asked Leslie to order for us—fried this and that, bar food, wine for her, and gin and tonic for me. We talked about Meagan, Kari, Mark, John Candy, marriage, cancer, death, "the business," northern California, Connecticut, our families—all with a throw-it-to-the-wind ease and lack of restraint that was refreshing and emancipating. The skirt made sense. Leslie was, fundamentally, an East Coast woman who had never actually lived there. She had familial roots in Connecticut but had been born and raised in northern California. She had attended a San Diego college for a year but had left school to work and earn her own money. Initially, she had visions of becoming an agent. She got a job as a secretary to a talent manager based on the Sunset Strip in Hollywood. But after two years of selling performers like meat, she left and took work in television production, first as a production assistant, then as assistant director, stage manager, postproduction supervisor, and now switcher. She had assisted directors Marty Pasetta and Jeff Margolis on the fifty-ninth and sixty-first Academy Awards broadcasts. Leslie loved talking about people she encountered in "the business," like her best friend, producer Suzy Friendly. We shared a shorthand as we regaled each other with the hoots and horrors of the business of show, emphasizing the excesses, egos, and outlandishness of the whole enterprise. We nodded with recognition as one of us made a point or got to the punch line of a story. I took comfort in the familiarity of our separate but interlocking experiences around celebrities and film and television production.

Leslie placed laughter high on her daily list of things to do. She was attractive, with a conservative streak in her clothing and appearance. She was a mother raising an only child. She had a solid work ethic that drove her life. She couldn't stand being dependent upon anyone, whether it was parents, husband, or friends.

After four hours of nonstop conversation, Leslie said that she had to be on the *Drew Carey* set the next morning so, sadly, we had to curtail the evening. I didn't have to be anywhere. My job was to feed Nutmeg, originally Kari's cat, now my fourteen-year-old companion. I also had to try to get interview work. Leslie had a place to go. I didn't. I was discomfited by what I felt was a big disparity in our working lives.

By the time our evening came to a close it was the day after Valentine's Day. Restaurants everywhere had totaled their gross receipts. I drove back to Leslie's calm suburban neighborhood. We walked to her front door, stood in the first silence of the evening, and looked at each other. We embraced and kissed, a short kiss with an undeclared promise of more. Jack barked as Leslie quietly closed the door behind her. Suddenly I was aware of the late-night winter chill. I got in my truck and gazed at Leslie's house. I had just met a woman who I could tell was admired by coworkers, friends, and family. She had earned their trust, respect, and dedication through her goodness, honesty, and determination. She loved her daughter, her younger brothers, Michael and David, and her divorced parents. Family was everything to Leslie.

As much as we shared, there were dissimilarities: Leslie was married, though separated; I was single. She had a daughter; I had a cat. She had a real job in the morning; I dealt with the fantasy world of editors and publicists. She had a steady paycheck; I had no idea when my next check might arrive in the mail. She liked Seal; I liked the Beatles. She was seven years younger.

The Mazda's engine turned over.

What if? What if this could work? What if Leslie is the next woman in my life? I knew one thing for sure—Leslie was someone I wanted to know.

43

Same Shit, Different Century, 2000–2001

The new millennium began with a hope of happiness and peace of mind and body, which for me was a one-way road out of the burg of death and sadness. Leslie was looking for a demarcation line from her unpleasant separation and subsequent divorce. She wanted a fresh start, too. Most important, she wasn't going to raise Meagan in a shack-up situation. Leslie wanted the legitimacy of marriage to help build solidarity in our new family.

Leslie and I got married on July 15, 2000, after a four-year courtship. The low-key ceremony took place at the Westin Maui a couple of hundred feet from the Pacific Ocean and was well attended by family and friends from as far away as New Jersey and New York. Leslie and I exchanged rings during the simple ceremony—a slim, platinum band with six small baguette diamonds for her, a silver and platinum band for me. I thought of Kari and how we had purchased our plain rings at an Indian craft store. I shared cocktails with Leslie's father and our stepfathers before the ceremony, the first and only time these dearly beloved were gathered together. Many attendees packaged the nuptials with their own vacations in Hawaii. We hired a saxophone player as entertainment and scrapped all the insipid pre- and postwedding photographs. I didn't need anyone telling me to "have fun, smile!" I was on Maui, in love, getting married, and surrounded by friends and family.

Alas, we had to return to the mainland, to real life. Nutmeg had joined Kari in the great beyond, and Jack had stayed with Leslie's ex as part of the divorce, so Leslie and I acquired a six-month-old German shepherd named Chloe from a rescue facility in Burbank, and Leslie,

280

Robert and Leslie Crane, Ojai, California, 2014 (photo by Niki Dantine; author's collection).

Meagan, Chloe, and I settled into our new lives together behind a metaphorical white picket fence.

TV's *E! True Hollywood Story* and A&E's *Biography* were at their height of popularity at that time, and I took Meagan to the taping of an *E!* episode on John Candy in which I was to be one of the talking heads. I spoke with as much candor as a ten-second snippet would allow. I missed John on a daily basis and knew that had he been alive, he and his family would have been in Hawaii celebrating my nuptials. *E!* was also constantly rerunning a sordid hour episode about my dad, which contained an interview with my sister Karen. She had taped her segment at an unoccupied office down the hall from my dad's studio at KNX Radio in Hollywood. Karen had told the off-camera interviewer: "Who could have done this? Why would they do this? Everyone loved my dad. . . . Once the condolence cards and flowers stopped coming, that's when the sadness started and the realization of it all hit hard. . . . That wound will never completely heal for me. I suppose there's really no way that it can."

Also at this time, like the cyclical cicadas crawling out from the ground after a decade of dormancy, Patti and her son, Scotty, now thirty, emerged into the ether via the Internet. They started a website that offered the more squalid aspects of my dad's biography: crime scene photos, autopsy reports, and (drum roll, please) their real little moneymaker: fifty disturbing, XXX-rated photographs and videos from my dad's private archive of sexual liaisons involving him and various women—all for a monthly subscription fee of $19.95. The site also offered T-shirts with a black-and-white image of Patti's husband and Scotty's father in flagrante delicto with a consenting female. I felt more shame from that hideous money-grab website than from anything my dad had ever done in his private life.

Patti reeked of hypocrisy. She had professed to be the angelic wife who had had to sue my dad for divorce in 1977 because he allegedly showed pornography to their six-year-old son, Scotty. As a result of her accusations my dad was ordered by the court to seek psychiatric help. Patti leaked the information to the press, which seriously harmed my dad's reputation and his ability to secure employment. And, now, here was Patti, with her overexposed son, selling the products of my dad's wayward hobby on the Internet. Online, Patti denied any responsibility, claiming, "Scott owns it [the website]. I have nothing to do with it."

When I scanned the site I yelled out loud, which made Chloe, lying by my feet, sit up and bark. I screamed at the computer, "Who supplied Scotty with the images?" Patti told the press and her newly christened Yahoo Groups chat room that "she had millions of feet of film and video showing what a great father and husband he [my dad] was." Why, then, did she and Scotty decide to offer only my dad's sexual home movies to the world? Did those lurid black-and-white images of his sexual misconduct represent the loving memory of my dad Patti wanted to share with all comers who had a couple of sawbucks to blow? Why was there no G-rated footage for the paying customers? My dad's videotapes didn't involve hidden cameras or malicious intent. It was all done in the open between consenting adults. And now Patti was exploiting my dad's personal pastime, ego trip, or addiction, whatever it was, with a public and press that would unleash the final blows onto an already chastised, satirized, and bloated corpse. I don't believe my dad was ever on such an ego trip that he would have wanted to share this material with his fans worldwide. That was never his purpose. Patti was the wife of record, the executrix, the guard at the gate. She could have made any of several decisions regarding the tapes: keep 'em, burn 'em, lock 'em up in a safe deposit box in Switzerland. Instead she elected to share the tawdry images with the world, or at least a world that was willing to pay for them. Perhaps it was her final retaliation against her estranged husband. Patti always liked getting in the last dig.

Scotty claimed 5.6 million hits in the first week of the website that he and his mother created. He said, "I think if my father were alive, he'd be running the site himself." Comments like this only pointed up the chasm between my dad's two families. Scotty told the *Seattle Times,* "I'm protecting his [Dad's] image." Karen told the press scribes that Scotty was "the slime of the earth. . . . If there's a buck to be made, Scotty will go for it."

Patti and Scotty had gone through my dad's two jumbo life insurance policies of about $400,000 each, plus the proceeds from the sale of the Tilden Avenue house, nearly a million bucks, and the yearly receipts from the nonstop television replays of *Hogan's Heroes.* I guess they felt it was time to tap into the online cash cow booting up before them—the Web afforded Patti and her acolyte Scotty new opportunities.

Patti claimed she and my dad had reconciled in late April 1978. I found that amusing since I was living with my dad in Westwood at the time, and he was in the process of buying a home for himself in Sherman Oaks. Patti acknowledged the new home that my dad was going to move into upon his return from Arizona, but she falsely asserted that both their names were on the deed. Scotty chimed in with "They [Patti and Dad] were not separated or divorced; they were together." Patti claimed that my dad invited me to Scottsdale to celebrate my twenty-seventh birthday, but that I was so upset with their reconciliation I passed on the invitation. There was no such invitation. He was working, and I was transcribing a magazine interview on a deadline. According to my dad's divorce attorney, William Goldstein, the couple was so far apart there was absolutely no going back. My dad had told Chuck about the changes he wanted to make in his life, which included jettisoning Patti and "his pal" John Carpenter. I believed him. Patti told her website readers that she and I had wept in each other's arms after the murder. In fact, days after his death the sum total of her expressed emotion was her icy statement, "Your father's lifestyle caught up with him" while making a mental inventory of my dad's and my apartment.

Scotty added, "Bob [Dad] essentially disowned Anne's [Mom's] children in his will." That was the will that had had a codicil attached to it that eliminated my sisters and me from any inheritance. It was drawn up by his financial manager/attorney Lloyd Vaughn, the guy Patti got cozy with when my dad was working out of town. I've never been completely convinced that Patti and Vaughn didn't alter the will themselves without my dad's knowledge or consent. I must add that this is the same Lloyd Vaughn who was later disbarred and sent to jail for, among other things, embezzling more than $100,000 from my dad's bank accounts.

Patriciacrane1978@yahoo.com also pontificated about my dad's post-vasectomy sperm count to dissuade nasty rumors that Scotty was not my dad's son. Scotty used the forum to address something that had long bothered him—that editors, writers, interviewers, producers, and directors often dubbed me Bob Crane Jr. As I have said before, I have never asked for or assumed that moniker on my own, but it irked Scotty no end when I was referenced that way. Patti often went on rants against my dad's first family, my family, that were filled with inaccuracies, false accusations, and venom.

To add literary insult to injury, Scotty packaged more of the images his mother had turned over to him into a self-published coffee-table book that took the viewer briefly through my dad's childhood, radio career, and *Hogan's* but ended up portraying a lot of middle-aged, out-of-shape sex. I would say that it was a coffee-table book only if your coffee table was in the film *Boogie Nights*. The *Seattle Times* called it "a sad story"; the *New York Daily News* wrote that Scotty was "selling his family's dirty laundry." The whole enterprise reeked of a cheap reality show on a distant cable channel. When asked by the press for a reaction, I just shook my head and said, "This is not a celebration of my dad."

In one of my dad's unthinking, clueless states, he once showed me photographs of a threesome involving him, a willing Patti, and another woman. Those photographs were not in Scotty's book or on his website. So there was some selective editing, I presume, by Patti, showing her unwillingness to share her real self with her son. Scotty, sadly, was being brainwashed by the Jim Jones of home porn sales.

I was outraged by both Patti and Scotty. It made me wonder, what was more sordid—the pornography or the flogging of the pornography? One thing for sure, Patti was the pimp. Scotty heard about life with Father through the skewed, angry, victimized point of view of his mother. Maybe Scotty secretly would have wished to be his half sister, Melissa, who got out of Dodge early and headed for Texas.

But I tried to keep my outrage in check. I was newly married, father to a stepdaughter and a dog, trying to give my nascent family and rein-vigorated life my full attention. Leslie and I were in our second marriages and didn't want to repeat past offenses. I wanted to move forward with all things familial, but my father's life—and by consequence mine—was con-tinually turning into messy and embarrassing tabloid fodder. I was like Michael Corleone in *The Godfather III:* "Just when I thought I was out, they pull me back in."

44

Out of Focus, 2001–2002

I began 2001 with two priorities: to work hard at being a family man and to succeed as a freelance writer. However, on very short notice everything changed. While being that attentive husband, stepfather, and walker to, respectively, Leslie, Meagan, and Chloe, I was pulled back into a skirmish that I had hoped and prayed was over. The misinformation and tastelessness emanating from Patti and Scotty's website, chat room, and book, coupled with the announcement in the *Hollywood Reporter* that a film based on Robert Graysmith's book about the murder of my dad was in preproduction, propelled me into action.

I couldn't do anything substantive regarding Patti and Scotty's classless endeavors, but I could add my voice to *Auto Focus,* a $7 million film directed by Paul Schrader and written by first-time screenwriter Michael Gerbosi. The vitriol and ill feelings generated in me by Patti and her apostle Scotty had lain dormant for a number of years, but now they bubbled to the surface. Their words and actions roused this half-sleeping dog. It was bad enough that Graysmith, Schrader, and Gerbosi had never met my dad, but an inference in the trades that Patti and Scotty might be involved in the production literally kept me awake at night. The notion that no one from my dad's first family would be represented really kick-started me.

On the selfish side, I also wanted to meet Paul Schrader, who had written or cowritten three of my favorite films, *Taxi Driver, Raging Bull,* and *The Yakuza.* In 1976 my dad and I had attended a screening of Martin Scorsese's *Taxi Driver* at the Plaza Theatre in Westwood. At the time my dad was trying to get a part in another Scorsese picture, the big band–oriented *New York, New York.* We were both amazed by the intensity of *Taxi Driver,* but unfortunately my dad didn't get the role in *New York, New York.*

I cold-called Pat Dollard, one of eight producers or executive producers on the film. Dollard told me that Greg Kinnear had been signed to play my dad. I had enjoyed his Oscar-nominated performance opposite Jack Nicholson in *As Good As It Gets* and was aware of the similarities between his career and my dad's. They both started on the radio and then moved to television. Kinnear was a good actor: bright, funny, and handsome. He was perfect for the part, I thought. The intense and occasionally frightening Willem Dafoe was set to play John Henry Carpenter. I was impressed. This was going to be a first-class project. I had to meet Schrader.

It's important to note that *Auto Focus* was going to be made with or without my participation, but I wanted to at least read the script. I met with Dollard, who arranged a meeting between Schrader and me at the Focus Puller Inc. production offices on North Gower Street in Hollywood, triangulated between the old Columbia Square home of KNX Radio; the former Columbia Pictures studio, home of *The Donna Reed Show*; and Paramount Pictures, where the first two seasons of *Hogan's Heroes* were filmed. I was comfortable and at home in that neighborhood.

Schrader was lucid and serious, perhaps a reflection of his Calvinist upbringing. Comedy was not a part of his repertoire. I liked his dramatic side, but the man never laughed. I now understood that *Auto Focus* was going to be a sobering look at a sex-addicted television actor, but I was concerned because there didn't seem to be any humor in the mix, and comedy was such an essential and important element in my dad's life and career. Schrader told me he had been talking to Patti and Scotty, who had somehow managed to get hold of a copy of the script. They were trying to produce their own take on events with a script called "Take Off Your Clothes and Smile," and their attorney, A. Lee Blackman, was bluntly communicating to Schrader and the producers that his clients were upset with what they'd read in *Auto Focus*. Word quickly spread through the offices that Patti and Scotty were intractable pains in the ass, representing the negative and certainly litigious branch of the Crane family tree.

Schrader loaned me a copy of the script and suggested I write notes addressing the "voice" of my dad. I immediately went through the pages, marking up all but a few. Schrader and Gerbosi were locked into the scenes and events, but I offered alternatives with regard to the way my dad would express himself, the words or phrases he would use, as well as the look and sound of his radio show. I gave them background on the filming of *Hogan's Heroes*, conversations between my dad and me, and the look and sound of my family. I also suggested dialogue snippets, such as my dad's seeing new things like the color orange, which made it into the film but was transferred (by Schrader) from his real-life chat with Chuck to a cinematic scene between my dad and the twenty-year-old Bobby (me).

Leslie and I had dinner with Schrader one evening at his haunt Chateau Marmont off Sunset Boulevard. While we spooled pasta and polished off a bottle of pinot noir, we went through the script page by page. Schrader was very receptive to my insights. Besides seeing that the participation of Bob Crane's first son brought authenticity and veracity to the piece, he appreciated that I loved film, was a fan of Schrader and Kinnear, and wished only the best for the production at hand. I might also add that I was easy to work with, had no hidden agenda, and am one hell of a nice guy. Whereas Patti and Scotty had tripped their own landmines, resulting in persona non grata status on the production. I was still concerned about the film, but at least I was sleeping better.

A less successful dinner meeting took place at another of Schrader's favorite Old Hollywood locales, Musso and Frank's Grill on Hollywood Boulevard. Leslie and I invited Schrader to meet my mom and Chuck. My mom viewed Schrader as an enemy, cruising for trouble, leaving depth charges in her calm, tranquil Tarzana sea. It was not a congenial evening, and it would be their sole meeting. Though she knew almost nothing about him, my mom did not feel safe with Paul Schrader.

On the other hand, when I told Mom of a phone call I had received from Rita Wilson, the actress who was to play my mom in the film, asking for a luncheon date with the former Anne Crane, she perked up noticeably. "Where and when?" she asked right away.

Mom loved Rita as an actress and thought lunch sounded like fun. In fact, Wilson was doing an actor's research. She wanted to pick my mom's brain, watch her conduct, listen to her speech patterns, get an insight into her clothing choices, smell her perfume. So Mrs. Tom Hanks and Mrs. Chuck Sloan spent a couple of enjoyable hours dining at Bistro Garden in Studio City. Whatever transpired at that lunch must have been significant, because onscreen Rita Wilson *is* my mom. With a minor assist from wardrobe, hair, and makeup, she uncannily inhabits Anne Crane. I found it almost eerie, but it reaffirmed my admiration for truly great actors. It's a shame my mom never saw Rita's performance. She would have gotten a kick out of her lunch date's metamorphosis.

The character of John Henry Carpenter needed the same treatment I

PAUL SCHRADER

October 22, 2001

Dear Robert,

Here's the latest draft of "Auto-Focus" as well as a picture book on the San Fernando Valley I promised your stepdad. Thanks for dinner.

Buckle up. The script, I'm sure, will be more and less than you imagined. My first interest is not in writing and directing a celebrity biopic. I want to use Robert Crane's unique life to explore, firstly, a male psychology, secondly, the psychological contract between two men and, thirdly, American male sexual identity 1964-78. The script is a character study and character is the greatest mystery of all. The mystery is not "Who Killed Bob Crane?" but the mystery of why one's man's life takes the course it does. Such mysteries can be explored but never solved.

On the other hand I have no wish to willfully distort history. Yes, some characters become composites (all the agents become one), yes, events shift times frames a bit, and yes, events are imagined based on evidence, the needs of narrative and my sense of the characters.

I look forward to your reaction. Based on my initial reaction to your mother (a charming woman), I suspect this is something she might not feel comfortable knowing about in detail. I respect your discretion in this.

Yours truly,

Paul Schrader

Paul Schrader's correspondence with Robert Crane, 2001 (author's collection).

had given my dad—the input of someone who had known him well—but it was up to Mark Dawson, son of *Hogan's Heroes* costar Richard Dawson, the man who introduced Carpenter to my dad, to handle that job. He was hired for his insight into his friend Carpenter. Mark and I both became technical advisors on the film.

As part of my duties, I met with Greg Kinnear at a delicatessen in Santa Monica and shared photographs and memorabilia with him along with my thoughts and observations about my dad. I tried to give him a flavor for the way he spoke, his conscientious striving for likeability, his smile, his laugh, his quickness, the loudness of his voice, the way he carried himself. I offered Greg the use of Colonel Hogan's leather jacket and khaki shirt for the *Hogan's Heroes* sequences in the film. Kinnear was genuinely touched and honored.

I worked with Julie Weiss, the costume designer, suggesting the sort of clothes my dad wore. James Chinlund, the production designer, and I went through piles of photographs and tossed around ideas for the 1960s look of our home in Tarzana and the furniture that filled its rooms. Chinlund referred to the "accreditation of clutter." My dad "got messier, tangled in more and more video cables" toward the end of his life.

I also assisted the Sony Pictures Entertainment legal department in the clarification of factual errors in the script. That same legal department was being hounded by Patti's emissaries, and I felt it incumbent on me to add my voice to the cacophony in a constructive manner.*

I was helpful, serious, dedicated. I offered assistance to any department that requested it. I wasn't hanging out at the craft service table downing M&Ms and drinking coffee. Any prejudgment the cast and crew might have had about Crane's kid—"What's he like? Does he have a chip on his shoulder? Is he an asshole? Is he a sex maniac?"—evaporated rapidly. I became an unexpected asset to the film. Schrader allowed me in, albeit at arm's length because, after all, this was a Paul Schrader film. He operated on a lone-wolf premise, very much like my dad in the way he trusted only his own creative instincts. I was circumspect, participating in key scenes where I felt the "Welcome" mat was out and staying away from others, like those in the murder sequence. While I was the only person working on the film to have walked through the actual murder scene, this was to be Paul Schrader's take on it, and therefore the look would represent Schrader's own biases. Having seen the real thing, nothing was ever going to be worse than those images burned into my brain.

I had never been interested in being part of the actors' club, but Kinnear and Dafoe heard about my interactions with many of the film's

---

*See appendix C, "Robert Crane's Letter to Sony Pictures Classics Legal Department Addressing *Auto Focus* script, 2002."

departments and also about my respect for their work. They both made me feel welcome and treated me as one of their own. They recognized that I wanted them to do great work.

The company shot several scenes at the long-shuttered Ambassador Hotel in the mid-Wilshire district. The Ambassador was where Robert Kennedy was assassinated, and it housed the most popular nightclub of its day, the Cocoanut Grove. Leslie and I walked through the once-luxurious showplace, imagining Barbra Streisand, Nat King Cole, or Sammy Davis Jr. on the darkened stage performing for Los Angeles's elite. My mom and dad had attended many glamorous openings at the renowned venue during his radio days. Now, it felt like Leslie and I were Shelley Duvall and Jack Nicholson at the Overlook Hotel on the set of *The Shining*.

One morning during a casting call for some of the minor roles in the upcoming scenes, Schrader peered out of his office with a devilish grin. "Hey, Bob," he yelled, motioning me into his office.

I had no hint of what was coming my way.

"There's this interviewer in the film from a Christian magazine who's going to interview your dad about what makes his life and career successful." Schrader paused. "I want you to play it."

I immediately flashed on Barry Van Dyke. I wasn't sure I could give Schrader what he wanted, but I thought it would be a great experience. And how could I possibly fuck it up? I was going to play a magazine writer interviewing my dad. A little surreal but fun, I thought. Besides, in the postproduction phase, the film editor, Kristina Boden, would obviously edit the scene in favor of Greg Kinnear. I had nothing to lose. "Sure," I said.

Recalling my endless repeats of Kevin Costner's dialogue helping John Candy rehearse his *JFK* scene, I ran my five lines over and over in my head until I couldn't remember them at all, but hell, I was a veteran. After all, I'd held my own with Chevy Chase ad-libbing on the radio, with John Candy in *Delirious* (Candy: "Hi, Bob." Crane: "Hi, Jack."), and with Dave Thomas on *SCTV* (no dialogue). I'd faced John Carpenter in court, Nicholson and Beatty backstage at the Academy Awards, and Koko the signing gorilla in front of her jealous four-hundred-pound mate, Michael. This would be a piece of cake. In casting me, Schrader showed his confidence in me, and I was damn sure I wasn't going to let him or Kinnear down.

So on a beautiful Southern California Sunday morning in January, the hair department removed my beard and shortened my locks to create an extremely conservative 1960s look. The wardrobe department kitted me out in a baggy dark suit, white shirt, and diagonally patterned tie with metal clasp. The makeup department coated my face with foundation and powder, deciding to remove my eyeglasses because they were from the wrong decade and would reflect the lights and camera. I felt exhilarated and completely naked. Plus, because I'd worn glasses since I was five years old, my visual inadequacy enhanced the intense irrationality of what I was experiencing. It certainly brought new meaning to the film's title.

I walked to the hotel swimming pool set, shook hands with Schrader and Kinnear, and exchanged a few words with a *Premiere* magazine writer covering the shoot. I was pretty nervous until I sat down in a poolside chair facing Kinnear. Then I said to myself, "Fuck it," and entered my version of a method acting state where I was just going to be in the moment. I told myself, "Listen. Don't think about your dialogue. Just listen to what the other person is saying and play off of that."

It seemed to me the crew perked up a bit at this next setup. All involved in the production worked their asses off fifteen hours a day, and as far as I was concerned, the talent level made up for the relatively small budget. The picture looked terrific so far. But now a living, breathing genetic remnant of the number one character name on the daily call sheet was in their midst. Kinnear and I ran the lines once with the camera pointed at me. Schrader would get my shot out of the way first and work with his star next. The set grew quiet. There were some final lighting adjustments. The assistant cameraman again measured the distance between the camera lens and my pancaked punim.

"Everyone settle," the assistant director yelled. "Quiet, please. No movement."

My heart was racing.

Disconnected voices chimed in. "Roll sound."

My heart skipped a beat. Concentrate, De Niro, concentrate.

"Speed."

A clapboard displaying the scene number and take snapped inches from my face. "Action!" Schrader barked.

I was playing a journalist attending a *Hogan's Heroes* press junket at a hotel. Crane (Kinnear) and the interviewer (me) sat poolside, Crane periodically checking out the female sunbathers. I fiddled with my reel-to-reel tape recorder as I held a microphone toward Kinnear. The interviewer wanted details from the *Hogan's Heroes* star about balancing career and family life.

Interviewer: "What's your secret?"

Crane: "Three simple words: don't make waves."

Interviewer: "You're a fortunate man."

Crane: "Yes, I am."

"Cut," Schrader yelled. "We're going again."

I had contributed the "don't make waves" line to the script, referring to my dad's philosophy of life, a clueless but affable world where everyone said yes and stood aside. I looked Kinnear in the eye and listened to his words as if it were the first time I'd ever heard them. Schrader knew of my years of interviewing celebrities for magazines and books and knew I was perfect for the small role. More important, the producers would now be able to list "Bob Crane Jr." as the interviewer in the credit roll and maybe get a nibble or two from some more attentive members of the press. Sorry, Scotty, but I had nothing to do with the credit.

Schrader didn't give me any direction. I couldn't be directed. I'm not an actor. A couple more takes and the camera turned around on Greg Kinnear. Since I was now off camera I decided to take my jacket off. Big mistake. The glare on Kinnear from my white shirt was like a klieg light. Nice going, Bobby. I could hear John Candy laughing somewhere in the firmament. With the pressure off me I could relax and just enjoy Kinnear's transformation into my dad—the smile, the wiseass wit, the good looks, the seeming self-assurance. Kinnear was perfect.

Thus I faced "my dad" armed with the tools of my trade, a tape deck and mike. I had spent three years putting together the *Jack Nicholson: Face to Face* book and had written for *Oui* magazine before my dad's death, but unfortunately he had missed my work for *Playboy* and my later books. He had missed my career. Now, I hoped he was witness to the ultimate Fellini Excursion—his real-life son interviewing him, via Greg Kinnear, saying his real words ("Don't make waves") from my script notes in front of a director (Schrader) whose script (*Taxi Driver*) had amazed us one evening in a Westwood theater long, long ago. Even Fellini himself would have been impressed by the magnitude of this Fellini Excursion.

The film wrapped after a few more weeks of shooting. The actors and crew were spent. Patti, Scotty, and their attorneys were now throwing stun grenades at the Sony Pictures legal department in an attempt to keep *Auto Focus* permanently in the can. To show his appreciation for my con-

Auto Focus set: Robert Crane and Greg Kinnear, Los Angeles, 2002 (courtesy Sony Pictures Classics; author's collection).

tributions, which I had been giving gratis, Paul Schrader paid me $20,000 out of his own pocket. Tom Bernard, the principal of Sony Pictures Classics, the distributor of *Auto Focus,* invited me to tag along on part of the movie's publicity tour. The fact that I had written for several first-tier publications as well as having spent years as John Candy's publicist weighed heavily in their decision to utilize "Bob Crane Jr."

Leslie and I attended press screenings in Los Angeles. One of them was crashed by Scotty and his model-wannabe wife, Michelle. It was the first time we had seen each other since Dad's funeral, twenty-four years earlier. He appealed to me to intercede so they could get into the screening, but I refused. They were ushered out by security. This exact scenario would repeat itself like a bad acid flashback a couple of weeks later at a screening in New York.

I was in no frame of mind to offer Scotty an olive branch. It would be too hypocritical. There had been too much artillery launched between the two families, and the situation would only escalate over the coming months. *Auto Focus* didn't reflect Patti's vision of her life with my dad, and she and Scotty would tell as many people as would listen the "real story." No producer would touch their script. It had always been

Generalissima Patti's way or the firing squad. In this case, Sony Pictures disarmed them. The studio had a film to sell to the public, but Patti and Scotty were about to ignite their counterpress offensive from their West Coast trench.

I had been impressed with Paul Schrader's filmmaking. *Auto Focus* was edgy; it was devoid of humor but a decently told tale chronicling the era when the sexual revolution started to roll. The performances, the look, the soundtrack, all worked cohesively. In the days of double features *Auto Focus* and *Carnal Knowledge* with Jack Nicholson would have made the perfect double bill, serving up the American sexual awakening from the 1950s through the 1970s with a sizable side of dysfunctional male ego. I was able to put aside any arguments or quibbles I'd had regarding story points or liberties taken by the film's artists and stand back and praise the film on a purely cinematic level. *Auto Focus* was a film my dad and I would have gone to see in Westwood in the '70s. It and *Hogan's Heroes* represented the most important creative projects my dad was ever affiliated with. Leslie and I saw *Auto Focus* four times, including at the Toronto Film Festival, where I appeared on a panel with Schrader, Kinnear, and Dafoe. I also made the rounds in New York, appearing on ABC's *The View* (with other guests director Michael Moore, Sean Hannity, and O. J. Simpson's attorney Johnny Cochran). Judging by their comments and questions, it seemed the *View*'s cast members already had their views made up.

Joy Behar: "What we didn't know was offscreen Bob Crane indulged in a reckless hobby of filming himself engaged in various sex acts and orgies, all of which is now the subject of a new movie, *Auto Focus*."

Lisa Ling: "So your father actually showed you X-rated pictures when you were young. How old were you and what was your reaction?"

Meredith Vieira: "How would you describe his sexuality? You're an adult now looking back. Was it a healthy sex drive, overly sexed, sexaholic, pervert?"

Star Jones: "I saw the movie and I found it depressing and pathetic. That someone would look for that kind of acceptance in sex constantly."

Leslie had warned me. Sex sells. Or was it, I wondered, that the hosts were really fans and admirers of my dad who felt they had been let down by their hero and were hostile as a result? Why was it that Pam Anderson, Colin Farrell, Paris Hilton, and many other young actresses and actors could build their careers by "leaking" self-produced sex tapes? It was de rigueur for a certain kind of star-making machinery in Hollywood, but my dad was being tarred and feathered for it, even though he never intended his films for public consumption.

Joy Behar: "He was a sex addict before his time. Nowadays, we realize there is a sexual addiction. People go into rehab for this . . . the movie is really sick to watch. Very entertaining, however. . . . You're a consultant on this movie, Robert. Why do you want to get yourself involved with this, expose your father for a pervert or some kind of sex addict?"

That was the best pitch they'd thrown me. I took my best cut.

"Because already the second family brought out a website that I'm opposed to. I think it's awful. . . . Paul Schrader was doing this film, and you either join or you don't. It was going to be made. . . . I gave him my two cents' worth on behalf of the first family. . . . I think my dad would have been really happy with Greg Kinnear. Greg nails the essence of my dad. . . . My dad would be proud to be in a Paul Schrader film . . . after I saw *Taxi Driver* with my dad . . . he looked at me and said, 'God, those are the kinds of movies I'd love to be in.' . . . The movie [*Auto Focus*] is an hour and forty-five minutes long. My dad's life was a little longer than that. He had a great first marriage to my mom . . . it ran out of gas after twenty years . . . it was a Donna Reed family life."

Joy Behar concluded the segment by hitting the ball out of the park herself. "Except for one little, tiny thing he was perfect. He was also very funny."

My armpits were damp. Backstage, Leslie looked into my eyes and kissed me. She didn't say, "I told you so." She knew the importance of the trip to New York—I was speaking on behalf of my family—playing Red Adair, fighting fire with fire, standing up for my dad when it seemed like he had become an easy target for the press and Patti's scandal sheet. My next stop was Fox News' *The O'Reilly Factor.* O'Reilly didn't waste any time on pleasantries.

Bill O'Reilly: "This is not for children. . . . Let's face it, your father wasn't the perfect husband. He's running around, jumping on anything that moves, photographing it, and . . . reveling in his debauchery. . . . He has a mental illness, don't you think? . . . Your father was basically a pervert. . . . The basic theme of the movie is these two guys [my dad and Carpenter] are out of control and your father gets murdered. . . . I don't think your father was real popular in a lot of circles for what he did. Do you respect your father?"

Me: "I respect him career-wise for what he did, where he got to. . . . He was a good father to my two sisters and me. We had a lot of fun times. . . . There wasn't anything perverted at home as far as I know."

The interview continued for what seemed a very long time, and never got any softer. I needed a long, hot shower. I much preferred asking questions to deflecting them.

We attended the *Auto Focus* premiere at the New York Film Festival at Alice Tully Hall at Lincoln Center. I joined Schrader, Kinnear, and Dafoe onstage afterward for a Q&A.

Schrader began by saying, "*Auto Focus* is the All-American, heterosexual version of *Prick Up Your Ears.* Bob Crane aspired to be one thing but acted in a counterproductive manner."

Greg Kinnear, who, more than anyone, was focused on what made my dad tick, added, "Bob was a different person when he first came to Los Angeles. I think he was affected by the show business element. . . . John Carpenter was a very unfortunate association for Bob to have come across."

"There's a husband and wife quality about them," Willem Dafoe interjected, adding, "They abet each other's weaknesses. They had this incredible intimacy and dependency on each other."

"Bob came at you with both headlights bright but he's a superficial man, clueless man, who didn't have much of an interior life," said Schrader, who always looked at the bigger picture. He continued, "I don't think Hollywood makes good people go bad. I think bad people come to Hollywood in order to be bad. When *Hogan's Heroes* and Bob's first marriage went down, his level of hypocrisy went down with it. He allowed himself to become more of the person he always was, but he couldn't see why his behavior was such a problem for others. He undermined everything he'd accomplished because of a private, personal obsession. Bob Crane made a career out of being likable—the charmer, the glib, funny guy. When someone is that personable, attractive, and semifamous, we tend to let them get away with murder."

Kinnear summed it up. "The thing that's interesting about Bob is the contradictory nature of who he appeared to be and who the man really was. This guy was so cool and always heroic and funny. I was a fan."

I didn't have much to add. I felt as though I were eavesdropping on a psychiatrist's group session.

The film generated an enormous amount of press, not all good, not all bad, and much of it not about the film at all, but about what was rapidly becoming an incendiary exchange between Scotty and me. In his piece "Video Killed the TV Star," David Edelstein of *Slate* wrote, "The son from one marriage regards his father's life as a sordid mess; the son from the other thinks his dad was a sexually liberated hero and has uploaded the hard-core films and tapes to a Web site for public consumption (I would report on their quality, but they kept crashing my Internet connection). . . . *Auto Focus* is a cautionary tale of addiction."

Susan Wloszczyna of *USA Today* wrote, "Not even Richard Dawson would touch this family feud. . . . 'I knew this [*Auto Focus*] wasn't going to be a titillating piece of garbage' . . . says the older brother [Robert]. . . . Scotty . . . calls it 'horrible' and 'sensationalistic.' . . . It also riles Scotty that Robert often is referred to as Bob Crane Jr. Oddly, both sons are named Robert: Scotty is Robert Scott, Robert is Robert David. . . . Robert says it goes back to the question his reporter character poses to Kinnear in *Auto Focus.* 'What is his secret to a long marriage?' The answer: 'Don't make waves.'"

Kate Nolan of the *Arizona Republic,* in her article "Tawdry Tale Sets Crane Sons A-feuding," wrote, "From the start, Scotty slammed Robert's involvement, saying the script was a distortion. . . . 'You don't ask Sean Lennon about the Beatles, you ask Julian,' he [Robert] says, apologizing for striking a parallel between John Lennon and Crane. . . . Scotty retaliated by telling 'The Arizona Republic' recently that Robert could be a likely suspect [in their father's murder]. Scotty's theory: Robert became enraged that Dad was reuniting with Patricia and killed him. Robert scoffs at the allegation, saying he had never visited Scottsdale until after his father's death. The police have never considered Robert a suspect."

This last salvo from Scotty precipitated a kind of Hatfield and McCoy blood feud fought out in the mud of Tinseltown. I repeated to Lynn Hirshberg, a reporter from the *New York Times* magazine what I had said to the Scottsdale Police and the Maricopa County district attorney: since Patti was the only one to profit from my dad's death—that's a fact, not my opinion—and needed it to happen before the divorce was final, she was the only person with any kind of motive, and therefore, I said, her whereabouts and involvement should bear some scrutiny. Jeez, you'd have thought I had publicly accused her of murder. Well, maybe I had, and hell hath no fury like an heiress with a checkbook.

There was, naturally, an immediate backlash. Lee Blackman (Patti and

Scotty's attorney) went on TV to say, "I will only say that any accusations or insinuations that Patricia Crane had any involvement in the murder of her husband Bob Crane are outrageous, defamatory lies."

Scotty, too, got in his two seconds' worth. He said, "His [meaning me] claim is ridiculous. She [Patti] was thoroughly checked out by the Scottsdale Police. There's no evidence that even suggests [her involvement]. She was 1,500 miles away at the time of the murder. I was with her at the time of my father's murder. *Hogan's* hadn't kicked into syndication yet. His estate wasn't worth anything. Actually, it was a financial loss to us when he died. He was out on the road making quite a bit of money. When he stopped doing that, the paychecks stopped. He's [again meaning me] a dangerous person. He's disturbed. He'll do anything to promote this movie [*Auto Focus*]."

Patti wrote to the *Times* objecting to "the false statements and insinuations made by 'Auto Focus' director Paul Schrader and 'technical advisor' Bobby Crane, the son of my husband's first wife." She was outraged that "The Times even printed Bobby's suggestion that I killed my husband. Bobby knows that there is total and absolute proof that I had nothing at all to do with his murder. I loved my husband, and we were reconciled at the time of his death. A respectable journalist would not have, by omitting key facts, so clearly taken one side in this matter. It is shocking to see this brand of tabloid journalism in a publication such as yours." Patricia Crane, Seattle.

Attorneys were now fully deployed. Maggie Heim, Sony Pictures' vice president, assistant general counsel, sent me copies of two letters from Patti's legal advisors. They questioned Sony Pictures over scenes involving Patti's character, played by Maria Bello. They objected to her portrayal as "a drinker," "a home wrecker," "a violent person," and "greedily and vindictively demanding." The First Amendment was mentioned, the lawyers arguing that Patti was not attempting to "'chill . . . free speech rights' or force SPE [Sony Pictures Entertainment] to 'make her look good in every way and to leave out anything that might be conceived as negative.' Mrs. Crane, however, only complains about the portions of the movie that are both negative and false." In other words, all of the scenes involving the character of "Patti."

The missive also addressed Paul Schrader's "false and derogatory statements about Patricia Crane" to the press, including his telling the *New York Times* that Scotty's book included "photographs of Patricia

Crane nude and 'with a woman,'" that Schrader "know[s] she did girl-on-girl stuff," and that "the movie's potential damaging effects on Mrs. Crane's health cannot be laid at his [Schrader's] doorstep because she is a 'lifelong . . . drinker.'" The letter continued, "The Daily News reported that Bobby Crane calls his stepmother a cross between 'Sante Kimes, Bonnie Lee Bakley and Adolf Hitler.' . . . On behalf of Mrs. Crane, I repeat the demand that Robert David Crane immediately cease and desist from making such statements, and that Sony Pictures Entertainment take immediate steps to ensure that such statements are not repeated. . . . Very truly yours, A. Lee Blackman."

I was, in fact, guilty as charged, having been enraged by the lies and hypocrisy from the Patti and Scotty camp, and while I thought it was funny at the time, I'm not particularly proud of myself for that little bout of mud wrestling. But, always needing to get in the last blow, Patti still had one more diabolical trick up her sleeve.

The *Globe,* on page 3 of its November 12, 2002, edition, splashed the headline "Bob Crane's Widow Digs Up His Body—And Hides It!" It happened like this: my sister Karen, the only member of my family to pay respects at my dad's gravesite at Oakwood Memorial Park Cemetery in Chatsworth after the actual day of the funeral, visited one afternoon only to discover, as the *Globe* reported, "the headstone missing, freshly dug dirt in the plot—and their dad no longer there!" A quote from me read, "My dad was buried next to his parents. . . . My sister asked what happened and the cemetery said the body had been relocated. She asked, 'Where is he? I'm his daughter!' They said, 'We can't tell you.' . . . It's simple human decency to let someone know that their daddy's body has been moved. My family was devastated. That's always been Pat's style— no respect for us. . . . She hates us, we hate her." After several hysterical phone calls, "Pat's lawyer revealed that the TV legend had been reburied alongside stars like Marilyn Monroe and Natalie Wood at the famed Westwood Cemetery. Her attorney Lee Blackman tells GLOBE Pat moved the body because it was her husband's wish to be buried at that cemetery. . . . Says Robert, 'Pat bought the spot next to him, so now Hogan and Hilda can be together forever.'" What was really missing from the whole story was a quote from Patti to the effect of "Take that, Bobby."

I wanted to keep this never-ending Fellini Excursion alive, so I pitched a Greg Kinnear "20 Questions" to Rezek at *Playboy.* I knew the piece had to be light and funny to fit in the "20Q slot," not at all replicating the heaviness of *Auto Focus* or the fireworks playing out in the media. I wanted to show Kinnear my real day job, and, after pretending to interview him, I wanted to do an authentic version for the record. Rezek gave me a thumbs-up. In the December 2002 issue, *Playboy Playbill* wrote of me, promoting the enclosed piece: "A deft and lively contributor to the magazine—he once turned in an incredible Q. and A. with Koko the Signing Gorilla—Crane returns this month with a singularly astounding entry: a 20Q with Greg Kinnear, who plays Crane's father in 'Auto Focus.' . . . So the stage was set for a fascinating conversation between Kinnear and Crane—read it."

Playboy: "How did you prepare for the explicit scenes in 'Auto Focus'? Was there a Thighmaster in your trailer?"

Kinnear: "There should have been, because I put on some weight to play Bob [Crane]. . . . No push-ups before scenes for me. It was basically hit the craft service table about 10 minutes before doing anything questionable."

Playboy: "You're known as being a nice guy in Hollywood. Have you disqualified yourself from playing a really dark character?"

Kinnear: "I'm a prick. . . . As an actor, there are few places I'm not interested in exploring. . . . There is just as much charm and inspiration behind a guy with a hatchet as there is in any other character."

Playboy: "In 'Auto Focus' you wear the jacket that was worn by Frank Sinatra in 'Von Ryan's Express' and by Bob Crane in 'Hogan's Heroes.' If that jacket could talk, would it say, 'Ring-a-ding-ding' or 'Colonel Klink'?"

Kinnear: "After 'Auto Focus,' it has a few other things it wants to say—some not fit for print. I have to go with Colonel Klink on that one. As you might understand, I am a little partial to the jacket. It fit like a glove and I'll be the first to bid on it when it's put up for auction on eBay. Give me 24 hours' notice."

Auto Focus was released by Sony Pictures Classics during the fall of 2002 in the United States and Canada.* For all the hysterical babble and family feuding, film festivals and talking head commentaries, rave reviews and pans, print and Internet articles and interviews, the picture managed only a pretty anemic gross of about $2 million. It was a disappointment that there wasn't an audience for a thought-provoking look at the sexual revolution and sexual addiction, or a behind-the-curtain glimpse at an everyman

---

*See appendix D, "Robert Crane's Piece for *Auto Focus* Website, 2002."

actor who played an iconic television character but lost his way. Perhaps not enough filmgoers wanted to auto focus after all. Tom Bernard, who ran the show at SPC, insisted that after international release, pay, cable, and DVD, *Auto Focus* would be in the black. I hoped so for all those talented folks' sake. I would miss the cast and crew, but I was glad it was over. Life is nothing if not about the accumulation of experiences, good, bad, or otherwise.

Shortly after the film's release I received a telephone message from Scotty asking me to call him in Seattle where he was living. I did call him back but got his machine. I said there were no hard feelings. It was always between his mother and me. I knew he didn't ask to be placed into the situation he was in. He was born an innocent, though now he was quite a bit less so, defending his mother at all costs, hearing about the history of the family through a one-sided, distorted mouthpiece. There was just too much poison, too many bad memories. We had all traveled too far, and it was way too late to turn around. We were part of a group thrown together by fate, genetics, and my dad's and Patti's egos. They were first, we followed, and then they were no more. I wished Scotty good luck and much happiness. I have never heard from him again.

The one voice that was truly missing from the *Auto Focus* Tower of Babel was that of the star of the hour, Bob Crane. I felt the need to share his voice with the public, bring his brightness and fun back from the dead. I knew instinctively that the place to go with my wild idea for an interview with a deceased but much in the news celebrity was the Coachella Valley. My old friend and former *Oui* magazine editor Stewart Weiner, after years of toiling for magazines like *TV Guide* and *Palm Springs Life,* had just created his own general-interest publication called *Hwy 111.* Weiner could be as funny as Rezek, but with a more fly-by-the-seat-of-your-pants attitude. He loved the idea of an exclusive "interview" with my dad (and the attention it would generate).*

Leslie and I attended the lavish *Hwy 111* launch party in Palm Desert. *Auto Focus* was on everyone's mind—either they couldn't wait to see it or they were avoiding it like an STD. Weiner was pleased with the Q&A and ordered a series of articles with luminaries who'd gone to the great press briefing room in the sky. For my part, I was thrilled. I was writing, I was making money, and the best part was I didn't have to deal with the talent's publicists or attorneys.

---

*See appendix E.

45

Nature Morte, 2003–2007

Life was full. I was conducting and writing interviews every month during 2003 for either Rezek at *Playboy* or Weiner at *Hwy 111*. At the highly competitive *Playboy* I captured seven of the twelve "20 Questions," my best year ever. I had pieces run with Juliette Lewis, Rachel Weisz, and Nicolas Cage, among others. In addition, I had half a dozen more Q&As with long-gone luminaries for *Hwy 111*, including tête-à-têtes with Marilyn Monroe, Frank Sinatra, and John Wayne. I really liked interviewing dead celebrities; they were easy to work with, and they never griped about the finished product.

I loved my wife. Leslie took 2003 off, retiring from the hellish hours of television production after Meagan threatened to throw her pager in the toilet. I was making enough for Leslie to relax and refuel and to spend her days guiding her newly teenaged daughter.

Meagan and I stepped lightly around each other, trying to find inroads, connecting points. She had a father, whom I would never attempt to upstage. I tried to give her a sense of logic, planning, and an awareness and consideration of other human beings by example. I loved Meagan because she was part of Leslie, but I didn't always like her. It was sometimes very tough going—she was thirteen and thought she knew everything there was to know—but Leslie's levelheadedness, decency, and dedication kept us together as Meagan and her parents continued to opt for the weekly visitation plan.

At the end of 2003, John Rezek was unceremoniously booted from the hutch after three dedicated decades at *Playboy*. The hierarchy came up with the brilliant idea of moving the editorial offices from Chicago to New York, where all aspects of running the magazine would cost more. Rezek wouldn't uproot his family and move, but the fact was that a new regime of high-mastheaded editors had taken over and felt it was time to clean house at the money-losing publication. I eked out two more interviews for the magazine—*Friends* costar Matthew Perry and *Star Trek* spin-off actress Jolene Blalock—before I, too, was cut loose. It was never done officially, but I would pitch thirty or forty names with no response, no assignment. Sometimes some of those pitches turned up in the pages of the magazine interviewed by someone else—someone more connected to the new editors, someone younger, someone hipper. Get the picture, old-timer? Over the twenty years that I contributed to *Playboy*, I conducted forty-five "20Qs" and wrote dozens of other articles, none of them, however, as fun, interesting, and unique as my interview with Koko. I often wonder how my dad would have reacted to his kid contributing to Hefner's empire. Besides being amused, his reaction would probably have gone something like this: "Bobby, who's Rachel Weisz? God, look at the tits on Miss July."

I continued to contribute interviews and humor pieces to Stewart Weiner's vision of a glossy, upscale monthly for another year until it turned into roadkill on Highway 111. For every Hefner, there were a thousand Weiners.

Leading any kind of creative life involves reinventing yourself periodically or running the risk of turning into a fossil, so I reinvented myself as a writer of books, working with Dave Thomas on *SCTV: Behind the Scenes* and alongside Chris Fryer on grizzled veteran actor Bruce Dern's candid, gossipy autobiography, *Things I've Said, but Probably Shouldn't Have*. That project alone took us two and a half years to complete. It spent one whole week on the *Los Angeles Times* Bestseller List. It was a good thing that Leslie had a new steady job.

I dedicated myself to work and family, but one day it ominously occurred to me that all was too quiet on the post–*Auto Focus* front. Five years had passed. The Patti and Scotty camp was mysteriously silent. Inasmuch as *Auto Focus* enjoyed constant pay-television showings, the initial prurient interest surrounding Patti and Scotty's website had crashed, their self-published photo scrapbook was stillborn, and the pulpit chat room was strangely silent. A few weeks later a friend told me to check an item on the Internet, and there it was: "Sigrid Valdis, 72; Sexy secretary on 'Hogan's Heroes' married its star. Lung cancer. Patricia Annette Olson Ateyeh Crane, twice-widowed, died October 14, 2007, in Anaheim, California, at daughter Ana Marie Sarmiento's home." Ana had begun as Patti and my dad's housekeeper and nanny for Scotty. She had apparently been adopted by Patti. Why was Patti with Ana? Where were Scotty, her daughter Melissa, her daughter-in-law Michelle, her five grandchildren, her sister Dale, and brother-in-law Hans Gudegast, aka Eric Braeden?

In a related piece Scotty was quoted, "*Auto Focus* was a strain for her [Patti], and she was in and out of the hospital quite a few times for stress-related illnesses. . . . Two years after the movie was released she was diagnosed with lung cancer." I turned off the computer and sat staring at the wall. It was the end of something. The memories came fast: a father straining unsuccessfully to make two disparate families one with virtually no support from any of the participants; Patti, a woman so unlike my mom, playing the older sister I never had, captivating me with stories of the Rat Pack and sleeping with half of Hollywood; Patti's growing jealousy, distrust, and intolerance of my dad's side of the family evolving into a poisonous cauldron of ill will that destroyed whatever it was that held their marriage together; Patti's insecurities driving her lust to be right all the time; my dad's constant appeasement, resulting in the sacrifice of his loosely held principles; my losing respect for my dad not just because he had become a slave to his own desires but because he allowed Patti to become his slave master; Patti's fear of losing her last blood relative and disciple—Scotty—and therefore having to rewrite her own history; creating the fiction of reconciliation; Patti playing the victim of my dad's penchant for pornography while simultaneously being the archivist and purveyor of it.

Now it was all over, packaged in a nice, neat paragraph in the newspaper. After all the years I'd debated with myself over who killed my dad, it didn't matter anymore. With Patti's death it felt as if I'd sloughed my final skin. Patti was dead. Carpenter was dead. My dad had been dead almost thirty years. Who killed him? Had Carpenter done it in a fit of rage at being cast off? Had he done it as Patti's henchman because she'd planted some demon seed in his not too sophisticated brain? Had Patti done it herself or hired a mob hit, providing the door key she'd most likely lifted from the apartment on her impromptu visit? Certainly it was one of those scenarios, but none of it mattered anymore. I had a new skin, shiny and vibrant and clean, and the debate about the murder was finished, as dead as the principals.

Patti slid into the sunset with the knowledge she had moved my dad up from "unfashionable" Tarzana to trendy Westwood, from lying low in the dust bowl of Oakwood Cemetery in Chatsworth to rubbing elbows with his idol Jack Lemmon and former costar Donna Reed at Westwood

Memorial Park Cemetery, from the simple plate that read "Robert E. Crane, 1928–1978" to a grotesque monument of Tinseltown and bad taste that announced, "Hogan and Hilda Together Forever," with Patti and my dad in character etched into the stone. The image of Patti shows her wearing Hogan's hat. Other engraved lowlights include: on the left, "Bob Crane aka Col. Hogan Star of Hogan's Heroes 1965–71 nee Robert Edward Crane, Father of Deborah, Karen, Ana Marie, Robert Scott Crane" and an autographed publicity still of my dad as Hogan reading, "I adore you Patty—647-646 Your Bob"; and on the right, "Sigrid Valdis aka Hogan's Hilda—Mrs. Bob Crane nee Patricia Annette Olson, Mother of Melissa Suzanne, Ana Marie, Robert Scott Crane" and a publicity still of Patti wearing a low-cut dress. Her own poetry completes the shrine: "Wild wheat against the sky / Once young now brown and dry / All signs of life are gone / Yet in still Earth the roots live on. Patricia Crane ~ Humanist." This final commemoration typifies the distorted remembrance of the distorted relationship between my dad and Patti. That relationship would have died had he lived, but lived because he died.

I wear my omission from Patti's monolith as a badge of honor.

46

Taps, 2009

After my dad's murder, one of the things I spirited away from our Midvale Avenue apartment was the uniform he wore on *Hogan's Heroes*. Comprised of a khaki shirt, leather jacket, and that iconic hat (which will live forever slung insouciantly over the spike of Colonel Klink's Teutonic helmet in the *Hogan's* end credits roll), the outfit was mustered out of service in 1971 after the show's unexpected cancellation.

Apart from a few post-*Hogan's* publicity gigs that my day did in character, he never wore these garments again, and after I liberated them from his bedroom closet, they were relegated to the dark confines of the hallway cupboard at my mom and Chuck's home. I would from time to time retrieve the suit bag from its nearly forgotten recess, unzip the long zipper, take the jacket off its hanger, and have a deep sniff. Was it my dad's smell? I couldn't remember, but the history of 168 episodes of *Hogan's* wafted alluringly as I filled my nose with its scent and my mind with a kaleidoscope of emotions and memories as I touched the fabric. These reunions usually ended with me mumbling, "What a waste," and zipping everything back into its sarcophagus.

One afternoon, shortly after my dad's funeral, I got a call from Patti regarding his *Hogan's* hat. She spun a long and tender tale about how much Scotty loved that hat. She asked if I knew anything about its whereabouts, and while I knew admitting I had the chapeau might easily trigger a SWAT team bashing in the front door, the generous part of my nature caused me to say, "Tell Scotty he can have the hat." Many fans of the series would argue that the hat best symbolized the whole shebang, but as I'd done with Kari's clothing, shoes, and accessories, I let it go. I don't know if the story about Scotty wanting the hat was even true.

I remained the custodian of the jacket and shirt, and in late 2001, when I met with Greg Kinnear, who was to become my dad for seven weeks during the filming of *Auto Focus*, I offered him the use of them, gratis. I did it because I greatly approved of the casting of Kinnear as my dad (and I think he would have as well). I was pleased that after Frank Sinatra and Bob Crane, the jacket was worn by another actor I respected. Since my family never discussed *Auto Focus* or, except for me, even saw the film, I felt using my dad's clothing was a moot point as far as they were concerned. I felt joyful just knowing it would appear on camera again. Like his predecessors, Kinnear filled the jacket perfectly, no alterations required.

The *Hogan's* garb meant different things to different members of the family. For my mom it symbolized her ex-husband, the father of her children, and the mostly good times they'd had together. For Debbie and Karen it was more emblematic of a difficult and trying part of their lives, when their father became a weekend visitor. For me it brought an amalgam of delight and sorrow, the memories of spending my aimless teen-aged summers camped out in a German POW camp mixed indelibly with the gnawing sadness that the laughter was now hollow and decades old.

My wife, Leslie, enjoyed trying on the jacket one day as she regaled me with stories of being a young *Hogan's Heroes* and Bob Crane fan growing up in Santa Rosa, California. Her memories brought a smile to my face, but the good cheer quickly evaporated. As I retired the jacket and shirt to its mothproof garment bag again, my heart told me it was time to say good-bye to these symbols of my dad's success, a success that was beyond everyone's expectations, and to a time when my family was still a family.

One morning as Leslie and I left the office of our Beverly Hills internist, Dr. Joe Ruiz, I spied a building just down the street on North Camden Drive that was adorned with Christie's signage. "Hang on a second," I said to Leslie, and I ducked into the building. I asked the receptionist a few questions about Christie's auctions. When I inquired about television memorabilia, I was directed to Christie's Pop Culture Division, headquartered in Rockefeller Center in midtown Manhattan.

I had sold things in the past, ranging from license plate frames to celebrity interviews. The only emotion ever connected with those commodities was my satisfaction as I cashed the checks. But the *Hogan's* shirt and jacket had a history with my family, and I wondered if divesting myself of them might mean losing the mixed emotions associated with them. Still, I felt I was the appropriate person in our clan to make the decision to shed these items, just as I had been the one to go to the murder scene all those years ago. If it had been put to a vote it would probably have broken down like this: my mom not equipped to bid a final adieu; my sister Karen against the sale, wanting any profit for herself; my sister Debbie, still angry with my dad for what she perceived as his favoritism toward his new family, a true believer like me that it was time to let go.

"Your father's uniform is an iconic piece of television history," said Simeon Lipman, Head of Pop Culture at Christie's during our initial telephone conversation. "My colleagues and I would be delighted if you would entrust Christie's with the sale," added Candra Gilcrest, an associate of Lipman's. I got a sense of elation and recognition from all the Christie's personnel I was in contact with during that spring of 2009. Colonel Hogan was not forgotten, at least not by people who were about to make a buck off him.

The sale was scheduled for Tuesday, June 23, 2009, six days shy of the thirty-first anniversary of my dad's murder. As Leslie and I entered the cool marble foyer of Christie's, the lack of hubbub and excitement struck me as odd. I don't know what I expected, but certainly not the hushed atmosphere of a catacomb.

We made our way upstairs to the preview rooms where the items for sale were on display: some, like an autographed Beatles' *Sgt. Pepper* souvenir poster, framed and on the wall—my friends beaming down on me, forever young in their psychedelic regalia—and others, like a handwritten poem by young Bobby Zimmerman before he became Dylan, in glass cases smudged with fingerprints. The merchandise ran the gamut: from a *Never Mind the Bollocks* album signed by Johnny Rotten, Sid Vicious, and the other Sex Pistols to Marlon Brando's personal script of *The Godfather* to Kurt Cobain's bass guitar from Sears to Harry Houdini's locking iron handcuffs (with keys). There were film posters, concert bills, souvenirs, and clothing—hundreds of items on the walls, in the cases, and displayed on mannequins—including the shirt and jacket worn by my dad for six years as Colonel Robert E. Hogan.

Standing in front of the headless torso, I could already feel the tug on my heart lessening. Just seeing the jacket in this room made the connection between that brown leather and me more tenuous. I was pretty sure I was making the right decision, provided, of course, someone actually bid real money for it. The estimate on the card describing the two pieces was $15,000–$20,000, and standing there in that room, surrounded by what some might consider merchandise from a Woodstock garage sale, I started to have doubts. Would that jacket mean anything to anyone but me? Was

Christie's catalogue: Colonel Hogan's shirt and jacket, New York, 2009
(author's collection).

Hogan's Heroes still even in the public consciousness? What if no one bid
on it? My nerves ratcheted up a few notches. It wasn't the money that
mattered to me; it was the idea that interest in the jacket would be a vali-
dation of my dad's career, his personality—indeed, his very existence. If
some unknown person was willing to plunk down cold hard cash to own
a piece of my dad, then it was as though he was still out there, still entertaining with his quick wit and mischievous smile. Then I thought maybe
the appeal of the jacket would have more to do with his gruesome exit, a
souvenir from a horror show, a ghoulish relic. It might be like owning a
German luger or the deck of cards Wild Bill Hickok was using when he
was shot in the back. I needed a drink.

The lots were brought onstage in the main auditorium one at a time.
There was seating for a couple hundred in rows of high school assembly
chairs, but there were fewer than fifty people in attendance, and only a
fraction of those actually wielded the green and white paddles used in the
bidding. The auctioneer stood at a podium, to her left a table staffed with
employees working on computers and handling the phones.

The items came and went with a crack of the auctioneer's gavel; some brought more than their estimates, some did not. Having never been to one of these shindigs before, I had no way to judge how it was going. As the lots fell away, I became more and more nervous. I couldn't sit, so I paced in the back of the room. The lads from Liverpool were carried in, and the bidding became quite spirited. Paddles were raised in the room, and the auctioneer monitored the almost imperceptible signals from her colleagues online and on the phone. When the gavel finally came down, the poster had sold for $52,000. Shortly afterward, Kurt Cobain's Sears-Roebuck special sold for nearly $45,000. A few other lots were hammered down, and then a small mannequin was rolled onstage. "Ladies and gentlemen," the auctioneer intoned, "this next unique item is actually six items. The lot is comprised of a shirt, trousers, shoes, belt, glasses, and leather jacket all worn by the actor Peter Dinklage* in the film *Death at a Funeral*. Let's open the bidding at $500."

The silence in the room took me back to junior high school when my algebra teacher, Mr. Brashears, asked who'd like to solve a particularly difficult problem on the board.

"How about $250," the teacher, er, auctioneer said jovially. "This is a beautifully made ensemble."

I thought of Ben Stein in *Ferris Bueller's Day Off* saying, "Anyone? Anyone?"

"One hundred. Who'll start at $100?"

People began looking around the room.

"Fifty? Can we begin at $50?" There was now a trace of pleading in her voice. "The leather alone is worth at least that."

A ripple of giggling went through the room. "Twenty-five," said a fellow in the front of the room. It was a mercy bid.

"Thank you," said the auctioneer, relieved, but with renewed energy. "I've got $25. Who'll say fifty? $50, I've got twenty-five; can I get fifty?"

Crickets, as they say in showbiz.

"Thirty-five?" she cajoled. "Can I get thirty-five?"

The silence was terrifying, broken by the gavel's shotgun crack. "Sold. $25. Congratulations."

---

*Peter Dinklage, the diminutive actor from *The Station Agent, The Chronicles of Narnia,* and *Nip/Tuck,* has since become something of a cult hero based on his role as Tyrion Lannister in HBO's *Game of Thrones.*

The man in the front raised his numbered paddle. Did he get an unreal bargain, I wondered, or would that outfit end up in the children's section at the Goodwill store?

"Jesus," I said to Leslie, "what if that happens to my dad?" I was sweating. "I gotta take a walk."

I left the reliquary and went to the men's room to splash some water on my face. Returning to the sale, I heard the gavel banged down on a sealed copy of the Beatles' *Butcher* album. "Sold for $40,000. Thank you."

The *Butcher* album was the original *Yesterday and Today* cover, with the Beatles posed in butcher's coats, covered with raw meat and dismembered dolls. It caused such an outrage that it was pulled from record store shelves and given a new, less incendiary look. I remember my friend and bandmate Dave Arnoff steam ironing off the new cover of his *Yesterday and Today* album to expose the original butcher version underneath. His cost less than five bucks.

More items came and went. I wasn't really paying attention. I thought again about how I feel about relics left behind by loved ones. My dad made that jacket live, just as Sinatra had before him and Kinnear after him. Without them in it, it was just so much cowhide to me. It was the same with Kari's things, or any of the items from John Candy that I'd received over the years. My heart longed for the people, not their props.

As I thought my big thoughts, Lot 182 was brought in. "Ladies and gentlemen, this next very special item consists of a khaki shirt and leather jacket. The jacket has military insignias and 'Colonel Robert E. Hogan' stenciled on the breast. This ensemble was worn by actor Bob Crane on the hit TV show *Hogan's Heroes*. Who will start the bidding at $5,000?"

I rubbed my fingers against one another. They were a little clammy. There was a terribly long silence. I thought, "Shit, what if he doesn't even get $25?"

"Thank you, five thousand. Do I hear six?" said the auctioneer. "Six, I have six—seven, yes, in the front. Do I hear eight?" There was a nod from the table on the right. "I have eight on the phone; do I hear—yes, nine on the left, ten, thank you."

On it went for several minutes, and then the bidding stalled. The digital money meter on the wall read 22,500. Well, at least it made the estimate, I thought.

"Twenty-two thousand, five hundred once," said the auctioneer, "twenty-two—twenty three."

A paddle went up. "Twenty-four, here on the left."

A nod, a paddle, and in a couple of minutes the gavel came down once more like a cannon report. "Sold. $32,000."

I took my first breath in several minutes. With the buyer's premium that Christie's tacks on, it turned out my dad was worth forty grand to someone. At that instant I was quite proud of him, and moved that somebody somewhere remembered him fondly enough to blow what is a good year's pay for a lot of people.

In the end, my dad's jacket was the fourth-highest-selling item in the sale. I was relieved and happy, and damn glad it brought more than the Peter Dinklage model. That three-hour auction represented 286 lots and hundreds of thousands of dollars in receipts for Christie's and its consignors. I was moved by the response to Hogan's jacket, and particularly glad it was sold in the company of the Beatles, Dylan, Brando, and Cobain. For a guy who ate at Du-Par's in the San Fernando Valley, my dad was posthumously sharing a table at the Four Seasons with some of the greats.

Leslie and I were buoyant as we walked out the front entrance of Christie's onto West Forty-ninth Street. With the bright sun on my face, I squinted up at NBC's studios in Rockefeller Plaza. This was, or had been, home to *Saturday Night Live*, *30 Rock*, the Fallon, O'Brien, and Letterman late-night programs as well as the original late-night show, *The Tonight Show*, which had featured Hogan's own heroes—Steve Allen, Jack Paar, and Johnny Carson.

The *Hogan's Heroes* jacket symbolized the pinnacle of my dad's career. But I wondered, standing there in front of that iconic edifice: what if contract renegotiations between NBC and Johnny Carson had broken down those many years ago, and my dad's three-night stint as guest host during Johnny's "sick-out" had turned into a permanent gig? "Heeeere's Bob!" Then what if my family had returned to the East Coast? I would never have known and loved Chuck, Diane, Kari, and Leslie. That thought immediately triggered a tug on my heart. Would I have spent all those years in John Candy's world? What if my dad had not been stung by the acting bug after watching Jack Lemmon and Gig Young? What if he had stayed with radio? He shared the same trail as his idols, if only bringing up the rear, but he kept moving toward a spot on the horizon that only he could see.

As I studied the building in front of me, I thought of my dad doing his work, living his life on his own terms. As I understand him now, he never really committed to his wives, his children, or his friends. Some souls have a mentor or guide, but my dad never trusted anyone but himself. He got to spend three nights in this building before Carson "got better" and returned to work. My dad went back to the narrowing trail that led past the glory of NBC Rockefeller Center, past *Hogan's Heroes*, and ended in a dark, squalid apartment in Scottsdale, Arizona.

I looked at Leslie. I didn't tell her what I was thinking. The auction had been a great success, an exciting event at a place I would probably never visit again. And it was all because of my dad. I looked up at the patch of cloudless blue between the skyscrapers and thanked him in my own quiet way for giving me this moment with Leslie in New York City on a beautiful afternoon. We strolled down the street to the sidewalk café at the Morrell Wine Bar, where we took a table in the sunshine and clinked our glasses together.

"Here's to Colonel Hogan."

Acknowledgments

A huge thank-you to author/editor Patrick McGilligan; the gracious and talented leader of the UPK pack, Anne Dean Dotson; and her equally talented colleagues Bailey Johnson, Amy Harris, David Cobb, Cameron Ludwick, Blair Thomas, and Mack McCormick for all their dedicated efforts; the 20/20 vision of copyeditor Robin DuBlanc; Wilbur Hanson; Bill Jones; John Cerney; Joe Coyle; Grace Kono-Wells; Niki Dantine; Leslie Bockian; Jill Cartter; and the queen of Colbath, Ona Harris.

And to Chris, thank you for traveling the long and winding road with me.

R.C.

Thanks, of course, to all those diligent and professional folks at UPK mentioned above. It's been a pleasure working with all of you. Thanks, too, to the sage Henry Morrison, to the prince of pixels, Nick Harris, and to Professor Rhonda Shary for her careful and insightful reading of early drafts of this book.

To Desly, beautiful and steadfast girl of mine, thanks for putting up with me, lo, these forty years.

I also have to thank Bob, my best friend and confidant since we thought we were secret agents in the seventh grade. It's been both an unalloyed joy and a tear-spattered heartbreak of a journey. Thanks for taking me along, not just the first time, but this go-round as well. As we've said many times, "Life's the strangest thing we've ever done."

C.F.

Appendix A

Bob Crane Interviewed by John Carpenter for an X-Rated "Swingers'" Magazine, 1969

Carpenter: Are there many single people in show business?
Crane: Yeah, there are a lot of single people, a lot of single actresses and actors. Being in show business you never really think of the person's home life, whether they are married or single.

In my particular case, I'm talking as a person now who's been married for 20 years and suddenly finds himself so-called single. It really hasn't changed much in my own way of life. In the business where you're on the set from 7:30 in the morning say until 7:30, 8 o'clock at night, you're basically living a single existence anyway.

As for dating I've always been the kind of guy that goes with one girl at a time so I'm not the kind that's going out to single dances or bars looking for friends or what not. I find somebody that I'm happy with and I stay with them. I guess basically I'm the married type person.

As for the other single people in the business, I think everybody's out for the same thing, they're eventually going to find somebody they're happy with and then they stay with them.

In our business of course it's easy to meet a lot of people and a lot of actresses especially. There are a lot of single girls. It's a funny thing, you eventually find out they're not single, that there's a married husband of theirs that's lurking somewhere in New York City or something and they're out here trying to earn a living. That, so many times.

I think that all single people should have a card verifying and signed by the pope or somebody that they are really single and bona fide so that

317

you don't find, you know, wake up some day with a gun in your head because you didn't hear footsteps.

You've got to be fast on your feet in this business. That's my advice. And especially if you go to ski resorts. I mean that's, especially where it's slippery, if you're not fast on your feet you're really in trouble.

Carpenter: Do singles stick together socially?

Crane: I don't think that singles stick to themselves. You find people you enjoy being with married or single. It doesn't make any difference. I don't think anybody has a stamp on their head that says I am single or I'm different than a married person. In fact, most everybody that I know in show business, as I said before, you forget that they're married, that there is somebody that's attached to them.

Carpenter: Is life more or less difficult for singles?

Crane: It's difficult when you're registering at hotels as a single. You put down your name and you feel that some time during your stay in that city you may not be passing that desk by yourself and will they somehow reach out and grab you and say, "Uh-uh, stay away from the elevator." And that can be embarrassing. So many times I will sign in as Mr. and Mrs. even though I'm by myself. Not that I'm necessarily thinking I'm going to get lucky. But I just don't want the guy at the desk to embarrass me as I'm walking by with somebody.

I have so damn many things that I love to do: tape editing, I love recording, I love music. So, this is why I say even though I was married for 20 years I really led a single existence as my wife always used to say. When I came home from work, I used to go in the back room, that's where my tapes were and my records, and they didn't see hide nor hair of me until I left the following morning to go to the studio. And that's basically the way I live now. Nothing has really changed. Except it's costing more, a hell of a lot more. And my advice is make a lot of money otherwise you can't do it.

I say there are disadvantages to being single. Not necessarily deductions. As I say, I find somebody that I enjoy being with and that's it. I don't like camping around with a lot of different people. I've always been that type of guy that's married. Even when I'm not married, I'm married. I enjoy one person and I go steady.

I'm doing a play—"Beginner's Luck"—that is written by Norman Barasch and Carroll Moore who wrote "Send Me No Flowers" which was a story about a man that thinks he's going to die and so prepares his wife for that day. She thinks he's going to leave her and there's a whole mix up where she's sure he's having an affair and his neighbor convinces him to admit it even though he's not having one.

In this new play, "Beginner's Luck," a married man sets out to have his first affair and his wife catches him when the building catches fire. He's seen coming out of the building with his bowling ball because he's supposed to be bowling that night. His wife divorces him right away without understanding. Later, she says, "If we had such a great marriage, how come you were up at that girl's apartment when the fire started?" He says, "I don't know. I guess because I'm human." She says, "Oh, you're not going to fall back on that old bromide." And he says, "No, I'm just saying human beings have faults, weaknesses, and they make mistakes. In my case, I also ran into a little bad luck." It's a very funny line and very true because if the fire hadn't started she never would have known.

We found out that married people who came to see the play got uneasy during the first couple of scenes when the man's having the affair because I think too many of them associated with what was going on. The men didn't want to laugh too loud because that would show recognition of the situation. The wives sure didn't want to laugh because there was nothing funny about a guy messing around especially with a gorgeous, young, single girl who works in his office. I think you can find more girls in offices than you can in show business. In fact, I'm going to get out of this business. I'm going to go work in an office.

Appendix B

Robert Crane and John Carpenter Telephone Call Transcript, 1978

MARICOPA COUNTY ATTORNEY'S OFFICE
SUPPLEMENTAL REPORT

SUBJECT: HOMICIDE	DATE: 9–12–90
FILE #: 90-099	INVESTIGATOR: Raines/Vassall
VICTIM: Robert E. Crane	ATTORNEY: M. J. Parker
CHARGE: Pending	APPROVED BY:

John H. Carpenter and Bob Crane, Jr. Conversation (date unknown)

The following is a transcript of a taped conversation between John H. Carpenter and Bob Crane, Jr. The original tape was presented to this investigator by Chuck Slone [*sic*], Bob Crane, Jr.'s step-father on September 8, 1990.

JC: John H. Carpenter   BC: Bob Crane, Jr.

JC: [I think Patti was] vindictive enough from what I heard in conversations.
BC: John, you haven't seen the will yet.
JC: You're right, I told him [Lieutenant Ron Dean] that, I said you and I have been in contact with each other. We're now amateur sleuths.
BC: Right.
JC: And I said we're trying to compare notes from what we read, he said well don't believe anything you read, and I said we don't know that.
BC: Yeah.

JC: You know, and I said the will is ridiculous—

BC: Right.

JC: I said this will is absolutely bananas. I said I was with Bob and many times he said the new house it'll be a great show place for Bobby.

BC: Yeah or the equipment for instance.

JC: Yeah and I said, I said to him, I said and would you believe I said Bobby was telling me that two years ago they left the equipment to Scotty.

BC: Yeah.

JC: He was only five then, what the hell would he do with all of the material from Bob.

BC: Right, i.e. Patti, you know.

JC: Yeah. And I, and I said well that's my own opinion and I said that's it.

BC: Yeah.

JC: Then he popped up with what, what's Dick Dawson's phone number and I know he had got it from before.

BC: Yeah.

JC: And I figured this is bullshit and like I said I called my attorney at home this morning and I said you know I said this is a crock and he says don't talk to them if you don't want to.

BC: Yeah.

JC: And so then they [Lieutenant Ron Dean and detective Dennis Borkenhagen] told me last night well you're going to be around the weekend, I mean for, the fly out Thursday and Friday and I said yeah and then Rita [Carpenter's extramarital girlfriend] popped up and she said no we're going to be late Friday because I have a hair appointment, she does.

BC: Yeah.

JC: And I said okay so fine I'll be home at ten o'clock. He says okay we'll be in touch with you because we're going to see quite a few people in town. And I don't even know if they have your new phone number.

BC: I imagine, well they, they can get it through Vaughn or, Lloyd Vaughn or Goldstein.

JC: Yeah.

BC: They're the two, you know, I went to Phoenix with. I mean if they don't talk with me it's ridiculous, now I imagine they're going to talk to Patti.

JC: I don't know, like I said they, like I told them last night you guys don't tell me nothing.

BC: Yeah.

JC: You come to me and ask me and now they're asking me stupid things like you went and bought a sun shade for your car, my lotus—

BC: Yeah.

JC: —and I said yeah, they said where did you buy it at. And I'm thinking to myself, what the fuck is this, man, we're talking, we're talking one o'clock in the afternoon the day before.

BC: Yeah.

JC: I mean you know this is fucking ridiculous, I told them what I had done during the course of the day and I went in and got the sun shade, they said where did you buy it, I said how in the fuck do I know where I bought it. I can tell you that I went down the street and made a left-hand turn and went into a, a car, car parts house—

BC: Yeah, yeah.

JC: —what did they sell, I said car parts.

BC: Yeah, yeah come on.

JC: You know and this is bullshit and then you know he says how are you sleeping at night, and I said great.

BC: Me too.

JC: You know I said fuck I'm sleeping great.

BC: I'm so exhausted after every day man I just I zonk out.

JC: This is fucking ridiculous.

BC: Stupid questions.

JC: I mean you know and after they left last night, I thought to myself this is, this is bananas you know.

BC: Yeah.

JC: If they, if they're accusing me, great you know at least I know where I stand.

BC: Yeah.

JC: You know and I went to Phoenix to give them my, my fingerprints, my blood type.

BC: Yeah.

JC: They say that there was blood on my car, this is bullshit.

BC: Yeah.

JC: And they say it's the same type as Bob Crane's and I said what type is that.

BC: Yeah.

JC: He says a very uncommon type. And I'm thinking to myself oh bullshit, and then the guy driving me to the airport says well you know he says it might not be his blood, you know and they break it down to inspect them to genes to this and that.

BC: Yeah.

JC: And I says I know nothing about it, you know, here you are you're still mentioning things to me, I says I know nothing about it. And I'm thinking to myself what the hell is this shit.

BC: No they're, they're searching.

JC: Boy they're, they're scratching and then they're scratching my back hard.

BC: Yeah.

JC: And I'm the one that's trying to help.

BC: Yeah.

JC: I'm telling them you know give me something, you want to know something about something that's different.

BC: What pisses me off is that they haven't talked to any family members, just for background or whatever, or for whatever I mean, my relationship with him you know—

JC: Yeah.

BC: —in terms of anything I could give them.

JC: Oh yeah they asked last night, where was Bobby Crane—

BC: Great.

JC: —living and I said they lived together as son, son and father.

BC: Yeah.

JC: It's a two bedroom, two bath big house. Uh-huh, I mean it's—

BC: Yeah well I'll probably be accused next so you know, it's okay.

JC: Well great friend except for one thing I called you on the phone as soon as I found out and you were sitting there working.

BC: Yeah.

JC: And that was what 2:30, 3:00 o'clock that afternoon.

BC: Right. That's—

JC: After I'd talked to Dean thinking it was a fucking robbery.

BC: Yeah.

JC: Like an asshole and I'm giving him my name, hey if something's been robbed, my name is John Carpenter you know bullshit.

BC: Yeah, yeah.

JC: Oh this is crap, you know I wouldn't mind it so bad if they were coming at me with you know can you help us Mr. Carpenter, that routine but no this guy comes up with and now I'm becoming reluctant ever since that first fuckin' night why did you kill Bob Crane, what did he ever do to you to get you so mad at him.

BC: Yeah, yeah.

JC: And I'm thinking to myself fuck I've never said a bad work [sic] to your dad in the twelve years or thirteen years that I've known him.

BC: Right.

JC: And I'm sure your [sic] glad, your dad felt very highly of me.

BC: Oh yeah.

JC: You know.

BC: I've told them this already, I've had like five phone conversations with either Dean and Borkenhagen, you know, just from the length of like asking me one question do you know Joe Smoe—

JC: Yeah.

BC: —to what can you tell us about John Carpenter, and I said you know the fact that I've known him through my dad for you know like I said twelve or thirteen years, I mean the complete character reference on you, you know.

JC: Yeah.

BC: Type, if my dad had any best friend, you know, or whatever you want to call it—

JC: Uh-huh.

BC: —it was you.

JC: Yeah.

BC: Because he wasn't, you know, as you know he didn't have a lot of—

JC: Right.

BC: —male friends or anything.

JC: Right. You know here's what got me too, what do you think about Bob Crane's death, and I said it's very sad, I said it's a loss, I said I'm very sorry, the man is a beautiful man.

BC: Yeah.

JC: He says is that all you got to say. And I said well that's my feeling.

BC: Yeah.

JC: He said well other people have said other things. And I said well I don't care what other people say, you asked me what I felt, I said he's a very beautiful man, we've had a lot of good relationships with each other, our friendships.

BC: Right.

JC: I taught him all he knows about video.

BC: Right.

JC: I said it's, it's a awful loss, he's a very good long friend.

BC: Yeah.

JC: You know, so.

BC: I guess they're waiting for you to just break down or something, you know.

JC: Oh yeah run out and say here take my blood. Well anyway I thought I'd let you know, you know.

BC: John, thanks for, don't you know, I don't know how I can tell you not to worry or anything but—

JC: I'm not, it's just the idea that it's starting to become frustrating.

BC: Yeah but I suspect that I will be called upon shortly.

JC: Well like I said told him the same thing you and I had discussed, you know the same thing.

BC: Right.

JC: So that's, that's, I'm not making in collusion with you, I'm simply just telling you exactly that [*sic*] I told them what my feelings were.

BC: Right, right.

JC: And you and I had already discussed it so I told them that too.

BC: Right.

JC: Okay big daddy.

BC: Okay well I'll let you know, you know I'll either call you at your office or home or whatever.

JC: Okay, whatever.

BC: If I hear anything or talk to them or whatever.

JC: Okay.

BC: So—

JC: I think what they're up to is they want to star gaze now.

BC: Yeah.

JC: You know, is basically what it turns out to be, oh I want to meet a movie star.

BC: It's so funny this guy Pat O'Brien from KNXT, he called because I asked him if I could get a bunch of tape from that whole period of a couple of days like I missed a lot of it you know like David Shenan (phonetic) [Sheehan] had a report and things like that on video tape.

JC: Uh-huh.

BC: And he says yeah it's, it's shaky in terms of when you start seeing these guys [Dean and Borkenhagen] wearing new clothes and wearing sunglasses and you know having new hairdos, you know, he was half fictitious [facetious] in terms of the Scottsdale Police you know because they're on camera so much.

JC: Yeah.

BC: He says the problem with them is they talk too much on, on camera.

JC: Yeah well he came up with a routine he says we haven't given out anything, the information that is all wrong he says has come from other sources and I'm thinking to myself sure.

BC: Yeah, yeah.

JC: But I'm not going to, you know, what the hell. Okay, dad, have a day, I've got to get back to work.

BC: Okay talk to you soon, John.

JC: All right, bye.

BC: Bye.

Appendix C

Robert Crane's Letter to Sony Pictures Classics Legal Department Addressing *Auto Focus* Script, 2002

Patti's smoking and drinking.

Patti smoked constantly, 24/7. The ashes would overflow the ashtrays in her car. Everyday, starting in the afternoon around four or five, the wine would appear. My enduring image of Patti is of her holding court in the kitchen nook at the Tilden Avenue home in Westwood, a glass of wine in one hand, a lit cigarette in the other. This would go on with an audience and afterward, all evening long. I remember seeing her sitting in the same position alone, late at night, more wine, more cigarettes, never ending, whether my dad was home or not.

Debbie Crane being unwilling to talk to Bob Crane.

Around 12 or 13, my sister Debbie started to forgo seeing my dad on weekends during his visitation. Karen would go on her own with dad. This went on periodically for a few years. Debbie was the middle child, strange, angry, getting back at my dad, I suppose, for leaving home. They were communicating and seeing each other in the last few years of my dad's life, though.

The nature of Bob and Patti's sexual relationship.

My father told me about, and I saw photographs of a threesome between Patti, my dad and another woman they had picked up at a club in L.A. The sexual encounter was held in their bedroom at the Tilden Avenue home in Westwood.

There are three other occurrences chock full of innuendo: Patti would occasionally receive massages from a masseur at home in the bedroom at Tilden Avenue which would go on for hours. The bedroom door was locked. My father would occasionally try to enter the room but couldn't and there would be no reply from inside.

Patti was intrigued with their attorney/business manager Lloyd Vaughn (who it turns out, stole around $100,000 from dad and Patti to help him finance his cocaine habit). They went out a few times to dinner and sporting events. The third episode involves me. Patti and I were sitting in the kitchen nook at Tilden one night. My dad was on the road. Patti and I were talking about a short film idea I had about a truck-stop diner. She would be the waitress. A trucker, who admires her, rips her blouse at one point. Patti, glass of wine in one hand, a lit cigarette in the other, stared at me and said, "I wouldn't mind if you saw my breasts." I was 24, uncomfortable, looking down at the floor. I changed the subject. Nothing happened. The film was never made. The trap was laid but I didn't bite.

Robert D. Crane
4-8-02

Appendix D

Robert Crane's Piece for *Auto Focus* Website, 2002

The following is a statement from Bob Crane's son, Robert Crane Jr., about his father and *Auto Focus*.

Like John Belushi in *Wired*, my dad, actor Bob Crane, in *Auto Focus* is a driven, meteoric show business phenomenon whose lack of self respect and naivete lead to an early demise. We read about or watched Belushi because he was an uncontrollable fireball who was hilarious and did things we fantasized about doing. We watched Bob Crane because he was an in control leader who said and did funny things always at the right time. Many HOGAN'S HEROES viewers wanted to be him. Belushi and Crane—fueled by the need to make people laugh. Unfortunately, because of time limitations, writer/filmmaker point of view and arc of story, the humor, the driving force behind Belushi and Crane, is left behind. Drugs, sex, and death take center stage. People slow down on the highway to view the accident. Some want blood, some want survivors, everyone must ease up on the gas pedal to take a look.

Sense of timing, razor sharp wit, better than average drummer, handsome, man's man, take charge, work your ass off, non-stop, do it better next time, are some of the adjectives that come to mind regarding my father. Also, love of jazz (Buddy Rich, Louie Bellson, Stan Kenton, Glenn Miller), photography, electronics, yes, and women. My dad was the sort of male who probably should never have been married. Yet, my dad, mother Anne, sisters Karen and Debbie and I had a blast. We made 8mm (film striped for sound) movie epics like I *Was a Teenager for the FBI*. My dad and I had the POOL LEAGUE, where we played a full schedule of baseball games against each other in our swimming pool in Tarzana, California. My father videotaped my rock power trio with Dave Arnoff and Ron

Heck playing live in 1967, long before MTV videos. Okay, it was in black and white. We went on what we called Fellini Excursions like attending a celebrity bocce ball tournament at Caesar's Palace in Las Vegas. We got to meet a very crabby Joe DiMaggio. At the end of the evening, my dad and I turned toward each other and said, "What the hell are we doing here?" *Auto Focus* doesn't pretend to be a biopic. It isn't interested in showing how much time Bob Crane spent with his kids. My dad was a big kid. He loved to have fun. My mother was the rock, the glue that kept our family together as long as it did. Although my mother only met Paul Schrader and Rita Wilson once, Schrader and Wilson capture her perfectly. She is a small-town, east coast product, who put family and sanity first. She is Ingrid Bergman, Grace Kelly and Donna Reed. Although she has been happily remarried for almost thirty years to Chuck Sloan, she still speaks of my dad with love and affection. We had great times.

Auto Focus is among Paul Schrader's best films. My dad and I saw Schrader's *Taxi Driver* together in Westwood, California, in 1976. I compare *Auto Focus* to Mike Nichols' *Carnal Knowledge* with Jack Nicholson and Art Garfunkel. If there were double features today, *Auto Focus* would be the darker second half only this time with Greg Kinnear and Willem Dafoe stepping in. Both films are brilliant and disturbing looks at male sexuality and the sexual revolution. They both capture the time periods in painstaking detail. Kinnear nails the essence of my father, non-stop pleasing of the world at large, the laugh, the beat, the timing, the smalltown thinking in the big bad world of L.A. Dafoe is the too-loyal sidekick, the Tonto to Kinnear's Lone Ranger. Dafoe captures the eternal hanger-on, the second tier, the pathetic. Rita Wilson is my mother, Anne Crane. Too sweet, too trusting for her own good. Maria Bello is the second wife, Patti. Ron Leibman (my longtime friend Chris Fryer and I have loved Leibman since *Where's Poppa?*) behaves, speaks and breathes as THE Hollywood agent. Kurt Fuller IS Werner Klemperer/Col. Klink. It's a great film but, guys, don't expect to get laid after you and your female companion see this film. It's not a date movie. In fact, you'll probably want to hang out with some of your buds and get drunk. My dad would have seen this film and headed directly to a strip club. If you want the biopic treatment on Bob Crane, read the book or watch *E! True Hollywood Story* or *A&E Biography*. Or, keep supporting Sumner Redstone's (Viacom) lifestyle by watching *Hogan's Heroes* via syndication. For you Belushi fans, *Saturday Night Live* is all over basic cable. Keep laughing.

Appendix E

HWY 111: Bob Crane's Ten Stupid Questions, 2003

Robert David Crane, Jr. goes online to interview his late father, Bob Crane, celebrating the occasion of the release of *Auto Focus,* the Paul Schrader film that stars Greg Kinnear as his father and Rita (*My Big Fat Greek Wedding*'s producer) Wilson as his mother. The film depicts his father's tabloid-worthy life.

Stupid: What did you think of the movie about your life, *Auto Focus?*
Crane: Outside of *Hogan's Heroes* and Angel Carter of the Classic Cat, it's the most important project I've ever been affiliated with.
Stupid: Who's a better Hogan, you or Greg Kinnear?
Crane: Me. Kinnear's too pretty and too small. The Hogan jacket fit me better. Werner (Klemperer, who played Colonel Klink in the hit series) told me, however, that he prefers Kinnear.
Stupid: I understand Frank Sinatra wore the jacket before you did in his movie *Von Ryan's Express.*
Crane: The jacket still had the Western Costume label. It was an honor. I recently met Frank and Dean [Martin] up here, incidentally. They don't live with the rest of us, however. They share a Neutra-designed house on a hill.
Stupid: Because of your second wife, Sigrid Valdis, and her X-rated web site, you're now more known as an amateur pornographer than the star of a hit TV series.
Crane: She needed the money. The *Hogan's* residual checks apparently ran out. Her acting career stalled after she played Hilda, Klink's secretary. It doesn't matter to me because here we're all naked all the time. I'm staring at Jayne Mansfield right now as we speak.

Stupid: You've been the subject of a book (*Murder of Bob Crane*), television documentaries (*The E! True Hollywood Story,* "Biography"), numerous magazine and newspaper articles and a Paul Schrader film (*Auto Focus*). Your career has more buzz now than when you were living. What's next?

Crane: Stanley Kubrick was disappointed that his career ended with a Cruise-Kidman film. He's here filming another take on sex: Eyes Automatically Focused. I'm doing an unpaid cameo as a strip club drummer.

Stupid: You were a better-than-average drummer. You appeared on variety shows and even released an album on Epic Records. Do you still play?

Crane: That was sad how Michael Jackson turned on Tommy Mottola, don't you think? Of course, I still play. My teacher is Buddy Rich, for God's sake. Yesterday, I jammed with Lennon, Harrison, Morrison, Entwistle and Keith Moon. I was the oldest one there. That Moon—what a nut.

Stupid: You were brutally murdered, bludgeoned to death. Who did it?

Crane: I don't know. I was asleep. John Carpenter's here now. He swears he didn't do it.

Stupid: Hogan, Klink, Schultz, and your producer, Edward H. Feldman, are together again. Are you thinking of a reunion film?

Crane: No. We have great crews available but we want to shoot film, not digital. Everything's digital here. And there's no SAG contract yet. I'm not going to be a scab.

Stupid: You were killed in 1978. You loved technology. *Rolling Stone* called you a "cool video sex pioneer." Yet you missed digital cameras, CDs, DVDs, and PCs.

Crane: More importantly, I missed Pamela Anderson, Anna Nicole Smith and the real Erin Brockovich. Talk about equipment!

Stupid: Last question. Are you happy with the way you're being remembered?

Crane: I don't mind. It's not important up here. We're all equal—except for Sinatra and Dino. I would like to say to my first wife, Anne, Rita Wilson played you magnificently in *Auto Focus*. There's an Oscar buzz around here.

And, by the way, Anne, Donna Reed says "Hi," and thinks you did a great job rearing our three children, particularly Robert David, who, up here, is considered a brilliant writer.

And to Sumner Redstone, CEO of Viacom, which syndicates *Hogan's Heroes:* We shot 168 episodes at $90,000 per. Viacom has grossed $90 million off *Hogan's* reruns which play internationally.

How about sharing some of the wealth with the surviving members of the cast and writers and directors who've made you a billionaire? I'm a volunteer gatekeeper here twice a week. Good luck getting in!

Index

Page numbers in *italics* refer to photographs.

337

Giannini, Giancarlo, 226
Gibson, Charlie, 260
Gibson, Mel, 208
Gibson, Toy, 125
Gilcrest, Candra, 309
Gish, Lillian, 74
Godfather, The (film), 44, 248, 309
Godfather 2, The (film), 103
Godfrey, Arthur, 7, 17, 52
Golab, Jan, 124, 126
Goldberg, Whoopi, 208
Goldfinger (film), 45
Goldstein, Bill, 13, 37–38, 60, 71, 130–33, 283
Goodall, Jane, 181
Goodman, Benny, 47
Goodman, Gary, 261
Gorillas in the Mist (film), 180
Gormé, Eydie, 19
Gould, Elliott, 92
Grant, Cary, 74, 102
Graysmith, Robert, 286
Great Escape, The (film), 45
Green Acres (TV series), 17
Greene, Ellen, 252, 255
Gretzky, Janet Jones, 262
Gretzky, Wayne, 230, 257, 262
Guest, Christopher, 103
Gus (film), 199
Gwynne, Fred, 74

Haas, Bob and Betty, 97
Haas, Diane, 142, 153, 158, 161, 163, 193, 275, 313; breakup with Robert Crane, 100; engaged to Robert Crane, 97–99; having an abortion, 107–8; in Mammoth, CA, with Crane family, 95; meeting Fred Astaire, 95–96; meeting Robert Crane at USC, 89–93
Haas, Kris, 140
Haley, Alex, 150
Hall, D. J. (Debra Jane), 158–59

Halprin, Daria, 113
Hanks, Tom, 173, 179, 215, 262
Hannah, Daryl, 215
Hannity, Sean, 295
Hanson, Dian, 145–46
Hargitay, Mariska, 185
Hargitay, Mickey, 21
Harrison, George, 179
Harry, Debbie, 126
Hart, Mary, 215
Hartman, Phil, 183
Hawn, Goldie, 148–49
Heck, Ron, 47–48, 68, 93
Hefner, Christie, 151
Hefner, Hugh, 2, 124–26, 144, 184–85, 304
Heim, Maggie, 299
Helgenberger, Marg, 183
Hellman, Monte, 112
Helm, Levon, 208
Hemingway, Mariel, 215
Hemphill, John, 246
Hernandez, Frankie, 200–202, 253–54, 259–62
Heston, Charlton, 19
Hildebrand, Deborah, 247
Hildebrand, Kari: asking Robert Crane to move out, 237–38; buying house with Robert Crane, 189–90; cancer's return, 223–31; debut of *Hostage for a Day*, 265–66, 313; on feminism, 166–68; getting cancer, 190–96; getting married, 164–66; making *Hostage for a Day*, 235–37; meeting Robert Crane, 159–62; moving in with Robert Crane, 162–64; passing of, 244–51; posthumous art show, 258, 261–62; Robert Crane moving back into their house, 243–44; surprise party for, 241; with Robert Crane during making of *Uncle Buck* in Chicago, 201–2

Vicious, Sid, 309
Viera, Meredith, 295
Vietnam War, 38, 49; draft lottery, 85–86; effect on Robert Crane's education, 77; the Moratorium, 88
View, The (TV show), 295
Vilanch, Bruce, 213
Visconti, Luchino, 225
Von Ryan's Express (film), 45
Von Sydow, Max, 164

Wagons East! (film), 252–61
Waks, Suzan, 257
Wald, Jerry, 20
Walker, Pete, 32
Waltons, The (TV series), 119
Ward, Sela, 183
Wasserman, Lew, 199
Watson, Toby, 158
Wayne, David, 74
Wayne, John, 63, 253, 303
Weaver, Sigourney, 142, 179–80
Weiner, Stewart, 124, 302–4
Weisz, Rachel, 303–4
Wellness Community, 261–62
Welk, Lawrence, 31
Wendt, George, 237, 246
What's My Line? (TV show), 52
Whitley, Patrick, 155
Whittinghill, Dick, 17
Who Was That Lady I Saw You With? (play), 21

Wicked Dreams of Paula Schultz, The (film), 73, 199
Wilder, Billy, 44
Willard, Fred, 126
Williams, Tiger, 176–77
Williams, Wendy O., 156
Wilson, Rita, 288
Winchell, Walter, 174
Windmill Dinner Theatre, 35
Winfield Apartment Complex (murder scene), 34, 36–38
Winner, Michael, 124
Winters, Jonathan, 15, 19, 21
Wloszczyna, Susan, 298
Woman Under the Influence, A (film), 88
Won Ton Ton, the Dog Who Saved Hollywood (film), 124
Wood, Natalie, 300
Work Experience (short film), 215
Wyler, William, 225

Yellow Submarine (film), 207
Yoba, Malik, 241
Young, Gig, 21, 42–44, 57, 73, 102, 214, 313
Young, Neil, 180
Ysasi, Eloy, 127

Zahedi, Firooz, 183
Zehme, Bill, 151
Zemeckis, Robert, 89, 243
Ziskin, Laura, 99–100, 242–43

SCREEN CLASSICS

Screen Classics is a series of critical biographies, film histories, and analytical studies focusing on neglected filmmakers and important screen artists and subjects, from the era of silent cinema to the golden age of Hollywood to the international generation of today. Books in the Screen Classics series are intended for scholars and general readers alike. The contributing authors are established figures in their respective fields. This series also serves the purpose of advancing scholarship on film personalities and themes with ties to Kentucky.

SERIES EDITOR
Patrick McGilligan

BOOKS IN THE SERIES